SCIENTIFIC AND TECHNICAL COMMUNICATION

SCIENTIFIC AND TECHNICAL COMMUNICATION
Theory, Practice, and Policy

edited by
James H. Collier
with David M. Toomey

SAGE Publications
International Educational and Professional Publisher
Thousand Oaks   London   New Delhi

For information address:

SAGE Publications, Inc.
2455 Teller Road
Thousand Oaks, California 91320
E-mail: order@sagepub.com

SAGE Publications Ltd.
6 Bonhill Street
London EC2A 4PU
United Kingdom

SAGE Publications India Pvt. Ltd.
M-32 Market
Greater Kailash I
New Delhi 110048 India

Printed in the United States of America

Library of Congress Cataloging-in-Publication Data

Main entry under title:

Scientific and technical communication: theory, practice, and policy
/ editor, James H. Collier with David M. Toomey.
    p. cm.
  Includes bibliographical references and index.
  ISBN 0-7619-0320-8 (cloth: acid-free paper).—ISBN
0-7619-0321-6 (pbk.: acid-free paper)
    1. Communication in science. 2. Communication of technical
information. I. Collier, James H.
  Q223.S248   1996
  501.4—dc20   96-25374

    98 99 00 01 02 10 9 8 7 6 5 4 3 2

Acquiring Editor:	Alex Schwartz
Editorial Assistant:	Jessica Crawford
Production Editor:	Astrid Virding
Production Assistant:	Karen Wiley
Typesetter/Designer:	Danielle Dillahunt
Indexer:	Mary Kidd
Cover Designer:	Lesa Valdez

Contents

Preface

One of the principal founders of modern science, Robert Boyle (1627-1691), conveyed the difficulty in concisely reporting his experiments: "I have . . . delivered things, to make them more clear, in such a multitude of words, that I now seem even to myself to have in diverse places been guilty of verbosity" (Boyle, 1772/1985, p. 63). Hoping to reflect the integrity and accuracy of his experiments to his readers, Boyle decided no detail or contingency was too small to include even if it meant that he "knowingly and purposely transgressed laws of oratory in one particular, namely, in making sometimes my periods (i.e., sentences) or parentheses over-long" (p. 64). But Boyle's lament does not just reveal the practical limitations of scientific writing; rather, it marks a recognition of the richness, intricacy, and power of the activity being described.

Textbook conceptions of effective scientific and technical communication have been captured by the twin visions of efficiency and efficacy. Consequently challenges to the scientific image, often expressed in the dialects of Balkanized disciplines, fail to be translated into recommendations for communications practices. Driven by science and technology's complex cumulative practices, specialist discourses have evolved into jargon-dense mediums. Jargon, if comprehensively understood and uniformly taught, can be an effective conceptual shorthand. Practitioners use jargon to "stand for" lengthy explanations. Supported by graphics, efficient scientific communication, however, often sacrifices depth. The contexts supporting the presentation, consideration, and reception of theories and facts are, generally, dismissed as irrelevant to scientific and technical end-products (including knowledge) and inappropriate to the most revered form of presentation, the journal article. The efficacy of context, as an identifiable, practical consideration for technical communicators, and as a means for framing and discussing ideas, has been ceded to science popularizers. Still, Boyle's fundamental challenge remains for all modern scientific and technical communicators: How do we more accurately and fully express scientific and technological practice for the audiences affected by it?

TRANSFORMING IMAGE
AND PRACTICE

An initial step in transforming and communicating the image of science and technology involves integrating the perspectives of different academic disciplines, professions, and institutions. These perspectives are linked to the economic, historical, philosophical, political, social, and rhetorical contexts in which science and technology take place.

Technical jargon does not inspire public interest, yet the activities hiding behind that jargon are preserved largely through taxes, tuition, grants and corporate sponsorship. When the prescriptions and procedures for scientific and technical communication are seen out of context, they reinforce our perception of science and technology as distant and inert. Students and practitioners face a host of new challenges as scientific and technical communicators: the presence of increasingly diverse audiences, the proliferation, ownership, and marketing of information, the ethical problems presented by developments in science and technology, and the need to balance individual and social responsibilities. They will assume important and unique roles in our evolving "technical society." They will serve as gatekeepers within professions by determining who has access to information. They will serve as mediators among the interests and concerns of professionals and laypersons. And they will serve as translators of specialist language to and from the language of other specialists and laypersons. These new challenges and unique roles will converge and shape, and be shaped by, the situated practice of scientific and technical communication.

THE STRUCTURE OF THE TEXT

The Reader

Part II of this book is a collection of provocative essays on a wide range of issues in science and technology by authors who represent a variety of backgrounds and interests. There are educators from communication studies, scholars from science and technology studies, and policy analysts. These articles were chosen for their importance, diversity of ideas, and sheer interest. It is hoped that the curious reader will find something in them of lasting value.

The Rhetoric/Reader Relation

We wanted to present scientific and technical communication in their contexts. The difficulty in presenting the contexts of technical documents is that there are many from which to choose—history, society, economics and ethics, to name a few. We decided that the best approach was a limited one—to relate the practices of scientific and technical communication to particularly appropriate contexts. So, the chapters in Part I of the book discuss concerns of all communicators (collaborative writing, audience, argument, and persuasion). The essays in Part II discuss issues related to those concerns. The book's halves are interactive. That is, you will better appreciate the information presented in a given chapter in Part I by considering the issues raised in the corresponding chapter in Part II. For instance, Chapter 1, "Scientific and Technical Communication in Context," is paired with Chapter 7 by Steve Fuller, "Putting People Back Into the Business of Science: Constituting a National Forum for Setting the Research Agenda." Together the chapters ask you not only to examine the contexts affecting technical communication, but to consider the implications the contexts and images of science have for public policy. Discussion questions and writing exercises are designed to help readers make the connections. Although every chapter in Parts I and II is self-contained, and although you may proceed usefully through the book in many ways, you stand to gain the most by bridging the chapters.

Interdisciplinary Communication

Interdisciplinary work in science and engineering has become less the exception and more the norm, and the trend is likely not only to continue but to accelerate. Where appropriate, this book shows strategies for communicating across the disciplines. Directly, Dale Sullivan's chapter addresses the rhetorical resources necessary for interdisciplinary communication to be successful. Chapter 4, "Understanding Audiences," provides a means for analyzing disciplinary boundaries that is especially useful for students investigating an area outside their own.

Reading

Textbooks in technical communication devote little space to reading—perhaps assuming either that it is easier than writing, and unworthy of time spent, or that it is unteachable. We think that both assumptions are misguided and do the student a disservice: Professionals in science and engineering spend far more time reading than they do writing. This book devotes a chapter to types of reading and suggests a means for adjusting reading practices to various documents.

PURPOSES OF THE TEXT

Scientific and technical communicators are affected by the linguistic tools they use and by circumstances surrounding them: historical and social issues, economic needs, and cultural interactions, to name a few. Logically, communication about science and technology also needs to be understood in these contexts. Indeed, scientific and technical communication is already being changed by developments in interdisciplinary communication, cross-cultural communication, and new communication technologies. This book acknowledges those changes and explores their effects; toward that end it has three interdependent purposes:

■ *Assist readers in understanding traditional technical writing concerns and to show techniques for expressing and transforming those concerns.*

The elements of scientific and technical communication are the means by which the artificial world (of corkscrews, bridges, and computers) is constructed; they are the means through which the natural world (of electrons, trees, and stars) is known. To understand this communication students and practitioners must recognize its forms; to engage in it, one needs to shape those forms.

■ *Enable readers to communicate effectively across disciplines.*

Systems engineering integrates the technological with the larger system of human behavior, economics, and the natural environment; the field is increasingly important, but its lessons have barely begun to influence related disciplines. In asking people trained within disciplines to communicate with each other, one is struck by the difficulties encountered. Further, people within disciplines rarely talk to outsiders about their studies. The situation would be merely curious and worthy of only passing interest if the world outside the academy did not ask for communication of people from different backgrounds. But it does. American corporations are currently undergoing a "flattening," the result of which is that each worker is made more responsible for the entire production process. More and more, scientists, engineers, and workers in all areas of technology will be expected to understand matters outside their area of expertise.

■ Provide readers the means to examine the ways science, technology, and communication influence their lives as professionals, citizens, and thinking persons.

In recent years, a number of scientific and technological issues have made headlines and stirred discussions and debate in the home, the office, and Congress. Unfortunately, intelligent and informed thinking in these matters is rare. Many of us are unwilling to determine the course of science and technology— preferring to see it as a force beyond human control. We may be afraid, or misinformed, or even apathetic. Such attitudes are dangerous: The forces of technological change are beyond our control only if we allow them to be beyond our control. Gradually, the situation may be changing. Colleges and universities are beginning to recognize their role in sparking policy debates. Communication courses now involve themselves with national science policy; biology curricula require courses in medical ethics; and more and more, all courses in science consider the social consequences of pure and applied research.

Orientation

This book integrates multidisciplinary perspectives on the relation of rhetoric, science, technology, and public policy making to the process and product of technical communication. The text is inspired by science and technology studies (STS), a field emerging from the history, sociology, and philosophy of science and technology and having roots in anthropology, economics, and political theory. This text reformulates the issues raised by STS within the context of technical communication.

The objective of this book is to forge a critical link between rhetorical theory, rhetorical practice, and public policy, to enable academics, students, and laypersons to assess critically the cognitive and social factors influencing—and being influenced by—science and technology, and to begin a dialogue among academics, students, and laypersons concerning the ways science, technology, and communication transform their lives.

Current scholarship in the rhetoric of science, the sociology of scientific knowledge, and science and technology policy provides new grounding for technical communication practices. Technical communication instructors and students comprise a group growing in both numbers and diversity of interests. Although generally housed in English departments, many technical writing courses have been farmed out to disciplines such as engineering and communication studies. Instructors in these areas may have concerns different from those whose primary training was in English; consequently, they may be less interested in grammar (for instance) than in peptide chains. Whereas some may draw on their work experience, others are forced to teach "cookbook" courses, or—more ambitiously—supplement standard textbooks with lectures and exercises drawn from other sources.

Hopefully, this text improves upon traditional textbooks by offering theoretical orientations that relate developments in the rhetoric of science to technical communication, providing analytical models from STS for understanding the contexts in which technical communication occurs, acknowledging the social factors affecting communication, and integrating cognitive models of the writing process with social ones.

Nearly 400 years ago, Francis Bacon advocated new ways of thinking and communicating that we call the scientific method. As the millennium approaches, we find ourselves again needing to think about science and technology in new ways and communicate about them in new ways. With Bacon, we can say that "the matter at hand is no mere felicity of speculation, but the real business and fortunes of the human race." Indeed, in a very real sense, our collective future is at stake.

BIBLIOGRAPHY

Boyle, R. (1985). New experiments physico-mechanical, touching the spring of the air. In S. Shapin & S. Shaffer, *Leviathan and the air pump: Hobbes, Boyle and the experimental life* (pp. 63-64). Princeton, NJ: Princeton University Press. (Original work by Boyle published 1772)

Acknowledgments

While dealing with communications practices whose fundamental goals are formally conceived as presenting and maintaining objective knowledge, this book reflects a process sustained by deep faith. Originating as a passing conversation among friends in the Williams Hall computer lab in 1991, this book bears the influence of untold historical, intellectual, and institutional contexts. We thank the people who have participated in these contexts by lending their time and expertise to make it possible.

Our deepest debts are owed to Steve Fuller for his genuine example, early and ardent encouragement, and ceaseless energy; Bill Keith for his uncanny ability to cut to the heart of the matter; and Joseph C. Pitt for his intellectual stewardship.

The Center for the Study of Science in Society at Virginia Tech remains, despite economic vicissitudes, a rich source of interdisciplinary debate that fires the imagination. Special thanks to Henry Bauer, Richard Burian, Gary Downey, Marianne DeLaet, Skip Fuhrman, Carolyn Furrow, and the participants in the Wednesday and Thursday seminar series for creating and reanimating such a heady atmosphere. Very special thanks are due to the STS graduate students, past and present, for their fellowship and insight.

We are indeed fortunate to be associated with the faculty and staff in the Departments of English at Virginia Tech and the University of Virginia. This book has grown out of conversations with Frieda Bostian, Virgil Cook, Fritz Oehlschlaeger, and Paul Sorrentino. Annette Averill, Evelyn Raines, Tanya Reece, Tammy Shepherd, Lorrie Sumpter, and Terry Whaling helped us through the institutional thicket with few scratches. Thanks also to the staffs of both university libraries.

Those who have participated in this book's past, Jane Kinney and Katney Bair, have, we hope, found safe passage. We thank them for taking the risk. Those who participate in this book's present and future, Alex Schwartz and the tireless team at Sage Publications, we thank for their patience and dedication. We are grateful to Richard Steele at Taylor & Francis and Steve Bacon at Research Corporation for their ready cooperation.

Our friends and family in Charlottesville, Richmond, Washington, and North Adams keep us going. And our friends in Blacksburg make us whole. Thanks to John H. Mitchell for his wisdom, generosity, and stories. For their irony, kindness, and good humor we thank John Christman, Mary Beth Oliver, Matt McAllister, Scott Patterson, and Diane Wilson. Our good fortune is to have Chris Ruckman as a contributor and advisor to this text. Gary Atkins and Jane Varley give us heart.

To our teachers, and especially our students, we take this book to be a first payment on our debt to them.

Thanks to William P. Toomey, who said "Go slow and look at it," and to Jacqueline J. Toomey, who said "Bill—it's only a machine."

For her grace, resolution, and inspiration this book is dedicated to Almera C. Harris.

The Rhetoric

CHAPTER 1

Scientific and Technical Communication in Context

S cientific and technical communication is a process of gathering, organizing, presenting, and refining information. It is also a process of persuasion that often appeals to objectivity to convince an audience. Finally, it is a process shaped by the contexts in which it occurs and that is improved when it recognizes these contexts.

Consider the three parts of this definition. The first part is that scientific and technical communication is *a process of gathering, organizing, presenting, and refining information.* Take, for example, a technical problem that most of us have faced: preparing a dish according to a cookbook recipe. When making the dish the first time, you closely follow each of the steps. And while satisfied with the result, you have ideas for making the dish better. Next time, you may not follow the steps in order; you may add certain ingredients, subtract others; you may use different utensils; you may cook the dish for a longer or a shorter time. Eventually, you may come to see the recipe as a rough outline to which you make adjustments to suit your taste or your guests' taste. In short, you have made a new recipe. You may document such changes in the margins of the cookbook, commit them to memory, or communicate them to others—in, say, a telephone conversation to a friend. The recipe evolves.

This analogy applies to the process of scientific and technical communication. When faced, for instance, with writing a proposal for the first time you are likely to follow a preestablished form slavishly. And while satisfied with the result, you may have ideas for adapting the proposal to make it more persuasive. Next time you may not rigidly follow a standard format; you may accent certain sections, downplay others; you may use different sources of information; you may prepare different versions of the same proposal. Eventually, you may come to see the proposal form as a rough outline to which you make adjustments as you learn more about its purpose, the needs of the audience, and your relationship to them. Although the formal elements of the proposal are constant, they are neither permanent nor should they dictate content.

The second part of the definition states that scientific and technical communication is *a process of persuasion which often appeals to objectivity to convince an audience.* Scientific and technical communication is fundamentally persuasive. When writing a proposal or manual you always try to convince someone of your recommendations. You hold a reasonable position you think others should hold. Still, an audience lends information greater credibility when it is considered objective. But strict objectivity is elusive—absolute objectivity is impossible. At best, the presentation of a study or experiment strives for the most honest and balanced account of what happened and so *attempts* to be objective. Scientific and technical communicators cannot help but have personal feelings and biases about their work: after all, it embodies their interests and beliefs.

When reading a lab manual, textbook, or journal article, you cannot see what happens "behind the scenes" as they are developed. And even though experimental articles in science may be based on fact, they typically derive from situations that are anything but objective. An objective text is the result of choices made by the authors about which information to present to a specific audience. Jumping ahead of ourselves a bit, rhetorical choices are made within the many contexts affecting scientific and technical communication. Neither science nor technology stands apart from the change born in a world of developing nations, interdependent economies, shifting political ideals, global communication networks, and diminishing natural resources. The arguments and evidence that convinced a congressional committee 10 years ago to fund a scientific project, for instance, may not convince the same committee today. Taking into account the conditions and contexts affecting technical communication, you can determine occasions on which persuasive strategies are most effectively applied. Scientists and technologists commonly appeal to concepts and themes such as rationality, pragmatism, experimental elegance, simplicity, success, and altruism to convince audiences, and each other, of the accuracy of their claims.

Finally, scientific and technical communication is *a process inevitably shaped by its contexts, and which is improved when it recognizes its contexts.* Context is typically understood in two ways:

- As the parts preceding or following a written or spoken word, phrase, or statement. Frequently, we hear politicians complain that a statement they made was taken out of context by a reporter, implying that the true meaning was lost or distorted.
- As the set of circumstances surrounding a certain event or situation. What we designate as an event—an experiment on Tuesday—necessarily takes place within the flow of other historical and social events—such as decreased state funding for the university sponsoring the experiment.

In both instances, context refers to a bigger picture we must recognize to reach a proper conclusion or take appropriate action. The difficulty lies in discriminating which contexts are significant to the practices of science and technology, how we account for and manipulate them, and how we communicate about them.

Understanding science and technology in context consists of examining and translating the language, theories, explanations, and interests of one group into the language, theories, explanations, and interests of another group. For example, one can talk about biology in sociological terms such as "values," "social class," "power," and "institutional structure." Similarly, one can talk about social behavior in biological terms such as "evolution," "mutation," "adaptation," and "heritability." Talking about one discipline or profession in terms of another shows certain similarities. As well, translation and communication across disciplines, like communicating with different cultures, brings to light differences of which participants are not aware. By considering the relation of science, technology, and society in context, one intellectually challenges the accepted notions and images of science and technology. By challenging those notions, your communicative practices will achieve greater depth, precision, and thoroughness necessary for effective scientific and technical communication.

Practitioners in science and technology typically view and interpret the effects of social, historical, and economic change on their work within cohesive organizational contexts. Professional organizations allocate resources, fix requirements for people entering the field, and establish and regulate relationships among practitioners. The organizational structure of science is so strong as to influence each stage in the research process—and each stage in the process of scientific and technical communication.

Over time, as scientific and technical fields became highly organized, something was gained—efficient production—but something was lost—critical, long-term scrutiny of practices beyond the laboratory and workbench. Researchers became confident in their methods as the natural sciences evolved and grew exclusively dependent on the work of others inside the field. Theories and facts were uniformly accepted by community members. The written text was neither the focus of scientific activity, nor was it the only means to convince people of the facts. To convince other researchers (and laypersons) of the truth of a particular claim, scientists could mobilize a number of "nontextual" resources such as laboratory equipment, formulas, and references to the work of other researchers. Subsequently, the goals of scientific and technical communication became indistinguishable from the goals of efficient scientific and technical production. Yet these goals often remain at odds with broader concerns about public welfare. Nevertheless, we confer a special status and authority on scientific knowledge. Scientists and laypersons share the belief that science is universal and unaffected by language and society. If we concede that science is autonomous from society, then many people argue that it would be best to leave scientific research to its own devices.

Science, on the contrary, is not autonomous from society. During the Vietnam war era, the public began to question the societal ends of science and technology. In what direction were science and technology headed? Was the "military-industrial complex" implicated in an immoral war? Should scientists make decisions regarding the public welfare? As taxpayers supporting research and development, the masses demanded a voice on how their money was spent. Scientists countered that the public made hasty judgments and failed to consider the overall benefits and complexity of scientific research—aspects of which were beyond a layperson's comprehension. Today, mutual suspicion among scientists and laypersons persists. On one hand, the public argues that scientists and engineers are corporate and government pawns. On the other hand, scientists and engineers claim that the public cannot render any judgments until learning firsthand about science and technology. The fears and presumptions of both scientists and laypersons continue to substitute for critical reflection and sustained dialogue.

UNDERSTANDING CONVENTIONS

Effective scientific and technical communication is essential to all professions and fields of study in an industrialized society. The qualities we attribute to effective scientific and technical communication—accuracy, clarity, efficiency, and completeness—correspond to our understanding of what makes science and technology work effectively. For example, a physicist writing a journal article must show clearly how specific ideas and procedures are used in order for colleagues to test an hypothesis. If the experiment is replicated, the physicist succeeds in doing good science, but only to the degree that they accurately and persuasively communicate their concepts to a specific audience. The methods and research of science and technology have evolved as the professional standards and conventions of scientific and technical communication have evolved.

The conventions of scientific and technical communication extend beyond writing to the way people speak, listen, read, and present and comprehend visual images about science and technology. Academic disciplines and professional organizations rely on standards for the proper presentation of information in newsletters, journals, manuals, and other sponsored publications. By learning and following the conventions of their profession, scientific and technical communicators have a specific idea of how to effectively communicate to their peers. However, the people who use and are affected by the conventions of scientific and technical communication are not just scientists, engineers, and academics but are taxpayers, neighbors, heads of households, and citizens casting a vote. Scientific and technical communication evolves from the complex social roles we all share. For scientific and technical communication to achieve focus, it must accommodate these complex social roles. We must learn not only how to use the conventions of scientific and technical communication but to realize where those conventions come from, what boundaries they set, how we understand their subject matter, and how they affect the choices we make.

Too often, the process of scientific and technical communication is presented *exclusively* as a series of prescriptions—how one ought to write a process description, how one ought to write a letter of complaint, or how one ought to give an oral presentation, for example. Formal prescriptions and standards are important and necessary tools of the trade. They encourage a technical document (whether proposal, business letter, set of instructions, or scientific article) to be comprehensive, organized, and "user friendly." There is a sound rationale for such standards: Scientific and technical communication is dense, highly specialized, and difficult to comprehend even for specialists; standards of presentation help to make such information understandable. Further, such standards suggest agreement within a community, shared knowledge, and the possibility of agreement between the writer and reader, or between speaker and listener.

But their danger is that conventions encourage us to do no more than duplicate standard formats and criteria; consequently, we forget their origins, their specific contexts, and their purposes. In a 1964 article, Nobel prize winner Sir Peter Medawar, a pioneer in the field of immunology, observed, "What scientists do has never been the subject of a scientific . . . inquiry. It is no use looking to scientific 'papers,' for they not merely conceal but actively misrepresent the reasoning that goes into the work they describe" (pp. 42-43). Medawar suggested that, in order to understand the process of science, the "objectivity" of published scientific research cannot serve as a guide. If true, then the process of scientific and technical communication involves much more than following the writing conventions of an academic discipline or profession, or uncritically accepting the assertions of scientists. On one hand, the structure of scientific and technical communication itself encourages an audience to believe in the ideas being presented. On the other hand, the images of science and technology we derive from journal publications and textbooks is of a systematic, dull, bloodless activity unaffected by the affairs of ordinary people.

Far from passionless, science and technology have many characteristics of other professions and activities about which people care deeply. By only following sets of procedures, one neglects the specific dynamics of scientific and technical communication. The practices you will be taught embody a series of historical choices and social negotiations that continue to be discovered and developed in light of what we learn about science and technology. To accurately portray the interplay of science, technology, and society, the communication practices we develop must not simply reflect change: They must affect change in allowing the critical analysis of scientific explanation in both traditional and developing presentation formats.

You will face increasing specialization in your profession and the professions of others with whom you communicate. Increasing specialization can lead to misunderstood technical communication on two related fronts. First, even though specialists are educated in much the same way, the meaning of technical terms and jargon can have subtle but significant variations. Terms such as "trait," "fitness," "selection," or "allele" vary in meaning among population, biometrical, or molecular geneticists. Absent reflection by the communities using these terms, variations in meaning can lead not only to miscommunication, but errors in research that can ultimately affect the direction of a given field. Second, there are common words often adopted as specialist terms. Words used daily such as "frequency," "success," and "solution" have specific connotations in given contexts. What, for example, counts as "success" for stockbrokers and experimental psychologists is, of course, two different things. However, beyond obvious differences, the unexplored use of common words by different groups can lead to unwarranted assumptions and groundless agreement.

Understanding the conventions of scientific and technical communication entails that we learn both their effectiveness and limitations. The standard use and maintenance of conventions helps promote the growth of science and technology. But these conventions only partially convey the subtleties of scientific practice. While science's textbook image is, arguably, necessary to safeguard a more robust image arises by augmenting technical communications practices to address contemporary explanations of scientific practice.

IMAGE AND REVOLUTION

In 1962, a philosophical treatise about the history of science written by a physicist was published by the University of Chicago Press—Thomas Kuhn's *The Structure of Scientific Revolutions*. In a May 1991 issue of *Scientific American*, John Horgan estimated that the three editions of Kuhn's book had sold over 1 million copies worldwide, including translations into 16 languages—an extraordinary feat for an academic book written for philosophers of science. Given its consistent citation and diverse readership, *The Structure of Scientific Revolutions* likely will be remembered as one of the most influential academic books of the twentieth century. When reviewed in 1964, it touched off intense academic debate (see Shapere, 1964) over whether philosophers in the first half of the century had mischaracterized natural science, and if so, how this mischaracterization could be revised.

During the 1920s and 1930s, positivist philosophers attempted to render the claims of science and philosophy into sentences that could be proved true or false either through the use of logic or by empirical testing. The positivists hoped to determine a set of formal principles from which scientific and philosophical inquiry could proceed. With these principles in hand, the confusion brought about by using imprecise and ambiguous language could be eliminated.

In *The Structure of Scientific Revolutions,* Thomas Kuhn (1962/1970) enumerated a number of omissions from the positivist account of science. Kuhn argued that the conduct and progress of science could not be reduced only to the logical analysis of language and the application of a set of formal universal principles. Rather, the development and use of scientific concepts, methods, and theories derive from historical circumstance, the social structure of a scientific community, and a scientist's individual experience. Kuhn observed that science is a communally structured activity in which similarly trained researchers possessing a common worldview attempt to solve a defined set of problems. Scientific progress begins with a commitment to a shared set of concepts, or *paradigm,* within which researchers work until they find questions they cannot answer. Eventually, researchers come to a point where they must abandon the old paradigm and adopt a new one. The moment of change makes for a scientific revolution. The clearest illustration of Kuhn's notion comes in the procession of paradigms asserted in physical theories of the universe (regarding the structure of the solar system) from geocentric theory to heliocentric theory and (regarding laws governing the physical universe) from Newtonian theory to relativity theory.

The Structure of Scientific Revolutions opens:

History, if viewed as the repository for more than anecdote or chronology, could produce a decisive transformation in the image of science by which we are now possessed. That image has previously been drawn, even by scientists themselves, mainly from the study of finished scientific achievements as these are recorded in the classics and, more recently, in the textbooks from which each new scientific generation learns to practice its trade. Inevitably, however, the aim of such books is persuasive and pedagogic; a concept of science drawn from them is no more likely to fit the enterprise that produced them than an image of a national culture drawn from a tourist brochure or a language text. (Kuhn, 1962/1970, p. 1)

Kuhn's appeal to historical evidence puts into doubt fundamental assumptions—held by researchers studying science and scientists alike—about the growth, conduct and outcomes of scientific practice. Many readers of *The Structure of Scientific Revolutions* concluded that, to avoid the mistakes of the positivist philosophers, an understanding of science *must come* from an interdisciplinary perspective including the history and sociology of science.

If Kuhn is right—if the image of science presented by textbooks is as shallow as the image of a national culture presented by a tourist brochure—then technical writers are partly responsible for constructing that image. The challenge for scientific and technical communicators is in getting from the "travel brochure" mentality to a more meaningful expression of the activities of science and technology. One solution is to integrate many perspectives on issues involving science and technology rather than being tied to traditional concepts. From the points of view found in a variety of disciplines, we will develop a critical appreciation of the practices of science and technology. Out of these contexts, we will construct ways of communicating about science and technology not only to similarly trained experts but also to laypersons.

Initially, the most prominent contributions to the study of science and technology were made by historians, philosophers, and sociologists. More recently though, insights have come from feminist theorists, psychologists, economists, political theorists, policy analysts, and rhetoricians. Although there has been much debate about the value and the aim of interdisciplinary approaches to science and technology, agreement does exist that if we are to fully comprehend science and technology we need to understand the circumstances in which they exist.

We will begin by looking at science and technology in their *historical, social, philosophical, psychological, economic, and rhetorical* contexts. Obviously, no one begins communicating about science and technology by going through a "context checklist."

And the work of scientists and technologists cannot (and should not) be reduced to "just social," "just rhetorical," or "just philosophical." Science and technology embody complex practices. But the issues found in the contexts mentioned above do influence the way we communicate about science and technology. As a result of our training—and communicating with people similarly trained—we take for granted certain ideas and methods on which an "outsider" or layperson might have insight. As industry and government attempts to deal with the problem of integrating and evaluating the activities of specialists, your understanding of various contexts affecting science and technology will help coordinate the concerns of different groups. An expert community, for instance, can be cushioned from unwarranted intrusions and kept informed about programs and ideas that would be of larger social interest.

The following examples offer a starting point from which one can begin to examine commonly held images of science and technology in light of new perspectives. Through these contexts, you can begin to uncover new ways of presenting subjects in scientific and technical communication.

HISTORICAL CONTEXTS

The form that scientific inquiry should take and what, ultimately, should count as knowledge was the subject of passionate, sustained debate in mid-seventeenth-century England. Perhaps the two most prominent participants were Robert Boyle (1627-1691) and Thomas Hobbes (1588-1679).

Boyle and a fledgling group of "experimentalists" advocated the use of experiments in settling disputes concerning natural phenomena; the existence and composition of a vacuum for example. Science, Boyle argued, was properly conducted in a space where experiments could be performed and witnessed. Experiments provided knowledge because results could be observed. Experimental knowledge did not require the type of faith necessary to believe in "things metaphysical." Still, requirements regarding when experiments were needed, who would perform them, and who would assess them did not go unquestioned. In the seventeenth century, science was not a profession as we now know it. The term "scientist" was not coined until the nineteenth century by William Whewell. Boyle, perhaps bowing to political exigence, advocated a scientific practice divorced from society.

Thomas Hobbes challenged Boyle's conception of experimental science. In "Dialogus physicus," Hobbes (1661/1985) goads Royal Society members in an exchange between unnamed interlocutors: "Cannot anyone who wishes come, since, as I suppose they meet in a public place, and give his opinion on the experiments which are seen as well as they? . . . Is this Society not constituted by public privilege?" The reply: "I do not have an opinion. But the place where they meet is not public" (p. 350). Advocating an open intellectual forum, Hobbes conceived of science as doing "natural philosophy"—a more speculative form of determining fundamental principles of nature through public debate. Opening inquiry to the public, Hobbes reasoned, would help avoid the corruption that went on behind closed doors.

One of the major differences between Boyle and Hobbes turned on who—experimentalists or natural philosophers—would serve as the model for a citizen pursuing knowledge. In seeking to professionalize inquiry, Boyle drew boundaries around the experimental enterprise. The experimental culture would have a particular way of life with unique rules of social and intellectual conduct. The community would demonstrate its usefulness by providing cures for disease, higher crop yields, and more accurate weapons. Further, inquiry would be free, ordered, and consensual. A balance would be struck between institutional and individual concerns. In short, the laboratory would work as a stable, peaceful civic society unlike the political order in which it existed.

Hobbes objected to building a distinct "scientific society." The experimentalists seemingly wanted to create an authoritarian hierarchy, one in which seemingly democratic inquiry was ceded to experts and professionals. Consequently, citizens were relieved of their responsibilities for directing knowledge production. Hobbes's condemnation of restrictions on empirical inquiry echoed Martin Luther's condemnation of the church a century and a half earlier. The experimentalists would be much like priests, interpreting the book of Nature for the lay public: a book, the contents and exposition of which, Hobbes felt, called for open debate, not expert exegesis. For Hobbes, knowledge was the product of human actions. To separate scientific knowledge from other public affairs was, at best, artificial.

With the restoration of Charles II to the throne of England in 1660, science became decidedly pragmatic. In granting the Royal Society its charter in 1662, Charles declared that the study of nature be conducted without interfering in, or interference from, the affairs of church and state. Accordingly, the experimentalists legislated against political speech and experiments about metaphysical and theoretical entities that could not be agreed upon as matters of fact by the community. Topics on which the community agreed were presented according to a negotiated set of standards. Boyle reiterated the king's sentiments by stressing the need for a restricted experimental space. The uneducated public—many of whom had questions regarding "metaphysical superstitions"—could not enter this space. Science required trained, credible witnesses who could properly interpret the outcome of experiments. Scientific practice required consensus. Although open in theory, experimental practice was closed to all but true believers.

Ultimately, Boyle's arguments triumphed. One reason given for the success of Restoration science in England was the ability of the experimentalists to adapt the activities of their community with the political landscape. Science survived where other intellectual enterprises were condemned because it protected the larger political and social order while offering the possibility of economic reward.[1]

The boundary between science and society is constantly being negotiated, as are the boundaries separating academic disciplines, professions, and their consumers. In some capacity, scientific and technical communicators help determine who gets access to certain information, materials, and resources. By restricting access, you empower some people and alienate others. Scientific and technical communicators must determine if certain subjects or procedures require open debate or should be closed off. Of course, the same decisions by other people—in government and in other positions of power—provide one with, or prevent one from having, information for making decisions. From an historical context, you can examine the basis for decisions in your own practice and for participating in public debates regarding the social influence of science and technology.

SOCIAL CONTEXTS

Well into the twentieth century, many anthropologists and sociologists conceived of "the savage mind" of primitive peoples as the underdeveloped precursor to the rational thinking of Western peoples. Initially, from the basis of armchair speculation, and then through fieldwork, researchers tried to establish the mentality of the "savage mind." Cultures such the African Azande were considered "primitive" due to their inability to distinguish abstract concepts from concrete objects.

According to anthropological observers, an Azande tribe member claims to "think with animal parts" in determining a personal course of action such as marriage or revenge on another tribe member. To the anthropologist, the tribe member looks to be manipulating an oracle (such as a poisoned fowl) to trigger an associated tribal custom or religious rite. Through repeated observation, the anthropologist tries to determine a series of "rules" governing oracle use. Initially, the anthropologist is confused when the tribe member regards a form of action as the "correct" one, when, according to previous "rules" of oracle use, an "incorrect" form of action is being followed. The anthropologist concludes that members of the tribe regularly break their own rules and thereby concludes that the tribe is irrational. Of course, the oracle is not what is really being manipulated. Rather, the poisoned fowl is a concrete model of an abstract process—thinking—unrelated to the manipulation of the oracle. The mistake made by the anthropologist is to impose a form of rule use and Western rationality on people of non-Western culture. Nevertheless, in our attempts to avoid similar mistakes by understanding behavior within its social and cultural context, we hastily assume all societies and cultures are equally good (or bad) in their own ways.

If we study science and technology as distinct cultures embedded in a larger society what do we find? Robert Merton, founder of the sociology of science, described scientific conduct as following from a set of four principles (or norms): universalism, disinterestedness, organized skepticism, and communalism. *Universalism* directs that claims of truth be evaluated by the standards of a community, not by an individual's standards. *Disinterestedness* directs the practitioner to value the advance of scientific knowledge rather than value personal gain. Accordingly, scientists should remain disinterested about their personal stake in the result of an experiment—their primary objective is adding to the storehouse of scientific knowledge. *Organized skepticism* directs the testing, confirmation, or falsification of claims empirically before they can be accepted as true. Finally, *communalism* directs the collaborative development and open sharing of knowledge among the members of the community. Merton's norms describe conduct that we associate with the virtues of the scientific method.

More recent studies of science—laboratory ethnographies (an anthropological and sociological on-site study of a laboratory, e.g., Knorr-Cetina, 1980; Latour & Woolgar, 1979)—conclude that a great disparity exists between the conduct of science and technology as reported in textbooks and journal articles and actual practice. Although a unique and powerful endeavor, science and technology share the complexities of self-interest and misapprehension found in all social practices. Additionally, Merton's norms were seen as defined by, and not defining princples of, scientific practice. Your own experience in a laboratory may bear out this conclusion. Rarely is research in science and technology straightforward and dictated by explicit conduct codes combined with a series of steps taken at a preordained time—except in lab manuals. Laboratory research can be disorderly, inconclusive, and pursued in direct proportion to the available amount of resources.

These examples illustrate the difficulty of comprehending the social life of cultures with which we have little contact—even for trained professionals. Certainly, most of us do not feel as far removed from the culture of science and technology as we might from the culture of the Azande. Still, we all have difficulties communicating among academic and professional specialties. Communication is difficult even within the relatively similar settings of the sciences: Biologists have difficulty understanding physicists; mechanical engineers have difficulty understanding electrical engineers.

Making the culture of science even more difficult to penetrate is the historical divide between scientists, engineers, and the lay public. A doctoral student, the first family member to go beyond high school, writes home to explain what goes on in the genetics research lab in which they work; their task, as you might imagine, is daunting. As a layperson, you may feel that without special training there is no way to understand the inner workings of science and technology. As a practitioner, you may feel there is no way to explain what it is you do to the uninitiated observer. The direction of the production of scientific and technological knowledge mirrors social needs and resources. When we consider our own knowledge and its social origins within a larger framework composed of students, parents, interested laypersons, and experts, we begin to draw necessary connections among our experiences and expertise and an audience's experiences and expertise. Consequently, as scientific and technical communicators, we need to be aware of the origin and impact of idealized images and the social interaction among science, technology, and society.

PHILOSOPHICAL CONTEXTS

Many of the categories and concepts we associate with science—confirmation, falsification, logical empiricism, objectivity, pragmatism, realism—follow from philosophical traditions. From analyses of questions involving scientific language and knowledge, philosophers of science have proposed criteria that try to capture the distinguishing features of scientific inquiry.

According to many philosophers, perhaps the best model of proper and successful science is physics. Physics has offered ever more accurate descriptions of the universe, it has emphasized mathematical expression and causal explanations, and it has produced fundamental "lawlike" statements about nature. Perhaps because physics succeeded so well and so obviously, other branches of science and academic disciplines adopted its language and methods. The first social scientists, for instance, sought to determine a "physics of human behavior" and began adopting natural science methods, such as a reliance on certain forms of quantitative analysis, to their disciplines. The efficacy of this strategy, as historically and currently practiced, is vigorously disputed by social scientists themselves.

What philosphers have traditionally identified as the unique features of science also inspires debate. While the effect of these disputed images remains unresolved, so do the philosophical notions. For example, Karl Popper claimed that the testability of scientific theories marked their difference from unscientific theories. He proposed the idea that a theory is potentially scientific if it could be *falsified* (refuted) through contrary observations. Popper also articulated a number of rules and criteria that should govern scientific experimentation. Richard Boyd speculates that, despite "technical difficulties," falsification hangs on today as a feature of scientific theories because of "the apparent commitment to an antidogmatic conception of scientific inquiry" (Boyd, Gasper, & Trout, 1991, intro., Sec. 1).

Interestingly, two sociologists, Michael Mulkay and Nigel Gilbert, interviewed 34 scientists to track the influence of Popper on actual scientific practice. Only a few scientists had read Popper in any detail, and many doubted the influence that philosophy of science had on laboratory practice. Mulkay and Gilbert (1981) determined that the reasoning of scientists "depends on highly personal judgments . . . (and) each individual scientist continually disagrees with his colleague's Popperian interpretations" (p. 393). Quoting from the 1958 preface to his *The Logic of Scientific Discovery,* Mulkay and Gilbert state that the norms Popper spells out derive from purely logical analysis and not actual practice. Popperian logical norms had been loosely interpreted by scientists to fit certain practices. Therefore, Mulkay and Gilbert conclude, rules are open-ended and do not entirely determine actions. If philosophers (or scientists) seek more effective rule use, the rules must be seen as part of social practice. As an example, Mulkay and Gilbert note how the rules of scientific publication lead to a relatively uniform product. In ways similar to the positivist philosphers, scientific and technical communicators failed to look beyond the rules guiding the larger scientific "game" and describe actual "play."

Philosophers have also focused their attention on technology. Technology has long been understood as applied science; as such, it was regarded as an irresistible force. For most of the nineteenth and twentieth centuries, technology was understood as *nothing more than* applied science. Technology in practice shows something quite different. For instance, automobile manufacturing over the past 70 years has undergone several great changes—not brought about by the technology itself but, rather, by aspects surrounding the technology. Historians and philosophers have come to redefine technology as part of a system composed of several integrated components such as machines, raw materials, workers, finances, management, and other systems. Technological artifacts can be studied as the point of intersection among several forces within a larger network.

Perhaps the two aspects of the philosophy of science that have had the most impact on scientific and technical communication are scientific realism and social constructivism. *Scientific realism* is the view that "the subject matter of scientific research and scientific theories exists independently of our knowledge of it, and that the goal of science is the description and explanation of the observable and unobservable aspects of an independently existing world" (Boyd et al., 1991, p. 780). In short, scientific realism holds that objects referred to in a theory would exist even if there was no theory describing them.

Social constructivism is the position that the subject matter of scientific research and scientific theories is wholly or partly a product of social interests, processes, and structures that construct the background theoretical assumptions of scientists and the order of the scientific community. In short, social constructivism holds that scientific theories and observations depend on, and cannot be separated from, society. For example, when a scientific revolution occurs—such as the shift from Newtonian mechanics to relativity theory—scientists, for a brief period, have no rational means for choosing between rival theoretical methods. Proponents of a particular theory seek to recruit adherents. The transition between rival theories and methods is socially negotiated through debates over the presented evidence. Consequently, scientists' notions of how the world operates, and the methods used to make that determination, are socially and linguistically negotiated.

The conclusions drawn from these positions offers profound implications for the practice of scientific and technical communication. Although the complex issues of how words refer to objects in the world cannot be tackled here, we need to begin to consider ways in which scientific and technical definitions and terms may depend on historical, social, and philosophical circumstances. Realists acknowledge, for example, that definitions and terms in science follow from theoretical discoveries, and could be revised given new empirical evidence. If you begin to explore the purpose and function of scientific and technical language beyond pointing out objects in the world, then you develop a more cogent sense of the possibilities for scientific and technical communication.

PSYCHOLOGICAL CONTEXTS

Scientific and technical communication is a cognitive process—you make hundreds of decisions as you write, listen, speak, or read. These decisions reflect your own thought processes, behavior, preferences, and abilities. The discipline in which you study and the profession you will pursue also organize your thoughts and behavior. The degree may be small or may be great: As suggested in the previous discussion of social constructivism, some psychologists hold that what a scientist actually sees in an experiment depends on an accepted theory. In coming to understand the contexts in which scientific and technical communication takes place, researchers have begun to examine how scientists and technologists think and behave.

Studies in the psychology of science have generally focused on personality, creativity and cognition. Thomas Kuhn, for example, claimed that the personalities and thinking processes of scientists such as Newton, Darwin, and Einstein are incompatible with inventors such as Edison, Tesla, and Gramme. Scientists, Kuhn suggests, are puzzle solvers who concentrate on solving one problem within a theoretical structure and deliberately moving to the next related problem. They think within strictures imposed by their discipline. Inventors, on the other hand, work outside those strictures.[2] Nikola Tesla (1856-1943) serves as a wonderful example of an inventor—a somewhat mad visionary who captured the imagination of supporters as diverse as George Westinghouse and Mark Twain. Although Tesla invented many useful and practical devices, he also believed he could harness wireless electricity to communicate with Mars or develop a "death ray."

If you accept Kuhn's premise that scientists dedicate themselves to thinking within the boundaries of accepted theories and defined problems, what happens to their thinking when traditional methods fail or contrary evidence begins to accumulate? How does their worldview change? Many of you have been confronted with such a situation. Ideas or beliefs you have held for along time—about personal relations or your perceptions of the environment and world around you—have been directly challenged. Your views about "the way things are" were perhaps profoundly shaken. Likely, you were reluctant to change your views; in fact, you held on to them in the face of contrary evidence. In science, changes in worldview can be as profound and as fundamental. The physicist Max Planck (1858-1947) observed that new scientific truths do not win the day because scientists suddenly see the light but, rather, because a generation of scientists dies off.

There are a number of examples illustrating how the perception of scientists influences the evidence generated by experiments. Perhaps the most infamous case involves the discovery of N-rays by the prominent French physicist René-Prosper Blondlot. In 1903, Blondlot, a professor at the University of Nancy and award-winning member of the Academy of Sciences, claimed to have found a new form of radiation, like X-rays, which he called N-rays. Within the French scientific community between 1903 and 1906, the effects of N-rays were observed and reported by over 40 people and became the subject of approximately 300 papers published by 100 scientists and medical doctors. N-rays, claimed Blondlot, could be produced by generating electrical charges in various gases and heated metals.

Scientists in England and Germany, however, had difficulty replicating Blondlot's results. While attending a meeting of the

British Association for the Advancement of Science in September of 1904, Robert W. Wood, an American physicist, was recruited to investigate Blondlot's claims. Wood enjoyed a flamboyant reputation—credited with fabricating one of the first photographs of an unidentified flying object. Blondlot showed Wood an experiment involving N-rays generated by a lamp, bent through an aluminum prism and detected on a phosphorescent surface. During the experiment, Wood secretly removed the aluminum prism from the apparatus. Nevertheless, Blondlot continued to find spectral lines in a refracted beam of N-rays—without the presence of the prism. A week later, Wood reported his encounter with Blondlot in the journal *Nature*. The scientific community agreed that Wood's findings thoroughly discredited Blondlot's experiments, although Blondlot continued to believe in the existence of N-rays until his death in 1930 (see Ashmore, 1993).

The case of N-rays poses interesting questions regarding the methods of science and the social psychology of scientists. At the time of his work on N-rays, Blondlot and his French colleagues possessed the facilities, prestige, and results attributed to the best aspects of scientific practice. But if we evaluate Wood's removal of the prism as a scientific experiment, it failed to meet the criteria attributed to "good science." Wood conducted the experiment surreptitiously, and it was not replicated (it would have been almost impossible to do so) by other researchers. Still, Wood's single experiment stood as a complete refutation of a body of work assembled by Blondlot and fellow researchers. How is it that one ingenious but essentially unscientific experiment achieved greater credibility than an entire body of research?

Wood's experiment is best understood not as a triumph of scientific method but as a study in Blondlot's state of mind and the social structure of early twentieth-century French science. If Blondlot had stopped seeing N-rays after Wood removed the prism, the experiment would have proved nothing. It was Blondlot's fervent, unshakable belief in what he saw that proved N-rays did not exist. Blondlot's work came at a time when decentralized French science programs competed for international recognition. N-ray research generated much the same enthusiasm and promised the same rewards as had Wilhelm Röntegen's discovery of

X-rays in 1895 and Noble prize in 1901. In this climate of desire and expectation, Blondlot and the French scientific community allowed each other to see what was never there.

In 1949, psychologists Jerome Bruner and Leo Postman exposed individuals to images of playing cards projected in quick succession, each image for a few hundredths of a second. The images alternated between normal playing cards and those in which color and suit were reversed—a red 10 of clubs, for example. At first, when individuals were presented with a reversed card, they identified it according to traditional colors and suits; to borrow Bruner's term, they *regularized* the card. Soon, however, they began to hesitate. They would proclaim something "wrong" with the display, noting that although a card was the 10 of clubs (conventionally black on a white background) it had a red border. Eventually, individuals would identify the reversed card *as* a reversed card. Once they discovered the first reversed card, they would identify others more quickly. Bruner and Postman concluded that when people encounter incomplete or confusing information, they make it conform to their own expectations (see Bruner, 1986; Bruner & Postman, 1949).

In the natural sciences, there is perhaps no better illustration of the phenomena that Bruner and Postman described than the wave-particle duality of light. Depending on the type of experiment to be performed, light can be described as either a wave or a particle. The duality of light initially confused experimenters who expected it to act one way or the other. However, as they came to understand that light had both properties, experimenters could offer descriptions accounting for them.

The structure of scientific and technical communication, like an accepted scientific theory or the grammar of a language, helps order our thought processes and our behavior. Out of this order, certain ways of thinking and learning become available to us as others remain unexplored. Inasmuch as the structures of scientific and technical communication direct our thinking and behavior, we need to step back, critically assess, and, if necessary, revise these structures. The reading selections in Part II are intended to enable you to develop this critical perspective.

ECONOMIC CONTEXTS

In 1983, the Washington, D.C. lobbying firm of Cassidy and Associates, hired by Catholic University and Columbia University, convinced Congress to direct the Department of Energy to appropriate funds supporting their laboratories. There were no hearings. The scientific community made no recommendations. Quite simply, the lobbying group was hired to get the funds and they delivered. Science entered the arena of direct federal appropriations—porkbarrel politics.

From 1983 to 1985, Congress appropriated approximately $165 million directly to laboratories and research project recipients on the basis of lobbying. Government agencies made no requests to release the funds, and no hearings were held. For the first time, money was appropriated for research without the submission and outside review of proposals from individual scientists. Members of Congress saw the value in getting direct support for projects at universities and research centers in their districts. In 1985, the Senate Appropriations Committee approved nine direct appropriations, but Cornell University's president, Frank Rhodes, turned down the money in arguing for the necessity of merit-based funding. Accordingly, the National Science Board found direct appropriations to be a threat to a peer-review, merit-based system. The recipients of the money in 1986, however, did not raise any objections.

Although scientific research and technological development is funded by local agencies, private industry, and private foundations, the biggest contributor is the federal government. The role of Congress in directly earmarking funds for projects in representatives' particular districts remains a highly contentious issue. As the congressional session of 1990 drew to a close, for example, both Senator Robert Byrd of West Virginia and Congressman Tom Bevill of Alabama secured $10 million for projects in their respective state and district. The 1990 Clean Air Bill contained a $19 million appropriation, anonymously authored, for the study of methane emissions from cattle. As the bill was modified in committee the provision was dropped but found its way to the Senate version of a farm bill. When the Senate and

House reached a compromise on the farm bill, the provision was again dropped. However, the provision found its way back to the Clean Air Bill, where there was a final, failed attempt to remove it. President Bush signed the bill and the appropriation survived. The anonymous author of the provision remained anonymous.

In 1991, the budget contained at least $270 million in pork for academic research, according to one researcher. Until recently, the trend toward earmarking funds directly for scientific research was rising. While universities initially resisted the allure of federal pork, university administrators found it increasingly difficult to legitimate turning down funds to boards of trustees—especially in this era of budget reduction. In coming to accept these funds, some university officials, recognizing that porkbarrel projects are funded at the expense of peer-reviewed projects, argue that direct funding spreads the money around to institutions that would not normally get funding. Consequently, the universities that "have not" would get two chances at the federal funding, one through merit review, the other through the "fair" and direct appropriation of federal dollars.

Most of federal dollars go to support "big science" projects. "Big science" refers to large-scale, resource-intensive programs such as the failed superconducting super collider (SSC), the Hubble space telescope, the human genome project, the Mars observer, and the planned space station. Invariably, "big science" projects come to dominate the direction of particular disciplines at the expense of "basic," or pedagogically oriented, forms of research. Certain areas of research are neglected or abandoned completely in favor of distributing funds to renowned researchers at prestigious institutions. As well, scientific talent accumulates where the money and prestige are, thus possibly fruitful avenues of research suffer as a result. The rich get richer as the gap between basic and cutting-edge research grows. The interests of the majority of scientists, most of whom perform basic research, are considered only in passing. Also, a lack of consensus exists in the scientific community about the ultimate value of these programs. A minority of the biology community opposes the genome project as harmful to the overall development of the discipline. Still other biologists wonder if the results predicted by those involved with the project could not be gained more rapidly by a decentralized research program. The split in the physics community over the SSC was drawn essentially along the same lines. Congress, however, prefers "big science" projects because they are concentrated, seemingly easier to manage, and offer individual representatives the opportunity for securing porkbarrel projects.

The economic contexts of science and technology confront scientific and technical communicators both as practitioners receiving funds and as interested taxpayers concerned with how their money is being spent. In either instance, you will be faced with weighing decisions regarding your individual and social interests, and the funding of science and technology. Although the impact of the federal and private finances on science and technology is not completely understood, the shape that knowledge takes reflects economic decisions. Perhaps the most profound influence on the direction of scientific and technical communication in the twenty-first century will be economic.

RHETORICAL CONTEXTS

The term "rhetoric" invokes a host of synonyms from "exaggeration," "embellishment," and "overstatement" to "lies," "fraud," and "concealment." In conversation, we use phrases such as "political rhetoric," "empty rhetoric," or "that's just rhetoric" to suggest a lack of genuine meaning.

Our impressions about rhetoric can be traced to Greek philosophy during the time of Socrates. Then, the "art of rhetoric" primarily referred to applied techniques for public speech making. Highly skilled orators were both admired and feared for their ability to inspire public action. In this charged political atmosphere, Socrates insisted that Truth be regarded as the highest virtue. He understood right-minded speech as a means to conceive of, and pursue, the Truth. Following Socrates, Plato declared that right-minded speech was available to everyone who sought it.

Opposing Socrates and Plato were the Sophists, who regarded language as a resource that might assist anyone to achieve a variety of ends. Moreover, the Sophists argued, as people have different communicative skills, not everyone has access to the same linguistic resources. For a fee, the Sophists made these linguistic resources available by offering training in the verbal arts. Socrates and Plato claimed that the Sophists were immoral both because they charged for their services, and because they did not instruct their clients/students on the ethical use of their newly acquired skills. Perhaps ironically, Socrates' prowess in debate won the day. He depicted Sophists as dishonest brokers of techniques that could be used to dupe innocents. Hence, we call the art of verbal trickery "sophistry."

At first glance, scientific and technical communication appears to emulate the ideals of Socrates and Plato. Following this ideal, scientists depict the goal of scientific description as capturing the natural world truthfully and accurately. Accordingly, scientific language should be objective. Facts should speak for themselves. But facts do not speak for themselves—people speak for them. Language, even *objective* language, gets in the way. All words, all our choices involving communication, carry or denote a set of values. Scientists must convince audiences that what they are seeing, hearing, or reading is true. The scientific community does not immediately hail new discoveries and theories as undisputed triumphs. Researchers have a personal stake in seeing certain theories succeed and certain theories fail.

Members of disciplines urging the transformation of their field into a science, or a branch of the natural sciences, seek to recast their problems in ways yielding to scientific analyses and solutions, thereby gaining scientific authority and status. As a result, the language and presentation of information (e.g., the use of mathematical tables, logical notation, and visual aids) of many disciplines has become "scientific."

Language is always used within particular contexts. Many people would argue that agreement in science exists because the claims being made are true, as demonstrated by observation and confirmation of results. But consider your own experience. If you are among several people witnessing an event—a movie, a classroom lecture, an automobile accident—you know that each individual has a slightly different account of what happens. Through discussion, and through several viewings (as with a movie), you may reach a consensus about what has happened. And you reach it through rhetoric.

NEW CHALLENGES AND ROLES

Science and technology will continue exerting extraordinary cultural influence while becoming more specialized. It is likely that most other professions will follow the trend of specialization. Ironically, as professions become progressively specialized, our own expertise and skills—absent constant retraining—progressively lose their value. All of us, scientists and nonscientists alike, will become part of the lay public on a growing number of issues involving science and technology. The situation will be complicated as the public—ourselves included—demand a greater voice in how business is conducted (especially environmentally), how local and national policy priorities are set, and how our tax money is spent. Communicating across the borders separating professions, government agencies, and interest-groups will involve something similar to trying to use a language with an incredible number of dialects. We cannot hope to learn all of these dialects but will nonetheless be asked to take positions and make appropriate decisions. But on what basis will our decisions be made? Here is an example of the roles that scientific and technical communicators can play.

In the late 1960s, the federal government proposed a standard for passive restraints in automobiles. The automatically inflating air bag was promoted as a "technological fix" to traffic deaths and injuries not solved by seat belts. For almost two decades, automobile manufactures, insurance representatives, government officials, engineers, scientists, and consumer advocates disputed the "facts" concerning air bags. Automobile manufacturers argued that the costs of air bags outweighed the benefits. Consumer groups estimated that between 2,000 and 12,000 lives a year could be saved. Experts lined up on both sides: Either they questioned the validity of tests using humanlike dummies, or saw a positive correlation between crash forces and human injuries. For years, each side produced "facts" and experts that generated opposing "facts" and experts.

One role for scientific and technical communicators will be to alter the conduct of similar debates. By understanding science and technology as inseparable from their social and rhetorical contexts, the endless procession of experts could have been avoided. Once convinced by historical examples that overwhelming scientific evidence would not win the day, debaters could have cast their arguments in new ways—perhaps in economic and political terms. In fact, this is what happened. The length of the debate allowed more people to get involved. Ultimately, social and political concerns—punctuated by the late 1970s' oil crisis, the demise of the United States automotive industry, and foreign manufacturers' initiatives for including air bags in mid-1980s' models—rather than scientific evidence—settled the debate. The air bag controversy illustrates how scientific and technical communicators could mediate public debates by translating technical issues into social ones and by providing means of communication that would allow various constituencies to be heard in a timely manner.

A FINAL WORD

C. P. Snow's 1959 Rede Lecture outlined the dangers of the widening intellectual gulf between scientists and nonscientists—what he called "the two cultures":

> I believe the intellectual life of the whole of western society is increasingly being split into two polar groups. . . . Literary intellectuals at one pole—at the other scientists. . . . Between the two a gulf of mutual incomprehension—sometimes (particularly among the young) hostility and dislike, but most of all lack of understanding. They have a curious and distorted image of each other. Their attitudes are so different that, even at the level of emotion, they can't find common ground. (pp. 4-5)

Like many, Snow felt that society was being transformed at an alarming rate by scientific and technological advances, one result being the creation of a split between two groups of specialists—each knowing little about the other, each mistrusting the other. Snow worried that this division would harm society as a whole.

Keeping Snow's sentiments in mind, one presumption of the field of science and technology studies is that sustaining an interchange of ideas, methods, and techniques among members of the "two cultures" will transform the work of the academic disciplines and professions. Through theses exchanges, new standards for effective communication, knowledge distribution, policy, and action—to which all practioners hold themselves accountable—will evolve. Ultimately, the result would be not only a greater tolerance among intellectuals, but a more open society in which the general public could make informed decisions about the aims of scientific and technological research. The issues confronting the two cultures will neither be settled by simply showing how—through technological by-products—scientific research is relevant, nor by insisting the public become "scientifically literate." As scientific and technical communicators, you share parts of each of Snow's cultures; consequently, you will be uniquely positioned to bridge the gulf between them. You can help craft the language required for exchanging ideas across boundaries. And, possibly, the syntax for this "exchange language" will come out of learning, exploring, and manipulating the contexts that direct, and are directed by, scientific and technological communication.

Discussion

1. One of the claims of this chapter is that the study and practice of scientific and technical communication often neglects the contexts in which it originates. What other contexts, not listed in this chapter, are important for practitioners and the lay public to know? Why is it important for you, in learning to become a practitioner in a field of study, to know the history of that field?

2. Consider the debate between Boyle and Hobbes presented in this chapter. Why should laboratory experiments not be witnessed by laypersons? Why should scientists not debate their claims in an open public forum? How do you think science would be different if Hobbes's arguments won the day?

3. Compare and contrast the views that Thomas Kuhn and Peter Medawar express about the role of scientific and technical writing in textbooks and in scientific articles. How do their

claims compare to your experience? How can consumers, yourself included, penetrate the images of science and technology provided in textbooks, news articles, and technical documents? Which professions do the best job of following the practices and rules given in textbooks and journals?

4. Who, in the debate between Socrates and Plato and the Sophists, was right? Explain. Why should scientists and technologists either embrace or maintain a distance from the rhetorical aspects of communication? Can one rightfully claim that *all* scientific and technical communication is rhetorical? Explain.

5. In the classroom and in textbooks we are often taught that professions adhere to certain standards of conduct and rules of practice. The "scientific method" is one example. Why is there a difference between what scientists *should* do and what they actually do? What does classroom laboratory experience tell you about actual scientific practice?

6. How is science and scientific knowledge situated in, or independent of, society? How do you think the state institutions, social order, political climate, public policy, economics, and trade influence the profession you intend to enter? How and why is science different in this regard?

7. Have you encountered what C. P. Snow calls the split between the worlds of the humanist and the scientist? In other words, have you seen scientists and humanists trying and failing to understand each other? Or, have you seen a place where scientists and humanists should understand each other but do not try? Have found yourself on one side of this split?

8. Referring to Chapter 7, Part II of the text, discuss how Fuller's notion of "democratizing" science addresses the following concerns. In 1919, the *New York Times* published a series of editorials on the lowly state of the lay public's understanding of contemporary developments in physics: namely, Einstein's work on relativity. Democracy was threatened, according to editorial writers, by the widening intellectual gulf between experts and laypersons. Astrology, mysticism, and religious fundamentalism were on the rise in the first quarter of the century. What parallels do you see between the arguments,

trends, and relationships regarding science and the lay public at the turn of the century and at the end of the century? How is democracy threatened by the gulf between intellectuals and the lay public? Why do scientific and technical communicators have a responsibility to educate the lay public about science and technology?

9. Discuss the similarities and differences between the definitions and functions of *context* forwarded in this chapter and in Fuller's analysis in Chapter 7, Part II.

Exercises

1. In the late 1940s, Gordon Allport and Leo Postman became interested in how rumor is spread. They performed an interesting experiment that allows us to replicate a Kuhnian paradigm shift in the classroom. Five or six students remove themselves from the rest—waiting outside the room or at least out of earshot. Everyone in the room is given the same photograph or drawing (offered as a slide or individual handout). Its subject should be a chaotic, confusing, and emotionally charged scene—an accident on a busy street corner, a political rally. Students in the room are given a minute to study the image. Then, one of those outside is allowed to return to the room but not allowed to see the image. The class describes the image—taking one or two minutes. The second of those outside is allowed to return; the first then recounts the description she has heard. And so on. If the experiment operates as Gordon and Postman's did, the description of the image changes greatly—many parts of it crystallize around a word or a few words.

2. In a one- to two-page memorandum, give a definition of one word or term common to two academic disciplines such as (feel free to choose others)—"formula," "result," "aggression," "submission," "depression," "migration," "experiment," "theory," "supply," and "value." Explain the similarities and differences in usage. Please provide the *etymology, history,* and specific *examples* of how the word or term is used in the

different disciplines. The etymology and history of the word or term can be found in the *Oxford English Dictionary* (*OED*), *Barnhart Dictionary of Etymology*, discipline-specific dictionaries, books dealing with the history of words and terms (e.g., Isaac Asimov's 1959 *Words of Science and the History Behind Them*), textbooks, and scholarly journals about linguistics. You may choose examples of how the word or term is used from any source or combination of sources. After comparing and contrasting how the word or term is used, consider the following questions in the recommendations or conclusion section:

- Can the word or term be used to explain or describe a similar phenomenon in different disciplines? For example, is the word "significant" used in the same way to describe experimental results in physics and experimental results in social psychology?
- How did these similarities and differences develop?
- Would the technically specific use of the term create confusion for lay audiences?
- Would curious lay audiences typically encounter this term?

3. In a one- to two-page memorandum, take an event or phenomenon that is normally explained by one academic discipline (this is only a partial list):

- How the universe started
- How (or why) capitalism works
- How animals evolve
- How mountains form
- Why we perform experiments
- How we gain and lose weight
- Why we have certain personalities
- Why certain groups of people are prone to poverty

Explain it in the concepts, terms, and theories of another discipline with which you are familiar. You need to redescribe the phenomena so that it might be discussed in the language of the second discipline. In providing your analysis, document any resistance you meet along the way in making the translation between the two disciplines. Do you think the practitioners of the first discipline would believe your analysis reveals something that interests them? How are your own ideas influenced as a result? What difficulties would practioners face by having their ideas or concepts explained in another discipline?[3]

4. In a one- to two-page memorandum, give an historical account of the development of the academic discipline in which you are now enrolled, or in which you intend enrolling. There are two parts to this assignment. First, by informally interviewing two or three instructors (of any academic rank), find out what they know about the history of the discipline or the field in which they perform research. Prepare a list of questions you might ask. For example:

▓ What is the history of the field before it was recognized as formal discipline of study?

▓ When did the discipline formally begin? Where? Under what circumstances?

▓ Who were the key players in beginning the discipline? What were their concerns?

▓ What is the current state of the discipline compared to its origins?

▓ What professional and social organizations govern the discipline?

▓ What types of people pursue work in this field?

▓ When did the discipline begin at your college or university? How many graduates have there been?

▓ What is the placement record of undergraduates in the department or discipline?

▓ What kinds of positions do graduates get?

The second part of the assignment is to perform limited library research. A number of scholarly treatments of the history of various disciplines exist, and most textbooks include some historical review. Compare and contrast the history of the discipline as presented by interviewees and in the research you survey. From your analysis of the two accounts, define your role in the discipline. What aspects of the discipline do you find interesting? How do you see yourself fitting into the historical context of the discipline as you now know it? What is the discipline's future? How do you define your role in that future?

NOTES

1. This paragraph offers a general summary of points made in Chapter 8 of Steven Shapin and Simon Schaffer's (1985) fascinating historical account of the Hobbes/Boyle debate.

2. This account follows the analysis presented in Thomas Kuhn (1977).

3. Exercises 2 and 3 are inspired by the Appendix from Steve Fuller's *Philosophy, Rhetoric, & the End of Knowledge* (1993).

BIBLIOGRAPHY

Allport, G. W., & Postman, L. (1947). *The psychology of rumor.* New York: Henry Holt.

Ashmore, M. (1993). The theatre of the blind: Starring a Promethean prankster, a phony phenomenon, a prism, a pocket and a piece of wood. *Social Studies of Science, 23,* 67-106.

Bazerman, C. (1988). *Shaping written knowledge.* Madison: University of Wisconsin Press.

Boyd, R., Gasper, P., & Trout, J. D. (1991). *The philosophy of science.* Cambridge: MIT Press.

Brennan, R. P. (1990). *Levitating trains and kamikaze genes: Technological literacy for the 1990s.* New York: John Wiley.

Bruner, J. (1986). *Actual minds, possible worlds.* Cambridge, MA: Harvard University Press.

Bruner, J., & Postman, L. (1949). "On the perception of incongruity: A paradigm." *Journal of Personality, 18,* 206-223.

Evered, D., & O'Connor, M. (Eds.). (1987). *Communicating science to the public.* Chichester, UK: John Wiley.

Fuller, S. (1993a). *Philosophy of science and its discontents* (2nd ed.) New York: Guilford.

Fuller, S. (1993b). *Philosophy, rhetoric, & the end of knowledge: The coming of science & technology studies.* Madison: University of Wisconsin Press.

Hobbes, T. (1985). Dialogus physicus (S. Schaffer, Trans.). In S. Shapin & S. Schaffer, *The leviathan and the air-pump: Hobbes, Boyle and the experimental life* (p. 350). Princeton, NJ: Princeton University Press. (Original Hobbes work published 1661)

Horgan, J. (1991). Profile: Reluctant revolutionary—Thomas S. Kuhn unleashed "paradigm" on the world. *Scientific American, 40.*

Krieger, J. (1990, May 14). Science education: Comprehensive approach urged. *Chemical and Engineering News,* pp. 4-5.

Kuhn, T. (1970). *The structure of scientific revolutions* (2nd ed.). Chicago: University of Chicago Press. (Original work published 1962)

Kuhn, T. S. (1977). *The essential tension: Selected studies in scientific tradition and change.* Chicago: University of Chicago Press.

Martino, J. P. (1992). *Science funding: Politics and porkbarrel.* New Brunswick, NJ: Transaction.

Medawar, P. (1967). *The art of the soluable.* London: Methuen.

Medawar, P. B. (1964, August 1). Is the scientific paper fraudulent? *Saturday Review,* pp. 42-43.

Mulkay, M., & Gilbert, G. N. (1981). Putting philosophy to work: Karl Popper's influence on scientific practice. *Philosophy of Social Science, 11,* 389-407.

Shapere, D. (1964). The structure of scientific revolutions. *Philosophical Review, 73,* 383-394.

Shapin, S., & Schaffer, S. (1985). *The leviathan and the air-pump: Hobbes, Boyle and the experimental life.* Princeton, NJ: Princeton University Press.

Snow, C. P. (1959). *The two cultures and the scientific revolution.* New York: Cambridge University Press.

Reading Scientific
and Technical Texts

Practitioners entering scientific and technical fields are confronted with an ocean of information—and the tide will constantly rise. As a reader, you will struggle to stay current with the literature in order to maintain and advance your position in your field. It is a truism that the task of reading all the information published in leading journals—in all but the most narrowly defined specialties—is impossible. The problem for you as a reader will not be reading faster, but learning how to select what is worthwhile to read slowly. As a layperson reading in areas outside your field of expertise, you will be confronted by a language not your own. The problem for you as a reader will not be to become an expert in dozens of fields, but to recognize the techniques for reading in your own field and relate them to other fields. In this chapter, we examine strategies for how to read and critically assess scientific and technical literature—from the perspective of the practitioner and the layperson—in an apt manner.

THE POSSIBILITIES OF READING

Approaches to reading vary widely and for the most part remain unexamined. Typically, reading is understood as a passive, individual activity about which one receives no formal instruction after childhood. Implicitly, it seems, individuals develop their own reading strategies. You may prefer to read in a certain place under specific conditions. Pressed for time, you may only read the introduction, conclusion, and subheadings to an article to be discussed in class that day. You may skip the words in a physics textbook altogether to get to the mathematical formulas. You may read a newspaper in a ritual manner—one section preceding the next. Although each of these strategies is unique, academic disciplines encourage certain possibilities for reading by regulating the expression, production, and presentation of a text; in part, how we read results from the activities going on "backstage" of the words we read.

Behind a text may lie the complex linguistic skills of a poet or the complex research skills of researchers in a laboratory. For poets, the activity of writing is generally private. Poets use imagination and personal insight in deciding what is true. However, consumers usually see the services of poets as minor. Reading poetry is associated with leisure. For researchers, the activity of writing is public *within their profession.* Researchers use each other's work in deciding what is true or factual. Consumers see research as valuable. Reading science is associated with accomplishing a task. What we face, in part, when reading a poem or research article is the organizational structure that helps write the text. As readers we approach poetry, rightly or wrongly, as the product of a less formal, highly individual process—which makes poetry seemingly more accessible. Reading poetry, one does not have to contend with the technical apparatus—graphs, charts, references to instruments, jargon, and references to other work—found in scientific and technical writing. Scientific and technical writing is less accessible. Further, readers of scientific and technical writing face an unusual dilemma:

> The peculiarity of the scientific literature is now clear: the only three possible readings lead to the demise of the text. If you give

up, the text does not count and might as well not have been written at all. If you go along, you believe it so much that it is quickly abstracted, abridged, stylized and sinks into tacit practice. Lastly, if you work through the author's trials, you quit the text and enter the laboratory. Thus the scientific text is chasing its readers away whether or not it is successful. Made for attack and defense, it is no more a place for a leisurely stay than a bastion or a bunker. This makes it quite different from the reading of the Bible, Stendhal or the poems of T. S. Eliot. (Latour, 1987, p. 61)

If Bruno Latour's irony rings true, reading a scientific or technical article is tantamount to going to war. Such a description runs counter to the general perception that "nothing happens" in a scientific text. Latour contends that if readers wanted to dispute a claim or enter a controversy introduced in a scientific or technical research article, they would confront an extraordinary array of resources available at the writer's command—laboratories, machines, instruments, chemicals, equations. In the face of these resources, and given a limited amount of time, almost all readers would abandon their challenge and concede the fact of the matter.

In mentioning other types of literature, Latour illustrates different reader responses to literary texts. Generally, the writer of a short story or poem invites the participation of the reader. Writers beckon readers in numerous ways—the use of language, dialogue, setting, tone, character, and plot devices. Latour points to the "demise" of scientific and technical texts because they chase away readers—the "defeat" of the reader is the goal of a scientific text! To achieve a "fact of the matter," the goal of the scientific and technical writer, from Latour's perspective, is to prevent challenges. Preventing challenges to a text is achieved by making it impervious to attack. The same textual devices making a poem or short story "reader friendly" are absent as a text appears more objective. If challenges are prevented, Latour suggests that the text should not have been written at all because no one, except a few experts, will be able to understand it. Absent challenge, the text is accepted as fact, abstracted, and received as another piece of knowledge fitting a larger puzzle.

Latour pinpoints many of the initial responses we have when encountering scientific and technical literature. As you know, scientific and technical writing can be dense and asks for (or *seems* to ask for) very close reading. Many scientific articles may intimidate you not so much by their content as by disciplinary jargon, long tables, and pages of footnotes. To provide a more mundane illustration, for the uninitiated, reading scientific and technical literature must be somewhat like reading the ingredients listed on the label of a can of soup. Words with common associations strike a chord in us—chicken, peas, celery—and lend an immediate basis for critical assessment and choice: "I like chicken, peas, and celery, so I'll buy the soup." Other words listed as ingredients—ferrous sulfate, thiamin mononitrate, monosodium glutamate—generate few associations and little basis for a choice. Until the reader has a context in which to place these terms, they remain meaningless. Perhaps, for the lay reader, these ingredients represent the centerpiece of a controversy about the use of food additives. The chemist may see these ingredients as the basis for a laboratory experiment having nothing to do with soup. The health specialist or environmentalist may see these ingredients as threatening to the interests they represent.

A FIRST READING

You may be surprised to learn that many technical documents are written *not* to be read. More precisely, documents are designed to allow certain readers to avoid reading certain parts: A company president, for instance, might read only the recommendation section of a final report; the project manager might read only the recommendation and conclusion; only a study group for a subsequent project might read the entire report. What allows this procedure is a commonly recognized format. Company presidents know there will be a recommendation section and know where to look for it: They open the document to the table of contents page, look to the bottom for a page number, and then move to it. When they have found the information they need, they file the report or send it to the next reader. A first reading of scientific and technical texts generally includes considering *what you need* and how you *initially respond to the text.*

Reading What You Need

Most readers are unaware of the mental models they possess that motivate their reading of a text. In scientific and technical fields, the largest percentage of reading (66% for students, 78% for people on the job) is done *in order to perform a task*. Readers tend to ignore lengthy introductions and manuals and strike out on their own. Reading in the sciences and technology is generally performed to gather information for practical application. As the readers of scientific and technical documents are, generally, practitioners in the field, the writer usually assumes the same or a higher degree of knowledge on behalf of the reader. By following familiar forms supplemented with indexical headings, scientific and technical documents direct a reader's movement through the text.

In a study of seven physicists in a variety of subspecialties, Charles Bazerman (1988) examined the basis on which the choices of what to read were made. Given the unbelievable amount of literature surfacing in physics, the researchers had to rely on time-saving measures to stay current in their fields. Bazerman's study suggested that scientists originally made choices of what to read based on the requirements of current or future work. In addition, choices about material on which to focus included a consideration of the author's reputation and the appearance of keywords in the title. Once these initial criteria were met the scientists moved to other reading strategies—selecting sections of articles to read, judging the significance of the research, determining how to use the material in their work, taking notes, and finally, re-reading the article. These schemes for reading, Bazerman concluded, were a combination of individual experiences (some dating to childhood) and the scientist's "map of the field," a conception of where the field is, where it will go, and how it will change.

Determining our needs for reading can be partially traced to the social roles we play: writers, editors, advocates, dissenters, experts, judges, and laypersons. The skills we acquire in becoming professionals—the ways we learn, think, communicate, and act—integrate novel, marketable expressions of individual talents and preferences with the goals of a particular group. Our contributions to the organization in which we work must be both unique and adhere to certain social constraints. Of course, the community in which we work molds, and is molded by, larger social groups, businesses, and institutions. As scientific and technical communicators assuming many social roles, we may feel a tension between more immediate roles, such as a parent and electrical engineer, and less defined ones, such as a member of a democratic society.

Different models offer explanations for how we read and process information. The design of texts—size of margins, length of paragraphs, use of subheadings, amount of white (empty) space on the page, placement of visuals—mirror assumptions about the reading process. For instance, your initial impressions from looking at a text—the size of the type, the number of references, the use of color—can influence your approach to a text or if you will read it at all. How you read indicates what your needs are. On one hand, the number of references an author makes in a text may suggest authority and knowledge of a field. You may read such a text closely to familiarize yourself with the current state of research. On the other hand, the number of references may intimidate you, and you may jump to the conclusion. In part, your decision of whether or not to read on is based on your assumptions and initial response to the text.

Responding to Assumptions

As you approach scientific and technical literature, consider the assumptions you bring to bear on a text and how these assumptions affect how you react to and read the text.

> ▨ *Presuppositions.* Consider what reactions or impressions you hold about a particular field or profession, its representatives, and its methods. On what grounds—personal experience, hearsay, news reports, reading literature in that field—are these reactions and impressions based? Laypersons sometimes allow their presuppositions to (a) prevent them from going outside their personal field of expertise, or (b) provide an excuse to ignore the work of others. This reaction can lead to (a) confusion with respect to legal,

medical, and insurance documents, or (b) a missed opportunity to bring insight to bear on your own work and the work of others. Everyone must deal with representatives of other professions. Compare the image of your profession or field to the one you approach as a layperson. By relating the images, language, and presentation of ideas of other professions to your own, you can build a context with which to understand the language of experts.

■ *Presentation.* Consider how you respond to the way the text looks. Are you impressed by the print quality? Is the text dense with words, tables, statistics, logical notation, and/or visual aids? Does the look of the text invite you to read it? Typically, readers have similar reactions to the way a text looks. On one hand, if a page has a number of pictures and visual aids the information presented may not be taken as seriously. On the other hand, a page with many words, tables, or mathematical formulas gives the information authority. The use of color, high-quality paper, and distinctive typeface suggests the financial commitment to the presentation. By comparing the look of past and present issues of a journal or the books in a series, you can get an indication of how the information is valued and why it is pursued.

■ *Presence of the authors.* Consider how you respond to the presence of the authors in the text. Do you get an impression of who the authors are and what they want to accomplish? Does the use of first-person and active voice make the information presented personal and therefore less legitimate? Does third-person and passive voice suggest that the findings have been confirmed by other researchers? The authority we place in a text, as readers, results from the mental picture we get of the authors. Ordinarily in scientific and technical communication, we get no feeling for the authors on first reading; rather, the research is presented as the product of faceless institutions or disciplines. Your reaction to the authors of a text creates a personal context that can sustain your interest in dense and complex material.

Characteristics of Technical Literature

Next time you visit the library, go to the periodicals section. Of course, depending on the library, the number of periodicals being received will vary, but survey the major journals in your field. Here, you will get some idea of the writing standards of your field and profession. In comparing the range of practices of journals published in the natural sciences, social sciences, and humanities you will encounter the following rough trends:

- Articles in the natural science disciplines (physics, chemistry, and biology) are more likely to have multiple authors than articles in the social sciences and the humanities.

- Articles in the natural sciences are more likely to be significantly shorter in length than articles in the social sciences and the humanities.

- Articles in the natural and social sciences are more likely to follow the same format (note the use of subheadings) than articles in the humanities.

- Articles in the humanities are more likely to have larger bibliographies, more footnotes, and refer to a greater number of different scholars than articles in the natural and social sciences.

- Articles in the natural and social sciences are more likely to rely on visual aids than articles in the humanities.

- Articles for each discipline have a good deal of jargon and specialist language; the audience for professional journals is usually small and consists of similarly educated specialists and professionals.

Scanning the Literature

As a potential practitioner, you will need to determine which sources of information best suit your needs. These needs will be quite different from your needs as a lay reader. As a lay reader, you may, for example, find secondary sources more helpful in acquainting you with the current debates in a particular field. Here are some factors that practitioners and laypersons can consider in choosing primary and secondary sources. Keep in mind that these factors should be considered together as a guideline, not as the sole basis for your choices. As you become familiar with the literature in a particular field, you will be able to more readily define the scope of your reading.

- *The press and/or journal.* Within specific disciplines, commercial and university presses, which publish books and journals, and journals, which publish articles, garner reputations based on who sits on the editorial board, commercial success, circulation, and the percentage of manuscripts accepted and rejected. With notable exceptions, high-prestige journals in a field have higher rejection and circulation rates than lesser known journals. Most journals and presses adhere to the blind review system in which a manuscript, with the author's name removed, is sent to a number of referees (usually between three and five). Each referee writes a report calling for the paper's acceptance, rejection, or conditional acceptance depending on the author's willingness to revise the paper.

The well-regarded journal *Science* rejects about 80% of the manuscripts submitted; the *New England Journal of Medicine* has a rejection rate of about 85%. In many cases, the author will resubmit a rejected manuscript to another journal. Given the proliferation of journals, tenacious authors can eventually find a home for their work. To determine how a paper has been received, examine the time lag between the original presentation of the manuscript and the actual date of publication. You can determine this by ascertaining when the paper was first presented at a conference (usually indicated in an acknowledgments footnote) or the dates of the original experiment. Knowing the specialties and rejection rates of journals and presses is the first step in evaluating information sources.

- *Title.* The title of a source will have keywords that allow you to determine its relevance to your needs.
- *Author(s).* Practitioners recognizing an author's name can select a source based on that author's reputation. The layperson unfamiliar with that reputation can consult citation indices, which, to a degree, help establish the regard the author's work has in the field or related fields.
- *Affiliation of the authors.* Just as the reputations of researchers can help you decide what sources to read, so can the reputation of the institution with which the researchers are affiliated. Usually, researchers are affiliated with either a university, a private laboratory, a national laboratory, or a think tank. Knowing the reputation or political leaning of a particular institution (especially in the case of think tanks) enables you to locate the strengths and potential biases of the research.
- *Support.* The federal government is the dominant source of funds for scientific and technological research and development. In 1987, according to one estimate, the National Science Foundation (NSF) funded slightly less than half of the research projects in physics; the major source for the other half of physics funding came from the Department of Energy. Over 80% of funding for research in civil engineering and anthropology came from the NSF. The extent of federal funding in certain research areas has triggered debate over how research priorities are set and how "politicized" the content of

science has become. Still, there are other sources of funding for research, such as private donors, pharmaceutical companies, and private foundations (e.g., the Heritage Foundation). Many of these contributors to research and development express clear interests and political agendas. As with knowledge of the affiliation of the authors, knowledge about the source of funds can give lay readers and practitioners a sense of the purpose, importance, and direction of the research.

Identifying Structural Elements

Journal articles in science and in technology have similar structures. This structure can serve as a basis for scanning and selecting relevant literature for both practitioners and laypersons. Before the article reaches the journal, it will most likely have been presented orally to a number of different groups and been commented on by audiences at conferences, as well as by reviewers.

Please note that other types of scientific and technical communication—proposals, instructions, oral presentations—follow well-defined structures. Your knowledge of the elements and derivations of these structures can serve as the basis for judgments—from the perspective of both a practitioner and a layperson—about the organization, thoroughness, and complexity of different types of scientific and technical communication.

Generally, journal articles contain the following elements:

■ *Abstract or introductory summary.* Given the explosion of the amount of technical literature, many scholars suggest tongue-in-cheek that the abstract *is* the real article. The abstract is perhaps the most important part of the article—clearly, it is the only part many people read. Abstracts may vary in length in proportion to the article's length. The reader can get a good idea of the content and technical density of an article from its abstract. Writing a clear, accessible abstract has become a necessary skill, as abstracts are used in access publications (publications that list and index abstracts) and on-line databases. Index and abstract publications, such as *Biological Abstracts, Chemical Abstracts,* and *Index Medicus,* and on-line systems, such as MEDLINE (*Index Medicus*), PsychINFO (*Psychological Abstracts*), and SCISEARCH, either selectively or comprehensively collect abstracts and article titles for literature searches. Both practitioners and laypersons can get the "feel" of a field of research by consulting abstracts in journals, access publications and on-line databases.

- *Keywords and phrases.* Not all journals provide a list of keywords and phrases. However, those that do either substitute keywords for an abstract or list them after the abstract. Keywords are reoccurring terms selected by the author. Like the abstract, the list of keywords gives an indication of the concepts and vocabulary with which you need to be familiar in order to comprehend the article. The title of the article also contains keywords necessary for cross-referencing in access publications.

- *Introduction.* The introduction of a science article lends an histori-cal context to the research by relating it to prior studies. In numerous cases, the research presented is performed to answer specific questions or to correct errors of previous research. Such research deals with points of contention internal to a narrowly defined field of study. Here, practitioners and laypersons can determine the relevance of the research to their concerns from its historical position.

- *Methodology section.* For the practitioner, the methods section may be the most important and substantive part of the study. The methods section presents the design of the study, the procedures followed, the means for data collection, and an evaluation of the procedure. Researchers evaluate the soundness of the methodol-ogy in determining the soundness of the results. If the methods are flawed, the data gathered will be flawed. However, a re-searchers' expectancy that following certain methods will lead to anticipated results may lead to self-deception. For the layperson, common sense provides a basis for critically judging the methods and results of certain experiments.

Some researchers have claimed that "thinking" animals—horses, dolphins, chimpanzees, apes—have the capacity to learn language and respond to questioning. At the turn of the century, German schoolteacher Wilhlem Von Osten announced that a remarkable horse, nicknamed Clever Hans, could count by tapping out num-bers with one hoof. Clever Hans would perform this feat not only for his owner, but for other audiences as well. Psychologist Oskar Pfungst investigated Von Osten's claims. Pfungst determined that Von Osten's expectations, unconscious cues, and the horse's ability to imitate his trainer were the actual reasons for the animal's ability to "communicate." The specter of this incident still haunts some animal researchers. Recently, for instance, the ability of apes to use sign language has been disputed on similar grounds. Of course, surveying the methods section of a scientific or technical article, it is unlikely that a layperson could draw conclusions about the validity of a researcher's findings. However, healthy skepticism of a researcher's methods or procedures based on personal experience with, for example, health care, statistics, or household chemicals and technologies, does have a place in critically scanning scientific and technical literature.

▓ *Results section.* Presented in a narrative form, the results section offers an analysis of the researchers' findings and contains tables, graphs, charts, and photographs. Again, the information represented may be incomprehensible to you as a lay reader, but your familiarity with the criteria for the presentation of visual information can be a basis for assessment. Tables and graphs that present too much information, for example, may indicate the author's confusion about the data's significance. The authors can offer interpretations of experimental results in this section or the discussion section.

▓ *Discussion section.* The discussion section reviews the study and may give ideas for areas of further research. Here the authors have room for apology, speculation, promotion, and instruction (for replicating the experiment). Depending on the authors' reputation and style, the discussion section allows them to "let their hair down." This section, for practitioner and lay reader, can be the most interesting. From a rhetorical point of view, it is important to keep in mind what the discussion *does not say* as much as what it does say. Disciplines have different attitudes toward presenting events that go on "behind the scenes" in an article. Research articles in the natural sciences, for example, give the reader an impression that the series of experiments was performed in an orderly fashion with few mistakes, interruptions, or disputes among laboratory members. Articles in some social science disciplines present a more introspective, critical treatment of their methods, procedures, and results—often citing limitations and failures. Lay readers can draw distinct impressions about the relation between the subject matter of the research and how results are organized and presented.

▓ *References or a bibliography.* Practitioners can determine how well the authors know the previous literature and also find relevant material for their own research. By knowing the literature of their field, practitioners make judgments about where the authors wish to position themselves with regard to previous research. Drawing comparisons between disciplines, the lay person can see how well-defined and organized a field is. For example, there tend to be fewer references in an article in the natural sciences than in an article in a humanities discipline. Some researchers conclude that writers in highly specialized disciplines have a precise idea of what their audience knows (or should know) and need to make fewer explicit references. Writers in less specialized disciplines, or with interdisciplinary concerns, must simultaneously educate their audience while legitimating their views to researchers with varying levels of expertise. As a result, the writer must appeal to a wider range of literature. From scanning the references section of journal articles over a period of time, laypersons and practitioners can identify the leading researchers and important techniques of a field by the number and consistency of references to a particular author or work.

A SECOND READING

Scientific and technical writing does not arouse readers, especially from outside a given subject area, to perform a second, more thoughtful, reading. As Latour (1987) suggested previously, one reason for this is the armor plating of the text—references and devices designed to take readers straight from the text to the laboratory. Lay readers cannot get around these devices. But reading is a truly interdisciplinary activity: We learn, at least implicitly, how to read a variety of material in a number of different ways. On a second reading, you can bring to light aspects of a technical text by techniques you have learned in other disciplines. In this section we will draw a comparison among reading literary and scientific texts. Both types of kinds of texts depend on shared and specialized uses of vocabulary and metaphor. In comparing and contrasting how vocabulary and metaphor work in science and other disciplines, we can take the first steps, as potential practitioners and lay readers, to understanding one of the unique rhetorical features of scientific and technical texts—witnessing.

Literary and Scientific Texts

We read texts from particular points of view. These points of view originate within the cultures, institutions, and classrooms in which we participate. Our reading and writing practices depend on a complex system of values. Neither can we "rise above" this system of values to offer objective readings or descriptions, nor do these values determine all our possibilities for expression. Although it is important to realize the social origins of how we read and write, it is also important to keep in mind that the boundaries separating disciplines and organizations are largely artificial. We can effectively bring the reading practices of one field of study to bear on other fields of study.

Scientific and technical writers are trained to *use* the conventional elements of documents such as the technical report and the experimental article, but they rarely *study* them. To study a technical article or scientific book the way you would study a short story or novel seems incongruous. If, for example, you enrolled in a course on Victorian prose, you would expect to study the literary and critical works of authors such as Matthew Arnold, Thomas Carlyle, George Eliot, and John Ruskin. Most likely you would not expect to study the theological, scientific, and mathematical works of William Paley, Lord Kelvin, Charles Darwin, and George Boole. But how does reading science compare to reading literature?

On the surface, reading scientific texts is nothing like reading literature. Properly speaking, of course, science writing is not storytelling. The imagination of a scientist is not the same as that of a poet or storyteller; it reflects the ability to see formal connections before they can be proved in a formal way. Scientific writing deals in general causes and procedures to get at testable hypotheses. Scientific writing seeks higher and higher abstraction to produce statements that can be applied in the most general way. Scientific knowledge is considered unique because it is subject to experiment. A literary text cannot be, in a meaningful way, verified or falsified. The facts of nature (e.g., the freezing point of water) exist independently of how well they are communicated. However, the seemingly unique aspects of science frequently translate into reasons why "outsiders" cannot comprehend its literature. For example, many people trained in humanities disciplines may not feel their interpretive skills apply to scientific and technical writing. In drawing this conclusion, we fail to recognize the shared standards of communication existing among disciplines.

Some theorists do not see scientific knowledge as having privileged status and argue that scientific texts can be treated to similar types of rhetorical and literary analysis as many forms of literature. If we entertain for a moment the notion that scientific texts *can* be studied like literary texts, what would our class in Victorian prose (mentioned earlier) look like? Literary critics

typically look at the features of a text—genre, narrative, description, dialogue, use of metaphor and irony, authorial presence (or
absence of)—and how certain texts compare to and influence
other texts. Although scientific and technical texts do not feature
all of the elements of literature, they do share many important
formal elements—narrative, word choice and arrangement, and
use of symbols. For example, one could study the features and
the ideas presented in Darwin's *On the Origin of Species* and trace
their development in the novels of George Eliot. As readers of
scientific texts, we neglect questions as to what influences
Darwin—or any scientist—might have felt, his rhetorical purposes, and how the reception and understanding of his work was
determined by later writers such as Matthew Arnold. Science and
technology are not just the source of ideas for literature; frequently, scientific and technical writing reveal literary themes
and devices.

While at Cambridge University, the famous English literary
critic I. A. Richards (1893-1979) presented his students with
unidentified poems and asked for their anonymous responses to
them over a week. In *Practical Criticism* (1935), he published the
findings of his experiment. According to Richards, students had
fundamentally misread the poems; they were unable to read the
texts in order to derive any meaning. Given the quality of the
students, he found it absurd that they had no instruction in how
to interpret a text. Interpretation itself, Richards contended,
could be taught. Students could be instructed on how to derive
the meanings of texts and then learn to make meanings in the
process of interpretation. Richards took up the task of instructing
students how to perform detailed readings of texts. The interaction between readers and words (or symbols) illustrated his idea
that readers do think not just about concepts, but with them.
From the principles of close reading, Richards made apparent the
need to pursue not only how meaning is made in the process of
writing, but the way meaning is made in the act of reading.

It is easy to see that how we write, say, in a humanities course
and an electrical engineering course is different. Because we write
differently in those courses, doesn't it follow that we would read
differently in them as well? We seem to think of reading, however,

as a universally applied process. You just "do it." As the example above shows, by examining science writing in, for example, the context of literary analysis, you can see how different reading techniques—like close reading—can shed light on subjects within various disciplines. The interaction between readers and words, demonstrated in the use of specialized vocabularies and captured in metaphors, shows that readers do think not just *about* concepts but *with* them.

Using and Translating Technical Vocabulary

You are coming into possession of a highly technical vocabulary. The disciplines and fields you study distinguish themselves by the use of technical terms. Although it is impossible to draw a sharp distinction between a technical vocabulary and general vocabulary, you can get an idea of a technical vocabulary by the frequency in which the words appear in ordinary conversation. Words such as "catalysis," "heuristic," and "homeostasis" would be unknown (although possibly recognized) to the ordinary person. Accordingly, technical terms originating in one field or used differently in various fields, such as "magnetohydrodynamics," "fermions," and "induction," pose a problem for practitioners who must communicate across professional boundaries. Here lies the problem of the absence of a shared vocabulary among experts and laypersons.

For the author of a text, one task is to determine the educational level of the readers and the best way to present information to them. For the reader of the text, one task is to derive the author's meaning. However, many scientific and technical communicators face the task of writing for multiple audiences, with multiple educational backgrounds. The simple solution to this problem has been to choose a "lowest common denominator"— determine a group's most basic level of technical knowledge and write or speak to it. Often, this solution offers more problems than it solves by being inefficient and possibly offensive to the reader. By examining the causes and possible solutions to the use of exaggerated technical vocabulary, you can devise strategies for presenting and reading scientific and technical documents for different audiences. Here are some causes of confusion:

- **Assumptions.** Although authors must make assumptions about the knowledge of the reader, they usually draw a series of inconsistent conclusions as a result. If the writer assumes the reader knows the meaning of "friction," then they may conclude the reader *must* know about convection, radiation, and the laws of thermodynamics. Assumptions on the part of the writer can develop into an almost endless chain of other assumptions and conclusions. Relatedly, the author may take the time to explicate an easier term while neglecting a more difficult one. The lack of consistency in the author's level of assumption can frustrate the reader and needs to be avoided by the writer.

- **Habits.** Authors and speakers fall into customary patterns of vocabulary use. These patterns are reinforced within disciplines and professions. As a practitioner in a field, you need to be aware that the habits you develop do not exclude diverse audiences.

- **Lack of recognition.** Practitioners in a field may fail to realize that the language they are using is indeed technical to a given audience. In attempting to define or simplify a term, the author or speaker can offer a definition as difficult or esoteric as the term itself. The definition reflects assumptions the author or speaker makes about the audience's knowledge, and can neglect how common terms have specialized uses. For example, "charm" can be defined as the fourth flavor of quark. Even with the proper context—subatomic particle physics—this definition gives no insight to the lay reader because it involves a technical term (i.e., quark) and an idiosyncratic use of daily language (i.e., flavor).

- **Specialized use.** As illustrated in the example above, another source of confusion between scientific and technical communicators and audiences is the use of words common to everyday speech in a specialized sense. Subatomic physicists in describing particles of matter not only refer to their "charm" but to "color" and "spin" as well. We are familiar with all these words, but their meaning is quite different in reference to subatomic particles. The specialized use of terms and concepts also changes over time. Scientific concepts such as force, matter, and time have historical origins and different applications in given theoretical frameworks. As theories have changed, so have the meanings of these concepts.

Here are some possible solutions:

▓ **Attention to use.** Paying attention to how you use technical vocabulary is, of course, necessary for both the writer and reader, keeping in mind the points of confusion mentioned earlier. By considering scientific and technical communication in context— the social and historical contexts in which the use of a word or term evolves (like mass or weight, for example)—you can begin to see beyond your disciplinary training in considering the perspectives of diverse audiences. Reading critically, you can begin to trace the source of confusion—assumptions, habits, lack of recognition, ambiguous use—between what the author tries to convey and what you are able to understand. In instances where the author uses everyday vocabulary in a clear, commonly accepted manner, the lay reader can establish grounds on which to understand technical vocabulary.

▓ **Word lists.** Some researchers suggest that the ultimate solution for bridging the communications needs of experts and laypersons would be to develop a list of words to which authors must confine their exposition. Once determined, this standard vocabulary could then be taught in schools. Specifically, such a list would be developed for writers—news reporters and science popularizers— who must convey highly technical information to lay audiences. Insofar as popular accounts of science and technology depend on a technical vocabulary the lay readers can understand (Tom Clancy's novels are an example), a word list does exist. Accordingly, proponents of scientific literacy argue that students be taught an essential vocabulary of words and terms so that they are prepared to make informed public and personal decisions about science and technology.

▓ **Word origins.** Most scientific and technical terms (medical terms are a good example) are formed by Greek and Latin roots, prefixes, and suffixes. Knowledge of these root elements enables lay readers to make sense of certain technical terms.

Interpreting Metaphors

Metaphors are figures of speech in which comparisons are implied in order to reveal similarities between seemingly unlike things. For example, Italian novelist Primo Levi, in the opening of *The Periodic Table,* compares his ancestors to the inert, noble, and rare gases: "The little that I know about my ancestors presents many similarities to these gases. Not all of them were materially inert, for that was not granted them" (Levi, 1984, p. 4).

Metaphors help ground common experiences among the writer or speaker and the audience.

Metaphors play a powerful, if somewhat disputed role, in scientific and technical communication. In appealing to a lay audience, for instance, technical communicators use metaphors to compare specialized concepts to objects in the audience's experience. Antibodies and interferons (a protein that *interferes* with the virus' attempt to reproduce inside the cell) are compared to a "defense system" that "attacks" an "invading virus." This kind of comparison is contentious in that it ascribes human characteristics to nonhuman objects, invites an unwarranted value judgment, and influences treatment. To extend the metaphor and the impressions it leaves, the virus is "bad" because it "attacks" *your* body when its "defenses" are "down." To "combat" this "invader," you devise a "battle plan" that may include rest, aspirin, and lots of fluids. You have probably heard doctors describe viruses as "sneaky," "tough," and "resilient." Of course, the virus itself does not embody these characteristics, but the treatment of viruses and diseases follows from a model of "attack" and "defense." Critics of cancer research claim, for example, that metaphors controlling our ideas about disease have closed researchers' and physicians' minds to alternative and inventive forms of treatment. Problems in treating cancer or AIDS appear intractable because the medical community is stuck in a rut in conceptualizing the function of disease.

Metaphors inspire a chain of associations that must also be critically considered. The leap from comparing diseases to "invaders" to reconceptualizing the treatment of cancer is at best treacherous and at worst malicious. As a reader and writer, you need to determine your critical priorities and how those priorities fit into the language of the discipline in which you study. In reading a textbook, set of instructions, or proposal, examine whether you understand the metaphor being used and if you see it as *essential* or *incidental* to the description given. For example, one of the root metaphors for science in the seventeenth century was of nature as God's clock. According to this metaphor, natural effects proceeded like clockwork according to the Creator's grand design. As a result, the purpose of experimental science was to examine the clock's mechanisms. Although God might produce the same effect through different causes, scientists could determine a *probable* cause for a natural occurrence because nature was regulated. The clock metaphor has been understood as essential to the conception and advancement of early modern science.

A more recent but quite different example of the use of metaphor in science is James Lovelock's Gaia hypothesis. Gaia, the ancient Greek mother goddess of Earth, is a metaphor for nature and the unity of all living things. The Gaia hypothesis postulates the Earth as a living organism existing interdependently with other living organisms. Earth itself is portrayed as a delicately balanced "superorganism." The hypothesis is highly controversial, and many natural scientists consider it New Age pseudoscience. Although Gaia as a metaphor is essential to Lovelock's hypothesis, it is incidental to the modern conduct of biology and environmental science.

As both a writer and reader, you need to determine the essential or incidental influences of the use of metaphors in scientific and technical communication. The values embodied by metaphor are expressed in the practices of a community. Describing nature as an earth goddess or a mechanical clock, for instance, leads to different notions of what it means to do research, perform an experiment, and report its results. Metaphor is a necessary element of technical communication that carries with it the values of a community—a set of values that requires critical examination.

Witnessing Experiments

"Show me." "Seeing is believing." Aside from being clichés, both statements capture the healthy skepticism we feel when someone, even an authoritative source, tells us something contrary to common sense. If we actually witness—among others who will confirm our story—the effects of room-temperature fusion in a jar, or the ascension of a "monster" from the depths of Loch Ness, then we will be convinced (at least partially) the phenomenon or object exists. The relation between seeing and believing is the basis for the experimental research article in science and technology.

Robert Boyle (1627-1691) and the English experimentalists strongly argued that if science were to be empirical it must be witnessed. In fact, Boyle (1772/1985) contended, the more times an experiment could be repeated with the same outcome—in front of an increasing number of witnesses—the closer one would come to establishing a fact. Debate persisted over who should witness an experiment and how observations should be reported and interpreted. Boyle faced the practical reality that the lay public could not be directly involved in the experimental process. Visual aids and a plain narrative reporting style were Boyle's solutions to the problem of actual witnessing. Accordingly, visual aids and narration were meant to "stand for" the performance of an experiment. In reading an experimental account supplemented with visual aids, the reader would virtually "see" the experiment taking place.

Since accounting for all the details and contingencies affecting an experiment is impossible, Boyle submitted to the practical constraint of choosing which details and contingencies to include in his reports. Today, we must recognize that authors' choices as well as other constraints (e.g., journal space, cost of printing and publication, and time) influence what counts as objective scientific and technical communication.

As many of you know from your experiences in the laboratory, writing a fully detailed narrative account of all experimental activities and contingencies is impossible. Your account would need to possess an endless array of details, mistakes, conjectures, speculations, and interruptions. Over time, the relationship that Boyle sought to foster between experimenters and witnesses has changed. By almost any standard, science and technology have achieved extraordinary success over the past 300 years. The need to convince public witnesses of the overall value of scientific and technical research no longer exists. Accordingly, failed experiments are only occasionally reported, and most experiments are not replicated.

The role of witnesses, for the most part, belongs to experts—peer reviewers and other researchers. Consequently, scientific and technical knowledge has been difficult to hold up to general scrutiny. Still, the legitimacy of specific research projects must be satisfactorily explained to government and corporate representatives, and the role of the "public witness" changes as science and society change.

Information Sources

In the sciences and technology, journal articles are the staple of published work. Journal articles are usually written for practitioners, not wide audiences. Recent changes in the editorial practices of some academic journals, however, are based on a desire to reach out to the lay public. Still, one of the better sources for understanding the communicative practices of your profession and other professions with which you will interact is the academic journal. Nevertheless, other information sources exist about which you need to make judgments. Determining whether a source of information is good or bad or appropriate or inappropriate depends on individual judgment, the methods and research being pursued, and the standards of the community in which you participate.

Roughly, information sources can be distinguished as *primary* or *secondary*. Primary sources are original works—journal articles, conference papers, monographs (textbooks, published symposia). Secondary sources—reviews, indexes, abstracts, data collections, dictionaries, manuals, literature reviews (in dissertations)— are derivatives of original works. An example of a primary source is Charles Darwin's *On the Origin of Species*. Secondary sources are (a) works that comment on Darwin's research, and (b) research using Darwin's findings as an empirical basis. The cumulative nature of science and technology, however, denies such a hard-and-fast distinction—almost all scientific and technical literature is secondary in that it derives from previous work.

Consulting Citation Indexes

The work of science and technology is cumulative. Through references and citations, researchers acknowledge previous work in an area, lend support to their own arguments, and look toward the future of the research. A reference gives credit to previous work, places the research being presented in that context, and demonstrates the author's familiarity with the relevant literature. A citation shows what the research being presented receives from other research and may lead the reader to future work in that area. If you looked at an article published in a sociology journal in 1992, for example, you might find a research paper offering an explanation for the rise of violent crime in the United States the previous year. Looking at research done on violent crime in 1995, you may see a citation, or a number of citations, to the 1992 paper. As your research progresses, you may find an increasing number of citations and references to the 1992 study in subsequent research. As a result, the importance of the 1992 research has been established. Nevertheless, you need to establish *why* and in what context the work was considered important. The 1992 paper may be cited as an example of a famous statistical blunder leading to misinformation about the causes for the rise of violent crime. Generally, however, the number of citations a paper receives indicates its confirmation and authority in the field. Roughly half of the available papers are cited in any one year, and of that half, 75% are cited only once.

Introduced in 1964, the *Science Citation Index* covers scientific and technical literature in the natural and behavioral sciences as well as in agriculture, engineering and medicine. The index is published every two months and is made up of three sections:

- *Source Index,* which covers current articles, is arranged alphabetically by the name of the first author of the journal article. Other source items are names of secondary authors, abbreviations of journal titles, volume, page, and year of the publication and the number of references it contains.

- *Citation Index,* which covers references appearing in these articles, is arranged alphabetically by the author's name followed by a chronological list of the author's cited articles.

- *Permuterm Index,* which covers keywords appearing in these articles, is used essentially as a subject guide to the article in the *Source Index.*

Bimonthly issues are compiled into an annual index, and five-year indexes have been compiled since 1965. Retrospective indexes have been published. There are also the *Social Sciences Citation Index* and the *Arts and Humanities Citation Index.*

Accordingly, *Journal Citation Reports* analyzes the frequency of citations to journal titles, noting which titles have been cited most and least frequently. The coverage of each of these indexes has continued to increase, mirroring the increase in the number of publications and citations.

The relevance of citation indexes generates a good deal of debate. The number of citations attributed to an author, paper, or journal has been taken as an indication of the impact and influence of the work or journal title. Put simply, the greater the number of citations, the greater the significance of the work. Through citation analysis, sociologists have studied the relation between scientists' productivity and the recognition of their work. Nobel prizewinners, for example, have citation rates almost 30 times greater than other scientists *after* they win the award. It seems that, with respect to citation, the rich get richer. Although peer recognition influences citation rates, it is, however, impossible to determine whether content or reputation is the basis for frequent citation as authors are not anonymous.

Sociologists and historians use citation sequences as the basis for claims about the progress and impact of certain ideas and techniques. The ideas and techniques presented in research papers may be picked up and cited in later work or completely forgotten. Frequency of citation can also be seen as a product of the number of articles published about a subject in a given year. As well, many researchers argue that even though a work has been cited, it may not have been read. In many fields, for a journal article to be considered relevant, an obligatory citation must be made to a standard-bearer in the field or to an article explaining a technique used by researchers. Self-citation is also customary in many fields. Many researchers cite their previous work as a bid for self-promotion. However, self-citation is not seen as statistically significant in comparing citation frequencies.

Still, given disputes about the merit of citation, these indexes can be powerful tools both for retrieving information and for evaluating the current state of the art. For instance, one way for a layperson to frame a current scientific debate would be to compare what the participants understand as the relevant focus of research with the number of citations to the topic in papers and journals.

Discussion

1. Consider the different contexts in which you read—for pleasure, for class assignments, for work. How do you approach reading in each of those contexts? How does having a choice of *what* you read influence *how* you read? What strategies do you employ in choosing what you read?

2. How do you approach assigned readings in class? In what specific manner do you read? Do you skip sections of the text? What triggers your attention? Particular words? Images? Equations? How much time do you spend reading each week?

3. What does Bruno Latour mean by "the demise of the text"? How are facts established in scientific texts? Why should facts be challenged? How is it possible for a layperson to challenge a claim of scientific knowledge? What role does the laboratory play in the writing and reading of scientific and technical texts?

4. What role do you think the reader's purpose plays in defining a reading strategy? How do your own social roles—as a student, parent, resident, voter, fan, employee—influence what and how you read?

5. In surveying how physicists read in their discipline, Charles Bazerman (1988) challenges that if an article is poorly written, readers cannot follow its argument or meaning. Generally, what do you think bad writing indicates? When reading bad or confusing writing, do you stop to reread the material or give up? What strategies does a writer use to write well and accessibly about complex or dense subjects?

6. The piecemeal reading of texts makes information seem personal. Frequently, the basis of scientific knowledge—from reading journal articles—is not a question of comparing experimental results against the framework of nature, but of

comparing them against personal frameworks. Often, re-searchers admit that if they know the writer personally—and the author's reputation is bad—they won't read a journal article by that person. How do these attitudes square with your image of how science is conducted? If reading practices are often personal, in what respects does that make scientific knowledge more personal than objective? Why should a person's reputation make a difference in choosing to read scientific literature?

7. How does reading on the job differ from other types of reading? When you are asked to read something—as a requirement of your job or performing a task—what do you assume about the writing itself?

8. Referring to Chapter 8 in Part II of the text, describe how reading is a reflexive process, based on Cooper's definitions of reflexivity. Does reflexive writing encourage reflexive reading? Is reflexive reading necessary in science? Why or why not? What are some of the inherent weaknesses that Cooper points out in the presentation of reflexive texts? How can a reader overcome these problems?

Exercises

1. During the semester, keep a reading journal. Document the kind of material that you read and how you read it. In the journal, consider (among other things) your personal habits—when you read, in what location, if you mark the text, if you read a text from beginning to end, if you read selections—your preferences, the way you select material, and how you read material selected for you.

2. Go to the library and select the current issue of a leading professional journal representing your discipline. You may ask an instructor their opinion about which is the leading journal, or look at journals sponsored by the professional society governing your discipline. Once you have selected the journal, find a copy of it (bound in the stacks) from 15 to 20

years ago. In a short report, compare the two journals. Consider, for example:

- Does the journal look the same—cover design, length, font type, print size, how the table of contents is presented, ratio of words to figures, use of graphics? What are the differences and similarities?
- Are there any common members of the editorial board from the two time periods? Is the journal still published by the same company or located at the same university?
- If you can find a statement of the purpose of the journal (perhaps on the back cover of the journal), compare the stated purpose of the journal and the editorial policies from the two time periods. Are there any differences?
- Are there differences in the journal articles themselves? Consider relative length of the articles, the number of footnotes, and the number of sources cited.

After comparing these characteristics (and others which you notice), draw some general conclusions about the health of the discipline. Here are some thought questions (you are not required to answer them directly) to help focus your analysis:

- Does the discipline appear to be growing and changing, staying the same, or declining?
- What are some of the characteristics you found in comparing the journals that lead you to your conclusions?
- What is the style of communication on the discipline?
- What are the characteristics of the prose (sentence length, use of person, use of voice, use of pronouns, use of jargon)?
- Emphasis on visuals?
- Generally, what is the rhetorical purpose of this disciplinary style?

3. In a two- to three-page memorandum give an account of the communication practices of the academic discipline in which you are now enrolled or in which you intend to enroll. By interviewing two or three practitioners or instructors (of any academic rank) in the field, find out what types of communication they consider more or less important. Prepare a list of questions you might ask. For example:

- What types of documents do you read most frequently (e.g., proposals, instructions, letters, memos, journal articles)?
- How did you learn to become an effective writer/communicator? Under what circumstances?
- Can you recall the first professional writing that you did on the job? What process did you go through? How was the product evaluated?
- Is public speaking (at meetings, conferences, in collaborative settings) an important part of your practice?
- Is most of your writing done alone or collaboratively?
- Is reading an important part of your practice? How, and how often, do you read?
- Over time, and given the advent of new technologies, what changes have you seen in communication practices?
- What would you consider to be the norms, or standards, of communication in the field?
- What passes for effective communication in the field? Are there examples that come to mind which you would have laypeople read?
- What communications skills do you think is important for a new practitioner to learn?

In comparing and contrasting the answers of the people you interview, offer a series of recommendations (to your instructor) as to how one could prepare a member of your field or discipline to become an effective technical communicator. Consider recommending what types of skills should be emphasized, to what degree they should be emphasized, and how you might teach these skills.

4. Before the modern scientific era, metaphor was used frequently, but with some hesitation, by early modern naturalists, scientists and inventors. The concept of Nature is often considered metaphorically. Today, metaphor is a device employed by popular science writers.

   Select two 500-word samples of scientific or technical writing from the same discipline—biology or economics, for instance. Each sample should provide an explanation of (roughly) the same phenomenon.

   The first sample should have been originally published before 1900 by someone now considered "a major contributor" (loosely defined) to the field, such as (there are many others from which to choose) Francis Bacon, Robert Boyle, Galileo Galilei, Isaac Newton, Benjamin Franklin, Michael Faraday, Jean Lamark, William Paley, and Charles Darwin.

The second sample should have been originally published since 1960 by someone considered a "science popularizer" (loosely defined), such as (again, there are many others from which to choose) Rachel Carson, Stephen J. Gould, James Gleick, Douglas Hofstadter, Carl Sagan, Alvin Toffler, and Robert Wright.

In a two- to three-page memorandum, compare, contrast, and analyze the uses of metaphor in the two samples. Some thought questions to consider (you are not required to answer them directly) are these:

- What metaphors do the authors use? What phenomena are they trying to describe?
- Do the authors use the same or different metaphors to describe the same thing? What accounts for the similarities or differences?
- From where do these metaphors originate?
- Who is the audience? From your analysis, what profile can you draw of the intended audience for these works?
- Is using metaphor objective?
- What impressions do these metaphors lend the audience?
- How does using metaphor help in, or detract from, understanding the concepts being presented?
- Does using metaphor persuade the audience to think of a phenomenon in a certain way? In what way? Is this way accurate?

BIBLIOGRAPHY

Bazerman, C. (1988). *Shaping written knowledge.* Madison: University of Wisconsin Press.

Boyle, R. (1985). New experiments physico-mechanical, touching the spring of the air. In S. Shapin & S. Shaffer, *Leviathan and the air pump: Hobbes, Boyle and the experimental life* (pp. 63-64). Princeton, NJ: Princeton University Press. (Original Boyle work published 1772)

Brennan, R. P. (1992). *Dictionary of scientific literacy.* New York: John Wiley.

Duin, A. (1988). How people read: Implications for writers. *The Technical Writing Teacher, 25,* 185-193.

Fuller, S., & Raman, S. (Eds.). (1991). *Teaching science and technology studies: A guide for curricular planners.* Blacksburg: Virginia Polytechnic Institute and State University, Science Studies Center.

Kronick, D. (1985). *The literature of the life sciences: Reading, writing, research.* Philadelphia: ISI Press.

Latour, B. (1987). *Science in action.* Cambridge, MA: Harvard University Press.

Levi, P. (1984). *The periodic table* (R. Rosenthal, Trans.). New York: Shocken.

Restivo, S. (1992). *Mathematics in society and history: Sociological inquiries.* Dordrecht: Kluwer Academic.

Richards, I. A. (1935). *Practical criticism: A study of literary judgment.* New York: Harcourt Brace.

Writing Scientific and Technical Texts

Writing is at once a highly individual and thoroughly social process. No two individuals approach the writing process in exactly the same way, just as no two individuals think and believe in exactly the same way. Also, as complex as our belief systems and thought processes are, so too are the processes of writing. Although writing is undeniably difficult, a writer's strategies and tasks originate within a set of existing community practices that, once understood, can be manipulated in creative ways. The forms of writing you use, the previous literature you have read, your knowledge of audience and purpose, your collaboration with colleagues, and your disciplinary training and work experience define the writing situation by providing a repertoire from which you can make choices. Your writing process, or processes, will be the unique expression of your choices within the social and historical contexts in which communication occurs.

The writing process does not occur in isolation. As you participate in an academic discipline or profession and become familiar with the literature of a particular field—textbooks, journal arti-

cles, technical documents, newspaper articles, popular literature—you enter an ongoing conversation consisting of certain
topics, accepted beliefs, and common questions. When, to illustrate, you come into a room and encounter a conversation among
a group of people, you listen for a subject on which you can
comment and then enter the discussion. The more you know and
learn about the issues and themes being discussed, the more
perspective you gain and the easier it becomes for you to participate. Accordingly, science and technology are institutions that
have "rooms" and conversations—separate fields and languages
of study and research—you can enter.

The forms of scientific and technical communication (e.g.,
proposals, instructions, and journal articles) represent an acknowledged set of guidelines that bring precedent and order to
bear on an exchange of ideas. These guidelines reflect the fundamental presumptions and goals, such as objectivity and succinct-
ness, of its practitioners. For instance, the evolution of the
experimental article in science came in response to changing
ideas about the nature of scientific knowledge. As a scientific and
technical writer, you need to critically evaluate the presumptions
and goals of the conversations within the community and justify
your acceptance of them. Still, the forms and guidelines of
scientific and technical writing are not an end in themselves. Your
unique interpretation of those guidelines comprises the voice you
bring to the process of scientific and technical writing.

A SHARED MYTH

Like science, writing is a process subject to myth. Francis
Bacon (1561-1626) originally formulated the scientific process as
a series of steps—observation, hypothesis, experiment, data, and
conclusion—we know as the scientific method. The writing process is also formulated as a series of steps—*inventing* (generating
ideas), *drafting* (presenting ideas and information), and *revising*
(reworking and editing). Like the steps of the scientific method,
however, it is a mistake to regard the steps of the writing process
as *anything more than a model* of actual practice.

Writing is never a neat, linear sequence of steps. No one produces a flawless first draft. We all experience fits and starts in the process of writing: revising one section of a document before going to another or performing research in mid-draft and changing the focus of the document as a result. Some days, you can write for hours; other days, the words will not come. Some writers panic and quit writing in the face of deadlines. For other writers, panic is a necessary motivation. You may think you have reached the conclusion of a document only to find after a second reading that you must change its entire structure. Writing is sometimes sloppy. Writing takes time. And writing is difficult—just like science.

Science is never a neat, linear sequence of steps. No one performs an errorless first experiment. Scientists experience fits and starts in the process of experimentation: revising a hypothesis, performing other experiments and research, and changing the focus of the original research. Some days, experiments work like a charm; other days, you cannot get results. Some researchers panic and quit working in the face of deadlines and funding cuts. For other researchers, panic is a necessary motivation. You may think you have reached the conclusion of an experiment only to find you must do it again and change its entire structure. Scientific practice is sometimes sloppy. Science takes time. And science is difficult—just like writing.

Due to their respective complexities, the practice of science and the process of writing are subject to myth. And these myths mirror each other. The myth of writing is that it is an innate creative "gift"—either you have "it" or you don't. The myth of science is that it is completely explained by the scientific method—by carefully following the method one can attain certain knowledge.

Science is perhaps best understood not as a single method but as a diverse set of practices that develops and changes over time. Scientific "method" includes *not only* observation, hypothesis, experiment, data, and conclusion but relationships among peers, argument, negotiation, serendipity, coercion, statistical sleight of hand, and fund-raising.

Writing is perhaps best understood not as an innate ability but as a series of distinct, directed tasks. These tasks *include* invention, drafting, and revising—connected to a self-conscious effort to define the elements of, and your place in, a conversation within a community.

The cognitive and social elements on which the writing process depends cannot be understood separately. Understood as a cognitive process, writing proceeds from a series of assumptions and existing ideas embedded in language. The writer takes those assumptions and ideas and transforms them through a unique manipulation of language and symbols. Understood as a social process, writing proceeds from a series of communicative conventions created by social groups and institutions. The forms of scientific and technical writing, such as analytical reports and abstracts, are conventions adopted by academic and professional communities. Although the specific elements of these conventions differ from group to group and from culture to culture, they structure thinking and how one expresses ideas. Thinking is enmeshed within a web of social relations. In turn, these social relations evolve out of your expression. Although we cannot map the impact of various and diffuse social relations on our specific thoughts, by understanding thinking and writing as social activities we get a better look at the broader contexts in which they occur.

SCIENTIFIC KNOWLEDGE AND THE WRITING PROCESS

Models of the writing process in scientific and technical communication reflect the profound influence of conceptions of the nature of scientific knowledge. Recently, however, traditional accounts of scientific knowledge have been challenged on social and historical grounds. Debates concerning the nature of scientific knowledge will continue into the twenty-first century. Undoubtedly, these debates will continue to influence individual and professional approaches to scientific and technical writing. In this section, we consider two views of scientific knowledge and examine how they impact our understanding of scientific and technical writing.

Philosophers of science, particularly in this century, became interested in determining *differences* between knowledge in the natural sciences and all other forms of knowledge. Viewed historically, the natural sciences furnish an incomparably successful and progressive source of knowledge. Philosophers and other professionals became interested in defining the features of scientific practice and knowledge to see if they could be applied to other subjects such as human behavior, economics, or philosophy itself. Scientific knowledge apparently possessed the unique trait of preserving its content in different social and historic contexts. No other form of knowledge can claim such uniform interpretation and agreement. Traditionally, philosophers of science attributed the universality of scientific knowledge to at least two characteristics: the pattern of reasoning employed in science and the repeatability of scientific experiments.[1]

Issac Newton (1642-1727) demonstrated that the force of gravity is the product of two masses and inversely proportional to the square of the distance between them. In other words, the larger the mass, the greater the gravitational pull. As the bodies are moved further apart, the force of gravity rapidly diminishes. Among other things, Newton's laws of gravity describe the motion of falling bodies on the Earth's surface as well as weight and ocean tides. As gravity is a natural, continuous phenomenon on Earth, its effect on falling bodies can be measured, predicted, and demonstrated through repeated experiments conducted at any time and in any location. From the evidence produced through repeated experiments, scientists conclude they have an accurate picture of how nature works—a picture that does not change with the current social and political climate. Newton's laws of gravity are an example of scientific knowledge that has only one universal interpretation that can be witnessed under different circumstances.

Given the traditional view of scientific knowledge, the goal of scientific and technical writers is presented as upholding uniform interpretation and agreement on information by writing a document that can be read in only one way.[2] Since scientific knowledge is universal, texts were written not to "get in the way" of scientists' representations of nature. The concept of scientific knowledge as constant across social and historical contexts meant that scientific and technical writing reflected the practices of science as a series of logical steps unaffected by factors such as funding, relationships among researchers, and institutional politics.

Sociologists of science, particularly within the past 30 years, became interested in determining the *similarities* between natural science, scientists, and scientific knowledge and other disciplines, practitioners, and forms of knowledge.[3] Responding to traditional views of scientific knowledge, many sociologists explain its universal acceptance in two ways. First, to become a member of a scientific community, scientists must adhere to uniform theoretical commitments. Second, scientists have only a limited repertoire for responding to information and ideas given disciplinary standards, writing formats, and disciplinary jargon.

Let's take another look at Newton's laws of gravity. From repeated observations and experiments, scientists elevated Newton's theory of gravity to a truth about nature. And we can agree that truth about the force of gravity that Newton and others demonstrated does not change; it is invariant and universal. However, language, even if objective, is *not* invariant and universal. Language, as demonstrated by *all other social interaction,* is an unreliable means for transmitting the truth. If we view science as an institution influenced by linguistic, historical, and social forces in *any* way similar to other institutions, then language remains a variable medium of expression. No matter what a writer does to ensure only one reading of an experimental article, inevitably there will be more than one interpretation of the information presented. Nevertheless, even if scientific knowledge was relayed by perfectly reliable linguistic means, scientists, just as ourselves, are imperfect knowers. We all process information differently. If you accept the idea that even if a scientific theory is true, its means of expression (i.e., language) and reception (i.e., cognition) are variable and imperfect, how can the universality of scientific knowledge be explained?

One explanation for the universality of scientific knowledge is that in order to become a member of a scientific community, scientists must adhere to the same theoretical commitments. In the physics community, for example, you cannot hold Newton's ideas with respect to the relation among *space*, time, and gravitation. Students learning to become practitioners in physics learn that relativity theory is *the* fundamental theory of nature. As a result, practitioners learn to perceive nature in the same way according to an accepted theory. In other disciplines and professions, even if practitioners hold the same theories and views about the world, they disagree on their interpretations. Even though critics of the traditional view of scientific knowledge would not deny the truth of relativity theory and its explanation of natural phenomena, they deny that the universal acceptance of the theory *is due to its unchanging nature.*

Another explanation for the universal acceptance of scientific knowledge is the scientists' limited choices in responding to information and ideas. Science is also unique in its reliance on a narrow range of communicative choices to convey information, governed by specialist jargon and defined writing formats. The uniform structure of the experimental article in natural science journals serves as an example. What counts as an appropriate expression of, or response to, an idea in science depends on how well writers follow disciplinary standards. If, for instance, scientific or technical writers presented their ideas in a narrative form using dialogue, the article would not be accepted by a mainstream journal. Authors must also use language and jargon appropriate to the discipline to have their views accepted. Critics of the traditional view of scientific knowledge claim that it, like all other forms of knowledge, is variable and contingent on time and circumstance. However, through institutional mechanisms requiring scientists to think and communicate along the same lines, scientific knowledge appears universal.

Questions concerning traditional conceptions of the nature of scientific knowledge pose interesting challenges for scientific and technical writers. One of these challenges involves how language is seen in relation to scientific and technical knowledge and information. From a traditional view of scientific knowledge, the function of scientific and technical writing is matching a word or symbol to the object it represents. On this view, language is representational—*mirroring* the relationship between science and nature. If we hold that scientific knowledge is variable and affected by social and historical (and other) contexts, the function of scientific and technical writing is shaping objects through words and symbols. On this view, language is constitutive and rhetorical—*constructing* the relationship between science and nature. However, even if scientific and technical writing practices are social, scientific knowledge is presented as largely unaffected by social contexts. In many instances, as studies of scientific laboratories have demonstrated, the picture we get of scientific practice and knowledge in journal articles and textbooks is highly idealized, if not misleading (see, e.g., Knorr-Cetina, 1980; Latour & Woolgar, 1979; Pickering, 1992).

STAGES IN COMPOSING

The processes of scientific and technical writing depend on an important mechanism: *recursion.* In thinking and developing ideas, recursion is the process in which the mind turns around on itself to consider its own inputs and to take stock of its capacities; an example is thinking about thinking. You have the ability to abstract, to "return again" and revise ideas and topics you had previously considered and see them in a new way. Throughout all stages of the writing process, you continually revisit the stages of writing (inventing, drafting, revising, and editing) and the elements and conventions of writing (ideas, formats, and sentence structure) within different contexts and with different intentions about what you want to say.

The process of recursion also applies to the institutional settings affecting your writing process. Like individuals, institutions have "memories" of past experiences, methods, and procedures. As a member of that institution, you develop memories that alter, and are altered by, your writing process.

One way of learning more about your own writing process involves examining the relationships between you—as a writer—your audience, and the subject about which you are writing. In scientific and technical writing, the relationships between writer, audience, and subject are woven into the relations among science, technology, and society. What you know about a subject, your purpose for writing, the appropriateness of presentation, and the characteristics of your audience are a part of your training, the discipline in which you participate, and its social image.

Making decisions about how to communicate in a particular situation involves understanding the relationship among the *writer, reader, subject,* and *previous texts.* Writing also requires performing *research* and distinguishing *audience, relationship, purpose,* and *content.* Each document requires different considerations of these concepts and certain constraints. The model that follows takes the view that your writing practices provide a deeper and more sophisticated understanding of science and technology by seeing language as not simply representational, but as constitutive and rhetorical. This model also characterizes science and technology as social institutions shaped by the contexts in which they participate. Effective scientific and technical writers recognize how those contexts interact with the writing process.

Inventing

At the time of Aristotle (384-322 B.C.), Athenian citizens learned rhetoric as a means for participating in an open forum. Classical rhetoric had its beginning as a practical course for training citizens in techniques for addressing live audiences. Speakers had to be intensely aware of their audience—they had to know it: its attitudes, emotional disposition, presumptions, desires, and prejudices. Knowledge of the audience primarily determined what was said and in what order it was presented. In this context, *invention* was defined as a process for choosing ideas appropriate to the audience, subject, and occasion. The intimate setting of the Athenian forum allowed speakers to closely profile an audience and establish a basis from which to begin the process of invention. Audience was the chief principle informing any kind of discourse.

We do not share the Athenian's intimate relationship between speaker and audience. Printing, electronic media, and telecommunications mediate our knowledge of the audience and audience reaction. These media also allow many different audiences access to our ideas. Still, scientific and technical writers must go through the process of invention to achieve the same ends as their Athenian counterparts. You must identify and explore ideas in relation to the audience, subject, and occasion. Nevertheless, because modern audiences are more diverse and complex, the process of invention requires you to constantly re-examine your ideas in relation to audience, subject, and occasion as you write.

Just as the writing process is recursive, so is each stage in the writing process. By learning more about your ideas, the subject, the audience, and the contexts in which you are writing, the content of your writing will change as you go back to re-invent, re-draft, and revise your text. Although we lay out the process of invention in separate parts, these parts are not mutually exclusive. As you plan and organize a document, you consult the standards of your discipline and the publication for which you are writing, you perform formal and informal research, brainstorm, talk with other colleagues, think about ideas, and learn about audience and occasion.

Planning and Organizing

Planning and organizing occur on two related levels. First, you must plan and organize strategies for writing. These strategies are based on your awareness of the circumstances surrounding each writing situation. Second, you must plan and organize what kind of document you will write under these circumstances, considering (among other things) structure, scope, style, and length.

In planning and organizing strategies for writing, consider under what conditions you do your best work: time of day, location, access to references, equipment, specific rituals, necessary distractions. Consider how you generate ideas—talking with other people, notes, lists, drawing pictures, outlining—and the time it takes. Map out your writing habits in relation to the constraints you will face: possible collaborators, research completed, results available, deadlines, budget, your knowledge and the audience's knowledge of the subject matter. Obviously, you cannot account for all your habits and constraints and those of others, but the time spent planning and organizing your writing strategies will reduce time spent drafting and revising.

In planning and organizing what kind of document you will write, consider the audience, your relationship to it, your rhetorical purpose, and the context in which you write. At this stage, it is important to have a clear idea of your audiences' needs in relation to the choices you make. Before mapping out your strategy in great detail, contact the primary reader(s) of your document. Electronic mail (e-mail) provides a wonderful medium for this type of exchange. By using e-mail, you give the reader the option of contemplating a response (or many responses), or responding immediately. E-mail also allows you to establish an ongoing dialogue with your audience. This dialogue can serve as a basis for defining audience and purpose, generating ideas, doing revisions, and setting the context in which the document is received. Of course, e-mail is not the only option for contacting the audience; a letter or fax, however, rather than a phone call gives the audience more time to assess your approach.

Formulating Ideas

About what will you write? What do you want the audience to know? For some writers, finding the "what" is the most frustrating part of the writing process. Writers perform different rituals to generate ideas. Some consult on-line databases and electronic networks, others browse through periodicals, references, and books in the library, and still others write lists, draw pictures, or prepare detailed outlines.

Much of the work of science is best understood as a cumulative or "puzzle solving" activity.[4] Scientific researchers enter well-defined disciplines and areas of study that do not necessarily require original research. Ideas and topics for research are often generated as a by-product of the structure and direction of the field or discipline in which you are a part. For example, undergraduate and graduate students entering the laboratory commonly work on projects begun by senior researchers. As scientific and technical writers you will not face the dilemma of essay writers who search for new ways to express personal experiences. The *cumulative* and *conventional* aspects of scientific and technical writing provide a basis for getting started.

Examine Previous Texts

Science and technology are *cumulative* in that the skills developed in lower-level courses are necessary for upper-level courses.

It is difficult, for instance, to do well in a sophomore- or junior-level physics class if you have not taken first-year physics and math courses. Disciplines and fields in technology and the sciences are differentiated by a shared literature, a literature on which research practices are based. Your knowledge of this literature—acquired as you move through school and your profession—gives you access to the accepted ideas and values of the community as well as what counts as good or bad practice. In sharing a common literature and cumulative practices, you share a clear idea of audience, relationship, purpose, and context within your field. In beginning to generate ideas for a paper, look initially to the shared literature of your field.

Use Conventions and Style Guides

The *conventional* aspects of scientific and technical writing are found in the general organizing principles for certain documents, and standards for writing are found in each discipline. These general organizing principles are given as templates (or patterns) for writing documents. These templates can serve as an outline for generating and organizing ideas in defining the necessary elements in the document. A word of caution, however. Many technical writers fall into the trap of believing that closely following a template is *all* that makes up technical writing. Nothing could be further from the truth.

The standards for writing in each discipline are found in professional style guides. Style guides are a list of requirements for preparing manuscripts for publication in journals. The dissimilar methods, professional standards, and goals of disciplines have caused each to create its own style guide. Professional organizations such as the Institute of Electrical and Electronics Engineers (IEEE), the American Chemical Society (ACS), and the Modern Language Association (MLA) have widely differing practices. Topics range from what subjects a professional journal addresses, how the manuscript is spaced, how quotations and footnotes are formatted, how illustrations are prepared, and how mathematical and symbolic notation is presented. By consulting style guides for the leading journal in your field, you can begin to see what ideas are currently being researched, how those ideas are received, and how they are presented.

Perform Informal Research

Research occurs on many levels and refers to different duties. *Primary* research refers to generating new or original information in working, for example, with microorganisms in a biology laboratory, conducting interviews with welfare recipients, distributing questionnaires to public housing dwellers, or compiling statistical correlations. *Secondary* research refers to looking at existing information in books, periodicals, indexes, and other sources available in libraries.

Primary and secondary research is usually goal-directed. You know, for example, the research topic and want to collect information. You locate an article using an on-line database, go to the library, photocopy the article, and go home. But research is helpful if conducted at an even earlier stage of the writing process—before you have a firm topic or idea.

During the process of invention, go to the library (or the Internet) and wander around. Don't have too many preconceived notions about the sources you want to locate. Go to the card catalog (computerized or not), look at references, pick through periodicals, leaf through books, and see if you are struck by other ideas.

Talk With Colleagues

Seek out different opinions on your ideas by talking with colleagues—classmates, lab partners, group members, and coauthors. Faced with vague ideas about what you want to write, talking *with* someone—or a number of people—can help clarify them. Encourage questions. Although people familiar with your ideas can impart their experience and give other sources of information, it also helps to speak with someone outside your discipline or field—a layperson. For example, you may tell that person "I'm thinking about writing a report on the use of radioactive isotopes in lab experiments on campus." The layperson could ask, "What does this have to do with me?" You respond,

"Well, once these isotopes are used, the radioactive waste must be stored in containers on campus." At that point the layperson could respond with a barrage of questions—"How is this material stored on campus? For how long? Where does it go? How does it get here in the first place? How many departments use radioactive isotopes in experiments? Can stored radioactive material affect the ground water? What are the university safety regulations regarding radioactive material?"

By having colleagues and laypersons (these are not mutually exclusive groups) ask questions and listen to ideas about your work, you make connections. You can get an indication of the audiences' concerns and reactions. And you can gauge your ability to explain ideas to people from various levels of knowledge.

Brainstorm and Free Write

Two related activities for curing "page fright"—the irrational fear of a blank page—are brainstorming and free writing.

The purpose of *brainstorming* is discovery—to uncover what you are curious about and in what you are interested. By listing your range of responses to a general topic, you can determine what ideas are important to it. Structured thinking offers obvious advantages, but brainstorming allows you to explore ideas that fall outside the structure. Frequently, these are the best ideas you will have.

Brainstorming is reminiscent of word association techniques used by psychologists. In this instance, you are trying to write down as many ideas as possible on your chosen topic. To begin, set aside 10 to 15 uninterrupted minutes. Write the general topic on the top of the page. As quickly as you can, list questions, words, phrases, and ideas about your topic. Use lists, not sentences. Try not to stop writing during the allotted time. Don't worry about spelling or word choice. Compose the list as quickly as you can.

Once you finish, sort out the list into ideas you think you can use and those you cannot. Set aside the list of ideas you cannot use, but save it. Ideas are a valuable, recyclable resource. From your brainstorming list you can compose an outline or begin free writing.

Free writing involves drawing connections between the elements in your brainstorming list and putting them into sentences or questions. Like brainstorming, the purpose of free writing is probing ideas through writing without a given framework or restrictions. Guidelines for free writing are much the same as those for brainstorming. Set aside a certain amount of uninterrupted time. Think about the general topic and write—this time using complete sentences when possible—as quickly as you can during the allotted time. If you get stuck, abandon the thought and move to the next one, or pose questions. Try not to stop writing during the allotted time. Don't worry about spelling or word choice. Compose as quickly as you can.

After you finish, you should have a mess—incomplete sentences, questions following questions, and awkward sentences. Much of this work will not find its way into the next draft. But scattered in the verbal wreckage you will find something you can use—questions that will guide research or sentences around which paragraphs are organized. Free writing gives you a chance to sift through your ideas and start linking them together.

Use Outlines to Think Rhetorically

Typically, outlines are used to break down the elements of a document, which are then arranged and refined. Later in the chapter we will look at patterns of developing ideas that lend themselves to these types of outlines, but during the invention stage, outlines can be used for another purpose: to think rhetorically.

Thinking rhetorically involves assessing the writing situation in terms of *problems* and *solutions.* Inexperienced writers often spend more time in the writing process analyzing the solution—adjusting items in the text itself—than the problem (i.e., studying the requirements of the writing situation). Often, when we analyze how great musicians play, cooks cook, dancers dance, or scientists "do science" we talk about the performance itself—how magically the elements just come together (Eureka!). One of the popular slogans of an athletic outfitting company is "Just do it"—as if, without preparation, you can shoot a three-point shot, run a marathon, or spike a volleyball. Almost all of "just doing it" is "just doing" years of practice. When we outline and draft documents we concentrate on the structure *exclusively* as the means to a solution: the document. To get to an effective structure, we must spend our time thinking about setting up the problem *we can solve.* One way to think about the problems you have when drafting a paper is to consider that you have not given yourself an equation you can answer. There are still too many variables. To eliminate some of the variables in writing, you need to assemble outlines that ask and answer questions regarding *audience, relationship, rhetorical purpose,* and *context.*

Audience

Who will read your document? The audience for scientific and technical writing is often cast as one of two seemingly mutually exclusive groups: experts and laypersons. However, such a distinction is useless unless understood as the endpoints on a broad continuum. Expert knowledge, for example, may apply only to a few people within a narrowly defined field of study. Professionals (e.g., physicians and lawyers) often look at journals in other fields—electronics, linguistics, cognitive science—to learn techniques and research results. These professionals are not laypersons in the strict sense of the term but are trying to learn new information. The knowledge of laypersons is also quite diverse. For example, a popular strategy for reaching wider audiences is through analogies: comparing features of a concept or technology with an idea or item within the audiences' experience. In contrast, shared experience limits, and defines, an analogy's reach.

In the *Phadrus,* Socrates notes one of the curious features of written texts:

> And once a thing is put in writing, the composition, what ever it may be drifts all over the place, getting into the hands not only of those who understand it, but equally of those who have no business with it; it doesn't know how to address the right people, and not address the wrong. And when it is ill-treated and unfairly abused it always needs its parents to come to its help, being unable to defend or help itself. (p. 275e)

Socrates points out a problem that all writers face. Once a document is out of their hands, writers can neither control the impressions of readers nor in whose hands a document will ultimately find itself. However, by making careful, educated guesses about audiences, writers need not worry about rushing to the "defense" of their documents.

Relationship

What is your relationship to the person(s) reading the document? The choices you make in writing a document (e.g., structure, vocabulary, tone) indicates your relationship to the reader. Generally, what counts as appropriate communication is a product of how relationships among people are defined. Writing to a potential employer, for instance, demands a different set of strategies and presumes a different set of values, than writing to a childhood friend. The formal tone you use in addressing a potential employer might seem artificial and raise concern when used with a close friend. All of our writing indicates our relationship to the reader. The standard structure and impersonal tone of a form letter lets readers know they are dealing with an institution, not an individual. Many people fail to closely read form letters because they *are* impersonal. In some cases, the relationships between writers and readers are traditional and easily determined—friendly, hostile, passionate, uncaring. As our society and our roles in it become more diverse, however, you must look at the aspects of culture—*and how you understand them*—in determining the relationships in which writers and readers are situated.

How each of us perceives relationships is a consequence of the culture in which we participate. The social roles that writers and readers play are often defined as a function of race, class, and gender. How we see ourselves and depict our relationships to others is based on a system of cultural values. This system grows out of the social institutions in which we are raised—family, neighborhood, religion, civic groups, schools, and careers. Our interaction with these institutions partially depends on our age, wealth, race, and gender. For example, writers of computer software manuals have a detailed profile of their consumers—who buys particular software, their level of education, their likely socioeconomic status, and their interests and hobbies. The tone and layout of the manual reflect the detailed assumptions of the reader profile. Although the relationship between the reader and writer occurs within a value system, keep in mind that "class," for instance, is an *abstract* concept, not a *concrete* thing we can see or touch. As a result, how a value system impacts, or informs, us is neither always clearly defined nor completely comprehensible. The social roles that readers and authors of scientific and technical writing play transform, and are transformed by, cultural values.

Rhetorical Purpose

Why are you writing this text? Texts are designed to achieve specific goals, but the purposes for writing are as varied as each writing situation. Your ideas begin to achieve greater intricacy as you consider why you are writing, who you are trying to persuade, how the information will be used, and how you will design the document to achieve those ends.

The idea that the goal of scientific and technical writing is simply to inform the reader, or render an objective presentation, fails to consider how language shapes the needs of the audience. If readers are not given an alternative, they will read your document within the guidelines of their own professional language. For example, let's say you are the manager of a medium-size company and at work on drafting a new set of sexual harassment policies. Although the employees are generally receptive to your ideas, in this case, they are largely uninformed. You cannot simply draft the policies, hand them out and say "Follow these policies or else." One of your rhetorical purposes is to educate the audience: You must show how these policies meet *their* needs, not just federal, state, and corporate mandates. To establish rhetorical purpose, you must help create the context in which these policies are interpreted.

Context

What are the sets of circumstances influencing the meaning or rhetorical effect of the document? Generally, these circumstances remain unexplored in science and technology. The context in which experimentation and observation take place is seen as unimportant to the findings. However, as individuals and members of institutions, our communication practices are embedded within (at least) historical, social, philosophical, psychological, economic, and rhetorical contexts. These contexts are impossible to avoid. We are all social beings existing in a moment of history with access to different economic resources. We all think in different ways, yet share problem-solving abilities and techniques with similarly trained members in our chosen fields. We all use language and concepts uniquely, yet communicate by sharing those concepts in our practices.

In writing to familiar audiences, it is easy to forget how shared assumptions affect the way we communicate. It is easier still to forget that other audiences don't share those same assumptions. By understanding scientific and technical writing in context, you begin to critically examine the elements that affect your writing; with a knowledge of those elements you can construct new contexts for diverse audiences. You need to know where the audience is and, through your knowledge of the contexts that affect the communicative situation, convey a shared sense of need and purpose.

DRAFTING

In the process of drafting, you choose a format for the text, begin writing, and begin designing visual aides. Drafting is a unique process for each writer. Yet we all face common fears, constraints, and objectives when writing.

Writers move from inventing and planning a text to drafting sentences and paragraphs in different ways. Some writers refer only briefly to notes and begin writing; others follow detailed outlines in a ritual manner. Some writers rush to complete the first draft quickly; others revise as they go. It is a mistake, however, to try and compose a flawless first draft in one sitting. If you are a thoughtful writer, you will see how maddening (and impossible) it is to start, stop, do further research, and revise ideas, sentences, and word choice in one session with a pad of paper or facing a computer screen. Begin with modest expectations of your first draft.

It is difficult, if not impossible, to determine when a writer is "ready" to draft a document. Faced with a blank piece of paper or blank computer screen, we get nervous and often abandon the elements we put together in planning the document. We look for distractions—urgent errands we must run, urgent dishes we must clean, urgent telephone calls we must return. Finding distractions is, for some, a part of the drafting process, a habit you need to account for in meeting deadlines. To get over the hump in drafting a text, you must, at this stage, just do it. But try to do it quickly and consistently.

Once you begin to draft a text, don't stop. Set a time limit, say, 45 minutes, and work without stopping. If you hit a snag, leave a note in the text and get back to it later. If an idea comes out of the blue, include it. Don't revise, change word choice, correct spelling or check grammar—just write. Write a phrase or sentence, then another. Get the raw materials with which you can work on paper (or disk). Draw associations. Wander through the ideas you generate and make connections where you can. "Mistakes," "errors," or "accidents" in the drafting process often reveal connections among ideas you may not have considered. "Errors" and free associations are the raw materials that are refined to produce a final document. When you reach the end of the time limit, either stop in the middle of a sentence or paragraph or write yourself a note specifying what comes next. This strategy will give you something with which to work when returning to the draft. If you are prone to writer's block, stopping in mid-thought or -sentence can provide a place from which to begin the next round of drafting.

Although the drafting process should be free of concerns about the later stages in the writing process, you need to prepare the draft so as to *use* it. Here are some hints for preparing usable first drafts:

▓ **Leave yourself enough space** so you can expand the document, add ideas, and revise sentences. If drafting on paper or note cards, skip lines. If drafting on a computer, skip lines and use a readable font. Use space to help organize and provide transition among ideas.

▓ **Consider using different writing media.** Many writers rely solely on computers in drafting texts. And computers offer several advantages. However, people forget how the physical act of writing can facilitate writing. If you use computers exclusively and are stuck putting together a first draft, try handwriting. The motion of the hand across the page can help generate ideas. If you are still stuck and must type, shift positions and move the keyboard. In moving from one draft to the next, writers using computers often like to look at the hard copy of drafts. Seeing printed prose affords you different perspectives on how the ideas are organized and developed. If you stare at a computer screen (or piece of paper) for hours, you lose the visual cues a draft has to offer.

▓ **Start with what you know.** Drafts often begin in the middle with a topic or idea the writer knows well. Writers forget that what is often assumed by them is not assumed by their audience. Fleshing out the details of a subject with which you are familiar can lead to related ideas. No rule exists that you must "begin at the beginning" and draft a text straight to the conclusion.

▓ **Draft the introduction last.** The weakest parts of most documents are the introduction and the conclusion. Writers drafting a document from start to finish often try to "predict" what they will say in the body of the text. Then, as with a self-fulfilling prophesy, the writer drafts the text to fit the prediction in the introduction. The result is a text that relies on developing generalities. And those generalities usually survive to the final draft. As the elements of the introduction are based on points elaborated in the body, it is helpful to know what points have been made rather than predict what points you will make.

REVISING

Once you have completed a draft, let it rest. You are too close to it to be able to assess what elements to revise. Try to give yourself as much time away from the draft as possible. Do other things and forget about the draft. Distance from your work is necessary in order to revise anything deeper than spelling errors and awkward sentences. To figure out how much "down" time to give yourself and your document, *realistically* assess the patterns and characteristics of your writing process. Then return to the draft.

Revising is as idiosyncratic as planning and drafting the document. Again, taking into account your own habits, consider the following techniques.

When you return to your draft, concentrate initially on *organization* and *coherence.* Keep in mind that none of the components of a draft are exclusive to one another, so revising its organization will likely make the draft more coherent. In scientific and technical communication, one of the nice things about having a standard format for many documents is that the format can serve as a template for organizing your draft. Be forewarned, however. Many scientific and technical writers, in their strict devotion to these templates, neglect the content and style of their writing. Writing becomes, as a result, an exercise in plugging in the appropriate response to the requirements for a particular document. The ability to "plug and chug" is often the strength of many mathematicians, scientists, and engineers, but it is a weakness if the other aspects of writing are neglected. Nevertheless, the templates for scientific and technical documents provide a good organizational outline and provide topics for headings.

Organization

To check organization initially, look at the headings in the text. Keeping your audience(s) in mind, see if the headings offer a logical progression for the document. Also, consider headings in reference to the requirements to be fulfilled for a specific document such as a proposal or set of instructions. Looking at the length of each section under each heading, you get a sense of the emphasis you have given each topic in the document. In the drafting stage you may have either outlined more topics than you substantively address, or may have given extensive treatment to topics that you may wish to divide into subheadings. If you have outlined more topics than you substantively address, consider whether you need the section at all. If not, eliminate it. If so, you need either to combine undeveloped topics into a broader topic or independently develop the topic. Let the detail and treatment of each topic reflect your emphasis. By sight, the audience may make an immediate determination about (a) whether you have covered a topic sufficiently, and (b) the point of the document.

COHERENCE

In organizing your document, start at the beginning of it and read each paragraph. Look to see if each paragraph has a central point, topic sentence, or argumentative claim. A paragraph is coherent when each sentence clarifies and explains the idea expressed in the central point, topic sentence, or argumentative claim. Determine which questions or ideas each paragraph addresses for the reader. One strategy for doing this is to list—on a separate piece of paper—these questions and ideas in as few words as possible. Then ask the following:

- Does each paragraph have a central issue or answer a specific question? If not, eliminate it.
- Does each paragraph "deliver" on its promise to present an issue or answer a question? If not, either flesh out the details or abandon the idea or question.
- Does each paragraph have more than one issue or answer more than one question? If so, split the paragraph into each separate idea and question. Either develop each idea or question fully or eliminate it.
- Does more than one paragraph address the same issues or questions? If so, either combine paragraphs or eliminate the redundancy.[5]

Paragraph Revision

A paragraph is a group of sentences organized around a central issue or theme that contributes to the development of the whole document. Paragraphs are organized much like short documents. In the opening of a paragraph, readers look for a short opening segment. This segment introduces general issues or themes discussed by the rest of the sentences in the paragraph. The opening segment then narrows to a central point. Most textbooks and handbooks call this opening segment the topic or thesis sentence, but fail to recognize that the issues a paragraph addresses are usually expressed in more than one sentence. Still, the issues presented must be short and recognizable. A good analogy to the opening segment of a paragraph is a musical overture or theme.

An overture is a piece of instrumental music composed as the introduction to an opera or symphony, for example. The overture previews melodies and musical themes developed later in the piece. During the course of the opera or symphony, the elements of the overture or theme, which listeners recognize, are woven into other aspects of the music. These elements are the basis for improvisation and always remain recognizable at some level. As the musical piece unfolds, you begin to anticipate where a certain melody will occur. When you anticipate the melody correctly or are surprised by recognizable changes, the music holds your interest. But if a melody occurs at irregular intervals or is dropped from the piece, you become frustrated.

Writing and reading a paragraph is much the same. You introduce an issue or theme that serves as a basis from which you can improvise. Then you offer a central point. The supporting sentences in the paragraph explain, extend, support, and qualify the issues and themes you introduce. Like the elements in the overture, the issues and themes you introduce remain recognizable at some level. And the reader comes to anticipate when issues and central points will be introduced and which issues follow from the next. Readers look for issues and central points in two places: at the opening and at the end of the paragraph. These two patterns of development reflect deductive reasoning, which is a general point leading the paragraph followed by corollary points, and inductive reasoning, which is a series of specific points with a general point at the end of the paragraph.

Generally, paragraphs are organized around a central issue with four to six supporting sentences. But the number of sentences and length of a paragraph are a function of audience and purpose. Like long sentences, long paragraphs require more effort from the reader. Several one- or two-sentence paragraphs, however, suggest the writer does not have enough to say about a subject or that several ideas require combining. Paragraphs are usually classified as either *transition* or *body* paragraphs. Transition paragraphs summarize the point of the previous paragraph and show how it relates to the point of the next paragraph. Transition paragraphs are usually short (three or four sentences) and are often used for introducing another element in the document (e.g., long quotes, visual aids, sets of instructions, lists of items). Body paragraphs support the document's main point and fully develop a central idea. The integration of transition and body paragraphs and varying paragraph lengths serve to carry the reader through the document.

Scientific and technical writing reflects the reading habits and reasoning processes employed in science. When we read, say, an essay in a popular magazine, we tend to begin at the beginning and go to the end. Articles in scientific and technical journals are rarely read that way. The main points usually appear at the end. Readers may flip to the conclusion or results section to cut to the chase. Induction is the mainstay of scientific reasoning, and paragraphs reflect that type of thinking—supporting points leading to a generalization. Let's look at the opening and closing paragraphs of Darwin's (1859/1968) chapter "Struggle for Existence" from *On the Origin of Species*:

> Before entering on the subject of this chapter, I must make a few preliminary remarks, to show how the struggle for existence bears on Natural Selection. It has been seen in the last chapter that amongst organic beings in a state of nature there is some individual variability: indeed I am not aware that this has ever been disputed. It is immaterial for us whether a multitude of doubtful forms be called species or sub-species or varieties; what rank, for instance, the two or three hundred doubtful form of British plants are entitled to hold, if the existence of any well-marked varieties be admitted. But the mere existence of individual variability and some few well-marked varieties, though necessary as the foundation for the work, helps us but little in understanding nature. How have all those exquisite adaptations of one part of an organisation to another part, and to the conditions of life, and of one organic being to another being been perfected? We see these beautiful co-adaptations most plainly in the woodpecker and the mistletoe; and only a little less plainly in the humblest parasite which clings to the hairs of a quadruped or feathers of a bird; in the structure of the beetle which dives through the water; in the plumed seed which is wafted by the gentlest breeze; *in short, we see beautiful adaptations everywhere and in every part of the organic world.* (p. 114, emphasis added)

• • •

It is good thus to try in imagination to give to any one species an advantage over another. Probably in no single instance should we know what to do. This ought to convince us of our ignorance on the mutual relations of organic beings; a conviction as necessary as it is difficult to acquire. All that we can do is to keep steadily in mind that each organic being is striving to increase is a geometric ratio; that each at some period of its life, during some season of the year, during each generation or at intervals, has to struggle for life and to suffer great destruction. When we reflect on this struggle, we may console ourselves with the full belief that *the war of nature is incessant,* that no fear is felt, that death is generally prompt, and that the vigorous, the healthy, and the happy survive and multiply. (p. 129, emphasis added)

The opening paragraph is long by our standards, 239 words; the closing paragraph is a more manageable 150 words. The average number of words per sentence in the opening is 39; the average number of words per sentence in the closing paragraph is 30. Active voice is more frequent in the close than in the opening—half the sentences are in passive voice. Aside from readability, these numbers indicate how the ideas develop. Darwin obviously regarded the opening paragraph of this chapter as a transition paragraph linking ideas from the previous chapter to what he will explain later. The italicized phrase at the end of the paragraph is the central topic. Darwin gives several specific examples leading to the general claim (an inductive pattern), but interestingly, the examples are given in descending order, moving from the most general category "organic beings" to the most specific category (and smallest item) "plumed seed."

The closing paragraph follows a similar pattern of reasoning, moving from the specific "individual imagination" to the general "war of nature" and its characteristics. In offering the main points at the end of both paragraphs, Darwin develops the issue along with specific examples and anticipatory points—"individual variability" in the opening, "mutual relations among organic beings" in the close. Darwin's work is an example of developmental patterns commonly found in academic, scientific, and technical writing. The central point is located at the end of the paragraph. Still, many readers have difficulty with that type of organization.

Here are some guidelines for revising paragraphs:

■ *Locate the central idea near the front of the paragraph,* after the introductory or transition segment. If you do use an inductive pattern of organization, lead to the main point by making a series of clearly understood minor points.

■ *Support the central point.* In some cases, the central point is posed as an assertion, argumentative claim, new idea, proposition, or definition. The support sentences of the paragraph all speak to or explicate this central topic with specific ideas and details. Given the type of topic sentence, the support sentences may be directed toward offering evidence for an assertion of fact, giving examples to defend an argumentative claim, giving causes for the development of a new idea, explaining the components of a definition, or defending reasons for a proposition.

■ *Read your draft aloud* as if you were giving an oral presentation. Note where you stumble in reading the text. In so doing, you will highlight sentence fragments, comma splices, lack of agreement between subject and verb, unnecessary repetition, and other problems of mechanics and construction. Make the appropriate revisions based on the sound and ease of reading aloud.

■ *Find other people to read the draft.* As mentioned in the opening of this chapter, the process of writing is recursive; it loops back on itself. When you revise, you "see again" the ideas you have presented. At times, however, one pair of eyes is not enough. In significant and necessary ways you will always be too close to your own prose. The document needs to be reviewed by others. In selecting reviewers, consider your audience(s). Although peer review and open and blind refereeing are the basis for substantive revisions in certain types of publishing, drafts are often reviewed by experts for experts. Consider the different audiences your draft will reach and try to solicit views from those different audiences. In addition, consider the wisdom of a reviewer who knows little about your chosen field or profession. People familiar with the current debates in an academic field or the issues concerning a profession can "fill in the blanks" in your draft. Having a knowledgeable critic can be an advantage in delineating specific, internal points of content in your draft—but shared knowledge and expertise can lead to shared mistakes. Misunderstandings, mistakes, or ambiguities can be reproduced within a closed community until they become accepted practices. Chances are that lay readers will admit if they do not comprehend a certain point. Use your judgment to determine if their advice is sound.

■ *Consider your personal standards.* After restructuring your draft for organization and coherence, reading aloud, having others evaluate the draft, and making corrections and revisions, you must be comfortable with having your name on the document. Ask yourself if you like the work you have revised and determine if the draft did not say it better. You also must determine if the document meets the needs and standards of collaborators and of your discipline or profession. Be prepared to negotiate your desires in light of the desires of collaborators and publishers. In some instances, you will make sacrifices. This aspect of revision is not easy and illustrates that the production and presentation of knowledge is based on social negotiation. You must decide what you are willing to give up or revise for the sake of completing and publishing a document.

Editing

Text editing requires that a document is correct, consistent, complete, and achieves its purpose. The term *editing* refers to the work done by an editor, someone other than the author(s), who suggests strategies for revising a document for the reader's understanding and use, and who coordinates the publication of a document. Editing practices can be internal to the subject matter and intended audience for the document. For example, the background and practices of editors dealing with technical documents in business, science, medicine, and government will be geared toward how documents are *used* by readers for instruction and information. Of course, the purposes and audiences for documents vary, and specific editing practices are required to meet different needs.

Generally, text editing can be classified in two ways:

- *Substantive editing.* An editor makes choices in collaboration with the author(s) whether to amend the content, organization, and style of a document with respect to the intended readers and purpose and to ensure that the document meets institutional policies.
- *Copyediting.* An editor makes sure the document is correct in terms of language, mechanics, style, page design, consistency, and correspondence among appendixes, figures, footnotes, indexes, tables, and references.

Most editors are also responsible for managing the administrative and production aspects of publishing, which is known as *coordination editing.*

Like the writing process, the process of editing is best under-stood as a series of tasks, none of which is followed in a linear fashion and none of which is mutually exclusive of the others. Accordingly, the process of editing can be seen as occurring in two stages: *development* and *production.* In the development stage, the editor determines the intended audience and the purpose, scope, and format of the document. After the authors research, write, and revise the text, editors suggest substantive changes. After making these changes, the manuscript is submit-ted to reviewers outside the publishing house or journal. Given the reviewers' approval, the document goes into the production stage. The document is copyedited, proofread, and typeset (or printed from typewritten pages). The document is then printed, bound, and distributed.

COLLABORATIVE WRITING

In science and engineering, multiple authorship is common. In certain science disciplines, as many as 80% to 85% of the articles are coauthored. Studies estimate that as much as 75% to 85% of the writing done in the workplace involves collaboration with one or more people.[6] Many colleges and universities require collabo-rative writing for senior design projects and theses. Increased collaboration reflects a recognition of increasing professional specialization and access to information, and a realization that knowledge is socially organized and distributed.

Disciplines and professions are becoming more specialized. Even with greater access to information, individual practitioners are reduced to laypersons on an increasing number of issues. Greater specialization leads to inefficiency in the way that knowl-edge and information are used and produced. Overlapping re-search projects, unread journal articles, and the split between theoreticians and practitioners (or hardware and software design-ers) are symptoms of specialization. As specialties *increase,* the number of practitioners within each new field tends to *decrease.*

Collaborative writing attempts to address this problem by having more people involved in planning and producing docu-ments. By breaking down personal and social barriers, collaboration helps improve communication, and teaches people how to get things done in an efficient manner. Group members can bounce ideas off one another and learn different ways to solve problems. However, the homogeneity of a group of authors can prohibit the free flow of ideas. Members in a well-defined specialty with established procedures often succeed in confirming each other's biases and reinforcing familiar methods. What is done locally—in a specific lab or branch of a corporation—sometimes needs explaining from an outsider's perspective. In writing a proposal, for example, it is quite clear to you and the people with whom you collaborate why you need funding for new computers, but a government agency or corporate headquarters may not share your sympathy. Two or more heads are better than one, but you need to be aware of the purpose you want collaboration to serve.

Collaboration gives writers a wider range of experiences from which to draw. The cognitive and social aspects of the writing process are magnified when people collaborate. They exchange different ideas about how to plan, write, and edit a document. And depending on the writing situation, you may want to magnify different aspects of the writing process. Let's look at the advantages and disadvantages of collaborative writing in the context of the writing process.

Advantages and Disadvantages

Collaborative writing takes place within and between two broadly defined groups: people from the same background or discipline and people from different backgrounds and disciplines. In science and technology, collaboration takes place in the context of specialization, the rapid pace of scientific change, and shifting patterns of government funding. Collaborative writing emerges out of the tension between an individual's self-interest, the interests of the group, the interests of the profession, and the interests of larger society. These competing interests require a balanced consideration often only available when "outsiders" and "insiders" meet to discuss their needs.

The history of science attests to the advantages and disadvantages of having similarly trained people, who share a worldview, work on a defined set of problems. With scientific problems, methods, and standards for success historically defined, practitioners know what they must do to achieve their goals. Accordingly, social roles and standards are explicitly defined. For example, in a laboratory with a senior head, assistant professors, graduate students, and laboratory assistants, the responsibility and credit for research corresponds to academic rank. In collaborative research and writing, the laboratory head is the final authority, who approves the experimental results, edits the research, and is usually lead author of the paper. How tasks and responsibilities are assigned, who coordinates writing and presentation, and who has final say about a document is largely defined by the social structure of the research community.

There are several other advantages to working with similarly trained people. In many important ways you share the same beliefs. Your choice of profession implies that you embrace certain ideals. Lifestyles and work habits are often common to members of the same profession. Because you are similarly trained, you can count on a certain level of shared knowledge. Consequently, you can make a number of assumptions, based on the needs of the audience, about how to approach the collaborative writing process.

The disadvantages to collaboration, within the context of specialization, are intellectual inbreeding, self-deception, and self-interest. Even though many people are involved in the collaborative process, the content of a document may not reflect intellectual diversity. Usually, the first rule of thumb in recommending policy or procedural changes is *if it ain't broke, don't fix it.* But from an internal group perspective, it is frequently hard to tell if it is "broke." Collaborators with similar beliefs and backgrounds—even peer reviewers—may simply confirm group biases and patterned ways of thinking. If personal self-interest is served within the context of a group, there is no motivation to see beyond it. But if self-interest is not served, collaboration may suffer as a result. For example, if I am a nuclear physicist, I want unlimited funding for my field. And my allegiance to my research and specialty is tempered by the funding it receives. If funding dries up, as the pace of scientific change often dictates, I may try to define myself in other ways—as a researcher with many applicable interests—to keep my laboratory alive. My need for collaboration, then, may primarily reflect what is in my best interest or in the interest of my immediate field. Even in the process of collaboration there is a tendency to see one's own research as the center of all that is worthwhile.

In the framework of collaborative writing, specialists are confronted by nonspecialists who ask "Why do you do it that way?" Procedures considered successful are usually never questioned, unless witnessed by a naïve observer. When scientists are confronted by nonscientists (e.g., patent attorneys, insurance representatives, marketing agents) or laypersons, they must provide an explanation of why they do what they do. Historian of science Derek de Solla Price (1986) found that the perceived success of science and technology in universities corresponded to how well ideas and techniques are spread to people working outside the university. The process of collaborative writing, then, involves determining how to investigate and spread knowledge to diverse audiences.

In collaborating and making policy decisions, you need to force yourself to see your interests as not an end in themselves, but as part of much larger projects. But you cannot see the "big picture" alone; you need people from outside your discipline or profession to lend their insights as well. By examining the needs of others in light of your own needs, you gain a better understanding of different audiences and a basis for self-reflection. When people from different backgrounds and training collaborate on a document, the process is more difficult to organize, but the impact is often more widespread.

Collaborating and Composing

Individual writers have uniquely defined ways of approaching the writing process, but individual styles must be situated within the group dynamic. Many writers, for example, are shy about sharing their work with others, fearing rejection or personal insult. In collaborative writing, however, sharing work and ideas is a necessary part of the writing process. Keep in mind that because writing is a recursive process, collaboration in some parts of the writing process is more effective than in others.

Why Collaborate?

What is the reason for collaboration? Clearly, there are several overlapping purposes for assembling a group of people to write a document including personal choice, initiating new employees, the circumstances of the work, and management directives (or classroom assignment). Generally, three reasons are cited for collaboration (see, e.g., Ede & Lunsford, 1986; see also Burnett, 1994, chap. 5).

- Subject and purpose of the project
- Process and product of writing
- Interpersonal benefits

Subject and Purpose of the Project

While increasing specialization makes us laypersons on a widening number of subjects, the trend in government funding is granting the largest sums of money for "big science" projects requiring interdisciplinary cooperation. For these two reasons, scientific and technical writers depend on collaboration. Let's say you want a government grant to develop new computer technologies for assisting people who are physically impaired. In writing the proposal, you may need help from computer, electrical and mechanical engineers, experts on the needs of the physically impaired, and perhaps a professional technical writer. Expertise in all of these areas is not usually found in any one person. Consequently, a reciprocal relation exists between the subject of the document and the members participating in the project.

Reasons for collaboration roughly correspond to the purpose for writing the document. These reasons also influence the selection of collaborators. For instance, if, among others, your purpose is to

- report the group's actions and ideas with a group of laypersons
- propose funding from an agency outside your organization
- publish a paper in an interdisciplinary journal
- draft new policies to employees (if you represent management)

- assemble a progress report on the efficiency of your department for the university or corporate headquarters

you need collaborators from "outside" your specialty to lend you the perspective to reach out to your audience. However, if the purpose of writing is to

- report the group's actions and ideas with another group of experts
- propose funding from an agency within your organization
- publish a paper in a journal in your own field
- draft new policies among other managers
- assemble a progress report evaluating the efficiency of other employees for the laboratory head or manager

you may need collaborators to gather information and put the document together. Consequently, you may want collaborators familiar with the information in your field.

Process and Product of Writing

Since the collaborative process is more effective in certain parts of the writing process, the generalizations provided here need to be examined in light of your group dynamic and individual preferences.

Collaboration is effective in the process of invention, for it is often easier to generate ideas when a number of people participate in the process of brainstorming. Group brainstorming sessions require a facilitator and record keeper to keep ideas flowing, to get as many contributions from as many people as possible, and to generate a list of these ideas for future reference. Groups can meet subsequent to brainstorming sessions to choose which ideas to pursue, organize them, and assign subjects and deadlines to individual members.

The act of composing is a solitary activity embedded in all of the interactive aspects of thinking and writing. Although writers usually draft documents individually, they continue to perform research, talk with colleagues, and write and modify outlines. Even writers who think themselves alone are not alone. Because of increased access to information through electronic communication, shared databases, and information networks, each writer has become more reliant on other writers. Writers also rely on how databases and networks are organized and must have the available skills and resources to use them. Computer networks and electronic mail provide a medium for immediate exchange and feedback on drafts. Still, many writers prefer to draft alone and without interruption.

Collaboration is also quite effective in the process of revising and editing a document. People with a variety of viewpoints can evaluate ideas and their presentation. Written feedback allows you to systematically go back and revise your prose. Here the writing process becomes genuinely recursive when, after drafting the document, you go back to integrate your work with the suggestions of collaborators.

Document production is also aided by collaboration. Major proposals, manuals, and newsletters have a number of elements: photographs, tables, graphic art, appendixes. Under normal circumstances, individual writers cannot professionally reproduce all of these elements. In the production stage of document design, it is necessary to bring in collaborators; namely, editors and graphic designers, to aid in putting together the document.

Interpersonal Benefits

Collaborative writing acts as a social threshold over which employees pass. Collaborative writing provides a situation in which the standards and values of a profession are made known to new employees. Employees involved with different levels of a profession get a chance to exchange ideas and views about goals and policies. People like working toward a common, defined goal. Members of a team like competing against other teams and sharing credit and blame. Organizations can coordinate their efforts easily when teams work together as opposed to the same number of individuals working separately.

When professionals and researchers come together from different backgrounds, they construct aspects of a larger conversation in which questions of professional values and public welfare can be addressed. Interdisciplinary and professional collaboration is a social threshold that leads to the lay public. Science and technology, as well as other professions, are seen as socially insular. When scientists and technologists venture into the public sphere, they receive the benefits of consumers' wisdom concerning their products. In return, the public receives a needed education about two institutions that profoundly affect individuals' lives.

Recommendations and Guidelines

- Consider *when* in the writing process *overt* collaboration works best. All writing is in some way collaborative, but continuous interruption, under the guise of consultation, makes the writing process inefficient. Try to define when a direct hand is needed and when to work alone.

- Agree to a set of goals and the strategies and procedures for reaching that goal. After formulating ideas, the participants must determine what the subject of the document will be. Accordingly the audience, relationship, rhetorical purpose, and context for the document need consideration in light of requirements regarding deadlines, length, organization, and style. If you anticipate problems in coordinating meetings or deadlines, try to set up a fixed schedule as early in the writing process as possible.

- Define specific roles at the outset. In longer documents, the group can assign chapters to individuals or determine who conducts research for the group, does the actual writing, or checks and revises the draft. Be clear that all understand their roles and responsibilities at the outset to make the process as smooth as possible. Choose a coordinator as soon as possible to chair meetings, facilitate the exchange of ideas, and arbitrate disputes.

- Discuss openly the group dynamic. Consider two groups of collaborative writers and how they reach a consensus (see Fuller, 1988, chap. 9): The members of the first group come to agreement by deciding individually to do the same thing; the members of the second group come to agreement by a collective decision to do the same thing. Reaching consensus in the first group occurs, if at all, by accident. The reasons why I may have reached an agreement on a particular subject in a document is unrelated to how my collaborators reached their decision. Unless we thrash out our differences like the second group, we cannot justify our choices in the long run. Justification, especially in science, is an important feature in reporting research findings. In defining the goals of the group, consider how you want to reach them. Consensus among group members is not a necessary condition for successful collaboration, especially if that consensus is built on false assumptions and expectations.

Constraints and Limitations

Because the writing process is complex, we face limited knowledge about, and access to, some of its components. Most profound are our own cognitive limitations. We are imperfect knowers. Our knowledge of ourselves and the elements of writing—audience, purpose, relationship, and context—are neither complete nor fully available upon personal reflection. What we know about ourselves and our own practices is limited—*and made possible*—by our cognitive capacities and the social contexts in which we live and work.

Cognitive and Social Constraints

Our knowledge of the components of writing is filtered through the social institutions—academic disciplines, fields, professions—in which we participate. Knowledge and information are socially constrained and defined. Academic disciplines, for example, organize their subject matter by specialized word use, borrowing language from other disciplines, and determining criteria for what counts or does not count as knowledge. The boundaries around disciplines and professions are artificial—drawn at the risk of excluding the perspectives, methods, and insights of other disciplines and professions. As professional specializations and accompanying boundaries increase, practitioners isolate themselves from one another and the public.

The French physiologist Claude Bernard (1813-1878) defined the normal state of an organism's health as an equilibrium between blood and lymph flow (its *milieu interieur*). For example, to compensate for a rise in outside temperature (the *milieu exterieur*), a mammal's blood vessels constrict, allowing heat to escape from its body, thereby restoring the balance between the mammal's internal and external conditions. For Bernard, disease was defined from the patient's standpoint—a temporary inability to adapt to an organic imbalance. The job of the physician was to determine how well or poorly a patient made necessary adjustments to their surroundings and prescribe treatment accordingly.

Bernard's model of disease and treatment drew a strict boundary between experimental medicine and concurrent developments in microbiology and evolutionary biology in two ways. First, disease was understood as an organic imbalance not as an infection from a pathogenic agent. Second, from the physician's standpoint, an organic imbalance could, in principle, always be medically corrected. With the physician's help and given the right treatment, an organism could adapt to radical change in the environment. Theories regarding microbes and human evolution had no place in Bernard's concept of medicine. As a result, Bernard's discipline may have been partly to blame for the slow acceptance of microbiology and evolutionary biology in nineteenth-century France (see Mendelsohn, 1964; also Fuller, 1988). Our knowledge and actions are bound and liberated by the social contexts in which they arise.

Along with cognitive and social constraints are these practical limitations:

- Audience constraints
- Format and subject constraints
- Time constraints

Audience Constraints

Audiences for scientific and technical writing are varied. And like ourselves, our audiences are composed of imperfect knowers. Due to the perceived universality of scientific knowledge, uniform training, and the homogeneous population of scientists and technologists, the audience for technical documents is also portrayed as homogeneous. There is, however, an increase in the representation of women and minorities in science and technology. Laypersons are becoming more interested in the effect that science and technology has on their lives. These new audiences for scientific and technical writing have different backgrounds and expectations. You cannot expect an audience to pick up every point you see as important. Even technical language generates many associations and interpretations.

Audiences for technical documents have several reasons for reading them. Members of your audience will occupy different positions within an organization. Laypersons may want to read the document. All of these people will have varying levels of expertise, insight, and reason. If, for instance, you have been retained by the town council to report which proposed highway route would most benefit the town, you know you cannot just talk about how the road is engineered. Politicians, town residents, environmentalists, transportation officials, and other engineers will have access to the document. Unfortunately, you are unable to determine the needs and technical expertise of all members of the audience. Even in a memo distributed to a few people within your department, there will exist some discrepancy between what you think you say and how others understand the information.

As a result, you must attempt to respond to the needs of a variety of readers. Because you cannot know or anticipate all their needs, you have to make decisions about the level of technical complexity, organization, and design of the document. By considering scientific and technical writing in context, you increase your choices and ability to provide choices for readers.

Format and Subject Constraints

Scientific and technical writing is prescriptive. There are formats and standards for presenting material. These formats outline the choices required by the writer by framing the expectations of the reader. In so doing, document formats constrain the writer's and the reader's choices. Laypersons unfamiliar with the format of a document have limited access to its contents. If there is disagreement about a finding or results of a study, its uniform presentation smoothes over areas of discrepancy. You do not see, for example, a member of a research team who has some questions about an experiment providing a sidebar comment in a journal article. A document's prescribed format infers that the writers adhere to the values of a discipline, profession, and journal. Readers, especially outside readers, wanting to challenge the content of a document challenge not only the writers but also, to some degree, the sponsoring discipline or profession of the writer and the standards of the journal and publishing house.

Subjects provide constraints by their complexity. Scientific and technical writers use jargon to avoid unpacking concepts with which they are unfamiliar. Some subjects, by nature, appear impossible to convey to certain audiences. Although the subject and format of many scientific and technical documents are frequently preordained, writers must focus on details suitable to the audience's interests. In theory, no subject is too complicated for a lay audience to understand.

Time Constraints

Scientific and technical writers are always bound by time limits, often imposed by people who do not understand the demands of the project. The amount of time you have to complete a project, with respect to the project itself, limits the amount of other resources (e.g., research, collaborators, production quality) you can use in writing about it. Larger projects require extensive planning and will have intermediate deadlines requiring status and progress reports and revisions. Shorter projects may not require as much planning and only cursory revisions. Within deadlines for a project other things happen. People get sick. Computer hard drives and floppy disks crash. Research is delayed. Collaborators disagree. You change your mind about the contents of the document.

Many organizations provide computer software or use time management techniques and evaluation charts to keep writers on track. These strategies map out the relationship of activities in the writing process upon one another. When planning a writing schedule, anticipate delays. If, after careful planning, you determine that a writing project will take three months, add another 40% to 50%—a month and a half in this instance—to the final deadline. Remember, *it always takes longer than it takes.*

Discussion

1. In many activities—writing, painting, dancing, laboratory experimentation, playing sports or music, teaching—there is the persistent notion that great writers, painters, or scientists have a special ability that makes them great. This ability is ineffable—something that cannot be described—and cannot be taught to others. Do you believe that any practitioner entering a field must possess, to some degree, an inexpressible ability to perform certain tasks? Why? What are the implications of your position for the practice of scientific and technical communication?

2. Do you think writing is crucial to the conduct of science or engineering? Why or why not? Do you see similarities between how the writing process and the experimental process are carried out? What are the similarities and differences?

3. One of the ideas presented in this chapter is that the universal acceptance of scientific knowledge can be explained, in part, by the uniform way in which scientists write. Do you agree or disagree? Do you think it is in the best interests of producing and communicating knowledge—in science and your particular discipline—that practitioners express themselves in the same way? What are the advantages and disadvantages of having standard forms of communication?

4. How do you think social organizations—schools, academic disciplines, religious organizations, professions—shape the way you write? Do you agree with the idea that your self-expression is partially, or wholly, the product of factors such as race, class and gender? Why or why not? Do cultural values influence the way you write? If so, what cultural values influence your writing? Do you think these cultural values are understood or communicated by individuals to groups of people? What kinds of values do science and technology embody? How does scientific and technical writing convey those values? Give an example from a document that you prepared recently.

5. One of the primary considerations of modern scientific and technical communication is audience. This consideration was shared in the Athenian forum. But fear existed that unscrupulous speakers, given their intimate knowledge of the audience, could manipulate people to do things they otherwise would not do. In an age of increasing professional specialization, this fear has been revived in another form: namely, that specialists are content to write just for one another. Do you think familiarity with an audience is always a benefit to the writer? Do you think increasing specialization helps or hurts a writer? Do you think a writer's reputation helps or gets in the way of writing and reading a text? When do you think familiarity with the audience is harmful? Do you think professionals and experts must be encouraged to write so that a lay audience can understand what is being said? Why or why not?

6. Discuss how Keith's concept of "being rhetorical" (see Chapter 9, Part II) informs the concepts of audience and persuasion in this chapter. What rhetorical strategies does Keith provide that can be used in your writing process? Specifically, how do the contexts of communication that Keith maps out apply to a specific document on which you have recently worked?

Exercises

1. Begin a journal in which you honestly compare your writing process to the model of the writing process presented in this chapter. What are the similarities and differences between how you actually write and the recommendations offered in this chapter? What do you think are important aspects of writing that you follow that are not mentioned in the chapter? Try to keep this journal for the entire semester, documenting the ways you approach different assignments, different strategies you try, and the results.

2. One of the central claims in this chapter is that writing is both a social and a cognitive process. As a result, how one thinks is bound to the contexts in which one solves problems. In a

brief report, describe the thinking or problem-solving style encouraged in your field or discipline. For example, what research methods does your discipline encourage? Which of these methods do you use most frequently? How would you describe yourself as a problem solver? What kinds of problems are easiest or most difficult for you to solve? Do the questions posed have an answer, or are they open-ended? Is discussion or note taking encouraged in the classroom? In answering these questions, consider the role of writing in your field. In what ways is writing encouraged or discouraged? How do you see the problem-solving strategies you are taught translating into the writing process?

Once you have completed this profile, form a group with two people from different disciplines. After reading one another's reports, pick an issue or topic that is of common concern to each group or discipline. These issues may be environmental or legislative problems, funding, community concerns, the marketability of your (respective) degrees, public perception of the field, and public policy, among others. After choosing a specific issue, produce a collaborative synthesis of problem-solving styles and methods of communication in which the issues could be analyzed, discussed, and perhaps even resolved.

3. Many of you have previous experience with collaborative writing and peer review. In a brief report, tell students inexperienced with collaborative writing what you think the strengths and weakness of this process are. In writing this report, you can use the criteria listed in this chapter as a jumping-off point. Do some projects lend themselves to collaboration more readily than others? How did the group divide the labor? Did one person do all the work? Were drafts checked and approved by everyone in the group? Can peers assess each other's work honestly? Is peer review better when it is anonymous? If the instructor is using peer review in the class, what ideas or suggestions do you have for making the peer review session more effective?

4. Find a sample of "typical" technical writing in your discipline. The sample can be a textbook, an article in a leading profes-

sional journal, a technical manual, or a set of instructions. You need not be able to fully translate the technical jargon. In a report providing advice to students in your discipline on strategies to use to persuade audiences of a given position *outside* your field, use Keith's (Chapter 8, Part II) "algorithm" for thinking rhetorically (considering purpose, audience, context, relationship, rhetorical problems, and resources) to analyze the function of persuasion in the piece you have selected. You can construct your analysis and report around the questions and considerations that Keith poses.

NOTES

1. One the stated goals of science is to uncover the "laws of nature." Because laws of nature are universal you could, ideally, deduce an explanation of a naturally occurring event from a set of premises that included a statement of the appropriate law of nature and a statement of relevant conditions that caused the phenomenon to occur.

2. One definition of technical writing stresses that good technical writing conveys only one meaning so that the reader interprets the material in only one way (see Britton, 1965, pp. 113-116). By ensuring that a document has only one interpretation, the writer helps ensure the universal acceptance of specific knowledge claims.

3. The benchmark for this research is Merton (1977), but in this section we draw on ideas presented by Bazerman (1987) and Fuller (1993).

4. Thomas Kuhn (1970) in *The Structure of Scientific Revolutions* uses the phrase "puzzle solving" to illustrate the daily activities of scientists who rarely perform truly original research but work to flesh out details and answer questions about a defined subject.

5. These strategies were inspired by Chapters 2 and 5 in Middleman (1981).

6. See, for example, Ede and Lunsford (1986), Anderson (1985), and Forman (1992). Gallison and Heavly (1992) explain the development of pidgin and "Creole" technical languages in big scientific projects requiring many scientists and engineers from different disciplinary backgrounds.

BIBLIOGRAPHY

Anderson, P. V. (1985). What survey research tells us about writing at work. In L. Odell & D. Goswami (Eds.), *Writing in nonacademic settings* (pp. 3-85). New York: Guilford.

Bazerman, C. (1987). *Shaping written knowledge.* Madison: University of Wisconsin Press.

Britton, E. (1965). What is technical writing? A redefinition. *College Composition and Communication, 16*(May), 113-116.

Burnett, R. (1994). *Technical communication* (3rd ed.). Belmont, CA: Wadsworth.

Darwin, C. (1968). *On the origin of species* (J. W. Burrow, Ed.). Harmondsworth, England: Penguin. (Original work published 1859)

de Solla Price, D. (1986). *Little science, big science and beyond.* New York: Columbia University Press.

Ede, L., & Lunsford, A. (1986). *Collaboration in writing on the job: A research report.* (ERIC Document Reproduction Service No. ED 268 582)

Forman, J. (Ed.). (1992). *New visions of collaborative writing.* Portsmouth, NH: Boynton/Cook.

Fuller, S. (1988). *Social epistemology.* Bloomington: University of Indiana Press.

Fuller, S. (1993). *Philosophy of science and its discontents* (2nd ed.). New York: Guilford.

Gallison, P., & Heavly, B. (Eds.). (1992). *Big science.* Palo Alto, CA: Stanford University Press.

Hamilton, E., & Cairns, H. (Eds.). (1961). *The collected dialogues of Plato.* Princeton, NJ: Princeton University Press.

Knorr-Cetina, K. (1980). *The manufacture of knowledge.* Oxford, England: Pergamon.

Kuhn, T. (1970). *The structure of scientific revolutions.* Chicago: University of Chicago Press.

Latour, B., & Woolgar, S. (1979). *Laboratory life.* London: Sage.

Markel, M. (1992). *Technical writing situations and strategies* (3rd ed.). New York: St. Martin's.

Mendelsohn, E. (1964). Explanation in nineteenth-century biology. In R. Cohen & M. Wartofsky (Eds.), *Boston studies in the philosophy of science* (Vol. 2, pp. 127-150). Dordrecht: D. Reidel.

Merton, R. (1977). *The sociology of science.* Chicago: University of Chicago Press.

Middleman, L. I. (1981). *In short: A concise guide to good writing.* New York: St. Martin's.

Pickering, A. (Ed.). (1992). *Science as practice and culture.* Chicago: University of Chicago Press.

Williams, J. M. (1990). *Style: Toward clarity and grace.* Chicago: University of Chicago Press.

CHAPTER

4

Understanding Audiences

The terms *audience* and *reader* are sometimes used interchangeably. To avoid confusion, we can define audience as a group of people representing the collective interests and character of an institution—like science. In referring to a reader or readers, we point to the roles and backgrounds of people (usually not specific individuals) who will read the document. Only certain members of an audience may actually read the document. If you know the reader personally, you have firsthand knowledge of that person's reasons for reading. Because we cannot, in most instances, know the personality, capabilities, and desires of individual readers, we must define their general attitude and motivation and aspects of the audience in which they participate. By examining the characteristics of, and organizational roles in, professional fields, you can determine the needs of an audience or readers and ways to persuade them.

CHARACTERIZING AND
PARTICIPATING IN PROFESSIONAL FIELDS

You can begin to develop an audience profile by examining the characteristics of professional fields. Each field defines itself and the place of its practitioners by setting requirements for what counts as good practice. These requirements are reflected in the organization of the field and influence, and are influenced by, societal demands. Generally, the greater the perceived importance of a profession, the more difficult it is for people to become practitioners. The more difficult it is to become a practitioner, the greater the influence of the profession. For example, professions that exercise power in our society such as law, medicine, and science require practitioners to go through long apprenticeships as graduate students and, in most cases, to be licensed or certified by national, state, and/or professional governing boards. Although many of the professionals in the art field, such as writers, musicians, poets, and noncommercial artists, go through apprenticeships, entry into these fields is not strictly controlled. Loosely controlled fields tend to attract practitioners with diverse backgrounds. A diverse set of practitioners usually encourages diverse techniques for, and approaches to, problem solving. Tightly controlled professions tend to be homogeneous. Practitioners with similar backgrounds and training frequently take similar approaches to problem solving.

Science is different from other professions at the level that *professional conduct* organizes work. Professional conduct refers to the attitudes and fundamental beliefs held by a community. For example, in science, the "search for truth" or "quest for knowledge" is cast as the primary goal of research. To achieve that end, individual scientists must put aside personal desires for the collective good. Like other professionals, scientists do make decisions to further their careers and achieve personal gain. Disputes erupt among researchers concerning who "got there first" in making a discovery or innovation, but scientists do see themselves as closely identified with the community in which they work.

In the seventeenth century, "gentlemen amateurs"—wealthy, educated lay researchers roaming the countryside making observations and setting up in-home laboratories—populated early modern science. Physics, for example, was an informal pursuit; uncertainty existed regarding the methods one should follow. The tasks comprising "good" or "sound" scientific research were not yet identified. Communication about science and technology was also less formal and more "conversational." Scientific and technical subjects often received book-length treatments that included an author's commentary. Investigators openly debated the "facts" describing how certain phenomena occurred. As a result, early modern science lacked the kind of formal organization with which it is now associated.

Here are some factors to consider in defining the general characteristics of a professional field and of practitioners in that field:

- **Resource concentration**: What resources—laboratories, computers, warehouse space, materials—does it take for professionals to do their work effectively, *and* where are these resources located? The audiences with whom you will communicate rely on specific resources for professional production. Knowledge of these resources and how practitioners interact with them allows you to see the importance placed on certain aspects of communication. For example, laboratory equipment is housed in a central location. By necessity research communities come together in a laboratory to work. Accordingly, there is greater dependence and emphasis on collaborative communication. Within communities, collaborative practices can lead to particular ways of communicating, such as specialist jargon. Additionally, scientists rely on resource networks to support their products. For professional writers and poets, the primary product is a written text. Supporting the text is (usually) a single author's experience. For scientists, the product is also a written text, but supporting the text is a laboratory, with many machines and many collaborators. By determining the resources a profession has and how they are positioned, you can position the resources of your text.

- **Requirements for practice**: What requirements must practitioners fulfill to enter a field? The tighter the restrictions are to practice a particular profession (years of schooling, credentials, certification), the tighter the control that practitioners have over their own field; just as the fewer the restrictions, the more impact the lay public has on a field. In the retail industry, for example, the customer is "always right" and so exercises direct influence on the practices and products of retail professionals. In science, scientists exercise almost exclusive control over their profession. Research scientists do not answer to patients, clients, or stockholders as do doctors, lawyers, or business executives. By identifying the strength of boundaries surrounding a profession, you get an idea of the practitioners' level of education and how they perceive and appeal to people affected by their work.

▓ **Organizational control**: How is the profession organized? Who controls the profession? These questions address the boundaries that surround a profession. Science is controlled by scientists. Organizational control is internal. Research is organized around collaboration. Although differences in the authority of scientists exist, work is controlled through negotiations among peers. Peers constantly review laboratory procedures, attend conferences, and referee journal publications. Constant peer review, and constant revision of ideas and outcomes to meet community expectations, leads to greater uniformity in the way practitioners act, think, and express themselves. Other scientists decide whether or not someone is doing good work. By using each other's work as the basis for their own, scientists produce facts. Compared to other professions, scientists are relatively unaffected by public concerns. Most other professions, in the social sciences and humanities for example, lack this degree of internal control. Professional writers, for instance, can exist outside a formal institution like a university. Even though publishing is controlled by organizations such as journals and commercial presses, individual expression is highly valued and preserved. What counts as a good literary work is more often a matter of taste than community acceptance.

▓ **Workstyle**: Are practitioners encouraged to take their own initiative, collaborate, or perform as an organization demands? The style of work reflects the organization of the profession. In both science and professional writing, *successful* risk takers are celebrated and have prestige. Modern science is highly specialized and highly innovative. Specialized fields maintain strict entry requirements and organizational control by licensing and requiring certification of practitioners and setting educational standards. Beyond meeting these standards, practitioners must work closely together in coordinating their work. As scientific work is highly uncertain— there can be extraordinarily rapid changes in areas of research— science is less centralized (or bureaucratic) than other professions. In work that is more directly supervised or controlled (e.g., working in an automobile manufacturing plant), laborers exercise less discretion over their work. The tasks of an assembly-line worker are certain and instantly judged. Mass production requires a well-defined, hierarchical management structure. In science and other professions such as medicine and law, practitioners learn codes of behavior and systems of belief in lengthy graduate school apprenticeships. These systems of belief are transformed into the professional rituals witnessed in laboratories, courtrooms, and operating rooms. The almost mystical aura that surrounds science allows scientists to maintain distance from the laypersons affected by their work (see Fuch's, 1992, analysis).

In considering the professional contexts in which you write and write to others, keep in mind that professions do change. Science and technology, for example, continue growing and affecting audiences that seem far removed from the research process. Many of you will become involved in projects funded by the government and will have to answer to a tax-paying public. Others of you will become involved in projects funded by corporations and will have to answer to stockholders. Practitioners in diverse disciplines and professions realize the benefits of seeking various perspectives on a common problem. Increasingly, you will be asked to mediate among them.

CATEGORIES OF READERS

Scientific and technical writing has a *primary* reader. A grant proposal to the National Science Foundation is intended for a group of people who will decide whether to fund the project. Technical documents are meant for a specific task. As a result, they should be clear and free of ambiguous terms or fancy language. Intended readers and audiences for scientific and technical writing are well-defined; as such, writers often make legitimate assumptions about their needs. However, the strict borders surrounding readers and audiences and repeatedly un-examined assumptions can lead to inefficient action and to the perpetuation of false images. In writing to a primary reader, there are occasions when, instead of assuming that readers agree on a particular concept or course of action, you must define what you mean or what you think the general audience means in a given instance.

The primary reader makes decisions to act; the *secondary* reader is affected by the decision and takes action. If you write a sales proposal, for example, the primary reader may agree to buy the computer system you are selling, but the secondary reader will want to know what is being planned, when the system will be implemented, and its likely uses.

Immediate readers are persons who distribute documents through an organization. These people are usually managers at some level of the organization who act as administrative gatekeepers by ensuring that the right information gets to the right people. The role of immediate readers is often one of enforcing protocol—making sure the distribution of information corresponds with organizational responsibilities. Audiences on the receiving end of information pipelines are often *nominal* audiences. Nominal audiences receive documents but usually do not read them. These documents are sent to and filed by these audiences often for purposes of record keeping and reference.

External readers are people outside the immediate organization to which you write. A lawyer, for example, can be retained as an external reader for a manufacturer to see if a set of instructions absolves the company of liability.

Categories of readers are located on a sliding scale from expert to layperson. These classifications are based on audiences' knowledge of the subject and their social role in a specific organization or larger society. But these categories are constantly shifting. Given the rapid advancement and specialization of science and technology, and number of new journals and electronic networks, experts can quickly become laypersons regarding a range of issues.

Generally, readers can be classified in the following way:

Experts
Technicians
Operators
Managers
Professional nonexperts
Laypersons

The knowledge of readers on most topics is varied. A general reader obsessed with the federal budget may possess knowledge equal to or greater than financial experts on Capitol Hill. The general reader does not have the formal credentials of the expert and so lacks the expert's social status, authority, and influence. Readers' knowledge needs to be understood in context to their ability to act on your ideas. Further, if you want to facilitate the involvement of audiences not having standard credentials (like the general reader), then you need to provide a means through which they can act. You must educate diverse audiences concerning forums for action.

Experts

Experts are characterized by their theoretical and practical knowledge of a field or discipline, including its terminology, concepts, methods, and leading areas of research. Most experts in scientific and technical fields carry out, or have carried out, basic and applied research in a certain area. As research traditions, practices, and funding shift, expertise also changes. Typically in the sciences, cutting-edge or breakthrough discoveries are made by researchers early in their careers. As the field advances, the skills and techniques of the researcher become "less expert." Generally speaking, however, experts are often classified by having postgraduate degrees or equivalent experience in a particular area. As a writer, you can assume that someone who has a Ph.D., for example, is considered an expert in the field. When writing to experts you can use technical jargon and formulas. You can assume as well that experts have less difficulty understanding longer sentences and prose descriptions. But you should not confuse an expert's knowledge with the ability to decipher bad prose. Although some writers use graphics to substitute for prose, you can assume an expert understands sophisticated graphics.

Technicians

Technicians read scientific and technical writing in performing hands-on jobs and completing a process involving the use of equipment. Technicians can build, operate, or maintain machinery and are vital (although their roles are underappreciated) for the advancement of science and technology. Like experts, technicians often have narrowly defined areas of skill. Computer technicians are well-versed in some aspect of computer hardware, but are usually unfamiliar with how to fix copying machines. Technicians are usually hourly-wage employees with an associate's degree, undergraduate degree, or on-the-job training. Technicians are distinguished, in most cases, from experts by their respective lack of theoretical knowledge. Consequently, documents written for technicians—instructions, functional descriptions, physical descriptions—focus on safely and efficiently completing a defined task. Documents written for technicians include diagrams and illustrations, parts lists, and lists of commands in the imperative voice. Sentences are short. A common vocabulary is used. A common format lets the reader know where information is and where to return. Graphic aids reinforce the instructions or serve as substitute instructions. As such, they must be detailed, readable, and clearly labeled.

Operators

Operators use equipment exclusively. They are primarily concerned with clear procedures and instructions and less so with background and rationale. Workers on an assembly line require clear explanations of what they are expected to do. Yet as experiences during the 1980s indicate, management should not neglect explaining to operators how they fit into the process of production. Usually, this information is related orally in group meetings but not in sets of procedures. Most operators are hourly-wage employees who do not have a college degree but received on-the-job training. Procedures and instructions are written in concise sentences and need not include discussions of related topics or theory.

Managers

The role of the manager is to know the specific duties of employees and to organize their efforts. The manager of a restaurant, for example, has probably trained or worked each position within the restaurant. Managers of engineering firms ordinarily begin as work-bench engineers helping design and build a firm's products. Laboratory heads are managers in that they keep a lab running by writing grant proposals, helping design experiments, and assigning tasks to other lab members. Managers help coordinate and oversee the daily activities of an organization.

Management tasks are varied and determined on a local basis with regard to specific tasks. Generally, however, managers are salaried employees, with at least a college education. Management and management science are academic disciplines in which topics such as management/labor relations, collective bargaining, and systems theory are studied. Within certain organizations, employees rise to the position of manager by staying with an organization for some time, learning different duties, and accepting a range of responsibilities. To "manage" other people, such individuals must be able to relate to, and communicate effectively with, employees. Frequently, the basis for this relationship is shared experience and sense of purpose. In writing to managers, determine their technical background and appeal to the practical. Managers are trained to regard the schedule of production and the "bottom line" (profit and loss) over most other issues. Consequently, there is little concern with economic or labor theory. Managers look for ways to keep a number of balls in the air—money, schedules, organizational policies—while overseeing many individuals. In describing a technology, for instance, don't talk about how it works; instead, explain how valuable it is on the market.

Professional Nonexperts

Geneticists read papers published by statisticians. Accountants read marketing textbooks. Medical doctors read journals written for anthropologists. Professional nonexperts are people who read material outside their specialty or home discipline. Normally, some connection exists between these readers' backgrounds and the technical material they read. Consumers who want in-depth information on electronics equipment may consult electronics journals regarding circuits. Biologists doing research on mycobacterium may read a journal article on AIDS research—

a related field outside their specialty. Increasing specialization will make many of us professional nonexperts. These readers can be characterized as having a basic understanding of theory and concepts—enough to follow the discussion—but not an expert's level of knowledge. Professional nonexperts are decision-makers in other fields examining how other professionals do their job. As a writer, you may thus find it difficult to anticipate who will read your document from this perspective, for interdisciplinary audiences are increasing and the information you present may be used in ways you did not imagine.

Laypersons

Laypersons, a broad audience category, are defined by a lack of technical expertise. Laypersons represent the most misunderstood group with respect to scientific and technical communication. Scientists and technologists often fail to see the need for laypersons to participate in any decisions regarding their specialties. In writing to laypersons, offer relevant background, use short sentences, use active voice and informal tone, translate technical jargon by using metaphors and similes rooted in common experience, and legitimate your position and interest with respect to public concerns. In short, you must build a context for your subject within the audience's experience.

General readers are people who read popular science books, newspapers, and magazines from which they get information about science and technology. Science writing of this type is aimed at making scientific and technical information understandable, without offering a critical context. Newspaper reporters who cover science are generally uncritical of the science news they report; sometimes taking scientists' press releases and translating them for general consumption. Popular science topics in which laypersons are interested involve health and diet, exercise, and cutting-edge research. Popular science accounts offer eye-catching headlines that hook readers and narratives about the effect that science and technology will have on people's personal lives. General readers come from all different educational and social backgrounds and represent a variety of interests. Many newspapers aim at an 8th- to 10th-grade reading level.

Characteristics of Readers

Upon classifying readers generally, you can determine their characteristics by answering questions that apply to the readers' background. Classifying readers is an imprecise process because, for the most part, you won't know who will ultimately read your document. A memo by the president of a corporation is written specifically to a department head. But the department head may find the information important to employees, makes photocopies, and distributes the content more widely than originally intended. Nevertheless readers share certain characteristics and concerns that you must try to pinpoint. To refine the analysis, here are questions you need to ask about the persons you *know* will read the document. Knowledge of your readers is gained by talking to people in the organization (also known as networking), your familiarity with its *ethos* and reputation, and inference from personal experience.

What is the reader's name and title?

In writing cover letters for résumés, job advertisements sometimes ask you to address the letter to the "director of personnel." Copies of a preliminary report are often forwarded to "all branch managers." Knowing the job titles of people within an organization gives you a clear idea of the tone you should take, the information you include, and how it will be organized. The purpose of most scientific and technical communication is to enable people to do their job. However, addressing persons' titles without indicating you care about their needs, especially in a job search, leaves you at the organizational door with no invitation to enter. Try to find out the names of the people to whom you will be writing. Although direct appeals should be used with great care, providing a personal context for information (how this policy will affect *you*) establishes goodwill and the basis for an ongoing dialogue among interested parties.

What is the reader's role in the organization?

Determine the reader's job responsibilities and range of actions. In writing a feasibility study on performing a new type of enzyme assay for a chemical manufacturing company, the manager of the plant will want to know what methods you use and the possibilities for cost-effect alternatives. If the manager can mandate changes, you can offer a straightforward cost/benefit analysis. Still, the wider the distribution the feasibility study receives—to accountants and laboratory technicians—the wider the range of concerns and actions you must address. A cost/benefit analysis helps little in actually performing the assay.

What is the reader's educational background?

Knowing the reader's intellectual pedigree does allow you to place them in general categories, as discussed earlier. But you need more detail than knowing the reader has a B.S., M.S., and/or Ph.D. The answers to the following questions will likely not be readily available at the outset, but are important to consider and determine when possible:

- In what discipline did the reader receive their degree?
- From what institution?
- What is the reputation of the institution?
- Did they write a senior project, thesis, and/or dissertation?
- If so, who was the supervisor or major professor?
- When did they receive the degree?
- What did their program of study entail?

Many companies and institutions feel that education is an important stepping-stone to on-the-job training. What you learn in this book about scientific and technical communication, for instance, will undoubtedly be approached and taught to you in a different way on the job. Industries spend a great deal of time educating their workers on the way they do things. Try to determine the type of in-house education—seminars, training sessions, workshops—your readers received.

Knowing the educational background of readers allows you to determine what assumptions you can make, the background you need to provide, your rhetorical relationship to the readers (Are they an authority? Is your background more extensive?), and the tone and vocabulary used in the document.

What is the reader's professional background?

Most readers enjoy a variety of professional and work experiences to which technical writers can appeal. The longer a person is in the workforce, the more likely that person will have worked a number of jobs—sometimes within the same general area but frequently in related areas. After the extraordinary corporate expansion during the 1980s, the shifting economy required many corporations to reorganize and become "leaner." Subsequently, many executives and managers were forced to find jobs in related professions. During the early 1990s, the downsizing of the military forced a number of engineers to go into other professions involving computer programming and hardware and software design. Although scientists tend to remain in their fields, there is a general movement from intensive research early in their careers to management-oriented duties. As a writer, you can appeal to common work experiences between yourself and your reader by acknowledging the changing nature and demands of the workplace. By being aware of your reader's professional path and possible career trajectory, you can gauge the content and style of your document.

To what professional organizations does the reader belong?

Many of your readers are members of professional organizations, such as the American Medical Association, the American Society for Chemical Engineers, Teachers for a Democratic Culture, and local unions. For each profession, there is at least one professional organization (sometimes several) representing the interest of its dues-paying members. These groups are organized around ideological and professional concerns. Professional organizations sponsor seminars and presentations, provide forums (newsletters and journals) in which members can publish their research and personal views, and take action to secure worker rights and compensation. Professionals join these organizations to ensure their voice is heard at their job and within the larger community. By looking at mainstream professional publications, you can get a sense of your reader's beliefs, topics of concern, and the standards of the field. Although individual readers may not wholeheartedly share these beliefs and values, you can draw a better portrait of a field and its members with which you are not familiar.

How will the reader read the document?

A technical document can be read in many ways. In most instances, you can assume the reader does not have time to thoroughly read the report. You can also assume that readers of your document have varying levels of interest and knowledge of the situation about which you write. The amount of time, interest, and knowledge the reader possesses will shape how your document is read. The reader may simply file the document, skim it, closely read certain sections, or closely read the entire content. In organizing and designing the document, appeal to different types of reading. For example, the generous use of concisely worded subheadings allows someone skimming the document to get an overall sense of its content. Anticipate which sections the primary reader needs—the methods section of a journal article, the cost breakdown of a proposal—and concentrate on the details in those sections. Try to get as much feedback as possible about the needs of the reader to encourage ways of reading the document.

What responses can I expect from the reader?

By examining the rhetorical purpose of the document, you can get a feel for how the reader will react. If, for example, you discover in the process of writing a progress report that the project you planned is impossible to complete by the proposed deadline, you *can* expect disappointment from your boss. You *cannot,* however, simply state "This project is impossible." You must offer alternative plans of action and deadlines. Although you can anticipate reader reaction in such clear cases, you cannot anticipate all reader biases and preferences. Even readers within the sciences are predisposed to consider certain research topics worthy, others worthless. When possible, look at documents written by your readers to learn their preferences. Does the reader have a bias for or against certain topics? Does the reader prefer certain presentation formats? In accounting for your readers' biases, do not forget your own principles and beliefs. Educate the reader to see what you see.

What Readability Indexes Reveal

A readability index is a set of principles and formulas used to determine how difficult a text is to read and comprehend. The premise governing readability indexes is that short sentences composed of "simple" words are easier to comprehend than long sentences with "difficult" words. By one estimate, over 100 readability formulas exist. The word processing program you use likely has a style- or grammar-checking feature that calculates readability. Many agencies, firms, and research institutions use readability indexes to set guidelines for drafting and revising documents. As your professional writing may be evaluated according to readability standards, you need to know the components and problems of indexes.

To think that writing and its comprehension could be determined by a formula is somewhat appealing. Many of the difficult aspects of technical writing could be eliminated by simply plugging in a text, testing the result, making revisions, and distributing the finished product. But readability formulas fail to take into account that reading is a complex individual, social, and historical process. Let's look at an example.

Components of Readability Formulas

Several techniques exist for determining readability, such as the Flesch Check System and the Dale-Chall Formula. Of these, Robert Gunning's "Fog Index" is the most familiar because of its wide use. The following "Ten Principles of Clear Writing" form the basis of the index and serve as a list of goals against which a sentence or passage can be compared:

1. Write to express, not impress.
2. Make full use of variety.
3. Keep sentences short.
4. Use the familiar word.
5. Prefer the simple to the complex.
6. Avoid unnecessary words.
7. Put action in your verbs.
8. Write the way you talk.

9. Use terms the reader can picture.

10. Tie in with your reader's experience.

In examining these principles, you should note, for instance, the complexity of tying in with "your reader's experience." Readers' understanding of their experience and needs is often quite varied. Also, there are occasional rhetorical advantages gained by writing to impress and not to express.

The Flesch Check System serves as the basis for "grammar checkers" found in the word processing programs many of you use. "To find how easy your writing reads" according to Flesch's system, do the following:

- Take a sample of 100 words.
- Divide the number of sentences in the sample into 100 to get the average sentence length. On Flesch's scale, a 5-word sentence is rated "very easy," whereas a 35-word sentence is rated "very difficult."
- Count the number of syllables in the 100-word sample. On Flesch's scale, 120 syllables per 100 words is rated "very easy," whereas 200 syllables per 100 words is rated "very difficult."
- The "reading ease" score is determined by comparing the number of words per sentence and syllables per 100 words.

If, for instance, the passage you select contains 6 words per sentence and 163 syllables per 100 words, the "reading ease" score is rated "standard." The size of the sample also affects the score. Here is an example from the opening (Chapter 1) of Charles Darwin's (1859/1968) *On the Origin of Species* using a word processing program to compile the score:

> When we look to the individuals of the same variety or sub-variety of our older cultivated plants and animals, one of the first points which strikes us, is that they generally differ more from each other than do the individuals of any one species or variety in a state of nature. When we reflect on the vast diversity of plant and animals which have been cultivated, and which have varied during all ages under the most different climates and treatment, I think we are driven to conclude that this great variability is simply due to our domestic productions having been raised under conditions of life

not so uniform as, and somewhat different from, those to which the parent-species had been exposed under nature. There is, also, some probability in the view propounded by Andrew Knight that this variability may be partly connected with the excess of food. (p. 71)

In this sample of 146 words and 3 sentences, two thirds of the sentences are in the passive voice, the Flesch "reading ease" level is 19.4%, the Flesch grade level is 17, and Gunning's Fog Index is 24.8%. According to this readability formula, Darwin's prose is considered difficult to read. The length of the sentences and the use of passive voice, technical jargon, and complex vocabulary lead the index to suggest that the reader's level of understanding approximates the senior collegiate level.

Darwin's work was calculated as difficult to understand. Yet when *Origin* first appeared on November 24, 1859, the entire first edition—1,250 copies—was sold that same day. *Origin* was close to being considered *popular* literature at the time and was reviewed in a wide variety of newspapers and magazines. Widespread interest in Darwin's thesis and its immediate popularization, combined with then-current reading habits and educational practices, influenced the public's perception of *Origin*'s readability. The book became a contemporary classic. What counts as a "difficult" sentence or word in the Gunning index today may have been part of common parlance 100-plus years ago.

Other factors influence readability. According to one study (Huckin, 1983), format and organization affect readability more than sentence length and word choice. Also, approaches to reading and reading comprehension differ among social groups and communities. Not only do members of certain professions and disciplines read differently, so do members of demographic groups. Age, level of education, socioeconomic status, and the reader's interest are factors that also influence reading comprehension.

Another criticism of readability formulas is that they do not live up to the scientific standards to which they aspire. Further, it is a matter of dispute whether scientific methodology is appropriate or adequate for understanding the process of writing and practice of reading.

Scientism is the belief that natural science is the most valuable part of human learning. This belief rests in part on the historical assumption that science brought humanity out of the "dark ages" by eliminating religious superstition and into the modern era by supplying the groundwork for the Industrial Revolution. The unparalleled success and resulting authority of modern science is posed as a reason to emulate scientific practice. Scientism proposes that it is always good for "unscientific" subjects—morals, history, politics, even writing—to be placed on scientific footing.

COMMUNICATING ACROSS
DISCIPLINES AND CULTURES

The cultural, institutional setting in which scientific and technical communication takes place affects how messages are written and read. A great deal of technical writing takes place among people who share the same background, motivations, and interests. But there are also diverse and differently motivated audiences for technical writing. One way to determine the needs of your audience is to analyze the setting for technical communication.

The Rise of Disciplines

> Expressed in the briefest way, the task of scientific knowledge appears to be: Fitting thoughts to facts and thoughts to each other. Every favorable biological process is one of self-preservation, and as such is at the same time an adjustment and more economical than a process that is disadvantageous to the individual. All beneficial knowing consists of special cases or parts of biologically helpful processes. . . . In the knowing process one can otherwise observe the most diverse qualities; we characterize these as above all biological and economical, that is, as excluding pointless behavior. (Ernst Mach quoted in Blackman, 1992, pp. 133-134)

Following the Franco-Prussian War until World War I (1870-1914), the European imperial powers—Great Britain, France, and the German Reich—took strides to modernize their education systems. Educational reform proceeded along two related, yet irreconcilable, conceptual fronts. On one front, democratic theorists proposed throwing open the doors to educational institutions by calling for universal access to formal education to amend social and economic disparities among the classes. On the other front, reformers urged caution. Increased mobility among a newly educated populace would threaten the existing social order. And denying access to formal schooling might lead to civil unrest. Consequently, educational credentials set forth by government and professional organizations within academic disciplines (and by the disciplines themselves) were introduced in order to distinguish and stratify occupations. Education reform became synonymous with both increased educational opportunity *and* increased academic specialization. The question of access to education quickly became a question about the requirements of academic disciplines. The modern debate over intellectual specialization was born.

From 1908 to 1913, a series of lectures concerning science education took place in Germany. The participants in this highly charged debate were none other than Austrian physicist Ernst Mach (1838-1916), famous for his work in mechanics (the Mach number) and profound philosophical influence on Albert Einstein and the Vienna Circle philosophers, and German physicist Max Planck (1858-1947), originator of quantum theory (Planck's constant). Both Mach and Planck agreed that the natural sciences should be taught in secondary schools. But given educational reforms, how should science be taught, and for what purpose? How should one present the content of science and technology to students who will not become practicing scientists and engineers?

Mach contended that the value of science was in "economizing thought." Science provided mathematical equations and formulas that make complex phenomena easier to describe and manipulate. Economy of thought was part of a "biologically helpful" process, a phrase reflecting Charles Darwin's influence on Mach, for human self-preservation. Put broadly, Mach held that science was necessary for human survival, but it was not an especially ennobling process. In fact, he derided the practice of scientists who dignified research into odd and anomalous phenomena under the guise of "scientific curiosity."

To teach science, Mach claimed, one must draw a relationship between concrete daily experience and the phenomena discussed. For example, one might introduce the concept of force by referring to muscular effort. Mach championed examining the philosophical questions inspiring scientific inquiry as well as addressing science within its historical contexts. In teaching science, one should also teach *about* science—how ideas and theories are developed, applied, revised, and learned over time. Mach emphasized that science enabled people to have a direct, comprehensible relationship to nature. Nevertheless the time for abstract scientific thinking was, metaphorically speaking, at dusk.[1]

Planck attacked Mach by claiming that no great discoveries in physics took place by "fitting thoughts to facts and thoughts to each other" in the most economical fashion. He countered that the distinctiveness of science was its ability to support a single, unified theory accounting for all observations. Such a theory would deliver the same results to any inquirer located anywhere. For Planck, the invariant nature of scientific truth—available to all people (even "Mars dwellers") at all times—was the essence of science. Mach worried about the all-consuming authority of this view of science and countered, "If belief in the reality of atoms is so essential to you, then I will have nothing to do with physical ways of thinking; I will no longer be a genuine physicist. . . . In short, thank you so much for your community of believers, but for me freedom of thought is more precious" (pp. 138-139).

In part, Mach was responding to current developments in physics. Planck and his colleagues were busy pursuing the "atomic hypothesis" concerning the nature of atoms. Mach questioned whether this, or any, disputed scientific theory should be introduced in the classroom. If the theory turned out to be true, why not wait to teach it once the equations and applications were established? If false, then teaching the theory would give it an undeserved legitimacy. Mach's emphasis on the *utility* of science and technology and Planck's embrace of the *authority* of science provide a framework for considering the purpose of scientific and technical communication.

Ultimately, Planck's vision of science triumphed over Mach's. Scientists and laypersons share the notion that science is an authoritative institution unaffected by society. Scientific knowledge is distinguished from other forms of knowledge by preserving its content within various historical and social contexts. Scientific experiments, we believe, give us truths about nature; the knowledge of which gives us increasing control of our lives and our future. Yet perhaps we are too quick in abandoning Mach's views, for in accepting Planck's view of science, we face an interesting paradox that embodies the significance and challenge of scientific and technical communication.

Scientific and technical knowledge exists only as it is expressed in language and other social practices—oral and visual communication, for example. Accepting Planck's view, we would all agree that the truths about the world do not change, but communicating those truths is a different story. Language is tricky. Words and symbols require interpretation; often by various audiences possessing different levels of knowledge and understanding. Words have multiple meanings that change over time. The paradox is this: Given the unreliability of language, how is it that scientific truths remain "intact" over centuries in different cultures using different languages? One answer, perhaps, lies in the narrow range of communicative options, such as disciplinary jargons and writing formats, that scientists and engineers have.

Interdisciplinary Audiences

Interdisciplinary audiences are composed of people from different academic disciplines and professions and the lay public who have different agendas, training, interests, and levels of education. The traditional categories and characteristics of audiences and readers mentioned in this chapter do not readily hold. As no one method of problem solving works within an interdisciplinary context, emphasis is placed on joint meetings, presentations, methods, and collaborative action. Further, because the composition of interdisciplinary audiences cannot be determined ahead of time, knowing integrative techniques can help you communicate to these audiences.

The twofold purpose of scientific and technical communicators in an interdisciplinary context would be to help *clarify* concepts and skills and to help *resolve* different perspectives by integrating them. Here is an example of how interdisciplinary method would work. There are many concepts that disciplines share. As Klein (1990) points out the concept of "power" is relevant to almost all the social sciences. "Power" is also a concept used in literary analysis, the natural sciences, and engineering. Technical writers, for example, would highlight the ambiguities and assumptions of the definition of power within disciplines by listing its various definitions and finding the basis for integration. In proposing a composite definition, participants can challenge their conclusions from specific disciplinary perspectives. This process would take the form of the dialectic—an argumentative process in which contradictory propositions are asserted, compared, and synthesized. The length of this process depends on the participants' patience, interests, and resources. Scientific and technical communicators would act as mediators for members of an interdisciplinary audience.

COMMUNICATING ACROSS CULTURES: A CASE STUDY

Karin Mårdsjö provides a study of how technical manuals are written in Sweden. She illustrates how assumptions about the audience by technical writers are based on the kind of technology being used. Typically, the purpose of manuals was seen as purely instructing the user, leading writers to assume an authoritative stance and imperative tone in giving commands. She suggests that manuals are only part of the technologies' interaction with the user. However, technical writers, in the assumptions they make about the user (smart, ignorant, capable, incapable) and the tone expressing those assumptions, actually help create the audience for a technology. The relationship established between the writer and reader of technical manuals shapes what it means to live in a "technological society." [2]

Technical Writers' Image of Their Audience

We are living is what is sometimes described as a technological society. Technical devices and technological systems surround us and are a substantial part both of our surroundings and of the objects with which we interact. Living in this kind of society demands from its citizens an understanding of technology and knowing how to use it. The devices—or the systems—need instruction and additional information in order to be comprehensible: they are rarely self-explanatory.

In my analysis, I have focused on the communication process between writers of microwave oven and computer word processing manuals and their users. The three microwave manuals I analyzed were produced in major Swedish test kitchens. Two of the word processing manuals were produced in Swedish computer software industries; the third was produced in the United States and translated into Swedish.

The Image of the User

English sociologist Steve Woolgar conducted a long-term field study at a computer software industry. He noticed then how the system developers and the technical writers created their image of their users, by speaking of them as ignorant and strange persons, and not by having any personal contact with them.

I believe that this image of the users, which can, of course, be created in other ways than in the Woolgar example, is one important factor that determines how the technology development and technical writing are performed and adjusted to the presumed users. Steve Woolgar called this process "configuring the user."

There are, of course, other important factors in the production process. As far as the manuals are concerned, there are implicit and explicit rules for writing, company standards, "organization climate," and so on. It is reasonable to presume—and I have found support for this in a pilot study and dissertation research—that the context for writing is as important for the writers as their awareness of the audience.

Ways of Addressing Users

Very roughly, in the word processing texts the users are addressed in a rather direct (or authoritarian way) way: *Do this, do that.* This, of course, could be viewed as threatening the users' personal freedom of choice and seeing them as ignorant. But it could just as well, possible preferably, be regarded as a perfectly natural style and tone in this kind of genre. Or it could be interpreted as the tone of the high-status engineer toward the ignorant commoners.

The microwave oven manuals are quite different. The tone is less direct so as not to offend the cook:

> As always in the art of cooking, you and your ingredients are the most important factors in achieving good results. The microwave oven is an excellent and practical help for cooking good meals quickly, and saving time and energy. (Original text in Swedish, my translation)

In this example, the user has the main role, not the technology. That is another general difference between the two types of manuals. In computer software manuals, expressions like "the program can" or "the program will" occur now and then, which never happens in the microwave oven manuals.

The purely instructional parts of the manuals are fairly similar, with a direct way of addressing the users. The differences lie mostly in the introductory parts, where the "polite" way of addressing is more usual in the microwave manuals.

Changing Attitudes, Creating Conviction

There is also a difference in how the writers explicitly—or implicitly—help the users think in new ways and try to help them adapt to the new technology.

On the whole, the writers of the word processing manuals seem to regard their readers as generally adjusted to the new technology and do not put much effort into convincing them. (Which is done quite a lot in older word processing manuals, with, for example, analogies to cars: "The cars were also regarded as dangerous in the beginning—but see how familiar they have become.") In the microwave oven manuals, verbal and pictorial means are used to convince the readers that the technology is useful and not dangerous.

The stylistic methods used are mainly analogies to and metaphors for well-known technologies along with straightforward explanations of the differences between the old and the new. In the case of word processing manuals, explicit statements about these differences and what is specific for the technology are more usual, in the few cases where anything like this occurs. Where analogies are actually used, the step between old and new technology is not so far:

> *You can think of a word processing system (program and computer) as a typewriter with a built-in pair of scissors, tape and copying machine. . . . A word processing program mainly functions like a typewriter, but with many extra possibilities built in.*

The same message is conveyed also in the microwave oven manuals, where the advantages of the new technology are expressed with the help of analogies to ordinary cooking. But there is an interesting difference as well: The writers of the microwave oven manuals seem to have the image of the users as potentially afraid. There was a discussion of "the radiation danger" when the technology was newly introduced, and the awareness seems to linger on. It can be found in texts like these (from the introductory part of a manual):

> *Microwaves are a type of electromagnetic energy. Ordinary daylight and radio waves are two others. The only difference between these two types of energy is the length of the waves. . . . Just as the ray of light goes through glass, clear plastic and air, the microwaves can go right through materials like paper, glass, china, plastic and air. . . . The microwaves are reflected by metal in the same way as a ray of light is reflected by a mirror surface.*

These three short examples come from the same part of the text, altogether less than half a page. In this short space, the writer has found it necessary to make analogies to well-known and "safe" phenomena like daylight, radio waves, and mirror reflections several times.

Interviewing Technical Writers

In my study, I interviewed the authors of the manuals I had analyzed and some of their close colleagues. The companies involved in the study were different kinds, and thus the conditions for text production varied to a great extent. Throughout the interviews, three major types of manual production became apparent: the *negotiation type,* where the technical writers openly negotiated with other actors; the *evolutionary type,* where the manuals have been developed over a long period of time; and the *industrial type,* made in a company with a very large manual production and clear aims of giving the products a profile through the manuals.

These three major types of manuals created an overall pattern for the text production, a kind of general frame. During the interviews, I also confronted the interviewed persons with my text analysis. It became obvious that the text writers regarded the motivational aspect as primary. Instruction is, of course, vital, but it not only has a value in its own right, it is also regarded as part of the motivational aim. "If the users get started quickly and correctly, they will feel happier about the technology in general" was one expression voiced on that issue.

As far as the descriptive approach was concerned, company strategies differ. One of the word processing companies found it unimportant; the audience is regarded as already having reached that level of understanding. Another of the two word processing companies had, however, devoted a major part of their manual to that purpose. The ambition behind that decision was described as more than just managing a certain word processing program; they wanted to raise the general "technology level," and the deficiency of school teaching was mentioned as a driving force for that aim.

In the microwave companies, descriptive elements were mentioned as a part of the introduction of a new technology. The users were regarded as needing information for correct and flexible usage.

Emphasized by almost all of the interviewees was a personal interest in the technology and its development and a cultural concern for preserving "the Swedishness," which consisted both of language and of traditional Swedish cooking. Two aspects of their answers were particularly interesting. The first was that most of the text writers spoke with greater emphasis and more details about their interest in the technology, its function, and improvement than about the use of language as a technique applied (instructional technology) toward the users. This may have to do with the aim of further stressing their professional situation. The other interesting aspect, the cultural concern, can be interpreted as another professional strategy or as part of the Swedish ideal of comprehensibility and equality ("everyone should have a chance at understanding"). Legal factors were mentioned as relevant but not as restrictive.

Conclusions

The two main results of this study are that manuals can and should be regarded as texts with multiple aims and that they should be analyzed in their communicational setting. As technical manuals have multiple aims, it is, in practice as well as in research, no longer advisable to regard them as purely instructional artifacts. The writers of manuals must have this in mind in order to avoid confusing the aims and in order to clarify their intentions toward the users. For the production of manuals, it is also important to keep in mind that the manual is one important aspect of a technology's interaction with the user. Manuals must be created in order to cooperate with other aspects of the relationships: the technology design and other information sources. If they support each other, the users will have a better chance of comfortably using and managing technology in a technological society.

Discussion

1. Referring to the categories of readers given in this chapter, how do you think the evolution of telecommunications technologies, like the internet, will affect the boundaries between them? How will the anticipated wider distribution of information impact experts, technicians, operators, managers, pro-

fessional nonexperts, and laypersons? What will the greater availability of information mean to the conception of audiences within your field or discipline?

2. In discussing your answers to the following questions, begin to put together a general profile of practitioners in your discipline and profession: What type degree does one need to be a practitioner? What type of special licensing does a practitioner require? Is there an emphasis on collaboration or on individual work? Does the profession or discipline have a well-defined or loose "pecking order"? Are the tasks you perform handed to you by an authority, or are you free to pursue your own ideas and initiatives? What type of resources do you need—equipment, space, money—to accomplish tasks?

3. Given your academic training and work experience, who generally is the primary audience for your scientific and technical communication? Who is the secondary audience?

4. A recent focal point of many universities and colleges is helping resolve society's problems through, for example, economic planning and continuing education programs. Does your university or college see community outreach as an important part of its mission? Why should community concerns be a consideration of your college or university? In what outreach programs does your discipline participate? How do you participate in outreach programs? Who is the audience for these programs? How will the needs and demands of these audiences have an effect on scientific and technical communication?

5. Karin Mårdsjö's case study offers some telling insights of how Swedish technical writers consider their audience. From Mårdsjö's study, what is the relationship between the type of technology being used and the writers' conception of their audience? Which assumptions are justified? What problems do you see with the tone of the instruction manuals? Why is the explanation of microwaves, for instance, necessary? What kind of relationship should writers of manuals develop with their audience? What cultural differences do you see between how Swedish and American technical writers relate to audiences?

6. With whom do you agree regarding the purpose of scientific knowledge, Mach or Planck? Should higher education be available to all who seek it? What roles do educational credentials play in structuring our society? Referring to Dale Sullivan's case study (Chapter 10, Part II of the text), what part does disciplinary specialization play in the acceptance of evidence about mass extinctions? Ultimately, how do Raup and Sepkoski convince the audience of their claims?

Exercises

1. Find a copy of an advertisement for a product that introduces new scientific research, a new technology, or a technological advancement to one of the categories of readers mentioned in this chapter. In an analytical report, draw, as detailed as possible, a profile of the audience from the technical communicator's point of view (Karin Mårdsjö's essay may serve as an example). Consider, for example, what the advertiser assumes the reader knows. Is that belief justified? What images of science or technology are used to promote the product? How is scientific and technical evidence presented? Do you think mentioning science is effective in convincing the audience to buy the product?

2. Now that Johnson Engineering is winning contracts outside the United States, the company is experiencing firsthand the contingencies of hosting foreign guests and preparing staff engineers and their families to live abroad. As a training manager, you know that many large corporations maintain a division that trains and houses foreign workers, teaches languages, and helps sales staff and engineers understand the social conventions and business practices of other cultures.

Johnson cannot invest in a major corporate educational center right now, and with engineers and their families leaving for foreign cities on an unpredictable schedule, hiring an expensive outside training firm to offer seminars is not possible.

You have been asked, therefore, to write a short manual that will be given to employees who are going with their families to specific countries. The manual must be short—fewer than five pages of copy and carefully organized to emphasize the main points.

Your boss wants you to start by choosing any one of the following nations:

Saudi Arabia	Thailand
Singapore	Romania
Germany	Indonesia
Taiwan	Poland
Hungary	Peru
Egypt	Finland
Japan	India
France	South Africa
Nigeria	Kuwait
Mexico	Russia

Your boss asks you to keep two goals in mind while writing the manual.

The first goal is to inform the reader of cultural practices and to show strategies, through illustration and example, for successful communication based on those practices. One way is to compare and contrast American and "other's" cultural communication practices.

The second goal is to assess the current state of scientific and technological development in the country. Various agencies of the U.S. government (e.g., the State, Agriculture and Defense Departments) perform these assessments, which are found in the government documents section of the library and on the internet. Additionally, many journals present "cultural updates" on specific countries. *The Hungarian Quarterly* is an example of this kind of journal. Foreign press newspapers and their English counterparts are also available in the library.

As a starting place you are given this list of areas to consider:

- Legal status of foreign nationals
- Political system
- Social taboos
- Living conditions: water, food, marketing, health conditions

▓ Eating meals: styles and rituals

▓ Customs: greetings, men's and women's dress, exchanging gifts, tipping

Your boss asks you to place special emphasis in the manual on communications practices:

▓ Languages

▓ Patterns of greeting

▓ Negotiating styles

▓ Writing styles

▓ Presentation styles

▓ Any aspects of business, scientific, or technical communication you feel are important to know

Just as you turn to leave, your boss offers a few reminders:

▓ Although many nations do share general cultural and historical traditions, like the United States and Great Britain, standards of proper expression are often quite different.

▓ Information on both the customs and the current state of scientific and technological development may be, for given countries, limited. Different issues will require different emphases in a given manual. The reasons for emphasis on, or lack of information about, required information for the manual may need explanation.

▓ Interviews with people from, or familiar with, the country are often quite helpful.

3. In an analytical report, compare and contrast Karin Mårdsjö's and Dale Sullivan's concepts of how audiences function in the acceptance or rejection of technological innovation and scientific explanation. Based on the case studies, provide a reader profile. From Mårdsjö's and Sullivan's analyses, what common strategies do the writers employ to persuade varied audiences? How well do they succeed? How do multiple aims of users and readers complicate the technical communication process? How do the aims of professional technical writers and scientists compare? Are you convinced by the points and recommendations made by Mårdsjö and Sullivan? On what levels do the authors themselves succeed or fail in convincing the varied audience for this text? You may broaden your report to include insights into texts common in your discipline whose

purpose is to convince distinct and varied audiences of a given view.

NOTES

1. G. W. F. Hegel's (1770-1831) famous quote about the task of philosophy: "When philosophy paints its grey in grey, a form of life has become old, and it cannot be rejuvenated, but only recognized by the grey in grey of philosophy; the owl of Minerva begins its flight only with the onset of dusk" (Hegel, 1991, p. 23)

2. Karin Mårdsjö's case study is excerpted, edited, and revised for this text from her article "Technical Writers' Image of Their Audience: Word Processing and Microwave Oven Manuals as an Example" (1992). Quotes were taken from three manuals of each of the two types purchased in Sweden in 1988-1989. The English translations are Mårdsjö's.

BIBLIOGRAPHY

Burnett, R. (1994). *Technical communication* (3rd ed.). Belmont, CA: Wadsworth.

Darwin, C. (1968). *On the origin of species* (J. W. Burrow, Ed.). Baltimore: Penguin.

Fuchs, S. (1992). *The professional quest for truth: A social theory of science and knowledge.* Albany: State University of New York Press.

Fuller, S. (1992). Being there with Thomas Kuhn: A parable for postmodern times. *History and Theory, 31,* 241-275.

Fuller, S. (1993). *Philosophy, rhetoric and the end of knowledge.* Madison: University of Wisconsin Press.

Hegel, G. W. F. (1991). *Elements of the philosophy of right* (A. Wood, Ed.; H. B. Nisbett, Trans.). Cambridge, England: Cambridge University Press.

Huckin, T. N. (1983). A cognitive approach to readability. In P. V. Anderson, R. J. Brockmann, & C. R. Miller (Eds.), *New essays in technical and scientific communication: Research, theory, practice* (pp. 90-108). Farmingdale, NY: Baywood.

Klein, J. T. (1990). *Interdisciplinarity: History, theory and practice.* Detroit: Wayne State University Press.

Mach, E. (1910). The leading thoughts of my scientific epistomology and its acceptance by contemporaries. (abridged). In J. Blackman, (Ed.), *Ernst Much—A deeper look: Documents and new perspectives* (pp. 133-139). (Boston Studies in the Philosophy of Science, Vol. 143). Dordrecht/Boston: Kleuwe Academic Press.

Mårdsjö, K. (1992). Technical writers' image of their audience: Word processing and microwave oven manuals as an example. In A. Grinstead & O. Wagner (Eds.), *Communication for specific purposes* (pp. 38-51). Tübingen: Gunter Narr Verlag.

Markel, M. (1992). *Technical writing situations and strategies* (3rd ed.). New York: St. Martin's.

CHAPTER

Language, Persuasion, and Argument

The April 25, 1953, issue of the journal *Nature* included an article titled "Molecular Structure of Nucleic Acids," which presented for the first time James Watson and Francis Crick's now famous model for the structure of DNA. The article begins, "We wish to suggest a structure for the salt of deoxyribose nucleic acid. This structure has novel features which are of considerable biological interest" (pp. 737-738)—a straightforward opening to what seems at first a not particularly remarkable scientific paper. The tone is understated: The words "wish to suggest" rather than the slightly bolder "suggest" or the much bolder "found" implies humility, as does the modest claim that their model has "novel" features of "considerable biological interest." The presentation has a modest tone for two reasons. Scientific writing often presents itself modestly, suggesting that what it describes is not "constructed" but rather reveals itself to the scientist. It is modest too for a more practical reason: The tone guards the authors' reputation in case they are mistaken. However, the use of "we" (unusual in scientific literature) suggests that its authors are concerned with credit for the discovery; it makes the unmistakable claim that they got there first. In short, the rhetorical strategy of the article is so subtle that we may miss it on a first reading; finally though, it is both controlled and amazingly powerful.[1]

To describe Watson and Crick's opening as an example of effective *rhetoric* may strike readers as odd. One could argue that the study of science and rhetoric embodies two very different sets of values. Science deals with truth—establishing certain knowledge and matters of fact through observation and testing. Rhetoric deals with deceit—the indiscriminate use of language to serve the desire of a speaker. Science finds truth; rhetoric hides it.

But language in all its forms supplies the medium for the exchange of ideas and in determining the truth. The functions of language to persuade, to inform, and to represent ideas are interwoven with one another; they cannot be separated. The truth of science depends on its linguistic expression. If scientists, like Watson and Crick, cannot convince an audience that their research has merit, then scientific truths become a casualty of ineffective language use. Audiences in science and technology require persuading just like audiences anywhere else. But how does this persuasion take place? Is it simply a magical combination of words? To understand how science persuades its audience, we must first understand how language works.

SCIENTIFIC STYLE AND
THE FUNCTIONS OF LANGUAGE

Words are not windowpanes through which we view objects in the world. Language cannot be cleansed of its ambiguity. Words and symbols form an opaque medium of communication and knowing. In part, scientific and technical language serves the authority and interests of its practitioners. The language can be fuzzy as a result. Those of you who have ever followed a set of simple instructions know that even clear-cut wording leads to mistakes. Imagine trying to replicate a scientific experiment from its presentation in a journal article.

Consider the many ways you use language every day. You tell stories, offer explanations, persuade someone of your views, make jokes, write letters—the list is endless. Traditionally in science and technology, practitioners saw the primary function of language—words as well as mathematical equations and symbolic notation—as *representing* nature or technology in words and symbols. On this view, words and symbols "stand for" or "correspond to" objects in the world. Nature, however, is difficult to capture. Natural phenomena are vast and perplexing. Scientific and technical language often tries to describe objects we cannot see and forces we minimally understand.

By asserting objective representation as their only goal, many scientific and technical communicators ignore other aspects of language and possibilities for understanding nature. Still, because of its complexity and apparent accuracy, scientific and technical language retains authority and privilege over our more mundane observations of the world. The authority of science lies in its ability to persuade audiences. But how do practitioners both maintain the authority of science and persuade audiences? To answer this question, let's revisit some of the historical issues raised in Chapters 1 and 2.

The Development of Scientific Style

Before the Fall of man in the Garden of Eden, Francis Bacon (1561-1626) speculated that Adam spoke a "pure language." Adam expressed thoughts with a "nakedness of mind," reflecting the innocence and simplicity of God's children. When speaking, Adam called out the true name of all things. After the Fall, language, like mankind, was corrupt. Bacon insisted that the goal of philosophical language was restoring the purity that existed before the Fall. In 1667, Thomas Sprat in *History of the Royal Society in London* formulated one duty of society members as separating the use of rhetoric from the knowledge of nature.[2] Another member of the Royal Society advocated that Parliament act to stop the use of metaphors by preachers. Subsequently, the "plain style" of scientific reporting was to be free of ornamental speech. Metaphor and analogy were unacceptable. If frills such as "poetic expression" entered a scholarly text, a lack of genuine content was suspected. The career of French naturalist Georges Buffon (1707-1788), whose *Historie Naturelle* ran 250 editions, suffered as colleagues in the Académie Française criticized his "literary" style.

Robert Boyle (1627-1691) echoed Bacon's sentiments in articulating the hope that refining scientific language would atone for the confusion that engulfed humanity at the tower of Babel. Boyle's emphasis on experimentation and plain writing deeply influenced concepts of a scientific style. For Boyle, experiments were a microcosm for the process of reasoning at which scientists arrived at truth. When witnessed, an experiment communicated directly to the audience. An audience might dispute what a scientist said or wrote, but there were no disputes about what happened as observers viewed an experiment. The "way of experimentation" was not like "the way of talk." Talk resulted in confusion. Words led to different interpretations of events, which in turn inspired argument. Direct observation, for Boyle, led to fewer interpretations. Experiments remained unaffected by the situation in which they took place. Observation was objective. To achieve greater clarity, science writing should mimic the process of performing and watching an experiment.

Thomas Hobbes (1588-1679) recognized the rhetorical character of Boyle's experimentalism. Observations, Hobbes countered, were not unaffected by the situation in which they took place. The audiences for experiments were not naïve observers; rather, they were trained practitioners. This type of observation, Hobbes claimed, was biased. As the audiences became better trained, they raised fewer questions about experimental procedures. Once procedures were internalized it was unnecessary to verbalize them—an audience's silence implied assent to the methods used. Hobbes grew concerned about the lack of a critical self-awareness of observers. When verbalizing their questions, thoughts, and ideas—warts and all—an audience's assumptions and prejudices were on the table. Each instance of articulating an observation challenged both speakers and writers to revisit their thinking. Hobbes maintained that the rhetorical character of verbal or written discourse was easier to identify and revise than the rhetorical character of an unarticulated observation. As experimental practice became tacit, it grew more difficult to identify confusion and misunderstanding. In contrast, all that Boyle wanted was certain knowledge through experiment and observation. What he got was much more.

The outcome of debates in the seventeenth century about the role of experimentation—and its presentation—in early modern science is apparent in the following style characteristics of contemporary technical writing:

- *References to what is "behind the text."* In the sciences and other technical disciplines, writers refer to laboratory equipment, experiments, calculations, and research on which the text is based. If readers wanted to challenge the claims in a science textbook or journal article, they would move next to a laboratory full of equipment and procedures they likely would not understand. What stands behind the text in the sciences gives it authority. Science writers do not need many words to anchor their claims. As a result, the scientific writing style is shorter in length and includes visual aids and mathematical formulas that represent laboratories and machines.

- *Absence of an "institutional memory."* By institutional memory we mean how well an academic discipline, corporation, or agency remembers the historical and social origins of current practices. The instrumental success and cumulative nature of experimentation permits scientists to ignore the origin of their practices. After all, if a procedure works, why question it? There is no compelling reason to investigate who developed a technique, why, and under what circumstances. Emphasis on experimentation, then, allows scientific and technical communicators to forget the contexts in which practices were developed. As a result, the scientific writing style is often not reflective or contextual.

- *Emphasis on* **how** *something is said.* As modern science developed, so did restrictions regarding form. Form was posed as the key to content. To achieve clarity, Bacon, Boyle, and other early modern scientists demanded a uniform presentation. Attacks on "the rhetorical" and "the literary" required practitioners to abandon the pursuit of a personal style. Scientific style was institutionalized. An emphasis on experimentation, then, entailed a "plain" narrative style. As a result, the scientific writing style frequently stresses form in relation to content.

- *Self-censorship on* **what** *is said.* To obtain "certain" knowledge, members of the British Royal Academy decided not to speak of, or experimentally test, metaphysical (mostly religious) claims. Further, at the insistence of Charles II, scientists stayed away from matters of "morals" and politics. As long as science served the needs of the crown, the crown funded and allowed scientific practice. Scientists conformed to the intellectual boundaries set by the state. An emphasis on experimentation, then, allowed scientists to legitimate their practices to the state supporting them. As a result, the scientific writing style shows the strain of balancing the need for government funding, the desire to maintain autonomy, and the demands of the lay public.

Functions of Language

All language serves many functions and allows us to employ many voices, none of them mutually exclusive of the others. For simplicity's sake we may count three functions of language: *rhetorical, representational,* and *constitutive.* To understand scientific and technical communication, we need to recognize these functions within it. And to undertake scientific and technical communication, we need to learn to use these functions.

Rhetorical Language

A user of rhetorical language *attempts to discover the best means of persuasion for a given case.* Again, to many of you, "rhetoric" implies an underhanded and not-entirely-honest means of persuasion. Classically, though, the term and its subject were viewed quite differently: Aristotle, for instance, considered rhetoric a useful and respectable practice for speech making.

When you *recognize* rhetoric, you will better understand the means by which you are possibly persuaded, and, consequently, how you can persuade others. When you *use* rhetoric, you appeal to the assumptions and attitudes of your audience. Rhetoric has many functions: teaching, motivating, persuading, pleasing, and inspiring, to name a few. Such functions are necessarily a part of all communication, including scientific and technical communication.

Consider the following series of statements:

1. Battery technology must be improved before electric cars can be mass produced in America.
2. Because *battery technology must be improved before electric cars can be mass produced in America* our engineering firm, 21st

Century Technologies, is actively pursuing government and private funding for research on batteries.

3. The leader of Chrysler Corporation stated that because *battery technology must be improved before the electric car can be mass produced in America*, a "wait and see" attitude toward future plans for mass-producing electric cars would be recommended to the board of trustees.

Sentence 1 states a matter of fact. Taken in isolation, the statement is innocuous. Inserted in Sentence 2, Sentence 1—still a statement of fact—is taken as a challenge and opportunity for funding for the members of an engineering firm. Inserted in Sentence 3, Sentence 1 becomes a reason, or perhaps an excuse, for suspending plans for mass-producing electric cars. One can imagine that the stock price of the engineering firm in Sentence 2 might drift down slightly after the pronouncement in 3. In both Sentences 2 and 3, the interests expressed transform the meaning and persuasive impact of Sentence 1. The historical sequence of these statements also transforms the meaning of Sentence 1. If the leader of Chrysler heard of the engineering firm's pronouncement first, the recommendation may have been changed, albeit grudgingly. In either instance, Sentences 2 and 3 lend a mutually influential, persuasive context to an initially innocuous statement.

If you know the values of your audience and can find a means to appeal to those values, you are more likely to persuade. The problem is that values differ with audiences of various expertise. For an audience that shares your expertise you may outline your method much more rigorously and make your conclusion modest. For a more general audience, you may gloss over your method and concentrate on your conclusion, perhaps even adding a section concerning the implications of the conclusion. For an audience that shares your expertise, you may use specialized language and may refer to projects of which (you assume) your audience has knowledge. For a more general audience, you may need to educate *as* you persuade.

Similarly, when you are on the "receiving end" of the communication pipeline, an appreciation of rhetoric can still be helpful: Even when you do not completely understand the subject presented, recognizing rhetoric will help you understand the presenter's intentions.

Representational Language

If language is viewed as strictly representational, you *assume that a given word stands for a given object and does so unambiguously.* At some point, nearly all children ask questions like "How can I know what *you* see as green is what *I* see as green?" Many of us dismiss the question as unimportant or at least irrelevant to everyday experience. And many of us assume a common understanding because it is too much trouble to do otherwise. Technical communicators too, have assumed an understanding; traditionally, they have regarded language as strictly representational—that is, they have assumed that a given word accurately and unambiguously represents a given object. On one hand, the benefits of this assumption are practical and obvious: If we were continually wondering whether what I mean by a certain word is what you mean by it, we would have little time to *do* anything. On the other hand, seeing the world as a series of objective linguistic representations, we experience only a small part of it. Viewing language as strictly representational may expedite the work of technical communicators, but this view neglects the work in science and technology accomplished by using the rhetorical and constitutive functions of language.

From the point of view of daily experience, such a view of language as strictly representational appears somewhat simplistic. Our daily conversations can be careless—full of ambiguity and misunderstanding—or exact with respect to rules and accepted canons of use. A great deal of what we try to "represent" to one another are concepts, and, as you know, concepts can be hard to grasp. Think about the most recent disagreement you had with your parents or friends. Chances are you could trace the misunderstanding to what was meant by words like "expensive," "soon," or "fine." In some instances, you take advantage of such ambiguity; in other instances, you have been taken advantage of by such ambiguity.

From the point of view of science and technology, words and symbols can accurately represent objects in nature and be used to solve problems (e.g., $F = MA$, the periodic table of elements). However, scientists and technologists are finding out more about the phenomena they capture in equations and tables. Although Einstein's theories of relativity do not overthrow Newton's mechanics, we understand "force" differently today than we did in the seventeenth and eighteenth centuries. Prior to the discovery of oxygen, many scientists believed in the existence of phlogiston, a chemical released during combustion. Demitry Mendeleyev's (1834-1907) periodic table has changed considerably with the discovery of additional elements as has our knowledge of the elements themselves.

Jargon

Usually, we associate the term "jargon" with its pejorative definition as unintelligible talk or pretentious terminology. However, jargon is also the language or vocabulary particular to a group, profession, or organization. Part of becoming a member in a particular field or profession involves your correct use of its specialized language; it confirms your knowledge of the field and can provide more concise terminology than everyday language. A field's jargon also marks boundaries where nonmembers cannot enter and through which its members cannot easily pass. Subjected to "legalese," "insurancese," "academese," and obscure medical terminology, individual consumers and public advocates demand that these professions reform their linguistic practices to give an open accounting of their activities. Taxpayers make the same demands of scientists, technologists, and congressional representatives—that arguments for funding "big science" projects be made in a language the public understands so as to make informed policy decisions.

Your own use of jargon needs to be tempered with the sense that almost any profession you enter will involve direct public contact. Your responsibility as a scientific and technical communicator is to make an honest effort to present information intelligibly to allow for public understanding of your profession. But jargon can also be a dangerous source of power. Those possessing a specialized or technical language have power over those who do not and who require the services of a specialist or expert. One of the most obvious examples of the successful and unsuccessful exercise of the "power of jargon" is the law. When laypersons seek the services of a lawyer, they, in a sense, hire a guide. Lawyers guide their clients through the system and translate specialist language so that the clients can make an informed decision. If lawyers are knowledgeable and can help clients to comprehend the system, and, accordingly, their own best interests, the system can work. Nevertheless, the lawyer has a particular power over the client in knowing the discrete language of the justice system. As a professional, specialist, or researcher, you command a specialist language. Your use and reform of that language can either encourage or discourage the *equitable* participation of nonspecialists in your field.

Constitutive Language

A user of constitutive language *appreciates that the meaning of a given word is negotiated.* A conception of language as purely representational is deaf to the full range of meaning of a given word: All language is inseparable from a host of assumptions and prejudices—in fact, what you mean by a certain word *is* likely to differ at least slightly (and perhaps significantly) from what I mean by it. Any user of language—and any technical communicator—will benefit from this recognition.

Figurative language, the language of metaphor, is often constitutive. In other words, certain figurative language shapes the conception of the field in which it exists, often producing an immediate and profound effect. One example is the metaphor of the gene as a "master molecule," which is the key to controlling human development. Although the metaphor may or may not accurately represent its subject, its rhetorical power is undeniable. The metaphors of molecular biology were instrumental in persuading Congress to funnel huge sums of money into the Human Genome Project.

When you read, you overlay your meaning on the words and thereby complement and shade the meaning intended by their author. The resulting meaning may be similar to the author's, but it is likely to be at least somewhat different; you may associate a given word with other things, or the author's argument may remind you of another. So the final meaning of the text—that is, the meaning of the text *after* it has been written and read—is not entirely within the writer's control. Rather, the meaning is *negotiated* between writer and reader. And if language itself is constitutive, then the final meaning of a text is negotiated even at the most fundamental level: The meaning of even a single word results from a kind of unconscious compromise between its author and its reader.

Rhetorical Themes

Scientific and technical communicators have traditionally employed rhetorical structures at once larger and more implicit in their writing, namely, *themes* (or *topoi*). We may define themes as *ideas used by writers to appeal to the principles held by specific audiences.* Generally, linguistic choices within the sciences are made with this intent. For example, chemical engineers and animal behaviorists—even the group we may define as "all scientists"—communicate with and within themes that appeal to sympathies and expectations of the reader. Certain themes— pragmatism, accuracy, and brevity, for instance—appear in almost all scientific and technical writing. As a writer, you may make a text more persuasive by using any of these themes; as a reader, you may understand a text better when you can identify the themes it uses. Nevertheless, these themes are not disembodied objects of discussion and analysis that can be abstracted from a text. For instance, what passes for accuracy in the reports of experiments in chemistry and sociology are quite different things. As a writer, you need to be conscious of what themes you are using in relation to your audience; as a reader, you need to be careful not to impose on a text themes that are not really there.

Appeals to Emotion

Ideally, a scientific paper is free of emotion. In practice, however, a paper is affected by both the commentary and the disputes that precede it. Since both are inevitably emotional, the resulting paper is likely to absorb into itself some of that emotion. Further, the *vocabulary* of scientists and technologists often has emotional resonances. For example, the mathematician who uses the term "elegant" to describe a theorem believes that the theorem has value because it is simple and (perhaps) symmetrical. The belief is at some level emotional. The computer designer who uses the term "kludge" is also appealing to emotion—the word is an insult for a system that is sloppy and inefficient.

Appeals to Ethos

Ethos may be defined as the fundamental character and spirit of a culture, the underlying sentiment that shapes the beliefs, customs, or practices of a group or society. You have heard proponents of Americans in space talk about America's destiny, America's heritage of exploration. They are appealing to an American ethos. Similarly, when scientists or technologists speak to lay audiences, they may represent *themselves* as part of an ethos— the fundamentally good nature of science or the fundamentally prosperous and progressive nature of technology. Although ethos may be presented as an essential, constant, and natural part of a group or culture, it is not. The ethos of a group is a designation assigned to the group by itself or, for instance, by critics of the group. Also, the effectiveness of an appeal to ethos can be a matter of timing. For example, to get funding, proponents of space exploration could more effectively petition America's sense of destiny and exploration in the 1960s after the success of the Soviet *Sputnik* than they could after NASA's *Challenger* disaster. Taking into account matters of time and place, an appeal to a fundamental set of beliefs by writers is a common and persuasive ploy.

Appeals to Natural Law

Scientific and technical communication appeals to a belief in a universal natural law—the idea that the universe operates in an orderly or lawlike fashion that can be understood through scientific method and empirical study. Before the rise of experimental science in the seventeenth century, the validity of law was understood in explaining something as either conforming to, or deviating from, a set of existing standards. The laws of nature—

God's law—were seen as eternal, the evidence for which was found in natural phenomena. After the rise of experimental science, natural laws were seen in evidence as a *result* of conducting experiments. By going into the laboratory, scientists could control the background conditions of nature in order to produce lawlike conditions. Today, scientific and technical communicators use themes derived from this idea. These include (but are not limited to) precedent, prediction, verifiability, direct observation, and experimental repeatability.

The persuasive power of much of science is connected to the notion that the truth of science—scientific facts—is universal and demonstrable. In presenting the results of an experiment, then, scientists can appeal to the applicability and verification of their findings. One of the most remarkable features of natural science has been the almost unchallenged acceptance of its guiding principles and success by society. By appealing to natural law, scientists appeal to standards of method and conduct *they* have derived, not to standards derived by other groups or disciplines. The persuasive power in science, then, can be partially understood as an appeal to its own standards of conduct. Other academic disciplines and professions have either followed or turned against seeking scientific standards for justifying their practices. Certain disciplines and professions either try to establish the significance of their practices in terms of concrete outcomes and real-world effects, or refuse to be evaluated in any way except as being significant for its own sake.

ARGUMENTS

When we use the word "argument" in everyday speech, we usually refer to a disagreement or a dispute among people. You might, for example, get into an argument over which movie to see tonight or whether the government should fund new science initiatives. In the study of logic, or critical thinking, an *argument* refers to a set of statements in which *one* statement—the *conclusion*—is declared to follow from all other statements—the *premises.* An argument in this sense can have as many premises as you want, but only one conclusion. Before going further, however, let's define our terms.

In examining *locution*—particular forms of expression, speech, and uses of phrases (as found in conversations among members of a specific group)—it is helpful to examine the dynamics among *interlocutors*—persons taking part in a conversation or dialogue. If you have ever read the dialogues of Plato, for example, you find Socrates speaking with students or friends (interlocutors) with a sense of shared inquiry, responsibility, and resolution. Propositions are put forth, they draw responses, and the responses are examined. Almost none of our daily conversations proceed in this way; argument and conversation is a free-for-all. Still, the care we take in knowing our interlocutors, listening to what they say, and responding carefully shows a willingness to cooperate.

A *premise* is a statement or proposition preceding the conclusion. In logic, premises are usually presented explicitly—as is the case with our examples—in a similar sequence: premise, premise, "therefore," conclusion. These premises often begin with an adjective such as "all," "many," "some," or "few." Of course, premises can also be simple assertions—for example, "Bill Clinton is a U.S. citizen." In daily conversation, however, the premises of our arguments are presented in different ways and at many points before and after the conclusion. Still, we commonly use certain words and phrases in conversation to signal the premises of our arguments:

since	for
given	as
moreover	it is a fact that
additionally	for that reason
because	can infer
from	can deduce

A *conclusion* is a proposition derived from the premises of an argument. To clearly show how the conclusion follows from the premises, logic books place the conclusion after the premises, often separating the premises from the conclusion with a solid line, or a symbol ($\therefore$ meaning "therefore") indicting the conclusion. Again, we often have to determine the presence of premises and conclusions within the context of unstructured discussions. Yet we normally signal the close of an argument with the following words and phrases:

thus	consequently
finally	as a result
in other words	that is
then	therefore
it follows that	in conclusion
to sum up	

Validity

Here is a way to keep validity in mind and why it is important. Sometimes in the course of daily argument, we commit or run across blatant, fundamental errors in reasoning—contradictions. A contradiction in reasoning is usually easy to pick out because the assertion—for example, "Boy Born Speaking French" (from a tabloid headline)—runs completely counter to our intuitions about truth and reason. But contradictions in our daily arguments are not so straightforward. Premises and conclusions are expressed in true and false combinations. Rarely do we make a series of obviously true or false statements leading to clear-cut conclusions. Valid arguments give us a benchmark against which to compare true and false meanings, assertions, and conclusions. By definition, a *valid* argument is one that *if* all the premises are true, the conclusion *must* be true. True input *must* yield true output—you can count on a valid argument.

You will note in the definition of a valid argument the word *if*. Frequently, we make and hear claims and conclusions that may or may not be true, but the argument is still valid. With an *invalid* argument, however, you never know what you will get. It does not matter if all the premises are true or false, you may get either a true or a false conclusion. There is no benchmark for invalid conclusions. True input *may* yield true output, but it may not. You cannot count on the fact that true premises lead to a true conclusion. The concepts of validity and invalidity will later help us determine fallacious arguments.

Deduction and Induction

One may reach a conclusion through either deduction or induction. *Deduction* is the process of deriving a conclusion that necessarily follows from a set of premises. In a deductive argument, if all the premises are true, the conclusion must be true. For example,

All cats are mammals.
All mammals are warm-blooded.
Therefore, all cats are warm-blooded.

Induction is the process of drawing a conclusion or supposing, based on past observation, that a particular hypothesis is true. For example,

All previously observed birds have feathers.
Therefore, all birds probably have feathers.

In science, the process of *inductive inference* is presented as the process by which one moves from a specific case, or cases, to a general hypothesis. Each time someone makes an observation that corresponds to the general hypothesis—seeing another bird with feathers, for example—is taken as evidence confirming it. So, each time we observe birds with feathers we help confirm the general hypothesis that all birds have feathers. However, just as arguments in everyday conversation do not necessarily follow the patterns found in logic books, neither is there a pattern or set of rules for what counts as confirming evidence of a hypothesis.

Argumentative Fallacies

In daily conversation, we generally equate argumentative fallacies with false ideas or superstition. With respect to logic, however, fallacies refer to faulty arguments in which the premises are inadequate to support the conclusion. Among other places, you can find argumentative fallacies in advertisements, news reports, political campaigns, talk-radio shows, and press conferences. Fallacies are often presented in arguments concerning pseudo- and new-age "science," but legitimate scientists and engineers (and their critics) share in committing the sins of bad argument.

The reason not to commit argumentative fallacies is a practical one. To maintain and promote a rational form of public discourse in which arguments lead to true belief, we, as citizens and scientific and technical communicators, must act as rhetorical gatekeepers. Rhetoric and argument is the medium in which our ideas are expressed. In different social roles—as an engineer, neighborhood leader, juror, parent—you will face the same task distinguishing that claims, arguments, and evidence make sense. One tool for making rational determinations is critical thinking.

Our society listens to many voices. In the "marketplace of ideas," people bring forward innumerable claims and arguments. Tabloid headlines plead with us to examine the latest evidence ("leading experts agree") for UFOs and miracle diets. The dignified, traditional format of science journals demands our respect and trust. Our approach to these sources and claims is often contradictory. On one hand, we want to remain open-minded to new ideas and find lurid appeal in the bizarre. On the other hand, we desire certain knowledge, a foundation on which to make judgments and determine for ourselves what is sense and nonsense.

Before looking at fallacies, let's work on our intuitions concerning logic, reasonable action, and cooperation.

Using Your Intuition

In 1950, Melvin Dresher and Merrill Flood of the RAND Corporation formulated a paradox, tabbed by Albert Tucker in an article as the "Prisoner's Dilemma." Unlike many philosophical paradoxes, the "Prisoner's Dilemma" is a problem of reason and action that many of us will actually face in some form.

Suppose you and an accomplice, for whom you have no special feeling, commit a crime. You are promptly apprehended, thrown in separate jail cells, and not allowed to communicate with each other. The prosecutor approaches you separately and says that each of you is being offered the exact same deal. The prosecutor explains, "We have a lot of circumstantial evidence on both of you. In fact, if we prosecute both of you we will undoubtedly get convictions and you will do two years in jail. But if you help us out—admit your guilt—and testify as to the guilt of your *alleged* accomplice, we'll let you go. Given your testimony your accomplice will get six years. But if both of you decide to plead guilty, each of you will receive four-year sentences."

Knowing your accomplice has the same information, you face the following dilemma. On one hand, if you don't claim innocence and your partner squeals, it's six years in prison. In that case, you would be better off if you both admitted guilt—just four years. On the other hand, if your accomplice claims innocence, the best thing to do is admit guilt and testify—then you'll go free. What do you do? The answer and a variation on this dilemma are at the end of the chapter.

After confronting this paradox, you are ready to tackle argumentative fallacies.

Ad Hominem

Translated from the Latin, *ad hominem* means "to the man." This fallacy occurs when someone attempts to refute an argumentative claim by attacking a person's character. The argument is logically invalid because the premises are irrelevant to the conclusion. A person's character or social standing has no logical relation to the truth or falsity of a given claim. The form of this fallacy with which most people are familiar is known as an *abusive ad hominem*; the person attacked is considered by the opposition to have a disreputable background (professors, conservatives, atheists, police officers). Here are some examples:

> Professor Smith maintains that the Loch Ness monster exists. That's absurd! Everyone knows Smith is a communist.

> Professor Jones believes the Loch Ness monster is a hoax. I don't believe Jones because she's a Christian fundamentalist.

Another form of the ad hominem fallacy used frequently is the *tu quoque*, a retort charging an accuser with the same, or a similar, mistake or crime. A thumbnail version of this argument is "Who are you to talk?" (see Chapter 8 in Part II for a further look at tu quoque arguments). The fact that someone has made mistakes or performed some misdeed does not disprove their claim that you (or someone else) has done something wrong. For example,

> The attacks by Democrats against Oliver North are politically motivated. Anyway, plenty of Democrats have lied to Congress. Therefore, they should leave Oliver North alone.

> What do you mean I should pay back my student loans? You cheat on your income tax.

Ad hominem fallacies are committed when the point of the argument—the truth of the conclusion—is avoided by personal slander or appeals to the audience's prejudices. The question of personal character plays a role in the courts, for example, in challenging the veracity of a witness's testimony. However, the truth or falsity of a claim ultimately depends on the facts, not the character of the person asserting it.

Ambiguity

Fallacies of ambiguity occur when a person trades on the ambiguous use of words, phrases, and sentence structure to make false premises appear true or invalid arguments appear valid. For example,

> ***John:*** Energy can neither be created nor destroyed.
>
> ***Mary:*** Human beings are composed of energy.
>
> ***John:*** Human beings can neither be created nor destroyed.

If we hold strictly to Mary's definition of a human being, John reaches a valid conclusion. But humans are composed of other things besides energy, and John's use of the words "created" and "destroyed" is ambiguous considering commonly held ideas of birth and death. Here is a similar example:

> All science is reason.
> Frank Smith is reasonable.
> Science is irrefutable.
> Frank Smith is irrefutable.

A number of things go wrong with this argument. The words "reason" and "reasonable" are used interchangeably, and the words "science" and "irrefutable"—designating both a method and a person—refer ambiguously to two different things.

Appeal to Authority

Many disputes in science and technology are settled through appeals to authority and experts. On many occasions, the opinion of a relevant authority acts as evidence for a particular conclusion. Although the criteria for establishing authority requires critical assessment, the appeal to irrelevant authority (*ad verecundiam*) is a fallacy. Here is a common example:

> You should buy Hanes underwear because Michael Jordan endorses it.

In this case, Michael Jordan's authority is not established. He may, in fact, be an authority on underwear, but his expertise is not established. Your authority about underwear is as valuable as Michael Jordan's. Let's look at another set of examples:

> Extraterrestrial intelligence exists in the universe. You can have no doubt about this because Robert Stack said so and he is the host of the television show *Unsolved Mysteries*.

> Extraterrestrial intelligence exists in the universe. You can have no doubt about this because Professor Williams said so and he is a tenured professor in the Civil Engineering department.

There is an interesting difference in these two examples, indicating how we subscribe to authority. Both arguments are examples of appeals to irrelevant authorities. However, the appeal to Professor Williams appears more credible because of his status as a tenured professor in a discipline related to "things scientific." Robert Stack is a television personality. As a result, we may have a tendency to afford Professor Williams unwarranted authority on the same disputed claim. But what about the claim itself? Here's another example:

> Extraterrestrial intelligence exists in the universe. You can have no doubt about this because Frank Drake, a leading astronomer, has formulated an equation that estimates 10,000 to 100,000 advanced civilizations exist in the Milky Way galaxy alone.

Addressed scientifically, both the claim—extraterrestrial intelligence exists—and the authority appear even more legitimate. Once taken as an empirical matter—a phenomenon that can be proved or disproved by experimental (and mathematical) evidence—extraterrestrial intelligence in the last argument becomes a matter for scientific investigation. Can we check Drake's assertion? Certainly. In 1960, Drake began the search for artificial radio signals from other planetary civilizations. And his work is continued by other scientists around the world. But in the case of such a claim, what would count as sufficient evidence proving the existence of extraterrestrial intelligence? How long should such a matter be investigated? At what cost? Note how the assertion "extraterrestrial intelligence exists in the universe" changes in the context of each argument presented. The more "scientific" the authority, the greater credibility (rightly or wrongly) given the claim.

Is Drake a more legitimate authority than Robert Stack? Obviously. Still, as a society we have a tendency to quickly validate the authority of scientists even about disputed scientific claims. The fallacy of appeal to irrelevant authority is easy to determine in cases of transferring authority from one field to another, such as a television personality or a civil engineer asserting the existence of extraterrestrial intelligence. But submission to legitimate authority should not in itself be the sole basis for making decisions about science and technology in society. Even legitimate scientists and technologists hold disputed or pseudoscientific beliefs.

Straw Man

The Straw Man fallacy occurs when someone's argument is purposely misrepresented so that a person arguing against it can attack the false argument without tackling the real issue. An interlocutor constructs a "straw man" of the other person's argument because it is easier to knock down. Politicians often engage this tactic. For example,

> **Senator Adams:** Bill Clinton believes in cutting some agriculture subsidies. I don't understand how Clinton can deny the suffering of Midwest farmers after last summer's flooding.

Did Clinton say he denied the suffering of Midwest farmers? No, he merely stated a belief in cutting some agriculture subsidies. The issue of flood relief is different from the issue of farm subsidies. Senator Adams is not attacking Clinton's position directly on farm subsidies; rather, she appeals to an indirectly related popular issue. Another example:

> **Jane:** Physicists don't take cold fusion seriously because such a discovery would threaten their jobs.

Obviously, Jane misrepresents the position of physicists. The physics community has neither a unified position on cold fusion nor agrees on the implication of such research. Jane gives a caricature of physicists to prop up her belief that cold fusion is an issue deserving greater attention.

Begging the Question

The fallacy of begging the question (*petitio principii*) occurs when someone accepts the truth of the conclusion in order to accept the truth of the premises. In other words, in the context of an argument, when interlocutors assume the truth of the disputed point, they beg the question. Begging the question is a form of circular reasoning because it leads to no new discovery or information.

Say, for example, we are discussing the relative merits of scholarly pursuits and we assert, "Physics is the only *real* science. You study biology. You're not a real scientist." If you accept the premise that physics is the only real science, then you accept the conclusion. However, the argument begs the question in that one who sees the value in studying biology would not accept the premise. Here is a similar example:

Bob: All biologists assert that species change occurs because the principle of survival of the fittest is true.

Sue: How do you know the mechanism for species change is survival of the fittest?

Bob: Because all biologists assert it.

Bob's reasoning begs the question because he supports his assertion that the principle of survival of the fittest is true because all biologists assert it. Bob's reasoning is circular in that he refers to the argument's premise, for which no evidence is given, to support his conclusion.

You can often find instances of circularity in occupational definitions:

- Scientist: an expert in science
- Historian: an expert in history; an authority on history

Until you have a useful definition of science and history respectively, you have little idea of what a scientist or a historian does.

Poisoning the Well

The fallacy of poisoning the well occurs when an argument is posed in such a way that if interlocutors agree to the premise the conclusion is impossible for them to contest. This argument is a fallacy because the process of critical interaction is short-circuited. To elaborate the metaphor, once the water in the well is poisoned (the argument is corrupted), no one can drink from it (the interlocutors cannot debate). For example,

Lisa: Do you believe in ghosts?

Grace: No, I don't.

Lisa: Given your position, I cannot talk to you.

Because Grace doesn't agree to Lisa's premise, Lisa ends the argument, rejecting the importance of anything Grace has to say before she says it. The fallacy of poisoning the well takes more subtle and pernicious forms with respect to personal qualities or attributes:

> **Fred:** Men just have an innate sense of what it means to be reasonable. I can't even talk to Ellen. As a woman she can't hope to understand male rationality.

Fred has disqualified Ellen as an interlocutor before hearing what she has to say. Fred's sexism poisons the well and silences the possibility of an exchange of ideas—and denies an opportunity for personal enlightenment.

Loaded Question

Perhaps the most famous loaded question is the one asked a man:

"Have you stopped beating your wife yet?"

Posed as a yes or no question, either answer condemns the respondent. Answering yes implies the man has beaten his wife. Answering no implies the man continues to beat his wife. Within each loaded question lies a questionable assumption. *Any* answer to the question indicates agreement with its central assumption. To avoid the trap of the fallacy of a loaded question, you must reject the question on the grounds that its embedded supposition is fallacious.

▧ *Example 1*

Are you still wasting time and money on that research?

▧ *Example 2*

Professor: I've been studying the genetic basis for intelligence for 15 years and I know a great deal.

Student: Tell me, professor, why are some races genetically better suited for rational thought than all other races?

▓ *Example 3*

Reporter: Is Dr. Jones allowing his belief in political theory to hinder more rational pursuits?

Colleague: I never see him working on anything else, so evidently he is.

In each example, the dubious—and often pernicious—presumption built in to each question leads the interlocutor to agree to the existence of thoroughly questionable "facts." In Example 1, the fact assumed is that the research is indeed worthless. In Example 2, the student's question presupposed the truth of the notion that some races are genetically predisposed to intelligence—a thoroughly false notion. Finally, Example 3, and its subsequent answer assume that belief in political theory is irrational. In each instance, an issue is presented as a question about a state of affairs about which the interlocutors implicitly agree. Once you reject loaded questions, you can move to an examination of the ideas motivating your interlocutor.

Correlation Equals Cause

Laypersons and scientists, on occasion, confuse the correlation among two or more things and a cause-and-effect relationship. The argumentative fallacy is often one of committing the wrong inference. This is fallacious because the true cause is obscured. For example:

Many juvenile delinquents listen to heavy metal music. Juvenile delinquents who prefer heavy metal music engage in promiscuous sexual behavior, commit vandalism or physical assault and dabble in pseudo-Satanic ritualism. Listening to heavy metal music, then, causes deviant behavior and Satanism.

Research has determined that people in bars drink faster in response to slow country music than people in bars who listen to faster tempo music. Therefore, slow country music causes alcohol abuse.

Although listening to heavy metal music in the first example and slow country music in the second example may, in fact, correlate to Satanic worship or alcohol abuse, they do not cause the effect that is claimed. Heavy drinkers who enjoy country music may simply prefer country music as a context for drinking. But the music itself does not cause one to drink. In the first example, wrongly inferring that heavy metal music causes other deviant behavior leads to a cause-and-effect correlation with Satanism. In these examples, the arguer is guilty of allowing a simple moral equation "evil things cause evil deeds" to provide a practical account of cause and effect.

Answer to the Prisoner's Dilemma

Logic tells you to confess—four years. However, if both of you remain illogical and maintained innocence—and had been subsequently convicted—you would both be in jail for only half as long—two years!

In May 1983, Douglas Hofstadter presented a variation of this paradox in *Scientific American* that appears all the more relevant in this age of information exchange:

Assume you possess an amount of something (money, pictures, experimental results) you are willing to trade for something else (gems, industrial secrets, patent rights). You agree to trade with a person who is the exclusive source of what you want. Both of you agree to the amount of the exchange. The conditions of the exchange are that it must take place in secret and that neither one of you will ever meet again nor have any further dealings. Each of you agrees to leave a bag containing the item in a designated place. Upon doing that, you will go pick up the other's bag at the other's designated place.

The immediate fear of both parties is that the other person will leave an empty bag. Of course, there are other possibilities. Both of you may leave full bags and be satisfied. But the most intriguing possibility for both parties is leaving an empty bag and picking up a full one. What do you do? (pp. 715-716)

Discussion

1. Employing Robert Boyle's reasoning, argue why scientific and technical communication should be void of the use of metaphors and figurative language. What advantages and disadvantages do you see in a plain reporting style? If rhetoric, by definition, is the best means of persuasion in a given case, then how is the plain reporting style rhetorical?

2. The development of scientific and technical writing style in British early modern science appears to be the result of self-censorship. Scientists agreed about what subjects were and were not legitimate in accordance with the wishes of the king. Offer an argument for or against the idea that scientific expression and experiment should not be censored in *any* way. What subjects should not come under scientific investigation? How do scientists continue to constrain (or censor) their work in order to meet the demands of the government and/or private investors that support them? In what ways does meeting the demands of private investors and public officials make science and technology political institutions?

3. Give examples of jargon you encounter or use frequently. Where is jargon located? When do you use jargon? What are some rhetorical functions of jargon? How does jargon cause confusion among its users?

4. Arguments are part of our daily interaction. No matter how carefully we pay attention to these arguments, we get caught up in the emotion of the moment. Our personal interests, attention span, our feelings about the person with whom we argue, knowledge and concern about the subject—all of these elements, and more, cloud our judgment. Science has always been portrayed as a passionless form of inquiry. In what ways are arguments over scientific matters different emotionally and intellectually than everyday arguments? To be objective, do you think scientific and technical communicators should fully disclose the personal, emotional, and intellectual contexts that go on in the process of intellectual argument? Why or why not?

5. Referring to Chapter 11 in Part II of the text, what kinds of persuasive and argumentative strategies are used by the military regarding the performance of technology during the Gulf War? Would you consider the language used to describe the technology objective? What role, according to Raman, does metaphor play in shaping our perception of events in the Gulf War?

Exercises

1. In examining the logical fallacies presented in this chapter, listen to, or watch, a show with a debate-style format. Although the topics of many of these shows are political, science and technology are often the subject or supply the evidence for varied political positions. In a brief response paper, document the logical fallacies that occur during the show. In analyzing these fallacies, consider the following questions: How many, and what type of, logical fallacies are committed? What role does empirical or statistical evidence play in these debates? What role does anecdotal evidence play in these debates? Do the interlocutors note they are committing logical fallacies? Do you think it matters to the average listener that logical fallacies are being committed? Do you think the perpetuation of logical fallacies damages political and/or scientific discourse? How? How does political debate of this type compare to debate in science and technology? Are logical fallacies simply and unavoidably components of daily conversation and thought?

2. Buy a copy of a tabloid newspaper (e.g., *National Enquirer,* the *Star,* the *Globe,* the *Weekly World News*) heralding a scientific or technological breakthrough. In a review of issues, topics, or articles you select, provide an analysis of the arguments presented. Describe any logical fallacies that occur. Also in your analysis, provide a study of the type of language used to persuade the audience the claims in the article are true. Based on your analysis of the arguments and language presented,

give a profile of the audience for whom this article is intended. After formulating your analysis, check with journals or scholarship that seeks to debunk these types of claims (the *Skeptical Inquirer,* the *Zetetic Scholar*). Give an analysis of their attempts to debunk these claims. Do you think the criticisms are effective? Provide a study of the kind of language used by the critics to persuade the audience their claims are true. Who is the audience for these "debunking" journals? In an informal oral presentation, report your findings to your classmates.

3. A number of books deal with the current state of science and technology. For example, Jeremy Rifkin's *Algeny* offers claims about (among other things) the hazards of genetic engineering and the ultimate direction of the Industrial Revolution. However, many of these books seem long on proselytizing and short on argument. Find a book about science and technology that fits this general bill. In a book review to your instructor, develop a checklist for nonfictional accounts of science and technology. What are the characteristics that discredit nonfictional accounts of science and technology? Consider, for example, how language is used, the amount of documentation, and the argumentative claims forwarded by the author.

4. In a reflexive report (you may try some of the strategies of presentation outlined by Cooper in Chapter 8, Part II) analyze the language, types of argument and persuasive strategies used by Raman is her examination of Gulf War rhetoric (Chapter 11, Part II). Does Raman use some of the same strategies to persuade her audience that she accuses military strategists of using during the war? Provide examples.

NOTES

1. In the same issue of *Nature, 171,* Watson and Crick elaborate their position in "Genetic Implications of the Structure of Deoxyribonucleic Acid" (pp. 934-937). For a more detailed rhetorical analysis, please see Chapter 2 in Bazerman (1988).

2. Consult Sprat (1667) regarding discussion on the purpose and function of scientific discourse in the beginning of the Royal Society. See also Shapin and Schaffer (1985, pp. 55-79) on the role of "literary technology" in the early experimental form of life.

BIBLIOGRAPHY

Bazerman, C. (1988). *Shaping written knowledge: The genre and activity of the experimental article in science.* Madison: University of Wisconsin Press.

Boyd, R., Gasper. P., & Trout, J. D. (Eds.). (1991). *The philosophy of science.* Cambridge: MIT Press.

Gray, W. (1991). *Thinking critically about New Age ideas.* Belmont, CA: Wadsworth.

Hofstadter, D. (1986). *Metamagical themas: Questing for the essence of mind and pattern.* New York: Bantam.

Miller, H. (1980). *Arguments, arrows, tress and truth* (2nd ed.). Reynoldsburg, OH: Advocate Publishing Group.

Myers, G. (1990). *Writing biology: Texts in the social construction of scientific knowledge.* Madison: University of Wisconsin Press.

Peters, J. A. (Ed.). (1959). *Classic papers in genetics.* Englewood Cliffs, NJ: Prentice Hall.

Shapin, S., & Schaffer, S. (1985). *Leviathan and the air-pump: Hobbes, Boyle, and the experimental life.* Princeton, NJ: Princeton University Press.

Sprat, T. (1667). *The history of the Royal Society of London for the improving of natural knowledge.* London: Royal Society.

Watson, J. D., & Crick, F. H. C. (1953a.). Molecular structure of nucleic acids. *Nature, 171,* 737-738; reprinted in Peters, op. cit., pp. 241-243.

Watson, J. D., & Crick, F. H. C. (1953b). Genetic simplications of the structure of deoxyribonucleic acid. *Nature, 171,* 934-937.

CHAPTER

Participation and Policy

Not all of the public is attentive to issues of science and technology. But everyone expects science to have a role in curing disease, supplying alternative forms of energy, and maintaining living standards. The future of science and technology in the United States will likely be marked by increased public participation in national and local policy-making. Science and technology pervade all aspects of life. Locally, and perhaps most directly, you are affected by the building of highways, airports, power plants, and waste disposal facilities. Nationally, disputes over recombinant DNA research, AIDS research, the future of the space program, and international competition show that the development of science and technology continues to outpace the government's ability and mandate to offer comprehensive policies.

Over the past 25 years, there have been attempts to establish a framework for public participation in federal policy decision-making. Such involvement has been solicited in the National Environmental Policy Act (1969), the Federal Advisory Committee Act (1972) and the Freedom of Information Act (1974). More recently, the government publication titled "Technology for America's Economic Growth: A New Direction to Build Economic Strength" outlined long-term initiatives and goals for American science and technology. These goals include innovation and private sector investment, world leadership in science, mathematics and engineering, and a national information infrastructure. The report also recommends that federal information be made available to a wider audience through "high-performance computing" (e.g., the High-Performance Computer Act of 1991) and policies aimed at making federal information available to as many users as possible.

One source for the tension in policy-making decisions can be found in the conflicting images we have about science and technology as public nuisances or economic saviors.

Your private interests and values either as an ambivalent bystander, an active participant, or a practicing scientist or engineer receiving federal funds will sometimes conflict with the desires of other consumers and producers of science and technology. The resolution of these conflicts on both national and local levels requires a difficult and complex process of negotiation among a public with various degrees of expertise and interest. Some experts fear that increased public participation in science and technology policy will encourage endless personal demands, expectations of risk-free technologies, and increased disagreement, all of which will "gridlock" decision making. Nevertheless, the public has a right to oversee and influence the way its taxes are spent. An unaware public may allow corruption like the Defense Department boondoggles of the 1980s. In sum, those managing science and technology are trapped between the ideal of democratic participation and the practical problem of accommodating quite different levels of knowledge and interest.

IMAGES OF SCIENCE
AND TECHNOLOGY

Many see science and technology as massive, impenetrable, self-sustaining institutions occupied by experts who are separate from, and unaffected by, the forces that shape other social interaction. Others see science and technology as easily manipulable tools, as extensions of humanity's nobler instincts. As with many issues, the truth probably lies somewhere between the two. Most admit that science and technology have been instrumental in both human progress and human destruction as seen both in the wonders of space exploration and the horrors in the use of atomic weaponry. Broadly construed, these are the images on which our conception of science, technology, and public policy have been based. Public interest regarding national and local science and technology policy is captive to a set of manipulative and reactionary views. These views pull both the public and policy-makers in two directions, presenting science and technology either as the cause of humanity's problems or as the solution.

Attitudes toward policy-making generally reflect a common-sense notion of how science and technology are structured and how their products (including knowledge) are made and distributed. In the example of nineteenth-century psychology, the methods of natural sciences were understood to apply equally well to the study of individual behavior. In a sense, then, the "problems" of human behavior were understood as amenable to natural science solutions. The problems of science and technology policy have been cast in similar scientistic light. Given their own scientistic presumptions, science policy advisors often regard the problems of policy as amenable to scientific solutions. Nuclear fusion policy in the United States serves as an example.

Largely unnoticed by the lay public, funding and research into nuclear fusion in the 1950s and 1960s were the result of an alliance between experts and members of Congress. Promised short-term results, legislators began to press for some evidence of the progress of the program. In the 1970s, with public attention focused on the energy crisis and alternatives to fission reactors, funding for fusion research increased. In return for this increasing investment, scientists promised a return on investment after only another 50 years of research. In 1979, the Office of Management and Budget slated another $30 million for research. Fusion scientists, however, turned down the money given the lack of progress (at that time) of the program. In 1989, however, two Utah scientists announced they had successfully created a fusion reaction at room temperature. Scientists immediately sought funding to replicate the experiment. Although the experiment was not replicated and room temperature fusion was generally written off as the result of instrument error or fantasy, funding programs had been resuscitated.

This example illustrates the cyclical approach to science policy and funding. Public and legislative interest in fusion depended on several "external" factors such as the energy crisis of the 1970s, the defense buildup of the 1980s, and a claimed scientific breakthrough in 1989. Accordingly, once legislators realized the amount of money invested in research, they had difficulty scrapping the program. From a "scientistic" perspective, the promise that science will eventually find an answer to a given problem, coupled with a belief that supporting scientific curiosity and freedom will yield economic benefit (in the form of technological spin-offs), keep funding alive for many research programs. Beliefs in the eventual economic payoff of research are rational, according to policy makers, because of science and technology's history of success. Consequently, approaches to policy remain stagnant, critics argue (e.g., Fuller, 1993; Hollinger, 1990), because of the scientism of policy-makers who believe that scientific practices will eventually lend solutions to the problems of science policy.

The myth of the autonomous progress of science and technology is the basis for both scientism and Luddism and continues to vex policy-makers. Historian of technology John Staudenmaier (1985) cites a guidebook for the 1933 Chicago Hall of Science "Century of Progress" Internal Exposition that captures the myth: "Science Finds, Industry (technology) Applies, Man Conforms." Ironically, whereas scientists believe that scientific progress should not be hindered by cultural influences, Luddites believe that technological progress is inevitable and must be hindered by fundamental intervention. Both scientism and Luddism stem from the common belief that science and technology progress absent any cultural influences.

Policy-makers have also bought into the myth of autonomous progress which has led to an interesting case of circular reasoning. Although "policy" by definition entails influencing the direction of a particular program, the essential nature of science and technology, according to the myth, already assures its own progress. The only decision that policy-makers have to make is whether or not to help speed along progress by appropriating funds. However, although scientific and technological researchers may promise results within a specified time period (as in the example of fusion policy), such promises rarely hold. This is particularly the case with "big science" projects in which the promise of a return on investment will not be seen for decades. To complete the circle, researchers argue for continued funding on the grounds that (keeping in mind the myth of autonomous progress) an answer will eventually be found. Whereas Luddites object to the dehumanizing quality of technology and take action against it, many hold that because workers cannot stop progress indefinitely they must eventually concede to losing their jobs and learning new skills. Progress, from the scientist's, Luddite's, and policy-maker's perspective, is constant.

METHODS AND MYTHS

Another persistent myth that influences science and technology policy-making regards a single scientific method. The scientific method can be defined as a procedure involving an observation or controlled experiment that results in a hypothesis found valid or invalid through further experimentation.

The concept of the scientific method, as we know it, may be traced to several sources: most essentially a notion of reason derived from Cartesian philosophy, the idea that an individual thinker may separate their interests from a given situation and so make unbiased judgments about that situation. The notion was elaborated in part by Isaac Newton's (1642-1727) assertion that scientific explanations should be derived strictly from observation, and Francis Bacon's (1561-1626) argument that scientific reasoning should be based on induction, a process by which a conclusion is drawn about an entire class of objects through the observation of only part of that class.

Many of us assume that the scientific method works in part because the scientist retains an open-mindedness, a disinterestedness, and a healthy skepticism (see Merton, 1973). Further, many of us assume that researchers' scientific knowledge is derived only from experimentation and that their opinions do not influence their observations. We forget that scientists and technologists are human beings who, like all human beings, simply cannot be entirely objective. Several studies have shown that the qualities that compose scientific method only rarely shape actual practice. In fact, scientists and technologists are greatly affected by the world around them, and their scientific method is affected too (see Gilbert & Mulkay, 1981). Scientists have endorsed a great many theories not so much because they provided the best explanation or the most elegant set of mathematical principles, but because they were endorsed by a colleague or a professional society. Theories involving the discovery of oxygen, the motion of the planets, natural evolution, and special relativity gained acceptance over time not only through experimentation, but also because they became endorsed by influential individuals and groups. The lesson here, which should not surprise us, is that scientists and technologists can be persuaded by the same things that persuade the rest of us.

To understand the actual nature of science and technology and develop a basis for policy, we need to examine our view of the scientist and technologist.

COMMON ASSUMPTIONS
ABOUT SCIENTISTS AND TECHNOLOGISTS

Many of us have a "good guy/bad guy" view of researchers. On the one hand, we see them as saintlike pursuers of truth, a view reflected and reinforced by popular images of Albert Einstein, Albert Schweitzer, and Steven Hawking. On the other hand, we may regard them as corrupted by personal desires for power, wealth, and fame and (more recently) by corporate mandates, a view reflected and reinforced by Mary Shelly's Dr. Frankenstein and his literary and cinematic successors. A little thought will suggest that both these views are caricatures and often have little to do with actual scientists.

Many of us have a romantic image of the scientist as a individual genius. The popular imagination sees Isaac Newton,

Nicholas Copernicus, Galileo Galilei, Charles Darwin, and Robert Oppenheimer as mythic figures standing above society and politics and unaffected by the "ordinary" people who preceded and surrounded them. Again, common sense suggests that no one can remain apart from society and still contribute to it.

Many of us have imagined the scientist as a "great man," an idea that Newton or Einstein, for example, were influenced solely by thinkers of equal or greater historical significance, also familiar names. The "great man" (emphasis on both words) idea overlooks the wealth of influences from two groups: women and those not written into history books. Women's roles in science have been obscured and little regarded in most histories of science; but the contributions of women like Marie Curie, Rosalyn Franklin, and Barbara McClintock are enormous. Similarly, the roles played by skilled laborers like metallurgists and carpenters are uncelebrated, even unrecorded, but Galileo could not have discovered the moons of Jupiter until an anonymous glassblower had created magnifying lenses.

One aspect of scientific discovery, the "Eureka!" moment, is often portrayed as a researcher's personal revelation, the point in time when all the parts of the puzzle come together. (Watson and Crick's discovery of the structure of DNA is commonly perceived as such a moment.) Although this type of insight certainly occurs, we are wrong to assume, as many of us do, that it arises without context and is attributable only to "genius," whatever that is. Students of the history of science are particularly troubled by this assumption in that it implies that such moments are forever beyond our comprehension. Such is simply not the case: "Eureka!" moments can be understood when we examine them with a view to history and sociology, the contexts within which they appeared.

You may believe that men are better than women at scientific reasoning. The idea may be part of a common stereotype that all men are rational and logical and able to set aside the emotions and that all women are irrational and illogical and unable to approach a problem dispassionately. Obviously, such ideas are dangerous, among other reasons, because they set arbitrary and artificial boundaries on women seeking education and employment.[1]

You may believe that certain groups have innate abilities in fields related to science and technology. A popular recent stereotype holds that Asians have innate mathematical skills superior to non-Asians. In fact, the well-documented success of Asian students in the realm of science and mathematics has been attributed not to natural inclinations so much as to family structure and values (see Kaplan, Choy, & Whitmore, 1992). This myth, too, is dangerous simply because it limits human potential.

SOURCES OF OUR IMAGES
OF SCIENCE AND TECHNOLOGY

We derive our images of science and technology and scientists and technologists from news reports, textbooks, advertising, film and television, and, in some cases, personal experience. Except for the last, each of these sources is likely to offer an image that is incomplete and inaccurate.

Science Journalism

Today, you may have read a story in a national newspaper about a study just released in the *New England Journal of Medicine* concerning a new treatment for AIDS. The local newspaper may have begun a series on hazardous waste disposal in your community. An evening news anchor may be relaying a story about a recent discovery by scientists working on the Human Genome Project. Debate may still be taking place in popular weekly news magazines about the future of the electric car and high-speed rail or the fate of a space mission to Mars. In many instances, public attitudes and expectations—including your own—about science and technology originate with media coverage. If the public's primary source of information about science and technology is the media, what impressions do they receive? What criteria determine a journalist's choice of the "interesting" or "significant" stories about science and technology? Is media coverage objective? Why is coverage about science and technology structured the way it is? Finally, if public attitudes about science and technology primarily derive from media coverage, what are those attitudes, and should something be done to change them?

Science and technology do not get covered with the critical zeal and accompanying skepticism of politics. But this comparison may be unfair. On the one hand, politics follows a familiar script. A "political season" takes place with beginning and ending points, regular controversies, and clear winners and losers. Political issues are also presented in terms of the decisions that need to be made about them. That is, although many issues confronting voters are complex and beyond their expertise, media coverage and explanations reflect the voting public's eventual need to make informed decisions. On the other hand, the practices of science are unfamiliar to the layperson. Mainstream science and technology take place over a long period of time—usually much longer than presidential races with which people quickly get bored. For the most part, a controversy in the scientific community (a case of scientific fraud) or policy debate (funding a space station) must flare up before the news media and the public get interested. It is hardly surprising then that the focus on controversial (cutting-edge) as opposed to "textbook" (basic) science leaves the public with a skewed view of scientific practice. For this reason, scientists complain about public ignorance and thirst for the sensational while demanding a fair hearing in the press. Here, the lack of most journalists' expertise cuts two ways.

Many of the stories about mainstream science offer a watered-down version of the scientists' own press releases. Surprisingly, and because these claims are not of general interest, these press releases receive little critical scrutiny. In struggling to get an angle on a scientific or technological dispute, the journalists' impulse is to "go with what you know." Journalists often bring other types of expertise (e.g., in economics, politics, and consumer affairs) to bear on the dispute. In these instances—the cold fusion controversy, for example—the press latches on to what is at stake for people in their daily lives, and interest grows. Still, controversial science and technology are long, and life is short. The press and the public become bored when controversial "events" fail to happen at rapid intervals. Do you remember the outcome (if one has been reached) of the cold fusion controversy, the investigation into the *Challenger* accident, or any one of a hundred proclamations in medical journals about foods that cause cancer, reduce cholesterol, or increase longevity?

Textbooks

You may take for granted that the information presented in your science texts is true, and to a large extent you are right. Nevertheless the image of science those texts offer is often inaccurate. Many textbooks present science as an *entirely* rational process, proceeding deliberately and straightforwardly. In fact, scientific discovery is often a case of someone recognizing possibilities made evident by an accident.

Percy Spencer discovered microwaves when, standing near a radar set, he noticed that the chocolate bar in his pocket had melted. Like many, this find was a fortunate accident. Still, many textbook writers, because they ascribe to the myth of scientific practice as completely rational and because the necessary abbreviation lends itself to a cause-and-effect summary of events, present Spencer's discovery (and others like it) as the outcome of an inevitable process.

Further, science textbooks make scientific and technological controversy seem settled. Such presentations appeal to our worst consumer instinct—the desire to accept, uncritically, a prepackaged ideal.

Advertisements

You may have seen the advertisement demonstrating the durability of house paint under laboratory-controlled conditions that alternately heat and freeze a painted surface. Probably, you have also seen advertisements for stomach antacids and headache medicines that use images suggestive of X-rays of the brain or stomach or have read the catchphrase "years in the making" in a magazine advertisement for a new product. Each of these presentations suggests (a) that scientific method is the basis for technology and (b) that technology gains legitimacy from the high regard in which you hold scientific research.

Some of you are, and all of you know, owners of "smart" technologies like self-starting coffeemakers, programmable dishwashers, and computerized lawnmowers. You (or they) may have justified the purchase on the grounds that it makes work more efficient. Is this the real reason? Examine the advertisements for the products, and you will notice that they have subtler, less practical appeals. Because designs are sexy, they make their user seem sexy. Because such products suggest a knowledge of technology in general, they make their user seem intelligent. Because such products are expensive, they make their owner seem wealthy. Finally, because they are tools and extensions of their user, they make their user seem powerful.

You may have seen pharmaceutical commercials that use a spokesperson dressed as a pharmacist or a doctor; such advertising uses the image of the scientist (a kind of gift bearer in a lab coat) to lend a product credibility. Interestingly, the image spills outside the commercial: The scientist in the real world comes to be seen as trustworthy and caring.

"PUBLIC" POLICY

Almost easier to define than what the "public" is, is what the public is not. "The public," or citizens of a country, is not a homogeneous group of people with similar concerns. Members of the public do not occupy the same jobs, do not have the same levels of income and education, do not belong to one community or professional organization, and do not participate in decisions regarding the same policy issues. Perhaps the only feature common to "the public" is diversity. Given its changing profile, the prospect of an increased presence in policy-making touches off debate over whether or not "the public" has the background, ability, and wisdom to guide science and technology. To arrive at some form of coordinated action and policy, critics argue, the diverse parties in the process must reach consensus. This consensus is impossible because the differences among members of the public is irresolvable, and these differences lead to the gridlock of the process. However, the idea that consensus is necessary for policy-making and makes for coordinated action has also been challenged. The dynamics of policy-making do not ensure that the goals of the participants will not change. Further, participants in the process need to realize that they must serve the interests of others as a means of serving their own. Finally, as the process of writing the United States Constitution illustrates, it is not the consensus of the participants that matters; rather, it is their ability to arrive at a language and a set of procedures allowing the public to sustain its own interests in the pursuit of a defined but changing goal.

In the 1920s, the famous *New York World* editorial writer Walter Lippmann published a series of studies on the interrelationships between the news media and public decision making. He railed against the ineptitude and sheer ignorance of the public in engaging the issues of the day. Lippmann's thesis was that the "government elite" busily manufactured public support for their programs by manipulating the news media. As the readers of newspapers were a "feeble-minded" and "neurotic" public, they were ill-equipped to critically assess what went on below the surface of a news report. Lippmann saw his job as educating the people, doing the legwork they was supposed to do, by finding and disclosing "inside" unbiased information on the issues of the day for an unquestioning public to consume. In fact, Lippmann became America's first political "pundit."

The 1922 appearance of Lippmann's *Public Opinion* caused a great deal of controversy. The book was reviewed by John Dewey who argued that the role of "responsible" journalism was not simply to adhere to scientific standards of objectivity (which was impossible), but to inspire public and community debate. The press would enable communities to pursue the democratic process by helping them follow, criticize, and engage in public political debate. In their clash, Lippmann and Dewey portrayed the public in opposite ways. Dewey's public took part in vibrant debate to which the press contributed an intellectual and emotional context. Lippmann's public did not debate, accepting as fact journalists' accounts. Today, the Dewey/Lippmann exchange still informs our ideas of what the public is and what constitutes public debate. We are confronted, as a democratic society, with the paradox of endorsing public input in the policy-making arena as long as the public is informed. Yet in setting criteria for an informed public (note the recent rise in demands for "literacy" of one type or another), we begin to choose whose voices will be heard and whose will not. Many times, these choices are made against the backdrop of the unjustified fear of a violent response.

In the section above on images of science and technology, a part of "the public" in England in 1811 were the Luddites. Threatened by job losses caused by new manufacturing technology, the Luddites burned factories and murdered factory owners. The infamy of the Luddite response continues even today to shadow legitimate protests of American workers who, over the past 40 years, have been confronted by the increasing automation of the workplace and accompanying job loss. Although political protest is now a matter for the courtroom, the fears of workers and policy makers remain the same. In these examples, the public is roughly equivalent to the working class or those who do not have as much political clout as industry barons. In making public policy, politicians assume the role of spokespersons for the public and imbue "them" with certain qualities. We have all heard, for example, politicians refer to "mainstream America" and the policies of government officials as either inside or outside the mainstream. The public being addressed in these instances is an "ideal type," a theoretical entity representing the habits and choices of a group of people assumed to have nearly identical views and lifestyles. Policy-makers, whether they be politicians, lobbyists, or scientists, appeal to the interests of ideal types in arguing, for instance, how the development of science and technology leads to the creation of jobs, the assumption being that "the public" wants jobs, not promises of the possible discovery of esoteric knowledge and experimental techniques (a similar strategy was employed in selling the Human Genome Project to Congress).

The rhetoric of policy-makers personifies their image of the public as either a hindrance or resource in the policy-making process. On one hand, the public is portrayed as a mob too disconnected to know what they want. The diverse and sometimes ill-formed perspectives of the public are seen as an obstacle to the forming of coherent policy. On this view, policy-making demands a meeting of the minds and the ability of one view to win out over the others. On the other hand, the public is portrayed as a group that can be dealt with but also does not know what it wants. Here, the public perspective is to be brought into focus by policy-makers and technical communicators in the role of facilitators. On this view, policy-making demands the structuring of a language and a process in which different goals can be met by using a number of different insights.

POLICY

Policy is generally defined as a set of either explicit or implicit choices made by a social group among possible goals and objectives in which the means are specified for achieving the ends, the intended and unintended consequences of those choices are explored, and the effects of those choices are evaluated. Specifically, national science and technology policy has been defined as a governmental course of action intended to support, apply or regulate scientific knowledge or technological innovation (Barke, 1986, p. 12). The study of policy is the study of how different social actors—ourselves, community action groups, scientists, technologists, and local and federal government agencies—make choices about science and technology. These choices involve considering a number of interrelated elements such as expertise, ethics, risk assessment, and power relations at which we will look in this chapter. As a citizen, as a potential practitioner in science and technology, and especially as a scientific and technical communicator, you have an important role to play in the democratic formulation of policy, which calls for knowledge of the policy process.

Generally, the public is not interested in issues concerning science and technology. Jon Miller models American public policy formation on a pyramid. At the top are "decision-makers," the leaders of the branches of government who can make requisite, legally enforceable decisions, and who interact with "policy leaders"—heads of lobbying groups and interest groups. At the next level is the "attentive public" (very interested, well-informed), which in 1983, according to the National Science Foundation, represented about 24% of the adult population. At the next level is the "interested public" (not adequately informed), representing about 28% of the adult population. The base of the pyramid is represented by the "nonattentive public" (not interested), about 47% of the adult population, a decline from 62% in 1981. Still, the interest of the public regarding science and technology depends, of course, on the particular issue. The objective of policy leaders is to enlist the involvement of the attentive public in influencing the decision-making process.

In 1964, the Economic Opportunity Act was passed. This bill contained a provision that the Office of Economic Opportunity achieve the participation of the customers it served (mainly the poor) in the decision-making process. Although direct citizen participation received a great deal of criticism, the rights of citizens to determine the direction of federal funds in their own communities was established. During the 1970s, federal legislators enacted over 200 public participation programs in federal agencies such as the Environmental Protection Agency and the Community Development Block Grant Program. During the 1980s, many of these programs were rolled back due to budget cutting and deregulation. Given the lack of stability of these programs, the impact of mandated citizen participation on public policy is impossible to measure. The question of the government's responsibility in encouraging and maintaining citizen participation (especially with underrepresented groups) remains unresolved.

Aside from government sponsorship, concerned individuals have initiated a number of grassroots movements around local science and technology issues. People are more likely to become motivated or mobilized into interest groups over a policy issue directly affecting their community—the installation of power lines, road building, waste disposal, and environmental management—than they are over national issues. Nevertheless, whether the issue is national or local, if individuals see that they have a personal stake in the outcome of the issue, regarding their family, their freedom of choice, and their land, interest is necessarily heightened. Here the direct impact of science and technology is made palpable. National policy issues that continue to be debated on a grassroots level involve the use and distribution of reproductive technologies, the regulation of controversial drugs (e.g., Laetrile), and what can be taught in public schools (creationism and/or Darwinian theory). Of course, the merit of public wisdom also sparks debate. Interest groups can fan the fires of controversy for a moment in the national spotlight (radical environmentalists engaging in "tree spiking" to prevent timber harvests), and in so doing shift the character of the debate. Still, policy makers see the advantage of having a number of interests represented in the decision-making process. Too often, especially regarding issues concerning science and technology, the voice of the public is not heard and policy decisions are left to experts.

You can participate in making local policy in several ways, including public hearings, advisory boards, and study groups. Occasionally, however, these forums of participation present only the veneer of participatory democracy. Often, public hearings are held at times and locations that limit public access. Even if available to the public, hearings can occur late in the decision-making process so that many of the contentious issues have been decided; public debate at this point is only a formality. Citizens unfamiliar with the language of science and technology and the procedures of governments can become frustrated and confused by the process of hearings. Experts in particular scientific and technical fields and people familiar with rules of order and parliamentary procedure have a substantial advantage over other citizens. If traditional forms of participation are perceived as ineffective or biased, the public may protest, start a direct nonviolent campaign, or attempt legal redress.

To provide alternatives to unsatisfactory conventional processes, a number of suggestions and participatory experiments have been proposed. Suggestions include encouraging interactive procedures during hearings, technical assistance to lay participants (including the use of scientific and technical communicators as "translators" and mediators), and posthearing follow-ups (see Checkoway, 1980, pp. 6-7). Participatory experiments such as citizen courts and citizen review boards have also been proposed. The Science for Citizens Program sponsored by the National Science Foundation in 1977 was terminated in 1982, but during its brief existence it started six public service science centers. An example of one of these centers is the Boston Neighborhood Network. The purpose of the network, which eventually grew into an independent, nonprofit organization, is to direct research activities at Boston's universities to the needs of neighborhood communities, involving, among other things, broad environmental concerns, energy planning, and banking practices. Although the relative success of the Science for Citizens Program cannot be determined due to its short life, continued conflicts among policy-makers, experts, and the lay public illustrate the need to encourage innovative approaches to participatory politics.

Experts

An expert is a specialist who possesses a skill or knowledge of a field or profession and, through training and experience, is recognized as an authority. When you think of an expert you likely picture an attorney, doctor, professor (in some academic discipline), scientist, or engineer. Experts are among the elites of society, people who earn advanced degrees and occupy leadership positions in high-paying professions. Although experts have a prominent role to play in a participatory democracy, the particular aspects and consequences of that role require scrutiny.

One view (Stigler, 1984) offers that expertise is not only needed but should be encouraged as an efficient means to divide the "cognitive labor" of society. Because we cannot become experts in every relevant specialty affecting our lives (these specialties appear to be proliferating at an alarming rate), we need, as a society, to have experts in certain areas so we can "think about" our own business and field of expertise. Intellectual specialization, like economic specialization, is necessary for an efficiently run society. There is no danger, on this view, that experts will become narrow-minded and out of touch with the lay public. As the ideas of individual experts would be highly diverse and experts would look to interact with one another, the exchange among experts would result in new ideas that would spill over into the larger public arena. As public benefactors, experts would occupy a special position in, and exert special influence on, the political process.

Another view (Feyerabend, 1978) holds that expertise is dangerous and should be discouraged because it does harm to the public good. Experts threaten democracy. As experts constitute a minority of the population (and in very specialized fields quite a small minority), they should submit to the will of the majority of laypeople. In issues in which the advice of experts is pitted against the will of the majority of laypeople, the majority should prevail. Hypothetically, on this view, if the majority of laypeople wanted a new drug treatment for AIDS available for over-the-counter consumption, but Food and Drug Administration (FDA) experts ruled it dangerous, the will of the majority would prevail. The argument against experts, given this view, is that scientific knowledge is knowledge just like other kinds of knowledge and does not *necessarily* deserve privilege in arbitrating disputes. Besides, scientific claims, like those of experts at the FDA, could turn out to be wrong just like any other nonscientific claims. Since the truth resides in more than one place, policy-makers would be close-minded indeed to think that only experts possess it. Although the examples given apply to science and technology, they could easily apply to expertise in other professional fields and academic disciplines.

With respect to decisions regarding science and technology policy, which position on expertise should prevail? Should the lay public follow the leadership of trained experts, or diminish (and possibly abandon) the role of experts according to the principles of individual liberty? Those of you reading this book are preparing to become experts in some manner, keeping in mind that you will always be a layperson in regard to another field. Will you expect laypersons to defer to your expertise and authority? Will you defer to another person's expertise and authority? Or will you as either expert or layperson defer to the will of the majority? Perhaps these questions are best answered within a pragmatic context. For example, because individuals do not have laboratories in their homes (although home pregnancy tests provide an interesting counterexample), they might defer to the findings of national laboratory scientists with respect to the benefit or harm of a new drug or food additive. However, in instances where policy issues are woven into the political, economic, and social fabric of a community, experts should be seen as contributors to a larger debate that might ultimately be settled by a negotiated consensus.

Ethics

The process of policy-making is morally complex and often overwhelmed by the rapid growth of science and technology. Changes in science and technology have challenged the courts to adjust from a decision-making process based on tradition and precedent to one based on anticipating the future impact of research and development. Also, science and technology are not simply the objects of ethical and legal debate but are institutions influencing that debate. In fact, our personal and institutional ethical and legal frameworks are in significant ways bound to our knowledge of science and technology. In a survey of college students in 1980, for example, Jon Miller concluded that of the students considering themselves "more religious" or "less religious," 23% of the "less religious" students were "attentive" to organized science, compared to 14% of the "more religious" students. Miller concluded that although different aspects of religious belief were incompatible with "attentiveness" to science, the lack of attentiveness could not be attributed to any single belief (see Miller, Suchner, & Voelker, 1980, p. 184). Policy-making serves both to sanction and to restrict the expression of ethical standards in science and technology.

The relation between policy-making and ethics has generated the following questions (among others):

- Should policy-makers be guided by certain moral principles and guidelines? If so, what (or whose) principles should they be?
- Is it "ethical" to restrict the freedom of choice of individual consumers of science and technology?
- Do corporations involved in research and development have moral obligations to consumers?
- Should scientists and engineers be held accountable for how their research or technology is used?
- When is the lack of an explicit policy moral or immoral?

▓ What moral responsibility does the federal government have to its citizens who use federally funded research?

▓ Should costs be a factor in imposing ethical regulations?

In contemplating the last question, it was estimated by the Alcohol, Drug Abuse, and Mental Health Association that the cost in 1988-1989 for new animal care regulations for primates and dogs was $40,000-$70,000 per research grant. Surveying 126 medical schools, the American Association of Medical Colleges estimated that compliance with animal rights regulations from 1985 to 1990 cost schools approximately $17.6 million. Researchers applying for federal funding must justify the use of animals in experiments as well as document expenditures for their care. The concerns of animal rights activists coupled with the growing expense of taking care of larger animals have forced some researchers to change their experimental procedures, using smaller animals (such as mice) instead of primates or no animals when possible.

Another illustration of the complexity of ethical questions in science policy is found in the Human Genome Project (HGP). Expected to carry a $3 billion price tag over a 15-year period, the HGP is biology's equivalent of putting a man on the moon. The goal of the project is to map and decipher the complete code of approximately 100,000 genes that determine the traits of human beings. Originally, the HGP was touted by some biologists as contributing to the possible cure for all disease. This claim did not go unchallenged, however, even within the biological community. Proponents of the HGP shifted ground and advertised the project as generating new economic opportunities through biomedical research. Nevertheless, the ethical implications of the HGP, no matter which side of the debate one takes, are vast. Scientists, technologists, policy makers, and individual citizens will face ethical questions ranging from the "right" to alter the genetic makeup of the fetus in the womb (and the consequences of that process), to who should possess, organize, and distribute the knowledge resulting from the HGP research. One of the more intriguing aspects of the HGP and other "big science" projects is the possible effect of interdisciplinary cooperation (e.g., the role of computer scientists in the HGP) on ethical issues. When researchers and professionals from different disciplines and fields come together on a project, they clash. The participants are forced to re-examine the beliefs on which their disciplinary perspectives are based. Consequently, the transformation of disciplinary perspectives often leads to changes in moral standards and practices.

Risk Assessment

We face risk daily—driving a car, jogging, using tools and household chemicals. From our previous experiences and observations or from the experiences of others, we approximate the amount of risk these activities entail under a variety of circumstances and decide whether or not we will do them based on the perceived probability of adverse effect.[2] Whereas we make individual determinations of risk, there are a number of professions, including science and technology, in which risk must be identified, estimated, and compensated for in specific practices and policies. Risks can be classified as new, historical, individual, and social. Historical risks are known occurrences about which data have been gathered; examples are industrial accidents, automobile accidents, and natural disasters. New risks are never previously observed occurrences about which data have not been gathered; examples are new technologies and exposure to unknown chemicals. Individual risks are those willingly taken by each person according to one's own value system; examples are using drugs and/or alcohol. Social risks are those chosen for individuals by institutions (government, banks, industrial corporations); examples are federal regulations and the location of a prison site in a community. These four classifications can be analyzed in three stages consisting of assessment, identification, and estimation. Assessors generally use one of four methods for determining acceptable risk: risk-cost-benefit analysis, revealed preferences, expressed preferences, and natural standards (see Shrader-Frechette's, 1985, chap. 2 for a more detailed coverage of these classifications).

Risk-cost-benefit analysis (also known as cost-benefit analysis) is the most prominent method for evaluating risk. Given a particular course of action, risk is initially determined in context to all other possible courses of action and the risks associated with each one. Based on one of any number of quantitative and qualitative models, risk assessors draw a comparison between possible alternative actions and assign a monetary value to the probability of a consequence. The components of the analysis are assigned a number representing the value of each alternative. This number also represents the difference between the benefits of alternative actions, on the one hand, and the risks and costs of a given course of action, on the other. An example of risk-cost-benefit is the automobile insurance statement. Criteria such as one's past driving record, the type of car driven, where the person lives, the number of miles driven to and from work, marital status, and age are assigned a numerical value. These numbers are compiled to give a profile of the driver, and insurance rates reflect whether or not the company believes the driver is a good or bad risk. In roughly the same way, risk-cost-benefit analysis is performed to determine the value of a worker, the safety of a factory, and the probability that a new drug treatment will cause harm or death.

Since the passage of the National Environmental Policy Act in 1969, and the creation of federal regulatory agencies such as the Occupational Safety and Health Administration (OSHA), efforts have been made to gather information on the various risks to which U.S. citizens are exposed (e.g., acid rain). In 1982, the Risk Analysis Research and Demonstration Act was passed to define and improve methods and standards used in the application of risk analysis. Aside from many of the dehumanizing aspects of risk analysis, criticisms of the risk-cost-benefit analysis center on scientistic presumptions on which this analysis is based. Often, assessors have failed to come to grips with the ways in which ethical and cultural biases are factors in risk assessment. For example, if a laborer was educated about the risk involved in doing a particular job, was offered a higher wage designed to reflect and compensate for the risk, and decided to do the job, should the laborer's personal preferences be the deciding factor in allowing them to do the job and take the risk? Do the risks an individual laborer takes affect only one life? Can workers adequately assess their own risk preferences? What is the difference between a worker's perception of risk at work and the same worker's perception of risk outside work, with respect to the threat of a local waste disposal site or nuclear plant? The answers to these questions are not found in actuarial tables, but in submitting risk analysis to the same contextual analyses as the science on which its methods are based and the technology whose risks it seeks to determine.

Power Relations

Science and technology policy consists of integrated courses of action formulated to organize, produce, and use goods such as knowledge, information and capital. Once a policy is enacted, however, the distribution of these goods is rarely equitable. As a result, certain individuals, groups, and institutions gain power while others are marginalized or pushed aside. Of the products with which science and technology policy deals, knowledge is the one we most closely associate with power. We have a tendency to define power through a series of verbal equivalencies. Knowledge is power. Power is control. Power corrupts. Absolute power corrupts absolutely. A verbal equation such as "knowledge is power" expresses a truism we casually accept. But how is the concept of power distinguished within the context of scientific knowledge?

On one view, knowledge and power have been characterized as external to one another in science and technology. From this perspective, power operates upon science but does not operate within science. For example, a telling but inexact definition of science is that it is the best method we have for obtaining truths about the world. While scientistic, this definition underscores certain accepted aspects of scientific knowledge, its universality and its applicability. Unlike other forms of knowledge, scientific knowledge claims to be universal by being "lawlike." The mathematical laws governing the ways colors combine to make up white light, for instance, are not bound to a particular location. These laws apply on any occasion and in any location. We can apply our knowledge of the composition of light in making lenses or in other theories regarding optics. Knowing how things are, how the world works, gives us an opportunity to manipulate or control a situation. Knowledge is power in this instance because we can impose our wills on a particular situation. Still, power can be used to influence or thwart the acquisition of knowledge. The Catholic Church prohibited Galileo from doing scientific work in 1616. The political regime in the Sovet Union suppressed knowledge of Mendelian genetics. In either instance, where knowledge obtains power through its application, or a person or government exercises power to stop scientific investigation, the character of scientific knowledge and achievement—its rationality, objectivity, and universality—remains constant.

Another view holds that scientific and technical knowledge and power cannot be looked at separately. Power relations among people, institutions, and ideas circulate throughout science and technology and are represented within scientific and technical knowledge. Scientific theories do not merely offer a description of the world, but assume and define relations among people and ideas. Power is entailed in any set of defined relations but is best understood, on this view, as exercised within a web of interconnected relationships. Power is not localized in any one place or possessed exclusively by any one person. The practices of science do disclose the way the world operates, but they also transform the world and the way the world can be known. Feminist theorists, for example, argue that sexist scientific language reflects a male-dominated culture that portrays nature as material resource to be controlled and exploited. The masculine conception of power and dominance permeates scientific practice by insisting that objective, "disinterested" observations provide the basis for what counts as knowledge. Feminists suggest that women's experience and understanding, if developed within the framework of science (some feminists argue for a separate form of science), offer the chance for a less power-oriented approach to observation and experimentation and a different form of scientific understanding.

NATIONAL SCIENCE
AND TECHNOLOGY POLICY

The Executive Branch

During one of the presidential debates, President Ronald Reagan declared, "I'm not a scientist," a statement which could be attributed to any modern president. Without hesitation, we cast votes for presidential candidates with little or no background, and varying degrees of personal interest, in science and technology. In many cases, a president will receive recommendations from science advisors and delegate policy-making decisions to assistants and government agencies. Nevertheless, the Constitution empowers the president to take a direct, active role in science and technology policy making. Consequently, the president can be an architect of national scientific research and technological development for decades to come.

Presidential policy initiatives are conveyed on both foreign and domestic fronts. As commander-in-chief and principal negotiator of international treaties, the president can encourage the classification or declassification of scientific and technological research or recommend standards for imported and exported technologies. As a key participant in the legislative process, the president can introduce or recommend legislation to the Congress and sign or veto bills. The president also has the power to appoint administrative officers to federal offices and agencies and present nominees to the Senate for confirmation. Through executive order (e.g., halting fetal tissue research), the president can direct specific research programs.

In calling for a shift in national priorities regarding the direction of basic science research and technology, President Bill Clinton observed,

> American technology must move in a new direction to build economic strength and spur economic growth. The traditional federal role in technology development has been limited to the support of basic science and mission-oriented research in the Defense Department, NASA, and other agencies. We cannot rely on the serendipitous application of defense technology to the

private sector. We must aim directly at these new challenges and focus our efforts on the new opportunities before us, recognizing the government can play a key role helping private firms develop and profit from innovations. (Clinton & Gore, 1993, p. 1)

Clinton's "new direction" includes reorienting national science and technology policy toward job growth and economic growth in sectors of the economy such as communications and information. Although Clinton's message of "change" was prominent during his campaign, his sentiments on science and technology were anticipated roughly two-and-a-half years earlier by President George Bush: "More and more our nation depends on basic, scientific research to spur our economic growth, [as well as provide] longer and healthier lives, a more secure world and a safer environment" ("National Medals Are Pinned," 1990, p. A23). Bush's and Clinton's comments did signal a change away from the policies of the 1980s that centered on defense, "big science" projects (the space station, the Strategic Defense Initiative, the superconducting supercollider) and biomedical research. Science and technology policy makers currently face the task of "reindustrializing" America by rebuilding its infrastructure and converting defense research to broader applications such as high-speed rail.

The design of national science and technology policy changes with the degree of personal interest and expertise presidents bring to office, and the social agenda they represent. President Lyndon Johnson, for example, saw science and technology as a by-product of his Great Society programs. President Reagan considered science and technology as keys for economic growth and approved substantial funding increases for defense and basic science. Critics have challenged the cultural assumptions symbolized in presidential science and technology policy. Should, for example, science and technology be regarded as national resources open to public funding, scrutiny, and intervention? Or should decision-making about, and funding of, scientific and technological research be placed in private hands? The tension over what constitutes democratic control of science and technology is illustrated in the president's policies.

An interesting counterexample to the modern-day trend of electing lawyers and professional politicians to the presidency is

Herbert Hoover, who held the presidency from 1929 to 1933. A leading mining engineer, Hoover wrote a standard textbook on mining. After completing the textbook, Hoover, with his wife Lou Henry Hoover, set about preparing the first English translation of George Bauer's (Georgius Agricola) treatise on metal and mining, *De Re Metallica.* After five years and four complete revisions, Hoover and his wife published their translation in 1912.

A Brief History of Presidential Science Policy

Toward the end of World War II, President Franklin Roosevelt asked Vanavar Bush, head of the Office of Scientific Research and Development, to give a list of recommendations for continuing and strengthening the cooperation between government, science, and technology. The irony of the war (like those before it) was that it served as a catalyst for extraordinary scientific and technological development. World War II saw the establishment of national laboratories like Oak Ridge and Los Alamos, the development of radar, sonar, and the atomic bomb, and the discovery of a number of life-saving drugs. Roosevelt wanted a method by which the government could harness and stimulate the growth of postwar science and technology. The memory of the Depression still haunted most people, and science and technology appeared to provide a stable economic base on which to build the economy. As a future consequence of Vannevar Bush's report, the federal government, through a range of agencies (Bush wanted a single national science foundation to handle all science funding), assumed the dominant role for funding basic scientific research in the university. The peer review system was established to review grant proposals from individual researchers and teams of researchers.

Science and technology policy during the 1950s was a direct response to the cold-war threat of the emerging Soviet empire. The breakout of the Korean War saw the renewed involvement of scientists in the military, especially the air force. By 1950, the Office of Naval Research had established over 1,200 research contracts with approximately 200 universities. Emphasis was placed on research in high-energy physics, and research universities began to depend on the flow of federal dollars. The increase in naval research coincided with Admiral Hyman Rickover's development of the nuclear navy. The navy launched the atomically powered submarine *Nautilus* in 1955. Field tests of the *Nautilus* were so impressive that Rickover achieved national prominence and a reputation for being dictatorial in his meticulous attention to detail. Rickover's accomplishments came in the midst of President Dwight Eisenhower's "Atoms for Peace" campaign begun in 1953. Eisenhower thought that nuclear power could be harnessed for peaceful purposes and encouraged engineers to design a nuclear reactor to produce energy for civilian use. Eisenhower enlisted Rickover to head the project. The urgency of Eisenhower's desire to build and export civilian reactors to Europe was symbolized by Rickover's appointment as director of the project and the real possibility that the Soviet Union would enter the market first. Toward the end of the decade, however, the military became disenchanted with scientific research. Funding for the Pentagon faced renewed scrutiny and in 1957 the Department of Defense announced that it was cutting its research budget by 10%. A shock wave hit the scientific research community. Fortunately for research scientists, the Soviet Union intervened.

On October 4, 1957, the Soviet Union launched the first *Sputnik*. Fear that the Soviets would control the sky above the United States (this fear was revived in the 1980s) touched off a renewed round of Department of Defense spending on scientific research. The space race had begun. John Kennedy's election in 1960 and his promise to have a man on the moon by the end of the decade is perhaps the clearest example of priority setting in science and technology policy. Scientific research and development in the decade of the 1960s, through increased funding for the National Aeronautics and Space Administration (NASA), included planetary probes, satellites, and the pursuit of manned space flight. National research and development expenditures continued to rise from approximately $17 billion in 1960 to approximately $30 billion in 1969 (expressed in 1972 dollars). The Johnson administration, while continuing to fund defense and space research, trained the attention of science and technology on Great Society programs. Research was encouraged in the areas of personal health, pollution, and transportation systems to demonstrate that socially desirable ends could be reached through science and technology. Johnson's attitudes toward research were indirectly quoted by one scientist who heard him suggest that scientists had done enough basic research and it was now time to work on its application.

The Apollo program symbolized the great irony of successful, goal-directed policy-making. Scientists and engineers met Kennedy's challenge, and the country stood united in awe of the achievement. But the expectations of Congress were raised; now the people wanted to see an immediate, timely return on their investments in science and technology. Similarly, the success of the Apollo program found a number of scientists and engineers out of a job and left NASA scientists pondering how, or if, they could follow the act of putting men on the moon.

With the publication of Rachel Carson's *Silent Spring* in 1962, Ralph Nader's *Unsafe at Any Speed* in 1965, and Alvin Toffler's *Future Shock* in 1970, the national debate over the relation among the values of science, technology, and society shifted and intensified. Science and technology, once presented to popular culture as society's benefactors, were now posed as threats. The threat of DDT and the Corvair automobile, as documented respectively by Carson and Nader, sparked the beginning of the environmental and consumer movements. Toffler's best-seller found the impact of science and technology on society problematic in echoing the warning of C. P. Snow's 1959 Rede Lecture that a dangerous and widening gulf had emerged between the education and aims of scientists and humanists. The tone of much of the literature of the 1960s and early 1970s was negative toward science and technology. Interdisciplinary programs began at several universities to educate science and engineering students about the social impact of their work and the values expressed in science and technology. Many of these efforts were initially reactionary, fueled by growing protests against the Vietnam War. Nevertheless, impassioned critiques against the social consequences of scientific and technological development continued to have their effect. Basic research performed by industry (in industrial labs, for example) fell approximately 37% between 1966 and 1972. Like Congress, industry wanted short-term results that promised a return on investment.

As funding for the Vietnam War and the space program were scaled back, research into energy efficiency and alternatives received a boost. In sum, however, funding for basic research began to level off in 1970 and stagnate until 1975. President Richard Nixon's personal antagonism toward science (and protesting academics generally) led him to abolish the post of presidential science advisor and the President's Science Advisory Committee (PSAC). Nixon also placed control of the Office of Science Policy under the aegis of the National Science Foundation. Scientists took up the task of making the case for the relevance of their research programs and prepared for greater public participation in their projects.

From 1973 to 1974, the economy stalled. Locked in an economic recession that witnessed the advent of government-mandated price freezes, economists saw investment in science and technology as a way of contributing to economic growth. Technological change and scientific research, according to these economic models, provided the economy with new products that, in turn, created new markets. Science-based industries (e.g., chemicals, pharmaceuticals, and microelectronics) were seen as key to United States trade, and investments in science and technology facilitated the growth of "intellectual capital." The shift in thinking in the White House during the Gerald Ford and Jimmy Carter administrations from spending on (government overhead), to investing in (promise of return), science and technology invigorated the scientific community. Semantically, science and technology were now couched in economic terms. The growth and production of knowledge required capital and careful investment planning. Long-term financial commitment had to be made to ensure yields. Controlling knowledge meant controlling markets. The business of America was the business of science and technology.

In 1975, the scientific community realized it had a friend in Vice President Nelson Rockefeller. Rockefeller proposed that Congress reestablish the Office of Science Policy (later named the Office of Science and Technology Policy) and sought to bring industrial and scientific leaders back into the White House. President Ford requested the formation of two expert advisory panels for science and technology policy. On the panels sat senior executives from General Electric, Texas Instruments, and IBM

(International Business Machines) as well as scientists from the leading universities—Stanford, Princeton, and MIT (Massachusetts Institute of Technology). By the end of the Ford administration, spending for basic research had increased approximately 2%.

President Carter endorsed the trend toward the growth of science and technology but sent mixed messages to corporations by his commitments to the environment, labor, and conservation. Carter appeared to be holding up the banner of unfettered research in science and technology in one hand while reaching out to the groups who had benefited from Johnson's Great Society programs with the other hand. These groups demanded an equitable distribution of funds and once again called for explanations of the relevance of certain research programs. Although the social relevance of alternative energy research was obvious, Carter's science advisor Frank Press called for the government to balance its budgetary research commitments with private capital. From Press's perspective, the government should only help a research project until it became somewhat self-sustaining, after which private corporations would assume control. In attempting to strike a balance between private and government sponsorship of science and technology, Carter's policy initiatives were captive to policy makers representing either the interests of corporations, or the interests of the people.

Declared by many as the era of "economic recovery," the Reagan years were marked by a shift away from applied science (e.g., solar power, private sector research) to basic research (e.g., defense, public sector research). Consequently, cuts were made in applied energy research and agricultural sciences. The Reagan administration encouraged the dominant role of the private sector in funding applied scientific research, whereas the emphasis in basic research included advanced computers and biotechnology. A strict line was drawn between private and public sector interests. Science and technology were to be controlled as much as possible by the free market, and public money was reserved to "provide for the common defense." As the Reagan years unfolded, big-science research projects turned up on the agenda. The proposed funding of the superconducting supercollider, the space station, the Human Genome Project, AIDS research, and the Strategic Defense Initiative was reminiscent of the big-science, long-term projects of the early 1960s. During the 1980s, the dependence of the world economy on science and technology became obvious just as the outcome of big-science projects became dubious.

National science policy, as influenced by the president, appears cyclical. The pet projects of one administration die with the election of the next president, only to be reborn a decade later. As this chapter was being written, Congress stopped funding for the supercollider, and eliminated the Office of Technology Assessment (OTA). If the patterns of previous executive policy making hold, however, we can speculate that the issues surrounding the supercollider, and addressed by OTA, will be revisited by a future president seeking advice from a number of sources, including the appointed science advisor.

The Science Advisor

The legacy of Vannevar Bush, in fashioning the framework for funding of science and technology during the Roosevelt administration, was to establish the dominant role the federal government exercises in influencing university scientific research. Bush set a precedent not only for current policy makers to wrestle with but demonstrated the need for the president, who may have no extensive training in science and technology, to have a science advisor. Still, Bush's appointment as science advisor was informal, and James Killian became the first titled Science Advisor in 1958 under President Eisenhower. Interestingly, Killian proved an initial exception to the developing trend of appointing physicists to the position. A trained humanist, Killian rose to an administrative position at the Massachusetts Institute of Technology and in the process gained acceptance in the scientific community.

Aside from being a presidential appointee, the science advisor, after passage of the Office of Science and Technology Policy Act in 1976, is the director of the OSTP, a relatively small department consisting of approximately 70 staff members. The OSTP provides information on various aspects of science and technology for the president, comments on proposals, coordinates interagency policy, and acts as a conduit between the executive branch and scientific and technical communities. Senior staff members stay on the job usually no longer than the science advisor, so each time a presidential administration changes, a new staff is assembled. The science advisor also chairs the President's Council of Advisors in Science and Technology. Created in 1989, the PCAST consists of members appointed by the president from academia, engineering, industry, and science. Through the PCAST and the OSTP, the science advisor exerts persuasive influence over the president but little else. Much of the effectiveness of the science advisor rests on a personal relationship with the president.

Members of the larger science community, as well as the general public, have questioned the role of science advisors as both ideological cheerleaders and as experts giving advice about issues with which they are unfamiliar. One of the most common complaints about the science advisor is that he is almost always a physicist, albeit extraordinarily credentialed. Accordingly, another complaint is that the input of the other natural and social sciences has not been fairly represented or funded. Physics, often portrayed as the dominant science discipline, represents only one model of how scientific research can be effectively conducted. Critics complain that aspects of the physics model, its organization, methods, and history of progress, have been unreasonably translated into policy-making standards for all sciences. As one critic has noted, what the president really needs advice on is not the conduct of science per se, but how the government can support the growth and use of technology.

Although the science advisor comes predominantly from one discipline, the appointment has not been seen as politically motivated. However, Ronald Reagan's advisor George Keyworth broke with tradition in openly promoting the distinction between the public and private concerns of science and technology policy. Whereas policy had previously been directed toward promoting "national well-being," Keyworth seized the opportunity to blur the line between "well-being" and defense. Keyworth's strategy became evident in his open promotion of the Strategic Defense Initiative (SDI). The opinions of scientists who had doubts about SDI were not always passed on to the president. Consequently, disgruntled OSTP staff members quit. The White House staff also became displeased with Keyworth's outspokenness and took the opportunity to call for the abolishment of the OSTP. However, Keyworth resigned in 1985 and was replaced by the deputy administrator of NASA, William Graham, an electrical engineer.

The influence of the science advisor is constrained by the system within the White House and the president's own initiatives. The science advisor may be viewed skeptically or cut out of the process altogether. Nevertheless, even though the science advisor's power is limited, it is not apolitical. All science advisors must wrestle with their own advocacy of science and technology, the president's ideology, and the function of other federal agencies.

Beyond the Budget

Budget Controls Policy. The budget for scientific research is assembled by the Office of Management and Budget (OMB), which analyzes the budgets of all federal agencies before they are submitted to Congress, with emphasis on programs of interest to the president. Some of the criteria looked at in investing in research are prestige, spin-off applications and technologies, and national security implications. The OMB sets goals for funding, taking into account the needs of other federal agencies given the discretion of budget examiners located in several government divisions. Working with specific agency budget makers, members of the OMB negotiate fiscal allocation, priority setting and research funding. Budget negotiation takes place behind the scenes and is not subject to public deliberation. The OMB has played a prominent role in setting the financial agenda for big-science projects. Since 1991, caps have been placed on discretionary spending for defense, domestic, and international spending. Consequently, the power of the OMB lies in negotiating within the executive branch how money is allocated among specific programs.[3]

Several independent groups provide a link between the scientific and engineering community and the executive branch. The members of the National Academy of Sciences, for instance, are solicited to provide reports on issues about science and technology and to serve on panels and commissions. Other groups exerting influence on the executive branch include the National Academy of Engineering and the Institute of Medicine. Lobbying groups also exert considerable, yet not unquestioned, influence on federal science and technology policy. As of 1989 there were an estimated 6,000 public and special interest groups. Although lobbying groups are usually associated with legislative decision making, the agriculture and energy lobbies have an important role in directing policy.

The centralized authority of the president allows for a distinct advantage over Congress in setting research and funding priorities. Although agencies such as the OTA (in the past) and the Congressional Budget Office provide Congress with invaluable policy-making resources, the fate of the research dollar rests with the OMB. Perhaps the most striking characteristics about the process of executive science and technology policy making is that it is largely undemocratic, often relying on internal party politics and the advice of well-qualified but ideologically connected experts (see Barke, 1986, chap. 4).

The Legislative Branch

In opposition to the centralized authority in the executive branch, Congress chooses to decentralize authority in the policy-making process. Approximately 150 of the 303 committees and subcommittees of Congress (as of 1991) have some jurisdiction over research. In the 101st Congress the House had 22 committees and 146 subcommittees, and the Senate had 16 committees and 87 subcommittees. There were 9 select committees, with 11 subcommittees, and 4 joint committees, with 8 subcommittees. Significant committees with legislative jurisdiction over research include Public Works and Transportation and Space, Science and Technology in the House, and Labor and Human Resources and Commerce, Science and Transportation in the Senate. Through their longevity, many of these committees have become permanent fixtures by carving out their own turf. As you can see, given the number of committees and subcommittees, policy development in science and technology can be slowed by debate concerning who has control over what issue. Still, the people selected to chair these committees have the opportunity to exert long-term influence over the development of certain programs.

Just as is the case with most presidents, representatives generally have little or no training in the sciences and technology. Through support agencies such as the Science Policy Research

Division and the Technology Assessment Board, which governs the OTA, Congress has attempted to improve its access to the scientific and technological community. But congressional priorities shift. Founded in 1972, the OTA assessed the impact of technology such as coal-slurry pipelines and rural communications systems by producing reports, giving oral briefings and issuing memoranda. The importance of the OTA increased over the years as indicated in 1985 when Congress transferred $700,000 from the National Academy of Sciences to the OTA to study SDI. The OTA studied mine reclamation, nuclear waste disposal, and retraining workers displaced by technology. In September, 1995, the OTA was the first government agency eliminated under the "Republican revolution." OTA now exists on CD-Rom and the World Wide Web as a "virtual agency"—perhaps the first of many.

Aside from support agencies, Congress has several means of affecting science and technology policy, including appropriations, earmarking legislation, and public hearings.

Appropriations

Through the appropriation process, Congress possesses its most powerful means for controlling science and technology policy. The appropriations process consists of two stages: program authorization and appropriation. Authorizing committees report on programs under their jurisdiction and set spending caps for the maximum amount of money spent on a particular program. These committees are most effective when new agencies are created and when authorizing funds to initiate, upgrade, or end a program. Authorization bills are used to oversee how, and on what programs, government agencies spend money.

Once the president's budget reaches Congress, it is met by resolutions of committees in both houses that set spending limits in certain areas. Appropriations bills control the spending of authorized funds for programs. Consequently, authorized money cannot be spent unless it is also appropriated. For example, in 1980, the Magnetic Fusions Energy Engineering Act authorized $20 billion for research and development on magnetic fusion over the next 20 years. However, the money was not appropriated by the House Committee on Appropriations (and its 13 subcommittees), so actual expenditures for the program dropped to about $330 million in 1986 (Barke, 1986, pp. 25-26). In some instances, agencies affected by the president's budget receive more budget authority than originally proposed. As a result, appropriations committees try to modify the authorizing to earmark more funds for special projects.

Earmarking

Historically, the term "earmark" comes from the practice of cutting off pigs' ears before the animals were sent to graze in a common area. The owner could get credit, or a "mark," for stolen or slaughtered pigs by producing their ears. Today, the term refers to the direct appropriation of funds for a project by Congress. The earmarking process, although not widespread, is a tradition within the legislative branch. Powerful legislators can bring home the federal bacon (or "pork") in supporting local projects such as roadways or a sewage treatment plant. More recently, earmarking has made its way into the academic arena in the funding of scientific research.

The OTA defines a congressional earmark as a "project, facility, instrument, or other academic research-related expense that is directly funded by Congress, which has not been subjected to peer review and will not be competitively awarded" (Chubin, 1991, p. 87). One of the largest beneficiaries of earmarked funds according to this definition (among others) was the Soybean Laboratory at the University of Illinois-Urbana. Other definitions of earmarking have been used within Congress to procure or deny procurement of funds by legislators. The earmarking process has special significance within the scientific community because it violates one of the defining characteristics of scientific funding—merit.

Proponents of earmarking point to the fact that respected research has been produced by this practice. Also, earmarking serves to provide a form of equity between the "haves," major land-grant or research universities, and the "have nots," other academic institutions, such as historically African-American universities. Proponents of earmarking note that the peer review system is thoroughly biased and perpetuates the cycle of the rich getting richer. As a partial result, diverse views and backgrounds are treated as incidental to the process of science. Moreover, funds are distributed inequitably even by region.

Each major geographical region has a number of institutions that should be able to compete on equal terms for funds, therefore distributing centers of research excellence throughout the country. However, 40% of earmarked funds go to just five states, among them Massachusetts, New York, and Florida, and two-thirds of the rest of the states, among them Virginia, Nebraska, and Missouri, receive less than 10% of earmarked funds. Additionally, from 1980 to 1989, 20 academic institutions, among them Stanford, MIT, and the University of Washington, received 60% of all earmarked funds (Chubin, 1991, Appendix B).

The scientific community has always held that the merit of a research project, as determined through the peer review system, should be the primary basis for awarding federal funds. Even though the peer review system itself has come under heavy criticism, earmarking is seen as an even more direct assault on the equitable funding of scientific research. Opponents of earmarking point to the fact that projects worthy of funding do not receive a fair hearing when funds are directly appropriated. All research proposals should be treated the same way, and all proposals should be subject to peer review. Because the federal government faces the impossible task of equitably distributing funds to the nation's 3,400 colleges and universities, 1,300 of which award science and engineering degrees, agencies should use results as the primary criteria for awarding funds. The top 100 institutions commanding the largest share of overall federal funding produce most of the doctorates in science and engineering (Chubin, 1991, p. 90). Thus, opponents of earmarking argue, research funding awarded competitively yields results that benefit the entire nation.

Given that the history of academic earmarking is short, a thorough analysis of the effect of earmarked funds on scientific research has yet to be completed. The concern over congressional earmarking may be misplaced if earmarked projects are found to have an equal or greater impact on scientific research (given specific criteria) as projects funded through peer review programs. On the other hand, if earmarked programs are found to be inferior, a change in the funding system is in order.

Public Hearings

By holding public hearings and investigations, Congress can substantially affect the direction of science and technology policy without legislation. Whereas bills are drafted to meet narrowly defined issues, public hearings can have broad implications for policy. Hearings mobilize interest groups to lobby certain agencies and raise voter awareness on specific issues. Public hearings also offer a chance to see "democracy in action" and provide a glimpse into what happens when the worlds of science, technology and politics collide.

From February 26, 1986, to May 2, 1986, a presidential commission appointed by President Reagan and chaired by William Rogers met to determine the cause of the explosion of the space shuttle *Challenger,* a disaster that profoundly affected the American consciousness and raised questions about the effect of political expediency on science and technology policy. The following exchange is taken from the transcript of the proceedings that took place on February 26, 1986. "Mr. Hardy" is George Hardy, then the deputy director of science and engineering at the Marshall Space Flight Center for NASA. "Chairman Rogers" is William Rogers, then the presiding chair of the committee. "Mr. Mulloy," mentioned in the testimony, is Larry Mulloy, then manager of the space shuttle solid rocket booster program at Marshall Space Flight Center. He is giving testimony concurrently.

> **Chairman Rogers:** Not being an engineer, and because I am surrounded by so many capable engineers, I would like to ask a question that is not an engineering question. At some point, I gather, you have to, you will agree that the colder the weather the greater the risk. Is that accurate?
>
> **Mr. Hardy:** I am not sure that is an accurate statement. I would say, and again, I am going to look at that question from the other side of 51-L. (the *Challenger* launch)
>
> **Chairman Rogers:** But I mean at the moment you are inclined to say it doesn't make any difference how cold it gets as far as the risk is concerned on the O-Rings?

Mr. Hardy: At the moment I would say that the consideration of the effect of temperature on the joint is certainly an active failure analysis, and there are some features of the joint, indeed, where temperature can affect it.

Chairman Rogers: But that's a key question, it seems to me, because if you in the back of your mind, in the back of Mr. Mulloy's mind you said it really doesn't make any difference how cold it gets as far as the joint is concerned.

Mr. Hardy: No, sir, I don't believe I said that.

Chairman Rogers: No. I am asking now do you think that at some point the coldness of the weather makes a difference on the risk?

Hardy: Well, I am sure there must be some point because there is some point at which the structural integrity of the O-Rings just wouldn't be maintained.

Chairman Rogers: At what point would that be?

Mr. Hardy: I think that would be somewhere in the minus 40, minus 50 range.

Chairman Rogers: So insofar as you are concerned now, it wouldn't make any difference about the risk in connection with the joints if it was above 40 below? In other words, I am trying to see what your thought process was. I think most people, or a lot of people have felt that the worse the weather, the more the risk insofar as these joints are concerned, and I guess you are saying you don't agree with that.

Mr. Hardy: Well, I think probably there might be dozens and dozens of things on the vehicle that one could say—

Chairman Rogers: No, I am talking about the O-Rings now and the joints.

Mr. Hardy: I could not in my mind quantify any increased risk—let me make sure I say that correctly. I could not in my mind determine that there was any increased risk to safety as a result of the temperature that we were discussing on the night of the 27th.

(Presidential Commission, 1986, vol. 5, pp. 871-872)

The testimony given in the investigation of the *Challenger* accident would forever change policy regarding space exploration. NASA, for example, had planned to deploy the Hubble space telescope in October 1986. That plan was delayed until April 1990, at which time it was discovered the $1.5-billion telescope had problems with its mirrors, making the images it sent back no clearer than those of ground telescopes. The public has grown impatient with huge investments of public money that yield failed results. It seems fantastic that cold weather could cause a sophisticated piece of technology like the shuttle to fail. As Hardy responds in his testimony, perhaps "dozens" of factors could have been responsible. Rogers assumes a populist persona, deferring to the expertise of the engineers in the room while persistently looking for a single, understandable explanation. In so doing, he asks the same question several ways, always coming back to the problem of temperature. Hardy counters that thinking about risk and temperature cannot be quantified, and the technology, while dependable, is, after all, complicated. This section of testimony defines many of the questions faced by policy-makers, the lay public, and scientists and engineers. Should policy-making regarding science and technology be a democratic process? Can an informed lay public who are not trained scientists and technologists scrutinize and evaluate science and technology? Should the conduct of science and technology be changed? What kind of communicative possibilities exist among speakers from divergent backgrounds?

LEGISLATION

The primary function of Congress is to make and enact laws. The complexity of science and technology, however, can make the writing of specific legislation nearly impossible. As a result, laws and regulations pertaining to science and technology either suffer from being too general, as phrases like the "best available option" indicate, or too specific, as Vice President Al Gore pointed out by displaying pages of specifications for making ashtrays for government use. Science and technology present unique legislative problems not only through their social complexity, but through their rapid change. Scientific discoveries and technological innovations routinely outpace the legislation meant to regulate them. Further, as science and technology extend throughout the marketplace, so do the uses and effects for particular products. A suggested approach to legislative decision-making about science and technology is to do so "scientifically" through cost-benefit analyses. Although these analyses offer some general guidance in policy-making, calculations can be wildly off the mark. Rarely do complex political and social decisions fit into neat scientific calculations. Lawmakers then must wrestle with the unintended consequences of regulating particular industries and technologies, a task as difficult as predicting the future.

In 1970, Congress passed, and President Nixon signed, the Occupational Health and Safety Act to insure the protection of workers. The law also created the Occupational Health and Safety Administration (OSHA). Previous labor struggles by coal miners and autoworkers demanding cleaner working conditions inspired the legislation which, in principle, gave workers the right to participate in decisions about the conditions under which they worked. Rank-and-file union members found legal support for their position and began to press for greater control over technological decisions. The corporate community worried that decisions over which technologies could be used legally by particular industries would rest exclusively in the hands of the state. Corporate rhetoric heralded the end of democracy and the end of private enterprise smothered by government regulation. Labor and environmental groups heralded the dawn of a new democratic era in which workers and interest groups could actively participate in making employers socially responsible. Regulations, business owners complained, weakened the entrepreneurial spirit vital for industry and the costs of compliance would drive some industries out of business. Throughout the 1970s, the battle over regulating industry and technology was waged on a number of fronts. The language of the legislation was legally attacked in 1978 by the textile industry, which claimed the new regulations were unduly burdensome because the cost of compliance had not been fully considered by Congress. In 1981, after a series of lower court rulings, the Supreme Court turned back the textile industry's challenge by holding that Congress did not intend that regulations were meant only for the companies that could afford them. Economic considerations were to be excluded from worker safety considerations.

In the early 1970s, the chemical industry, through a cost-benefit analysis, predicted it would cost $65-$90 billion to meet regulations controlling the exposure of workers to polyvinyl chloride (PVC). Essentially, this cost would force the industry into bankruptcy. However, the chemical industry eventually found innovative ways to meet the standards and was encouraged by the government to invest in new plants and technology. The eventual cost of the regulations was less than $1 billion (see Dickson, 1988, chap 6).

AN OVERALL PICTURE

The executive and legislative branches of government have separate roles in the policy-making process based on principle obligations and responsibilities under the law, and the shifting nature of scientific and technological research and development. The social, political, and institutional complexity of science, technology, and the federal government often make long-term policy making difficult. Even big-science projects are not assured of surviving the changing winds of government funding. Each agency in the executive and legislative branches possesses its own turf and power over a process that is as cyclical as the election of each new administration. The OMB oversees fiscal issues; the OSTP coordinates information on which the president makes decisions. The budgets for science and technology are nested within larger budgets, and these budgets are considered by specific agencies without any sense of the overall health of the funding process governing science and technology.

In the confusion and questions surrounding the local and national politics that affect science and technology policy, where do you fit in? Some of you will become scientists and engineers, some of you will pursue other careers, and some of you will compete for funding, authority and prestige, but all of you are implicated in a common fate. And while all of you will not agree about matters of policy, you can set standards in which the various and often contradictory skills and ideas you possess lead to quite different goals. Policy decisions regarding science and technology have been cast as winner-take-all propositions in which opposing interests (e.g., the chemical industry versus government regulators) require that one side succeed at the expense of the other. This type of thinking has been perpetuated by the idea that parties on the opposite side of an issue remain steadfast in their positions. Although communication will not lead to consensus, it will provide ways in which different goals can be harmoniously pursued.

In the first half of this century, courses in "civics" were taught in American public schools. One aim of these courses was to instruct students how democratic government worked, what their obligations were, and what political mechanisms were at their disposal. Today, we call civic participation and responsibility "empowerment." However, with respect to science and technology policy, we often feel powerless. Science education is wonderful at distributing facts and figures. As members of a technological society, we enjoy the fruits of the labor of scientific research and technological advancement, but we do nothing to influence the direction that science and technology will take.

Scientific and technical communicators inherit a unique perspective and position in helping mediate among various levels of expertise and interest. By studying and using scientific and technical communication in various contexts, one can engage in public debate concerning policy on both national and local levels. The biggest stumbling block to the formation of coherent policies on science and technology has been miscommunication and lack of access to information. An "exchange language" for ideas among people with different interests and professional backgrounds can be created by integrating various sources on science and technology (academic, journalistic, private) in professional communicative practices and in the policy arena.

Discussion

1. Would you consider yourself "attentive" to matters of science and technology generally and to matters of science and technology policy specifically? If you are a member of one of the scientific or technical fields, do you feel qualified to render informed decisions (which may be required in voting, serving on a community board, and serving on a jury) about science and technology outside your field? Explain your answer.

2. One of the claims of this chapter is that, in general, the "popular" images we have of science and technology, ranging from textbooks to television, are one-dimensional and hence inaccurate. If you are in a scientific or technical field, what images first inspired you (perhaps as a child) to become a practitioner? How do those images compare to actual practice? Do you agree that the accepted image of science lacks depth? Whose interests are served by promoting common perceptions of science and technology? Do you agree with Fuller (Chapter 7, Part II) on this point?

3. Technology is often defined as "applied science." Given this definition, science—and scientific advancement—is the fundamental engine of modern progress: All technology, then, owes its existence to the development of scientific theories. How would you define "technology"? How do you define the relationship between science and technology? Can you think of any examples in which a technological invention or advance came before, or led to, the development of a scientific theory?

4. In what ways has technology shaped what you consider "personal" or "private"? How have you used technology to find out information about another person with or without their consent? How have technologies redefined concepts such as gender, sexuality, intelligence, health, and beauty with which we define ourselves? How will technology continue to redefine those concepts? Can you think of other concepts that technology has essentially redefined that influence you?

5. How do you see the relationship between women, men, and technology portrayed in our society? Which technologies carry

with them the attributes of masculinity or femininity? In science and technology, how does the race or gender composition of a particular discipline or profession (e.g., the medical profession) influence the selection of problems and projects?

6. What are the similarities and differences in the views of national science policy proposed by Fuller (Chapter 7, Part II) and Tobias, Chubin, and Aylesworth (Chapter 12, Part II)? How do the recommendations the authors provide about future policy compare? What problems are presented by scientific policy being supervised by someone who is not a scientist? What problems are presented by scientists supervising other scientists?

Exercises

1. Assemble into groups of three or four. In a collaboratively written report, provide an analysis of a scientific or technological controversy. Such controversies typically involve a dispute among individuals and/or members of a group about the value of a research project, implementation of a government policy, or development of a technology. The contexts for the dispute can be wide-ranging: economic, political, environmental, methodological, philosophical, historical, or statistical. During a scientific and technological controversy, many basic assumptions that we hold regarding, for example, clear communication, what counts as evidence and knowledge, and boundaries between public and private interests come under scrutiny. The purpose of this assignment is to have you examine from both a practitioner's and a layperson's perspective the roles that science and technology play in public discourse.

Contemporary controversies often appear in the *New York Review of Books*, *The Times Higher Education Supplement*, *Critical Inquiry*, *The Skeptical Inquirer*, and the Tuesday science section of the *New York Times*. "Letters to the Editor" sections in journals such as *Science* and *Nature* provide summaries of ongoing controversies. Sunday editions of most major newspapers can also point you in the direction of current controversies.

Controversies are also addressed in the disciplines in which you are studying. Proposed changes in, and the ensuing debate over, the Endangered Species Act will affect practices in forestry, biology, and environmental science. Evidence concerning the possible harmful effects of technologies (from genetically altered plants and animals to high-voltage power lines) and the liability of designers and engineers are topics taken up in many of your classes.

In her edited volume on scientific and technological controversy, Dorothy Nelkin (1979/1984) identifies four general contexts in which controversies occur:

- *Efficiency versus equity.* Local or community concerns with costs, benefits, and justice. Examples are building or modifying airports, power plants, highways, or landfills and environmental racism—building incinerators or landfills in impoverished and racially homogeneous areas. Questions of efficiency and equity also occur on national levels regarding the funding of "big science" projects. For instance, what benefits does society get from "big science"? Couldn't the money be better spent elsewhere—on poverty programs, for example? Examples are funding for the failed superconducting supercollider, SDI, the Human Genome Project, the Hubble space telescope, a planned space station, and a manned space mission to Mars.

- *Benefits versus risks.* Fear of potential health and environmental hazards. Examples are nuclear waste disposal, use of growth hormones or synthetic drugs in making animals more productive, occupational health standards (e.g., with what chemicals can people work and for how long?), damming, rerouting or using waterways for irrigation, the results of the Human Genome Project, or developing chemical weapons systems.

- *Regulation versus freedom of choice.* Restrictions imposed by the government on freedom of choice. Supporters of government defend regulation; opponents want less government interference. Examples are lack of immediate availability of certain drugs (e.g., experimental AIDS or cancer treatments), federal risk assessment procedures, regulation of the Internet (e.g., what information can be posted—is hate speech permissible?), intellectual property rights, federally mandated safety regulation on technologies, cars, powerlines, construction materials and methods, household technologies, environmental protection legislation, and federally mandated immunization programs.

- *Science versus traditional values.* Controversies over research procedures and science education in the public schools. Examples are fetal tissue research, biomedical research (recombinant

DNA), the use of animals in experiments, doctor-assisted suicide, teaching Darwinian theory and/or current geological theories at the exclusion of teaching creationism, and the problems, causes, and effects of transferring technologies and methods produced by industrial countries to developing countries.

Here is a fifth context in which to examine controversies:

▓ *Science versus pseudoscience.* Controversies over whether certain phenomena actually exist and cause particular effects and the uses of empirical evidence to validate or invalidate given claims. Examples are debates over the existence of the greenhouse effect, the efficacy of psychoanalysis, the methodological problems of studying other cultures (i.e., explaining Captain Cook's death at the hands of Hawaiian natives in the late 18th century), room temperature (cold) fusion, the rise of Satanism in the late 1980s, a relation between celestial phenomena and personal destiny, an afterlife as evidenced in near-death experiences, and repressed memory syndrome. Also included in this category are debates over scientific hoaxes such as Piltdown Man, N-rays, evidence of "alien visitations" (e.g., crop circles), and a "missing link" in the fossil record.

In analyzing controversies, (a) determine the participants in the controversy and define their views about science and technology in the context of the debate; (b) analyze the arguments, evidence, and terms presented by groups and individuals in the controversy; and (c) evaluate, given your analysis, and draw conclusions about the positions presented in the controversy.

Here are some specific strategies and issues to consider:

▓ Map out and identify the constituencies involved. What groups or individuals are participating in the controversy? What is the agenda of each of these groups? Do all the members of a certain group agree? About what issues do they disagree? Examples of constituencies are consumer advocacy and safety groups, unions, professional societies and associations, manufacturers, lobbyists, scientists, engineers, educators, government representatives (on national and local levels), and the lay public.

▓ Provide a history of the specific controversy—not a general history of the science or the technological artifact. When did the controversy arise? Under what circumstances? What other historical and social factors contributed to the controversy? Do the groups and individuals in the debate see and tell the history differently? What is significant about these differences?

▓ Show how evidence is used to make a particular group or person's case. How is experimental evidence interpreted? Do groups and individuals interpret experimental results in the same way? Why or why not? How are statistics and polling data used? If experiments have been performed, are they sound? Have experiments been replicated?

▓ Analyze how technical communication and language are used. What types of documents make appearances in the debate? What role does technical jargon play? How are visual representations used? What role do the media play? How do the participants try to convince opponents or one another? What rhetorical appeals (to, for example, freedom, choice, economic gain, expertise, truth, objectivity, democracy, autonomy, knowledge) are used in the debate?

▓ Examine the use of experts in the controversy. Who are the experts? How did they achieve their expertise? Why should one listen to experts? Do experts agree? Can agreement among experts bring the controversy to a close?

▓ Determine if the debate can be, or has, ended. Did overwhelming scientific evidence convince all of the participants? Can an experiment or technological invention bring a controversy to an end? How does a scientific or technological controversy achieve closure?

In selecting a topic, please keep in mind that the purpose of the report, and the chapters that comprise it, is to analyze an aspect of science and/or technology, which you define, in the context of the controversy. The purpose then is not to tell a story about the rise in reports about Satanic activity in the 1980s, for example, but to show how science and/or technology shaped, or was shaped by, the aspects of the controversy about which you are reporting.

2. A number of accounts have been written about the shuttle *Challenger* accident, among them three popular books that look at the Rogers Commission investigations: Malcolm McConnell's *Challenger: A Major Malfunction,* Richard Lewis's *Challenger: The Final Voyage,* and Joseph Trento's *Prescription for Disaster.* In reading one of these accounts, analyze the function of witnessing from the viewpoint of the lay public and the testimony of scientific and technical experts. In your

analysis, consider the following questions: Do you think that the lay public should be involved directly in witnessing experiments? Did the lay public see something fundamentally different from the experts? Does the use of technical language help the audience or experts see certain aspects of the explosion? What threats did the *Challenger* disaster pose to the way scientific experiments and projects are designed?

3. In 1850, Joseph Paxton built the Crystal Palace in London. The Crystal Palace was heralded as an unparalleled architectural and engineering achievement and stood as a symbol of the future of modern technology. The Paris World Fair in 1855, the Paris World Exhibition in 1878, and the Chicago World's Fair in 1933 had exhibits that predicted what effect science and technology would have on life in the future. Contemporary futurists like Alvin Toffler in *Future Shock* and futurist groups (e.g., the World Watch Institute) have made less optimistic predictions of our time to come.

   Divide into groups of three to five. Each group researches a world's fair futurist exhibit, or contemporary future predictions and collectively writes a short, informal essay analyzing visions of the future based on scientific and technological forecasts. In analyzing the success or failure of predictions in the exhibits, or the probable success of recent predictions, consider what attitudes toward science and technology are demonstrated. In an informal oral presentation and class discussion, compare and contrast the findings of your research in considering how participants in different historical eras came to see both the promise and peril of science and technology.

4. To participate in social debates concerning science, technology, and your professional and personal interests, you must learn to argue your case in a clear and incisive manner. Prepare a debate on the merits of a controversial issue regarding science and technology. The issues raised in this chapter provide a general framework with which to consider the issues, but no specific guidance. Here are a list of possible resolutions:

- What passes for "science" these days is so big that it is better seen as a kind of transnational corporation than a knowledge-producing enterprise.
- Science and technology gain strength from having clear disciplinary boundaries.
- Science can refute all criticism made about it from nonscientists.
- Laypersons should regard the claims of the natural sciences and the social sciences in the same way.
- Knowledge is powerful because only a few people have it.
- Laypersons should/should not be involved in the process of determining science and technology policy on any level (national, state, or local).
- Critics of science and technology understand the nature of science and technology better than scientists and technologists do.
- It takes a special psychological makeup to become a successful scientist or engineer.

Divide into groups of four. Two of you take the affirmative side of the resolution and the other two the negative side. In typical debates (such as Oxford-style debates), resolutions are presented in somewhat vague terms. The opening move of debaters is to give the resolution a specific interpretation. The negative side must address that interpretation. Both sides do research and work collaboratively to lend the debate coherence. The affirmative side has 20 minutes, the negative side 10 minutes for rebuttal, and then 20 minutes to present their position, with 10 minutes for affirmative side's rebuttal. Fifteen minutes are dedicated to unrehearsed questions from the audience. This exercise is designed to simulate the following features of real-world policy debates:

- An audience uninformed about the issues but potentially receptive to what you have to say
- A time constraint
- Taking a clear position that the audience understands.

The policy arena at the local, state, and national levels has its own character that must be addressed by professionals but is often lost on academics and classroom training. In lobbying to the public, government officials, or even officials within the same industry, you will need to integrate academic, journalistic, and professional sources in analyzing the political agendas of science and technology and in constructing a persuasive argument.

An alternative to oral debates is to debate the same resolutions in a writing assignment. Split into groups of four, with two of you presenting the affirmative argument and the other two the rebuttal and negative argument. Those of you on the affirmative side offer a conclusion.[4]

NOTES

1. Research into the cognitive ability based on gender has reached no consensus (see, e.g., Halpern, 1986).
2. K. S. Shrader-Frechette (1985, p. 18) cites Lowrance (1976, pp. 70-74) in her definition of "risk," which we have modified.
3. Chubin (1991, chap. 3) provides more detail on the function of the OMB and other interest groups on research funding.
4. This exercise is inspired by Fuller (1993, appendix).

BIBLIOGRAPHY

Barke, R. (1986). *Science, technology and public policy.* Washington, DC: Congressional Quarterly Press.

Checkoway, B. (1980). Public hearings are not. *Citizen Participation, 1,* 6-7.

Chubin, D. (Project Director). (1991). *Federally funded research: Decisions for a decade.* Washington, DC: Office of Technology Assessment.

Clinton, W., & Gore, A. (1993). *Technology for America's economic growth: A new direction to build economic strength.* Washington, DC: Government Printing Office.

Dickson, D. (1988). *The new politics of science.* Chicago: University of Chicago Press.

Feyerabend, P. (1978). *Science in a free society.* London: New Left Books.

Fuller, S. (1993). *Philosophy, rhetoric and the end of knowledge.* Madison: University of Wisconsin Press.

Gilbert, G. N., & Mulkay, M. (1981). Putting philosophy to work: Karl Popper's influence on scientific practice. *Philosophy of the Social Sciences, 11,* 389-407.

Gude, G. (Project Director). (1987). *Expertise and democratic decision making: A reader.* Washington, DC: Government Printing Office.

Halpern, D. (1986). *Sex differences in cognitive abilities.* Hillsdale, NJ: Lawrence Erlbaum.

Hollinger, D. (1990). Free enterprise and free inquiry. *New Literary History, 21,* 897-919.

Kaplan, N., Choy, M., & Whitmore, J. (1992, February). Indochinese refugee families and academic achievement. *Scientific American*, pp. 36-42.

Lowrance, W. (1976). *Of acceptable risk*. Los Altos, CA: Kaufmann.

Merton, R. (1973). *The sociology of science*. Chicago: University of Chicago Press.

Miller, J., Suchner, R., & Voelker, A. (1980). *Citizenship in an age of science*. New York: Pergamon.

National medals are pinned on 30 scientists. (1990, November 15). *The Washington Post*, p. A23.

Nelkin, D. (Ed.). (1979). *Controversy: Politics of technical decisions*. Beverly Hills, CA: Sage. (2nd ed., 1984; 3rd ed., 1991)

Nelkin, D. (Ed.). (1985). *The language of risk: Conflicting perspectives on occupational health*. Beverly Hills, CA: Sage.

Peterson, J. (Ed.). (1984). *Citizen participation in science policy*. Amherst: University of Massachusetts Press.

Presidential Commission. (1986). *Report of the Presidental Commission on the space shuttle Challenger accident* (vol. 5, pp. 871-872). Washington, DC: Government Printing Office.

Rouse, J. (1987). *Knowledge and power*. Ithaca, NY: Cornell University Press.

Sassower, R. (1993). *Knowledge without expertise: On the status of scientists*. Albany: State University of New York Press.

Shrader-Frechette, K. S. (1985). *Risk analysis and scientific method*. Dordrecht: D. Reidel.

Studenmaier, J. (1985). *Technology's storytellers: Reweaving the human fabric*. Cambridge: MIT Press.

Stigler, G. (1984). *The intellectual and the marketplace*. Cambridge, MA: Harvard University Press.

The Reader

Introduction to Chapter 7

We are familiar with many images of science and technology. We see science as the relentless and progressive pursuit of truth. We regard science and technology as self-governing, monolithic institutions standing as a tribute to human rationality and pragmatism. We heed science as dealing strictly with facts—supported by a foundation of objectivity, a universal acceptance of logical principles, and the scientific method—and as the arbiter of disputes concerning knowledge and superstition. We assume that science supplies theories, and technology applies those theories. Ultimately, we believe that our faith in these images will be rewarded in the future by the products of research we cannot now imagine. To a significant degree these images of science and technology, and our faith in them, are misleading.

Much of our national policy has been cast in light of this image of research. Many argue that because scientific and technological research is highly organized, technically sophisticated, and yields results, it should be, at best, left alone and, at worst, left in the hands of experts. In effect, the governance of science and technology should be the responsibility of the same scientists and engineers who receive public funding. As taxpayers, we are asked to leave our money at the laboratory door and wait to see what the result will be. And yet as taxpayers, we demand an accounting of the costs we are expected to pay and the benefits we expect to receive.

When we place science and technology in different contexts, we receive new, accessible, and accurate images. We learn from philosophy that science is more than the logical extension and application of axiomatic systems derived from physics. We learn from history that science is not just a timely procession of revolutionary geniuses and that technology can, in fact, predate the scientific theories explaining it. We learn from sociology that the goals of scientists are not just driven by a quest for truth but often reflect negotiations and compromises with colleagues, sponsoring departments, and grant-giving agencies. As a result, we begin to see a new image of science—an image that would bring fresh approaches to science policy and stress to nonscientists the importance of understanding science and technology. Science and technology are as diverse, intriguing and affected by change as other social institutions. Looking behind the technical prose and jargon, we can investigate the factors influencing research and development. By attending to those factors in our communicative practices, we can, as Steve Fuller suggests, bring people "back into the business of science."

Steve Fuller challenges us to examine our assumptions about the relationship between science and democracy while presenting us with a new picture of how scientific inquiry takes place. Discussion and debate involving national science and technology policy, Fuller argues, continues to be overshadowed by the unfulfilled promise of large-scale, cutting-edge science projects. The focus on these projects ignores both needs for basic scientific teaching and research, and questions concerning social and educational welfare. We ignore these needs and questions because we defer to, and invest our faith in, the authority of traditional *images* of science. How then, as citizens in a participatory democracy, can we become participants in managing science? Fuller offers three strategies for developing an accountable science policy process, based on historical and sociological accounts of scientific research.

CHAPTER

Putting People Back Into the Business of Science
Constituting a National Forum for Setting the Research Agenda

STEVE FULLER

Science occupies the sacred space of modern democracies. Generally speaking, modern democracies are hard to govern because they must balance issues of *equity* against those of *efficiency* among diverse and mobile constituencies.[1] The time it takes to deliberate over who deserves what (equity) works at cross-purposes with the need to deliver what is deserved in a timely fashion (efficiency). Small wonder, then, that democratic theorists have been willing to make trade-offs. On the one hand, market liberals have argued that equity will take care of itself as a by-product of private individuals tending to their own interests. On the other hand, proponents of the welfare state doubt this rosy free market scenario and prefer instead to ensure that everyone's minimal needs are satisfied, regardless of the inconvenience that this poses for some people. How does *science* figure in the democratic balancing act?

The general problem of democracy is compounded in the case of science because of the awe and mystery surrounding it. Witness the persistent failure of nerve and imagination modern democracies have displayed in their attempts to articulate the exact relationship between science and societal goals. In fact, "more science" is such a pervasive part of the solutions proposed to standing social problems that few people have taken the trouble of thinking of science itself as a social problem.[2] Billions of dollars are annually "invested" in scientific projects, the ultimate value of which is assumed on a faith that largely goes unexamined. This faith is epitomized in the credo: "Even if science never quite solves our social problems, nevertheless it is a good in its own right that can do no harm if left to its own devices." In what follows, we shall subject this profession of faith to some critical scrutiny. Our considerations are framed by a pair of questions: What are the consequences of science as it is practiced today on both its cutting-edge contributors (who work in the major research universities) and its more peripheral participants (who work in the small teaching colleges)? Are their lives enhanced or diminished by their involvement in the conduct of scientific inquiry?

SCIENCE POLICY IN AMERICA TODAY—
DECENTRALIZED AND TRICKLE-DOWN

Science enjoys an especially sacred status in the United States, the world's largest producer and consumer of scientific knowledge products. The sacredness of science is immediately evident from the verbal impediments one faces in trying to comprehend it in a policy context. In its treatment of science, the U.S. Office of Management and Budget appears to follow the common religious practice of referring to a sacred object only under a partial description.[3] Thus, the federal budget allotment for "research and development" (R&D)—the expression policymakers use to refer to scientific knowledge production—is never discussed in its totality but is indirectly referred to in line items of the budgets of particular mission-oriented agencies. These include the Departments of Defense, Energy, Agriculture, and Health and Human Services, the Environmental Protection Agency, and the National Aeronautics and Space Administration. Unlike most nations today, the United States lacks a cabinet-level Department of Science & Technology. The only federal agency that specifically mentions "science" as part of its mission—the National Science Foundation—ranks a mere fifth among the recipients of federal R&D funds. Add to this already diffuse image the fact that the most expensive and most glamorous scientific projects of the last decade—the Human Genome Project, the Hubble space telescope, the orbiting space station, and the superconducting supercollider—have received their funding directly from Congress, for the most part bypassing the usual agency channels.

As this brief survey suggests, despite the periodic calls for Americans to "take back" their government, the public's reach fails to grasp the governance of science. On the one hand, Americans are clearly dissatisfied with a trickle-down economic policy that relegates most workers to the status of consumers of whatever investment opportunities the government happens to encourage in the rich. On the other hand, we have yet to question this country's even longer standing policy of trickle-down science. This is a policy that reduces most of us to willing—or not so willing—consumers of machines, potions, and symbols—products the design over which we exert little control. This difference in attitude to trickle-down approaches is a lesson that has come hard in the economic sphere and remains unlearned in the science sphere, namely, that the aims of all policy—even science policy—should focus more on the *employment of people* than the *manufacture of products.*

REPRESENTING THE DIVERSE AND
TROUBLED WORKFORCE OF SCIENCE

Like any other large-scale, multi-billion-dollar public works project, the success of America's long-term science policy will depend on the cooperation of its citizens. Most of us will be involved not just as grateful consumers but as workers committed to getting the job done. Typical of recent attempts to include a wider segment of the population in science policy is the 1992 Carnegie Commission Report, *Enabling the Future: Linking Science and Technology to Societal Goals.*[4] This report calls for an independent "National Forum" consisting of representatives of various groups that have a stake in the research agenda of tomorrow. So far so good. However, these groups must be imaginatively selected. The federal government has already set a good precedent for including women and ethnic minorities in other agenda-setting forums, but science policy introduces classes of stakeholders, most of whom have yet to be properly heard. These classes are not neatly categorized as either "clients" or "consumers" of scientific research. Their impact on the production and distribution of scientific knowledge is rather direct. Who, then, are these missing voices?

To answer this question, let us begin with an important sign of the Carnegie Commission's deafness to the missing voices. The report calls for the representation of both "top down" and "bottom up" approaches to science policy at a National Forum. Usually, the highlighted terms refer, respectively, to "establishment" and "grassroots" organizers. But a quick inspection of the Carnegie report reveals that "top down" corresponds to Washington politicians and policy makers, whereas "bottom up" corresponds to eminent scientists and engineers. Still more indicative of the elitist cast of these proceedings is the report's recommendation that safeguards be taken against a national forum becoming a vehicle for groups traditionally hostile to science and technology, such as environmental activists.

However, the troublesome groups are not about to disappear. If excluded from the policy process at the outset, their voices will only be heard later and perhaps more loudly. They will simply refuse to accept new scientific knowledge products. The annals of big business are littered with cases in which ideas that looked great on paper were stillborn because they were alien to the needs and interests of potential users. A subtle variation on this theme can be detected in the case of "big science," a phrase frequently used to describe the gargantuan character of post-World War II scientific research.[5] What we see here is not a few backward souls, "nature lovers" who fail to appreciate the gifts bestowed by modern science and technology. On the contrary, the biggest potential source of opposition to cutting-edge scientific research is found among science educators teaching in institutions of higher learning not primarily devoted to research. These institutions include both community and liberal arts colleges as well as most state university campuses. This group may include nearly every teacher of science outside of the thirty universities that have shared 50% of federal R&D dollars in recent years. What interest do such teachers ultimately have in supporting research, little of which is ever likely to make its way into the undergraduate curriculum? Only a trickle-down mentality would assume there is a natural fit between the research carried out in those top 30 schools and the teaching carried out in the other 2,000 institutions of higher learning in America.

This last point receives indirect support from a study undertaken by Carnegie Foundation President Ernest Boyer.[6] In his widely acclaimed 1990 report, *Scholarship Reconsidered,* Boyer formally identified and analyzed one of the open secrets of higher education, namely, that the scholarly perspectives of the most prestigious members of an academic discipline do not represent those of rank-and-file practitioners. Although the average faculty member strongly identifies with the discipline in which she was trained, the skills and qualities she associates with her discipline depends on her place of work. Consequently, physicists working in research universities tend to believe that cutting-edge research is what their field is all about, whereas physicists in community colleges believe that teaching is the core of their field.

Boyer's report hardly conveys the impression that teaching-oriented faculty are eager consumers of research. Rather, the image is more one of teachers being increasingly forced to adapt their work habits to the research mode, as their home institutions seek greater academic status. Boyer sees his own task as one of discouraging those institutions from evaluating their scholarly missions by the standards of the large research universities. Such a yardstick is bound to prove frustrating for all concerned—administrators, faculty, and students. It can lead to a backlash effect, whereby teaching-oriented institutions boycott cutting-edge research, say, by refusing to subscribe to the expensive scientific journals that typically publish such research.

Why, then, should a National Forum foster the contraction of higher education's diverse scholarly missions by including only faculty who define their work in terms of cutting-edge research? Instead, it would seem that the Forum should include representatives of each of the nine institutional types identified in Boyer's "Carnegie Classification."[7] This level of inclusiveness would ensure that faculty in community and liberal arts colleges, as well as in comprehensive teaching universities, are given a voice alongside faculty in research universities.

At stake in these hypothetical deliberations is the delicate question of how a scientific discipline should be represented in a National Forum. Do all members of the faculty of physics departments count equally as contributors to the discipline of physics? The answer is clearly no, if we focus on who has the biggest impact on the research agenda of the physics community. But is that where we should focus? Boyer's report suggests that if each physics professor were to count for only one vote, the majority would call for research more teachable to students and more transferable across disciplines. For all its democratic reasonableness, the "one person, one vote" principle actually goes against the grain of contemporary academic scientific self-governance, whose sociological character most closely resembles that of an oligarchy of elders.[8] Between the democratic tendency to represent scientists by their place of work and the elitist tendency of having scientists represented by their most distinguished colleagues, it may be argued that scientists are better represented by their professional associations. In many cases, professional associations challenge the self-serving research priorities proposed by a field's most prestigious practitioners. One recent case that received much publicity centered on the physics community. In 1991, the Council of the American Physical Society wondered aloud whether the future of basic research in the field was being jeopardized by tying up so much money in the multi-billion-dollar superconducting super collider project, about which more later.[9]

However, before the reader develops an unrealistic view of the democratic potential of professional associations, she would best see bodies like the American Physical Society as operating much as political parties do. They serve constituents who will maintain and strengthen their numbers in the local precincts of higher learning. Sometimes the associations do a good job of representing the interests of the rank-and-file disciplinary practitioners, but sometimes they cave in to the special interests of the more elite practitioners. Given the latter possibility, it is important that faculty also be represented in a National Forum according to the type of institution in which they work.

At this point, the reader may find it helpful to examine some collateral information about the social structure of science before deciding on the best way to secure representation in a National Forum.

SOME EVIDENCE FROM THE HISTORY AND SOCIOLOGY OF SCIENCE

Scientists often make it seem as though most scientific research consists of little more than solving the puzzles left behind by a revolutionary genius.[10] Typically, the work of such a genius—say, Newton's *Principia Mathematica* or Darwin's *On the Origin of Species*—is presented as an achievement of such magnitude that the rest of the scientific community gladly takes up the challenge of tying up the genius's loose ends. However, close inspection of the historical record reveals that these supposed works of genius were not immediately recognized as such. For example, the amazing powers imputed to Newton's mathematical vision of physical reality grew in direct proportion to the number of groups—both scientific and nonscientific—who found it in their interest to subscribe to Newton's way of seeing things. These alignments had less to do with prolonged exposure to Newton's own text and more to the work of partisans who translated "Newtonianism" into a variety of idioms, including those of education and politics. Whereas Newton actively promoted himself, less outgoing "geniuses," such as Darwin and Einstein, were fortunate to have in their corner such first-rate advocates as Thomas Huxley and Max Planck. Otherwise, they too would have joined the multitude of intellectually ambitious and technically proficient scientists whose works sank without a trace because of their inability to attract the support of a broad enough constituency.

Because relatively few scientists come to be recognized as either revolutionary geniuses or even distinguished technicians, it is tempting to conclude that science education at the graduate level sets students up for long-term career frustration. The pattern noted here is most pronounced in the natural sciences, yet that does not stop the social sciences and other fledgling fields from copying the natural sciences in their worst tendencies. All this does is to enhance the legitimacy of the more mature sciences, regardless of palpable differences in subject matter. For example, social theorists are perennially drawn to analogies between, on the one hand, intrinsic human agency and extrinsic social control and, on the other, the principle of inertia and the law of gravity.[11] One is then led to believe that society is nothing more than an elaborate network of mechanical pushes and pulls on people. Even though physicists now find such images of mechanism quaint, if not embarrassing, they continue to live on in the minds and theories of social scientists.[12] And what applies to research practice applies with a vengeance to research training.

Perhaps the most striking pattern of graduate science training is that it is devoted almost entirely to the development of cutting-edge research skills, with little, if any, attention paid to the interpersonal skills needed for teaching and administration. Yet most science PhDs who remain in academia are employed in teaching-oriented institutions. And even if a freshly minted PhD is fortunate enough to be employed in a research university, the value of her hard-earned skills is bound to depreciate at a rapid rate, *especially* if she trained in a field with a rapidly advancing research front. This last point helps explain why scientists tend to do their best work before they turn 40. Unless scientists continually upgrade their skills, they become obsolete as researchers within a dozen years out of graduate school. As a result, most scientists conduct the bulk of their professional lives in teaching and/or administrative posts for which they have received no formal training. Interestingly, these well-known facts have yet to elicit outrage from scholars of management and labor.[13]

On the contrary, the situation just described is often taken to be not merely normal but exemplary of science as a self-organizing enterprise. Indeed, the clearest reasons that federal policy-makers give for adopting a *laissez-faire* attitude to the allocation of R&D

funds turn on an analogy drawn between science's internal means of picking its winners—the so-called peer review process— and the "invisible hand" of the capitalist marketplace. The basic idea is that good scientists are in the best position to know—and to acknowledge—good science when they see it.[14] After all, are they not the primary consumers of scientific research? Without any special prompting from the government, science would seem capable of ranking its many practitioners according to the merit of their contributions. This hierarchy is more evident, the more mature the science is perceived to be. For example, in the more advanced natural sciences, it is not uncommon for 80% of the footnotes in journal articles to go to 20% of those publishing in the field.

In addition, more than two thirds of scientists who begin their professional careers by publishing research undertaken in graduate school will soon cease publication altogether. Typically, publication ends with the awarding of tenure, although often it results from discouragement born of the scientists' failure to generate interest in the "marketplace of ideas." The overall trend, then, is toward what sociologists call a principle of "cumulative advantage."[15] Scientists who distinguish themselves early in their careers—a group that nearly coincides with those who participate in the "old boy networks" of the prestigious research universities—tend to be the ones who distinguish themselves later on. As in capitalism, so too in science, the rich get richer, the poor get poorer. Of course, such a pattern is common to numerous large organizations. However, the difference is that in those other cases we often say that the organization suffers from a "structural bias" that systematically underutilizes the pool of available talent. Why not the same diagnosis in the case of science?

Lest the reader think otherwise, there *is* a strong positive correlation between initial R&D funding and the number of scientific publications subsequently generated. The most highly funded research universities produce the most professional papers. A similar tendency occurs at the international level, as nations with more lavish R&D budgets outpace the scientific publication of less endowed countries.[16] However, these facts address only issues of production, not of *productivity*: that is, the amount of scientific bang one gets for each R&D buck.

While no one denies that, in the modern era, she who has the largest budget generally has the largest impact on the research front, there lurks the more interesting question of the *proportional* impact of budget size on the direction that research takes. Unfortunately, there are no easy answers to this question, largely because the question can be framed in two quite distinct ways. Should scientists be seen primarily as adding to a potentially endless storehouse of knowledge? Or, should scientists be seen as inching closer to some ultimate goal, such as a unified theory of reality?

When appealing for public support, scientists like to conflate the two images, typically by presenting a torrent of publications in some field as evidence for scientists' closing in on nature's fundamental principles. But once examined a bit more closely, the two images do not fit so neatly together. On the one hand, there is evidence that the nations with the lion's share of R&D funding generate an even larger share of the total number of scientific publications. On the other hand, there is also evidence that each additional increment in R&D investment advances the frontiers of knowledge a little less than the previous one. In other words, *accelerating* the rate at which scientific publications are produced is perfectly compatible with *decelerating* the rate at which agreement is reached on the solutions to a field's fundamental problems.[17] The overall image of the dynamics of scientific inquiry, then, is one of a goal that seems to recede the more vigorously it is pursued: Tantalus would have appreciated the ruse![18]

The steady stream of professional papers serves to assuage the fears of those who worry about how scientists spend their time at work. Nevertheless, it is the image of scientists getting closer to unraveling the secrets of the universe that enables scientific inquiry to escape standards of accountability to which other productive enterprises are routinely held. Yet it is precisely here that we find the familiar phenomenon of diminishing returns on investment. An economic indicator of a "mature" science is that more resources need to be invested in order to make comparable advances. The main reason is that mature sciences work on increasingly specialized problems, solutions to which call for the manufacture of sophisticated instruments. These can be quite large and expensive, as in the case of the 53-mile underground oval tunnel known as the superconducting super collider, whose $10+ billion price tag proved too much for a budget-conscious U.S. Congress.

Upon completion, the supercollider would have been the world's largest atom smasher, presumably capable of experimentally testing rival accounts of the fundamental forces of nature. But the custom-made supercollider would have been good for little else, a point openly admitted even by its most eloquent defenders.[19] Moreover, if history is our guide, a set of decisive tests, or "crucial experiments," of the sort proposed on the supercollider would have yielded still more ideas for experiments requiring yet more customized equipment. Thus, plans were already afoot for a super-duper-collider! In fact, one would be hard-pressed to find a scientific research program that ever died a natural death, that is, as a result of having solved all of its own problems to its practitioners' satisfaction. None of this should surprise those who are used to the self-perpetuating tendencies of social welfare programs long after their effectiveness has expired.

Strategies for termination have had to be invented—often by those outside of the science concerned who nevertheless laid claim to the resources consumed by that science. Megaprojects like the supercollider, which are funded directly through Congress and not through a federal science agency, are forced to confront a truly formidable array of rivals. In fact, resistance may be strongest from big budget programs outside science altogether. For example, because weapons funding was possibly threatened by continued support for the supercollider, the Defense Department reversed its traditional pro-science stance and refused to intervene on the megaproject's behalf.[20]

Needless to say, the scientific establishment used the defeat of the Supercollider as an opportunity to decry these forced encounters between scientific and nonscientific projects. However, given the ease with which scientists themselves have been willing to claim long-term, large-scale public benefits for their most expensive efforts, it is perhaps not so unreasonable that they be made to compete against other projects that claim similar consequences, be they proposed by the Defense Department or the Department of Health and Human Services. Nevertheless, in what follows, I want to focus on a much narrower science policy arena: not where Nobel prizewinners face off against four-star generals but where biologists face off against physicists. It is to these contained strategies of termination—these institutionalized forms of "cognitive euthanasia"—that we now turn.

STRATEGIES FOR MANAGING SCIENCE SCIENTIFICALLY

At least three science-termination strategies have been proposed. None of them is in the least hostile to the pursuit of scientific inquiry. If anything, these strategies have been proposed in the spirit that science itself should be governed by the principles scientists use to govern their inquiries into nature. Thus, they should be understood as contributing to the general Enlightenment aim of extending the critical attitude of science to a wider sphere of social life—in this case, to the policy forums in which the research agenda is set.[21]

The first strategy, popular among West German leftists in the 1970s, would empower a government agency to monitor the growth of the various scientific fields. Once a field has secured widespread agreement over basic principles and its practitioners seem to be simply filling in the remaining details, the agency would offer financial incentives to divert the practitioners away from such fine-tuning and toward participating in interdisciplinary projects that addressed outstanding social problems, typically ones with a strong medical and/or legal component.[22] Although no country has yet adopted the German plan as a general science policy strategy, cancer research both in the United States and Europe has proceeded largely in this fashion over the past quarter century. Its pluses and minuses are thus reasonably well documented.

When scientists from different fields work well together, breakthroughs come more easily than if each scientist were left to the devices of her own discipline-based laboratory. Far from being an unmitigated good, scientists who have grown accustomed to the standards of their own disciplines often overlook research angles that appear quite plain to scientists operating from a different disciplinary perspective. This tendency—the mutual correction of disciplinary bias—turns out to be one of the big benefits of working in an interdisciplinary team. More generally, scientists tend to underestimate the extent to which practically oriented "applied" research has been the source of major innovations in theoretically driven "pure" or "basic" research. The impacts of agricultural and medical research on the development of biology and chemistry in the 19th century provide the clearest cases in point. In fact, only in the 20th century is basic research increasingly a source of innovative applications.

Of course, the possibility of fruitful interdisciplinary activity is predicated on scientists working well together, which is easier said than done. Highly specialized and accomplished scientists typically find it hard to adjust to an environment in which research standards and strategies need to be negotiated on a regular basis. Consequently, even the most serious of social problems (e.g., AIDS) requires large financial incentives to divert top-notch scientists from their normal research trajectories; yet the likelihood that a team of such scientists will enjoy a fruitful collaboration over the long haul remains quite small. The class of exceptions that proves the rule is the remarkable feats of interdisciplinary research done by all sides during the two World Wars. The stakes were survival itself, and the objects of concerted inquiry were "ultimate" instruments of destruction. Ironically, however, the "success" of these projects was credited less to the value of interdisciplinary teamwork and more to the ability of scientists to deliver on a herculean task when allowed to spend as much as they wanted for as long as they wanted.[23]

A second strategy for terminating expensive research enjoys the curious honor of having been originally proposed by Alvin Weinberg, who was then director of research for the U.S. Atomic Laboratories in Oak Ridge, Tennessee. Weinberg's funding principle was a simple one: The more expensive the research proposal, the more value it must have for fields outside the principal investigator's field.[24] The principle makes sense at several levels. In the first place, it applies to science policy the economic principle of "opportunity costs": that to invest resources in one course of action is, at the same time, to foreclose other opportunities for investment. Even if a research program is likely to succeed once it receives a certain level of funding, the value of that success must be weighed against the value of the competing programs that had to be terminated because of their failure to receive those funds. Armed with Weinberg's principle, policy makers will make funding decisions with an eye to the beneficial by-products that a given research program might have for researchers not directly contributing to the research.

This point about the opportunity costs of funding decisions dovetails with a deep point about the history of science. Major scientific breakthroughs tend to come out of left field, often as a result of people trained in one field moving to another one or of one field borrowing ideas and techniques from another. The inclusion of cross-disciplinary relevance as a criterion in science policy decisions would highlight such oblique paths of influence. Pursued to its logical conclusion, Weinberg's line of reasoning suggests that the field officially receiving a large research grant need not reap the largest benefits from the research done under that grant. Benefits may accrue to some third-party field whose own methods and theories are revolutionized by drawing on that research.

This conclusion may strike the reader as perverse. Nevertheless, the fact remains that no revolution in science has ever required the vast initial capital investment that is nowadays routinely sought for the most expensive and glamorous research projects. Neither Newton nor Darwin nor Einstein ever sought large research grants—and justifiably so. What government agency dedicated to the promotion of institutionalized science would find it in its interest to support research that promises—if "successful"—to displace most of the people working at the cutting edge of a large number of fields? That was, after all, the downside of the revolutions associated with these three scientists. After Newton, astronomers had to be knowledgeable in mechanics; after Darwin, biologists and geologists could no longer ignore each other's work; after Einstein, no physicist would be taken seriously without a theory of measurement.

It is worth recalling the consequences that scientific revolutions have had on the value of scientists' labor. When supporters of the supercollider touted the "revolutionary" character of its expected findings, they were not proposing a shift in worldview equivalent to the shifts attributed to Newton, Darwin, or Einstein. Locating the top quark or the smallest particle of matter, for all its apparent momentousness, would be intellectually no more significant than being the first to reach the top of Mount Everest. The last thing that the supercollider's supporters wanted was to have to retrain thousands of scientists. Rather, they trumped up the value of their high-energy physics puzzles to a level that was commensurate with the amount of funding that they were seeking from Congress. If a genuine scientific revolution were to have occurred in the aftermath of supercollider research, it probably would have been in any field *but* high-energy physics. Both the field's internal power structure and its balance of power vis-à-vis other scientific disciplines could have only been *strengthened* by the level of funding that Congress was asked to commit to the supercollider.

Still, scientific revolutions do not come cheap, although it is often hard to count up the costs. While such revolutions are certainly labor- and capital-intensive affairs, the necessary investments are rather diffuse both in terms of their sources and their recipients. Only a relatively small part of the overall labor and an even smaller part of the capital are invested in the designated "genius" of a given scientific revolution.[25] Part of what gives a scientific revolution its seemingly miraculous qualities is that historians and policy-makers fixate on the revolutionary genius to such an extent as to suggest that one person's efforts could move the world in a way that entire armies could not. In this context, it is sometimes claimed that truth is efficiently revealed to the honest scientific inquirer, whereas the artifice of politics requires constant coercion, manipulation, and, in any case, *effort.* However, in the case of the greatest scientist of them all, Sir Isaac Newton, this distinction simply does not hold up under scrutiny.

Living before the "Age of Grantsmanship," Newton earned a modest income as a mathematics professor at Cambridge University. Because his now classic *Principia Mathematica* was a rather hefty tome with pages upon pages of arcane geometric proofs, no publisher thought they could profit from printing it—that is, until Newton's friend Edmund Halley (of Halley's Comet fame) subsidized the entire operation. But Newton realized that publication alone would not turn many heads in the scientific community, since his advanced mathematical formulations were enough to intimidate even potentially sympathetic readers. He therefore embarked on a campaign of instructing likely reviewers of *Principia* in how they might represent his main arguments without including the higher mathematics. Newton went out of his way to invite challenges from scientists throughout Europe, especially France, whose major scientific societies sponsored competitions throughout the 18th century to refute this or that Newtonian claim. Although Newton is unique in the extent to which he orchestrated the revolution that bears his name, his example illustrates the number of levels on which activity must occur in order for a revolution to succeed. While no government agency need be in the business of fomenting scientific revolutions, it can foster the sorts of situations that characterize such revolutions by encouraging certain rivalries both within and between disciplines as well as cross-fertilizations.

Truth be told, "cross-disciplinary fertilization" is often little more than a policy maker's euphemism for the fact that universities poorly adapt to changing job markets. As a result, a surfeit of scientists are produced who need to find work in fields other than the ones in which they were trained. Barely a third of recent natural science graduates have found employment related to their chosen field of study, a figure that is comparable to supposedly "unemployable" graduates in the humanities and social sciences. The fact that most of the other two thirds have managed to find some form of employment testifies not to the "versatility" of scientific training but to the resourcefulness of desperate job seekers. One wonders whether those who eventually found jobs in, say, accounting or systems analysis would have gone through the trouble of majoring in high-energy physics had they anticipated their fate in the job market.[26] Indeed, it has yet to be shown that science graduates enjoy an advantage over other graduates in competing for these jobs. On the contrary, it may well be that the highly specialized nature of the science curriculum renders students ill-equipped for jobs not directly tied to that training. Like a species that has become overadapted to its ecological niche, science graduates may be incapable of survival in a radically changed labor market.[27]

To be sure, historically speaking, a tight job market often explains the emergence of new disciplines, as ambitious people trained in an oversubscribed field have found professional fulfillment by colonizing an undersubscribed field with their oversubscribed skills. Suppose you were Wilhelm Wundt living in the highly competitive environment of German higher education in the 1870s. Fortified with considerable self-possession and a doctorate in the elite discipline of physiology, he proceeded to apply the field's experimental techniques to the mind-body problem in philosophy, a field that had fallen into disrepute and hence allowed relatively easy career advancement. In this way, Wundt "invented" the science of psychology, a field that would remain largely in philosophy faculties until the end of World War I.[28] Cases such as Wundt's force the policy maker to consider whether this mismatching of supply to demand *need* be the principal cause of scientific innovation. If so, then given that most First World universities have failed to curb their intake of science students since the end of the Cold War, we should expect a ferment of innovation as unemployable scientists scramble to repackage their skills to unsuspecting employers. After all, a fifth of all scientists worldwide—and a third in countries like America and Britain—held military research contracts during the final days of the Cold War.[29]

The third strategy for scientifically managing science promises to be the most democratic by demanding the most changes in how scientists put forth their research agendas. It starts from the observation that science policy-makers typically find Weinberg's criterion of interdisciplinary relevance very difficult to put into practice. The main source of the difficulty is that research proposals are ordinarily evaluated by peer review, which means that scientists are encouraged to write their proposals with an eye toward impressing experts in their own field, each encased in its own standards and jargon. Thus, a given proposal is judged for its ability to advance the frontiers of knowledge in the particular field. The peer reviewer is not invited to ask larger questions having to do with whether the particular field of knowledge itself is worth promoting indefinitely: Is there a point at which we would be better off shifting our investments from high-energy physics to molecular biology? Because there are no opportunities for raising a question of this sort, proposals end up being accepted or rejected largely on grounds of "technical proficiency." In other words, the cross-disciplinary comparisons that are needed to implement Weinberg's criterion simply never arise in the normal course of events. Indeed, without a complete overhaul of the science policy apparatus, the disciplinary structure will simply be reproduced year after year, as each field allots its share of the available grants to technically proficient scientists.

However, the situation would be quite different if scientists from different fields were required to defend their proposals to one another in an open forum, such as before a congressional appropriations committee or perhaps even a university symposium. Historians, philosophers, and sociologists of the scientific enterprise could be called in initially to design procedures for publicly examining the scientists' claims. However, provided with an incentive to interrogate one another's claims, the scientists themselves will be in a position to intensify the investigation, stripping away gratuitous jargon, overstatement, and all-around obfuscation that might otherwise mystify nonexperts. In that way, what originally appeared to be a matter of apples and oranges— such as the theoretical benefits of a branch of physics and the practical benefits of a branch of biology—would now be rendered comparable in discourse. In fact, some philosophers and sociologists of science today believe that most of the seemingly "deep" differences in subject matter between the sciences are due to the lack of open communication channels across the corresponding disciplinary communities.[30] If such communities were routinely accountable to each other, then much of the aura of expertise and esoteric knowledge that continues to keep the public at a respectful distance from scientists would be removed.[31] Here two points are worth recalling. First, scientists themselves constitute part of the lay public for every branch of knowledge that goes beyond their specialty. Second, to call for science to be conducted in a "civil tongue" is not to end all disagreements among scientists. However, the cross-disciplinary turf wars that now produce more heat than light are likely to diminish.

Good models for thinking about criteria for evaluating competing claims in our science policy forum may be found in welfare economics. Of particular relevance are schemes for income redistribution based on competing ways of compensating the losers in a policy debate. These schemes have been given widespread currency in one of this century's leading works of political theory, *A Theory of Justice* by John Rawls.[32] According to Rawls, in the just society, people will tolerate income inequalities if they believe that the poorer members of society can somehow derive benefit from the income of the wealthier members. This idea is common to all modern theories of public finance, ranging from the investment tax breaks favored by the Right to the higher tax rates on the wealthy favored by the Left. The problem of public finance is central to modern democracies that operate within a capitalist economic framework: How can everyone benefit from wealth that remains concentrated in relatively few hands? Modern science is implicitly forced to ask a similar question, given the vast disparity in costs and benefits across the disciplines. A useful way of thinking about this disparity is through the concept of *epistemic fungibility*.[33]

Some forms of inquiry are more "epistemically fungible" than others. Consider the difference between high energy physics research done on the supercollider and psychological inquiry conducted by means of public opinion surveys. The supercollider was normally presented as a scientific instrument expressly designed to test certain theories in physics. No other discipline was likely to benefit directly from working on the supercollider, as no other discipline requires particle accelerators for testing its theories. In addition, the dimensions of the supercollider were nonnegotiable: One did not consider "big" or "small" versions of the supercollider, and it would make no sense to speak of "half" or "three quarters" of a supercollider. The supercollider would not have been usable at all until it was completely built. The decision whether to construct the instrument was thus an all-or-nothing matter, a fact that contributed to its controversial history.[34]

Together, all of these features rated supercollider research low on epistemic fungibility. In contrast, public opinion surveys are common to a variety of disciplines in the social sciences, so that even if most of the work were initially done by psychologists, sociologists and political scientists may stand to benefit and subsequently contribute to that line of research. Moreover, one can tailor the scope of the survey to the amount of funding available. While surveys that question more people are normally regarded as more representative of an entire population, one can determine the "statistical significance" of findings reached on any sample size. These opportunities for negotiating the dimensions of the project make survey research more epistemically fungible.

If policy makers regularly thought about science funding as a branch of welfare economics, they would require scientific teams to draft proposals not only for accomplishing their own goals but also for compensating other scientists with whom they are competing for funds. Moreover, the burden to provide compensation would be greater with the amount of money that the teams sought. Imposing such a requirement may cause certain disciplines to scale down their funding demands, as they reckon that the intrinsically esoteric nature of their inquiries precludes the incorporation of practitioners from other disciplines into their proposals. Of course, the other alternative available to these nonfungible fields would be to seek full funding from industrial and philanthropic concerns in the private sector. In that case, if the trend toward increasing specialization in science is truly irreversible, we should see the "privatization" of science, which, some predict, will incline society to think about the products of scientific research much as we think about works of art today. In effect, a privatized scientific enterprise would convert all knowledge to intellectual property.[35]

Not surprisingly, many scientists balk at the prospect of privatization. Historically speaking, most of the power that elite groups derive from specialized knowledge is directly traceable to that knowledge being shrouded in secrecy or, in some other way, rendered inaccessible to most people. Privatization, it is feared, would only increase that tendency, as certain wealthy "patrons of the sciences" could emerge as majority shareholders in the knowledge produced by particular fields. To stave off this unsavory possibility, it is reasonable to suppose that some scientific communities would start to reconceptualize their practices to increase the fungibility of their fields. For example, high-energy physicists may decide that rival theories in their field can be just as effectively tested on relatively inexpensive computer simulations as on the $10 billion supercollider. After all, geneticists, psychologists, and economists have long used computer simulations for analogous purposes, as they have tried to get around the unfeasibility of staging direct tests of their theories. Here it is important to recall that nothing in the formulation of a scientific theory dictates the method by which it must be tested. Indeed, it has become commonplace among historians of science to reveal the complicated negotiations that result in a community of scientists agreeing to test a particular theory by a particular method.[36]

However, perhaps truest to the spirit of welfare economics would be for high-energy physicists to try to persuade a coalition of inquirers from different disciplines to participate in some successor to the ill-fated supercollider project. For example, social scientists interested in understanding large-scale organizational behavior in isolated settings would find the community that surrounds the supercollider (Waxahachie, Texas) an ideal site for study. In fact, some of these social scientists may be already seeking grants to investigate different communities that have similar characteristics. If the physicists were willing to take the trouble, they could persuade the social scientists to join their team instead. Such an invitation not only would save money but it would also eliminate much of the rancor and mutual suspicion that currently accompany interactions between natural and social scientists—interactions that all too often have threatened the fate of innovative interdisciplinary research.[37] Of course, as with all compensation schemes, the wealthy would have to pay, which, in this case, would mean that the physicists would lose some of their privacy, as they allow the social scientists to roam around the supercollider facility, regularly recording observations and asking questions, most of which will range from the pointed to the pointless. In the not too distant future, one could even envisage the social scientists remarking on ways in which the scientific worksite could be improved. Such are the first painful steps toward a democratic science.

INCORPORATING SCIENCE'S
SILENT COLLABORATORS

The success of coalition politics, such as the one fostered by welfare economics, ultimately rests on the political system's ability to identify the degree of compatibility and conflict among different interest groups. This ability, in turn, depends on correctly identifying all the relevant interest groups. So far we have looked at some of the issues surrounding adequate faculty representation in the National Forum. But including nonfaculty representatives is equally vital to the success of any science-based coalition. And here I do not mean representatives of industry and government, which the Carnegie Commission report makes a point of including at every turn. Rather, I mean the less exalted class of technical and support personnel, as well as relatively recent PhDs—"postdoctoral fellows"—who have yet to find regular academic posts. The numbers of this latter group, increasingly known as the "unfaculty," are large and growing, now routinely filling one out of five academic positions in America's research universities[38] Together with less credentialed staff colleagues, they are the unsung heroes of the research process. Underpaid and undervalued, they often make all the difference between success and failure: What if the project secretary is unfamiliar with the work rhythms of the researchers, or the lab technician has not been consulted on the overall scheme of the project, or the postdoc's judgment is trusted only in matters of technique? Just as consumers need to be incorporated in decisions taken at the level of production, so too these "implementers" need to be incorporated in decisions taken at the level of project conception.

Indicative of the neglected state of nonfaculty voices is that the Carnegie Commission report calls for the revamping of university research facilities without saying a word about the people who would staff these facilities and ensure that projects proceed according to plan. The trickle-down science policy mentality apes a top-down research management style, in which the sheer brilliance or utility of a project idea supposedly calls forth the appropriate personnel. This policy is propelled by romantic images of research teams inspired by visionary directors. Back on earth, however, studies of corporate management style show the cult of the irreplaceable individual is a formula for megalomania, rude awakenings, and failed enterprises. If the actions of any one individual—even the scientific "genius"—are seen as disproportionally more significant than those of anyone else, then work and responsibility are not distributed to make optimal use of the talents of all the team members.

Admittedly, deliberations at a national forum may take an unexpected turn once secretaries, technicians, and postdocs are allowed representation. In particular, they may want to lend neither their opinions nor their approval to the science policy process until the status of their labor and the terms of their employment reflected the seriousness with which they were now being taken. Some scientific traditionalists may hesitate at the introduction of such issues. Nevertheless, these staples of labor-management relations follow from the realization that success of science policy in a truly democratic society is measured not merely by the quantity of the goods that science produces—nor merely by the quality of those goods—but by the quality of the interactions of the people who are employed in producing those goods. One can only hope that a national forum on science and technology goals will soon be designed so as to enable our research priorities to be set both *by* and *for* all the people entrusted to get the job done.

SUMMARY AND A POSTSCRIPT
FOR THE NEW MILLENIUM

Like the Almighty God of Scripture, science in America today is both everywhere and nowhere—at least if the accounting procedure of the U.S. federal budget is taken as one's guide. The invisible pervasiveness of science reflects our faith in science's inability to do harm if left to its own devices. On the contrary, I argue that this refusal to examine science critically does harm to democratic governance and public welfare by tying up large amounts of money that might be better spent elsewhere. In addition, such an uncritical science policy perpetuates an attitude toward knowledge that both devalues education and wastes and frustrates the talent of those who pursue scientific careers. Moreover, this attitude is currently spreading throughout institutions of higher learning and across academic disciplines. Armed with some insights from the history and sociology of science, I have proposed three strategies for the "scientific" management of science. Each would make science more open to democratic forms of accountability without necessarily compromising the quality of the science done. However, these proposals can work only if we adopt a more expansive view of the range of interests that need to be taken into account in the science policy process. And this means bringing into our discussions not only cutting-edge researchers but also teaching faculty and postdoctoral fellows as well as secretarial and technical support staff. We will have then made a systematic shift in our understanding of science from the manufacture of products to the employment of people.

Appealing to scientific authority has proven politically to be the most palatable means for democratic governments to coerce the populace. However, these governments are now saddled with enormous budgetary deficits, mostly arising from the need to buffer the effects that rapidly changing economic conditions have on their constituency. Under these circumstances, it is easy to see why an expensive scientific project like the Supercollider would be regarded as dispensable. But what if this is only the beginning of a trend toward governments divesting their financial interest in the education and research of the scientific community? Historically speaking, this would be equivalent to *secularizing* science, in the sense that Christendom was secularized when the emerging nation-states of Europe in the seventeenth century refused to grant a single church special economic and political privileges. This led to a period of evangelism, in which religious believers competed to attract believers who would materially sustain their efforts.[39] Analogues of such proselytizing efforts can already be seen among the defenders of New Age knowledges who broadcast their "infomercials" on late-night cable television. They promise custom-made enlightenment at a price (of a video, a book, or a therapy session). In the next few decades, we may find IBM or Shell Oil publicizing their virtues in terms of the major projects in high-energy physics or molecular biology they have supported—which may be used to excuse whatever political or ecological indiscretions were involved in their support. It will be interesting to see the role that will be played by all those disappointed natural science degee holders who were misled into thinking that there was a market for pure inquiry.

BIBLIOGRAPHIC NOTE

James Bryant Conant, president of Harvard University (1933-1953) and a leading architect of U.S. science policy after World War II, is usually credited with the argument that science's unique historical trajectory means that it cannot be evaluated by the standards used to judge other social institutions. His *Science and Commonsense* (New Haven, CA: Yale University Press, 2nd ed., 1951) was the most popular of several books he wrote for nonscientists. Kuhn's very influential *The Structure of Scientific Revolutions*—cited in this article (see note 10)—is dedicated to Conant.

A new round of questioning about the role of science in society began after the Soviet Union launched the first artificial space satellite *Sputnik* in 1957. This event was taken to indicate that the United States had fallen behind the Soviets in the "science race," a thinly veiled symbol of the arms race. Science policy debate over the subsequent decade is conveniently gathered in Edward Shils, ed., *Criteria for Scientific Development: Public Policy and National Goals* (Cambridge: MIT Press, 1968). Here the reader will find the articles from *Minerva* (a journal edited by Shils) cited in this chapter. (The relevant "race" today is over "economic competitiveness," and some old foes, Germany and Japan, have returned to haunt us.)

The 1960s witnessed the emergence of some notable critics of science's involvement in "the military-industrial complex." The theoretically sophisticated *Scientific Knowledge and Its Social Problems* (Oxford: Oxford University Press, 1971), by Jerome Ravetz, attracted considerable attention in its day. However, in the long run, the most influential theorist of "critical science" has turned to be the more radical Paul Feyerabend, whose books *Against Method* (London: Verso, 1975) and *Science in a Free Society* (London: Verso, 1979) called for "the separation of Science and State," on a par with the constitutional separation of Church and State.

The critical science movement has always been more powerful in Western Europe than in the United States. The reader can get a vivid sense of the more explicitly democratic, even populist, tendencies in this literature by having a look at Mike Hales, *Science or Society? The Politics of the Work of Scientists* (London: Free Association Books, 2nd ed., 1986). However, the scientists have recently begun to strike back at the critics. Especially notable in its "knowledge of the enemy" is Paul Gross and Norman Levitt, *Higher Superstition: The Academic Left and Its Quarrels with Science* (Baltimore: Johns Hopkins University Press, 1994). Gross and Levitt provocatively argue that science critics are making it harder, not easier, for the social goals of the Left to be realized. A good source of responses from the "academic left" is *The Science Wars*, eds. Andrew Ross and Stanley Aronowitz (Durham, NC: Duke University Press, 1996).

The best survey of the history of attempts to mask the political character of scientific research is Robert Proctor, *Value-Free Science? Purity and Power in Modern Knowledge* (Cambridge, MA: Harvard University Press, 1991). Closer to home, David Guston and various interlocutors have explored the "essential tension" between science and democracy in the history of American political thought in a special issue of the journal *Social Epistemology* (vol. 7, no. 1, 1993).

NOTES

1. For an analysis of the various appeals that are made to balance issues of equity against those of efficiency, see Brian Barry, *Political Argument* (Atlantic Highlands, NJ: Humanities Press, 1965).

2. See Sal Restivo, "Modern Science as a Social Problem," *Social Problems* 35 (1988): 206-228.

3. The following account of the federal science budget is taken from a wide-ranging report conducted by the research arm of Congress, the Office of Technology Assessment (OTA): *Federally Funded Research: Decisions for a Decade* (U.S. Government Printing Office, 1991), chap. 5.

4. Available from the Carnegie Commission on Science, Technology, and Government, 10 Waverly Place, New York, NY 10013.

5. "Big science" was popularized by the quantitatively oriented social historian, Derek de Solla Price, in *Little Science, Big Science* (Harmondsworth: Penguin, 1963).

6. Ernest Boyer, *Scholarship Reconsidered: The Priorities of the Professoriate* (Princeton, NJ: Carnegie Foundation for the Advancement of Teaching, 1990).

7. Boyer classifies institutions of higher learning according to the kind and number of degrees awarded as well as the range of subjects in which they are awarded.

8. This point was first forcefully raised in science policy circles by the philosopher Stephen Toulmin in a critique of Michael Polanyi's influential vision of the scientific community as a "republic of science." See Toulmin, "The Complexity of Scientific Choice," *Minerva* 2 (1964): 343-359. See also Polanyi, "The Republic of Science," *Minerva* 1 (1962): 54-73.

9. It was in this context that OTA senior analyst Daryl Chubin coined the expression "quark barreling" to characterize the self-serving arguments used by physicists on behalf of the supercollider. The Council of the American Physical Society's concerns are reported in *Federally Funded Research*, p. 159, n. 40.

10. The most influential work to present this position is Thomas Kuhn, *The Structure of Scientific Revolutions* (Chicago: University of Chicago Press, 2nd ed., 1970). Kuhn's position is systematically contested in Steve Fuller, "Being There with Thomas Kuhn: A Parable for Postmodern Times," *History and Theory* 31 (1992): 241-275.

11. In Newtonian mechanics, "inertia" refers to a body's motion before it has been subjected to an outside force, such as gravity. Soon after Newton proposed the principle in his First Law of Motion, philosopher began to see similarities between this idea of "natural motion" and the theological concept of "free will" in humans. Following the example of sociologist Emile Durkheim, many social scientists have envisaged the normative strictures of morality as akin to gravity in being an invisible external force that curbs the inertial tendencies of the individual's pursuit of self-interest.

12. For a spirited and learned attack on the attempt by social scientists—economists, in this case—to derive legitimacy from defunct physics, see Philip Mirowski, *More Heat Than Light* (Cambridge, UK: Cambridge University Press, 1989).

13. The first cries from economists can be heard in Paula Stephan and Sharon Levin, *Striking the Mother Lode in Science: The Importance of Age, Place, and Time* (Oxford: Oxford University Press, 1992).

14. The virtues and vices of the peer review process are discussed in Daryl Chubin and Edward Hackett, *Peerless Science* (Albany: SUNY Press, 1990).

15. The locus classicus of this line of sociological research may be found in Robert Merton, *The Sociology of Science* (Chicago: University of Chicago Press, 1973), pt. 5.

16. Thomas Schott, "The World Scientific Community: Globality and Globalization," *Minerva* 29 (1991): 440-462.

17. Derek de Solla Price (see note 5 above) is responsible for the arguments that suggest that larger R&D budgets make for a more productive scientific community than smaller budgets. Such arguments generally appeal to "economies of scale." In fact, Price found that scientific productivity was closely correlated with electrical energy production. See Price, "Toward a Model of Science Indicators," in Y. Elkana, J. Lederberg, R. Merton, A. Thackray, and H. Zuckerman, eds., *Toward a Metric of Science* (New York: Wiley-Interscience, 1978), pp. 69-96. The idea that science may suffer from "diseconomies of scale" (that is, "bigger is worse"), especially if scientific inquiry is seen as aiming for the ultimately comprehensive account of reality, is pursued in Nicholas Rescher, *The Limits of Science* (Berkeley: University of California Press, 1984).

18. Tantalus is the source of the word "tantalize." In Greek mythology, Tantalus suffered a cruel fate. Cursed with an unquenchable thirst, whenever Tantalus moved toward a juicy fruit, the wind blew the fruit out of his reach, causing him to redouble his efforts, only to have the fruit elude him yet again. His torture thus consisted of being repeatedly frustrated just at the moment of consummation.

19. See the highly romanticized defense of the supercollider presented in Steven Weinberg, *Dreams of a Final Theory* (New York: Pantheon, 1993).

20. Such was suggested in the October 24, 1993, *New York Times* editorial written in the wake of the supercollider's demise.

21. The Enlightenment is a general cultural movement that began in 18th-century Europe and is strongly associated with "modernity." Enlightenment philosophers—in whose ranks include Voltaire and Kant—held that the popularization of scientific modes of thought would foster the criticism and reform of traditional religious and political practices.

22. This science policy strategy is generally known as "finalization." The word itself suggests that a mature science coasts on its own inertial tendencies, unless it is explicitly given direction, and in that sense, "finalized." See Wolfgang Schaefer, ed., *Finalization in Science* (Dordrecht: Reidel, 1984).

23. In the American context, this was the lesson drawn by Vannevar Bush, director of the Manhattan Project, which developed the atomic bomb. In a very influential treatise published soon after World War II, *Science: The Endless Frontier,* Bush argued that the success of the war effort justified the establishment of a "National Science Foundation," whose goal would be to encourage discipline-based basic research but in the policy environment that scientists enjoyed during the war.

24. This view was first presented in Alvin Weinberg, "Criteria for Scientific Choice," *Minerva* 1 (1963): 159-171. It has since been discreetly endorsed by the OTA in *Federally Funded Research,* pp. 139-140. To prevent confusion, Alvin and Steven Weinberg are not related. In fact, Steven is quite hostile to Alvin's views, a point he makes in *Dreams of a Final Theory,* pp. 59-60.

25. To put it in the terms of R&D policy: More money is spent on "D" (the networking of interests that enables an innovation to spread) than on "R" (the work that originally goes into making the innovation). Contrary to the common view that traces D's dominance of R to the rise of Big Science, this tendency can be found throughout the history of science. See John Cockcroft, *The Organization of Research Establishments* (Cambridge, UK: Cambridge University Press, 1965).

26. The employment figures were provided by Jane Fielding and her associates in the Sociology Department at Surrey University, UK, in the context of a debate that the author had with UK government science policy advisor, Robert May, in the pages of *Financial Times* (Britain's answer to *The Wall Street Journal*) on November 18, 21, and 28, 1995. The author was responding to May's concerns about the decline of university science enrollments across First World nations. Good anecdotal evidence that recent physics PhDs regret their career choice may be found in the campaign statements of the four write-in candidates for the 1994 election to the Council of the American Physical Society.

27. A good survey of the full range of problems raised in this paragraph may be found in "Careers '95: The Future of the Ph.D.," *Science* 270 (October 6, 1995): 123-147.

28. In the sociology of science, Wundt's career path is regarded as a classic case of "role hybridization." See Joseph Ben-David and Randall Collins, "Social Factors in the Origins of a New Science." *American Sociological Review* 31 (1966): 451-465.

29. "R&D Budget: Civilian Gains Outpace Defense," *Science News* 137 (February 3, 1990): 71.

30. Advanced readers interested in pursuing this thesis should see Steve Fuller, *Social Epistemology* (Bloomington: Indiana University Press, 1988).

31. Readers may be interested in finding out about the tactics that scientists currently use to appear authoritative before policy-making forums as well as the countertactics that have been developed to challenge those displays of authority. For the former, see William Wells, *Working with Congress: A Practical Guide for Scientists and Engineers* (Washington: AAAS Press, 1993). For the latter, see Brian Martin, *Strip the Experts* (London: Freedom Press, 1991). Freedom Press is located at 84B Whitechapel High Street, London E1 7QX, UK.

32. (Cambridge, MA: Harvard University Press, 1971).

33. This concept was first introduced in Steve Fuller, *Philosophy, Rhetoric, and the End of Knowledge: The Coming of Science and Technology Studies* (Madison: University of Wisconsin Press, 1993), p. 295. In economics, "fungibility" refers to the ease with which one good can be exchanged for another—and hence the ease with which it can serve as a means of satisfying the ends of its owner. A fungible good is one that can be had in different amounts without destroying the good's integrity. For example, a half-bag of groceries may provide half the nourishment of a full bag, but a half-automobile will not get you halfway to where you want to go. Thus, only the groceries are fungible, not the automobile. By calling this kind of fungibility "epistemic," I am stressing the fact that the goods in question are forms of knowledge.

34. Of course, once Congress voted to halt funding on the supercollider, various science interest groups competed to pick at the carcass of the partly built particle accelerator. Among the most publicized strategies came from the medical community, namely, to have it produce radioisotopes that could provide proton therapy to cancer patients. See Kim McDonald, "Fight Erupts Over What to Do

with Remains of the Supercollider," *Chronicle of Higher Education* (March 23, 1994): A23. However, these post mortem attempts to salvage something of value from the nearly $1 billion spent on the supercollider should not be confused with fungibility proper. The test lies in the question, "If one were keen on increasing the availability of proton cancer therapy, would supporting an expensive project in high-energy physics be the most efficient route?" (The answer, presumably, is no.)

35. For a wide-ranging discussion of the historical backdrop to this move, see Yaron Ezrahi, *The Descent of Icarus* (Cambridge, MA: Harvard University Press, 1990).

36. An interesting historical aside is that had computer technology been more advanced than particle accelerator technology in the 1930s, hypotheses in high-energy physics may have been tested by computer simulations (as is common today in science, e.g., climate modeling). After all, particle accelerators are themselves persuasive only as simulations of the first milliseconds after the Big Bang. For the best insider argument on the economic unfeasibility of continuing high-energy physics research, regardless of its symbolic and cultural value, see David Lindley, *The End of Physics* (New York: Basic Books, 1993).

37. A good case in point, which involved an anthropologist studying the gendered character of high-energy physics research, is documented in Sharon Traweek, *Beamtimes and Lifetimes* (Cambridge, MA: Harvard University Press, 1988).

38. On the demographic characteristics of the unfaculty, see *Federally Funded Research*, pp. 214-215.

39. A good brief analysis of the social processes of secularization is Daniel Bell, "The Return of the Sacred: The Argument about the Future of Religion," in G. Almond, M. Chodorow, and R. Pearce, eds., *Progress and Its Discontents* (Berkeley: University of California Press, 1982), pp. 501-523.

Discussion

1. One of the problems in managing science, Fuller claims, is that science is decentralized. Currently, the United States lacks a cabinet level position for a policy advisor for science and technology. Also, Congress can earmark funds for particular research. Science and technology appear to be both everywhere and nowhere. As science is pervasive and decentralized, science policy in the United States tends to be uncritical. The lack of a critical approach to science policy, suggests Fuller, devalues issues involving public welfare, science education, and the interests of laypersons. Explain why you agree or disagree with Fuller's position. How does the funding of social welfare programs compare to the funding of science? Why should science and technology be treated as

social problems to be regulated by the government? Why should science and technology be left in the hands of private citizens?

2. In looking at examples from the history and sociology of science, Fuller presents the reader with a paradox. Traditionally, the history of science has been presented as a series of advances by individual geniuses (e.g., Newton, Darwin and Einstein). On the one hand, Fuller implies that this historical rendering is false. All of these "genius" individuals had to convince contemporary audiences that their position was correct either by simplifying their views (Newton) or through the work of advocates (Darwin/Huxley, Einstein/Planck). On the other hand, Fuller argues that if one believes the progress of science *is* the movement from one genius to the next, then scientific advances from this historical perspective cannot be funded. Initially, what do you think a genius is? When can a community count on an individual genius to bring about radical change? Why do you agree or disagree with Fuller's argument against the role of the genius in advancing knowledge by claiming they would fail if their ideas could not be sold to the larger community?

3. Fuller offers three strategies for managing science "scientifically." Explain these three strategies. Why do you agree with the aims of these strategies? As a criterion for assessing the value of a potential scientific program, Fuller introduces the concept of "epistemic fungibility" in which he suggests the value of a particular knowledge claim, and the resources needed to produce it, can be assessed by how well the equipment and concepts transfer to another field of study. In introducing this principle, Fuller suggests that "big science" projects like the supercollider are wasteful because the experimental apparatus and possible determinations from its use can be comprehended and used by only a few experts. On one level, making a project fungible would entail that researchers present their knowledge in an accessible manner for would-be users in other disciplines and fields of study. From Fuller's perspective, the supercollider would not be "epistemically fungible." Do you agree or disagree with Fuller's concept? Why

or why not? Why would experts in a particular field object to this principle? Why would such a principle make science more accountable to the taxpayer?

4. Is science, according to Fuller, democratic? Whose interests are represented in the debate over "big science" projects? Why should the people who work to support the day-to-day activities of science—laboratory technicians, project secretaries, postdoctoral fellows—have a voice in the direction of a scientific or technological project? Is science funding distributed democratically?

5. If a truly national political forum concerning science and technology policy did exist, what general communicative strategies do you think experts would use to convince nonexperts of their position? How could nonexperts use the same strategies to convince experts? What strategies could nonexperts employ? How do individuals or groups with different types of knowledge persuade each other?

6. One could argue that cutting-edge or advanced research in science and technology (and any number of other professions) is so inherently complex that a layperson, with only a high school education, could not hope to understand it. What level of understanding or experience would a layperson need to make an informed decision concerning science and technology policy? Explain whether you agree or disagree with the following statement: Given the skill, time, and resources, *any* complex problem could be explained by a technical communicator so that a layperson could make a decision about its impact on oneself and others.

7. What social obligation or responsibility do you have to become involved in science and technology policy in the United States? What shape or direction would that obligation or responsibility take?

Exercises

1. Fuller mentions T. H. Huxley as Darwin's leading advocate. Huxley gained fame as "Darwin's bulldog" in an exchange with

one of Darwin's detractors, Bishop Wilberforce, at the meeting
of the British Association at Oxford in 1860. Huxley concluded
the debate by purportedly stating that he "was not ashamed
to have a monkey for an ancestor; but he would be ashamed
to be connected with a man [Wilberforce] who used a great gift
to obscure the truth." The debate can be seen as a turning
point for the more general acceptance of Darwin's theory.
Nevertheless, questions remain about the impact and future
of Darwin's work. In a brief essay, assess the current state of
public debate over Darwin's theory or any controversial scientific theory or technology. Where are the boundaries of the
debate? Who are the advocates on each side? What role do
advocates or spokespersons play in the debate?

In a similar assignment, research how breakthrough technologies and their applications—airplanes and air travel,
household technologies and household management, the potential of electricity, telephones, phonographs, and so on—
were pitched to consumers. In a short essay examine who
pitched these technologies and the techniques they used.
What type of images, language, and arguments were employed? Is there any association made between these technologies and freedom and democracy? Were laypersons
brought into the research and development manufacturing
process to consult with engineers and inventors?

2. Consider the following hypothetical situation:

    A bill has passed out of a committee in the House of Repre-
    sentatives authorizing the federal government to establish a
    national citizens board to review funding requests for scientific
    and technological development and research. The National
    Board for the Governance of Science and Technology (NBGST)
    would control the part of the federal budget, determined by
    Congress, allocated for the federal funding of science and
    technology. Given complete control of these resources, the
    NBGST would have the power to invest, shift, or eliminate
    money from any federally supported science and technology
    project. The NBGST could, for example, put its entire yearly
    budget behind a single megaproject, spread the money among
    various projects, or refuse to fund *any* project. The bill also
    requires that the NBGST "look like America." That is, the people
    appointed to the board by the president (subject to approval)

would necessarily represent diverse educational and socioeconomic backgrounds, social groups, beliefs, and experiences. Although scientists and professional experts may sit on the board, their numbers would reflect, per capita, the total number of scientists and professional experts in the nation. For the most part, then, those sitting on the board would be laypersons with no particular background in science and technology. Scientists and technologists seeking funding would have to apply and then testify directly to the board to request funding. Although the budget of the NBGST would be strictly maintained, if all new funds had been entirely allocated before the end of the fiscal year, the board could, if convinced by those requesting funds, shift money from one project to another. Funds would be allocated, shifted or eliminated on a straight up or down vote of the members. Each proposal could be presented only once a year.

You and other classmates (in this course) have been solicited, by the congressional representative of the district in which your school is located, to write a letter defining your position on the bill. The members in the class will either individually sign or abstain from signing the letter. Compose the letter considering the following questions:

▦ Should nonexperts (laypersons) be on the board?

▦ What do student practitioners preparing to become scientists and technologists think of the formation of the board?

▦ What do students who will not be scientists or technologists think? If there are differences of opinion among the groups, explain them.

▦ Should the board be empowered to spend its budget in the fashion outlined in the explanation of the bill or should their power be restricted? How?

▦ Do you think it's a good idea to have the board "look like America?" Why or why not?

3. One of the strategies that Fuller proposes for making the management of science more democratic is to change the peer review system. Proposals requesting funds from government institutions are reviewed *for* experts in a certain field *by* experts in that same field. Fuller argues that, as a result, peer reviewers do not ask larger questions about the relevance of certain projects as would laypersons. President Clinton's Secretary of the Interior Bruce Babbit proposed a new law regarding the management of federally owned grazing lands.

Babbit suggested that range management boards, which used to be controlled by ranchers, be composed of 15 people—5 ranchers, 5 environmentalists, and 5 residents of the area with no professional interests at stake. To achieve consensus, Babbit has suggested that each voting third of the committee must approve or disapprove any new policies. That is, voting would occur within each constituent block and then each block would register its approval or disapproval. Babbit's proposal sounds much like Fuller's. In a research paper, analyze the success or failure (at the moment of research) of Babbit's plan. How does your analysis of Babbit's plan shed light on the points made by Fuller?

Introduction to Chapter 8

One of Dutch graphic artist M. C. Escher's (1898-1972) most popular works is a lithograph titled "Hand with Reflecting Sphere" (1935), which shows a reflecting globe resting in the artist's hand. The globe acts as a mirror reflecting, somewhat distortedly, nearly all of the artist's surroundings. The room contains a window at the far end, tables, chairs, lamps, paintings, and books. Directly in the center of the globe sits the artist. He observes himself in the globe at the same time he observes and draws himself and his surroundings. As with many of Escher's works, the subject is self-reference. The self provides the basis from which one composes, and is composed by, one's surroundings.

Self-reference is a unique concern in the social sciences. Social scientists immediately affect, and are affected by, the actions and settings of the persons they observe. And although the subjects of natural scientific inquiry undoubtedly affect their investigators, their significance on an objective account of nature is disputed. Moreover, natural science methods rarely depend on subjects answering questions. Many social scientists concede that in any given instance what motivates human action is hard to pin down. Humans can act irrationally. They know only partially what motivates them. They lie. They use language in distinct ways. Consequently, the boundaries between analyst and analysand, stimulus and response, and cause and effect blur when humans interact with one another. Identifying how the interaction among subjects and objects affects social scientific explanations of, for example, why and how people vote, commit crime, and live in poverty seems thoroughly vexing—so much so as to forever deny solutions to persistent social problems. In addition, social scientists have an undeniable stake in their own descriptions and recommendations. They too arc affected by historical, political, social, and economic change and how people conceive of that change. How then, in the swirl of social interchange, can one be a member of a society, come to describe and understand it, and objectively prescribe social policies? These questions lead social scientists to confront the problem of reflexivity.

In the sociology of scientific knowledge (SSK), reflexive textual practices are characterized by the use and mention of self-referring narrative forms, devices, and literary styles. By self-consciously undermining the authority of assumptions held by writers and readers about the representational function of language, reflexive practitioners invite the active participation of readers in constructing the meaning of texts. The meaning of a scientific text, for example, would not rest primarily with the author's ability to match apparent linguistic referents with observable phenomena but would be related to disciplinary dialects, previous literature on the subject, and discussions among members of a given discourse community. Reflexive theorists hold a robust conception of language as constitutive of reality. Writing science is not just simply recording natural facts. Writing and reading science, rather, involve the creation of facts through social and rhetorical contexts. Consequently, traditional—often static—roles among reader, writer, text, and real-world referents in scientific texts have been redefined. Reflexive theorists invite readers to employ the same interpretive devices to scientific texts as they would to literature.

In a rather playful and provocative article, Geoff Cooper explores possibilities for reaching outside (and inside) the traditional forms of scientific and technical communication. To varying degrees, all of our communication practices are instances of self-reference and self-discovery. We all participate in contexts from which we cannot, at any designated instance, separate ourselves. The act of reading a scientific text is a study in self-reference in which one composes, and is composed by, one's aims and desires. But what happens if we consciously and directly take self-reference into consideration when writing and reading scientific texts? Geoff Copper explores several possibilities.

CHAPTER

Textual Technologies
New Literary Forms and Reflexivity

GEOFF COOPER

1. A POSSIBLE PREFACE

The following text has recently come to light (cf. Mulkay, 1991a, chap. 14). It dates from 1993 and, as far as can be inferred from its contents, was a putative contribution to a textbook on technical communications for engineers. As far as we know the book never appeared. The paper attempts an overview of "new literary forms," The term is more rarely invoked today, except in a historical sense; even at the time of writing, the author took a somewhat ambivalent stance toward its status as a genre. Nevertheless, the experimentation that the term denotes, and the theoretical motivations that inform it still have a considerable presence: in some respects, that presence is more widespread. It is therefore presented here with minor revisions.

AUTHOR'S NOTE: Thanks to Steve Woolgar for encouragement and constructive comments.

2. PROLOGUE: SOME MOMENTS
FROM THE CHAPTER'S PREHISTORY

My second request is to ask if you could recommend someone—
associated with the Discourse Analysis Workshops—willing to
contribute a compatible piece providing an overview of New Literary Forms. (in letter from Jim Collier to Steve Woolgar, August 18,
1992)

I would suggest Geoff Cooper. . . . He points out to me, however,
that if you wanted the piece written in [a] new literary form[s], he
might wish to defer to someone who has already published in this
vein. (in electronic mail message from Steve Woolgar to Jim
Collier, September 7, 1992)

I think it would be interesting to have the overview presented
through the use of an NLF, but I will work that out with Dr. Cooper.
(in electronic mail message from Jim Collier to Steve Woolgar,
September 15, 1992)

The piece need not be presented in a New Literary Form. (in letter
from Jim Collier and David Toomey to the author, September 22,
1992)

However, the relation between reflexivity and new literary forms
can be formulated in different ways: and the critical issues that
are raised by this flexibility form the focus of the chapter. Addressing this relation topicalises the question of whether this chapter
itself can adequately describe the work in question without making use of this literary technology, if such it is. (in abstract for the
chapter sent to Jim Collier, November 1992)

Geoff Cooper: I haven't decided whether to do it in a new
   literary form.

Malcolm Ashmore: You may as well. If you don't, you'll only
   have to talk about why you're not doing it that way.

   (from conversation with Malcolm Ashmore, February 17, 1993,
   as approximately recalled by myself)

3. INTRODUCTION

This chapter attempts to give an overview of the use of "new literary forms" in science and technology studies. It argues that the genre and its motivations have to be understood in relation to a concern with reflexivity. The latter, as we shall see, resists easy or singular definition; indeed, it can be construed as explicitly problematizing definitional work. However, to get things started, reflexivity can be provisionally characterized as an issue that arises when we address questions of representation: the statements that we make, or the knowledge that we construct about representational practice are themselves representations and thus implicated in what they describe.

Clearly, since representation is a crucial feature of scientific and technological practice, reflexivity can be seen as an important issue for those who study it. The use of "new literary forms" can be thought of, in general terms, as an attempt to attend to the implications of reflexivity for one's own representational practice. But, as we shall see, it is important to describe the relation between reflexivity and new literary forms more precisely.

To attempt an "overview" of this work immediately lands the would-be summarizer in a reflexive dilemma about his or her own representational practice, for the mode of presentation chosen will be seen to entail the denial of or subscription to some of the claims made by those who write in "new literary forms." Can this work, which places such store on moving beyond the strictures of the academic monologue, be adequately summarized in conventional prose?[1] Does the very notion of "overview" do violence to the instability and flexibility that new literary forms attempt to preserve?[2] In other words, the way in which this chapter is written will form a significant part of the arguments that it makes. In this respect, it shares with the texts that it discusses the key objective of showing as well as describing. The modes of writing throughout the chapter can therefore be thought of as a way of testing the assertion that new literary forms are necessary for an adequate engagement with reflexivity; the relative success of different strategies adopted will then be available for evaluation at the end of the chapter.

I begin by briefly elaborating some of the senses of "reflexivity" before moving on to look more specifically at new literary forms.[3]

4. REFLEXIVITY

"Reflexivity" cannot be described or defined as one entity; it is referenced in various domains and contexts, often in quite different senses. I do not intend to map out this diversity here, still less to try to reduce it to one central meaning. Rather, I will suggest that reflexivity can be understood, for our purposes, in terms of two, possibly three central dimensions, and that these can be seen to interact and shift in relative importance in some of the different usages of the term. A few examples are discussed in order to give an indication of the term's diverse meanings and the breadth of its application. The main concern here is with reflexivity as an issue for Sociology of Scientific Knowledge (SSK) (see Ashmore, 1989, chap. 2, for a comprehensive view of this diversity). However, it is my contention that, too often, discussion of reflexivity within this field has been hampered by a certain insularity and narrowness of focus and that placing reflexivity in a wider cultural context can recast and clarify the significance of some recurrent questions and their terms of reference.

Dimension 1: Reflexivity refers to those aspects of representation—intended here to include a spectrum from everyday language to more formal bodies of knowledge—that involve some degree of self-reference or self-implication. This can be termed structural reflexivity.

Dimension 2: Reflexivity refers to the capacity for awareness and reflection. In many instances, but not in all, this reflection might be directed toward or occasioned by, the self-implication described in Dimension 1. This can be termed cognitive reflexivity.

The shifting interrelation of these dimensions in different usages is complex. In SSK, advocates of reflexivity tend to see the second dimension as weaker and less interesting than the first; for whereas self-implication has the capacity to generate paradoxes and instabilities within texts, reflection is seen to suggest something altogether less exhilarating and disruptive.[4] But it is important to realize that this second sense is also crucial for their work, and in particular, for their attempts to find new forms of writing that can embody, sustain and explore these instabilities. For whereas Dimension 1 describes a structural aspect of representation, the use of new literary forms derives from reflection on and recognition of this first dimension. After all, structural reflexivity can be acknowledged but ignored in practice (Ashmore, 1989, chap. 4) or dealt with in different ways (Latour, 1988): The strategy of (attempting to) highlight structural reflexivity within a text implies a commitment to reflecting upon it as a part of one's representational practice.[5]

A third dimension can be tentatively offered.

Dimension 3: Reflexivity refers to the inseparability of representation and represented. This implies, for example, a rejection of the idea that the observation and description of phenomena can be seen as detached from those phenomena. This can be termed embedded reflexivity.

Embedded reflexivity itself admits of a range of emphases, from the need to take into account some version of the context of representation (but see Cooper, 1991) to the assertion that representations constitute or create the objects they describe (Woolgar, 1988b). The latter point resonates with a number of contemporary approaches to representation within the humanities and social sciences, whereas within SSK it can be placed at the extreme end of the relativism/realism axis. It should not be seen as a separate and distinct thread from structural and/or cognitive reflexivity. They are all rather to be interpreted as differences of emphasis. For example, embedded reflexivity can itself differentially be seen in structural or cognitive terms: In the latter case the stress would fall on the observer's reflection upon his or her degree of engagement in the phenomena of interest.

It is easy to see that, whilst these different strands of meaning are closely interrelated, they allow for a wide range of usages. Let us briefly consider a few. Reflexivity has been considered a defining feature of modernity in at least two distinct senses. Lawson (1985) considers it to be the central problem of modern philosophy, given that the recognition of the constitutive quality of language (3) gives rise to problems of self-reference (1). In the work of Beck and Giddens however, reflexive modernity refers to the capacity of citizens to reflect upon, monitor and critique their political and social environment (2) (see, e.g., Beck, Giddens, & Lash, 1994). Interestingly, this capacity for reflection may be conceptualized as deriving from the achievement of (cognitive) detachment from structural constraints. In other words, reflection may imply the very opposite of embedded reflexivity; and indeed this tension may be seen in the problems associated with "meta-reflexivity," to use Latour's (1988) term, within SSK (see Section 7).

By contrast, many other uses of the term stress the embedded character of reflexivity. In ethnomethodology, for example, reflexivity refers to the relation of accounts to the settings and contexts in which they are located, and which they describe: in Garfinkel's (1968) terms, they are "constituent features of the settings they make observable" (p. 8). This has a number of methodological consequences for social science which I cannot pursue here; but we can note that its significance is not restricted to the ways in which the social scientist would treat and interpret his or her materials where the latter are considered "data," The presence and interpretative work of the social scientist would itself be part of the setting being reported and subject to the implications of embedded reflexivity. Note here three approaches that entail different responses to this methodological issue, all of which entail reflection on the significance of the observer's presence as a way of improving the quality of the social scientist's account. Hammersley and Atkinson (1983) recommend reflexivity as a methodological device for avoiding positivism and naturalism in ethnographic studies. Work within feminist ethnography suggests that the gendered experience of the ethnographer in the field should be considered an important source of insight and part of the materials under study (see, e.g., Callaway, 1992). For Bourdieu (1990), the scientific status of the sociological or anthropological account can be buttressed by making the act of observation part of the phenomena of interest; in particular, the institutional constraints and structures of the observer's world are brought into focus.

Within the social sciences then, reflexivity arises both as a feature of modernity, and as a problem for method (to be solved by reflection). Before considering the question of reflexivity outside the social sciences, it can be suggested that reflexivity emerges as an issue of particular pertinence for certain disciplines and subdisciplines. For any body of work that takes as its central problematic language, representation, or knowledge, reflexivity will be of potential importance, even if responses to it within those fields might range from celebration, through management, to dismissal or silence. SSK is a conspicuous example here, but reflexivity is not, as some of its debates seem to assume, its exclusive property. For example, as Weber (1982) points out that psychoanalysis—a rational discourse on irrationality—can be seen as a discipline that has attempted to repress unavoidable reflexive questions (in a markedly reflexive manner) but asks "Can psychoanalytic thinking itself escape the effects of what it tries to think?" (p. xvi). Similarly, recent currents in literary theory and philosophy, such as deconstruction, which stress the constitutive character of textuality can be seen in part as responding to reflexive issues.

If the above remarks construe reflexivity as an issue for the social sciences and humanities, we should nevertheless treat claims that that it is not an issue for the natural sciences with considerable caution. Woolgar (1988a), for example, suggests that the natural sciences would acknowledge reflexivity as a "problem" "only if it was granted that electrons (like physicists) had belief systems, their own theories of interaction and so on" (p. 23). However, the validity of this assertion would appear to rest on the prioritizing and generalizing of what I have called cognitive reflexivity.[6] Bartlett (1987) points to a number of reflexive aspects in the natural sciences and mathematics which derive from structural or embedded dimensions: for example, proof-theoretical reflexivity in Cantor and Godel, reflexivity in topology, chronology, quantum mechanics, and biology (see also Hofstadter, 1980, on recursion in computer science, mathematics, music, and art; Steier, 1992, for a range of disciplines).

Self-consciously reflexive work within SSK can therefore be seen as having both differences and similarities with features of this heterogeneous collection of approaches; moreover, these will perhaps differ depending on whether we take its claims at face value or choose to read its texts more critically. But we can point to two emphases that, while not exclusive to avowedly reflexive work within SSK, play a large part in shaping its identity. First, in contrast to more overtly "humanist" approaches, the symmetries that concern it are at the level of textual representation: that is, symmetries that arise in description rather than in the embodied presence of the observer.[7]

Second, and closely related to the first point, it is committed to exploring rather than controlling the effects of reflexivity. Indeed, the development of "new literary forms" is precisely an attempt to go beyond that form of response to reflexivity that amounts to qualifying one's claims and carrying on as before; rather, a form of textuality is sought in which the paradoxes and instabilities of reflexivity can be both sustained and examined.

5. THE RATIONALE FOR NEW LITERARY FORMS

Woolgar (1982) is usually credited with the first reference to the need for new literary forms in SSK: "We need to explore forms of literary expression whereby the monster can be simultaneously kept at bay and allowed a position at the heart of our enterprise" (p. 489), where "the enterprise" is the ethnography of science, "the monster" is reflexivity, and "we" is a rhetorically constructed community of uncertain scope and status.[8] Of course, as its advocates are happy to acknowledge, the attribute "new" (noticeably absent from Woolgar's much cited original account) only has validity within this particular field. Other fields have experimented with textual forms as a response to, and as a part of, their own critiques of referential discourse; for example, work within deconstruction (see, e.g., Derrida, 1986; Ronell, 1989) and notably those parts of twentieth-century literature that can be read as a "revolt" against realist aesthetics (see Nash, 1987). Reflexive SSK has in some cases borrowed from the latter.

As I have already noted, the rationale for new literary forms is to facilitate the exploration and even celebration of aspects of reflexivity. In particular, the emphasis placed on the social construction of knowledge and the multiplicity of possible accounts that can be given of phenomena within SSK is seen as necessitating a different form of writing from the more orthodox realist and monologic (single-voiced) form of (social) scientific texts. As Mulkay (1991a) puts it, he saw a need to "devise a new kind of sociological language that could give expression to the conception of knowledge provided by SSK" (p. xvii). A key strategy here has been the introduction of more than one voice into the text.

But if Mulkay's saying that he had to devise a new language in order more adequately to represent a particular conception of what he is studying, what's so radical about that? In fact, it's difficult to imagine a more realist statement, isn't it?

Well, you might be right.[9] Or you might just be a token example of how the use of a different voice can be used to introduce instabilities into texts. And it would certainly be wrong to assume that new literary forms are just a means of putting more than one side of an argument; different voices are part of it. The belief seems to be that "whereas traditional, monologic texts were designed to hide their own textuality, that is, their own artful use of language to give meaning to the world, these other forms reveal and celebrate that textuality" (Mulkay, 1991a, xviii).

Designed to hide their own textuality? You must be kidding. Designed by whom? What is this, the conspiracy theory of scientific realism?

(et cetera)

Other claims can, have, and might be made for new literary forms beside the celebration of heterogeneity, the introduction of instability, and the foregrounding of the processes of textual construction. But I wish to draw attention here to just one further feature of new literary forms which is, if not always explicitly claimed, a common motivation behind many of these texts. This can be explained in terms of a distinction between what a text says and what it shows.[10] That is to say, the form of the text can be made to contribute to the points being made, either supporting or contradicting what is being ostensibly claimed. In this way, as Lawson (1985) puts it, "the move of reflexivity allows the text to indicate in the shift of meaning that there is something beyond what is merely said" (p. 113).

Let us move on to look at some examples of new literary forms. But let us (writer and readers) bear in mind two important provisos. First, the boundaries of new literary forms are not given, and indeed the entity itself is something of a construct. I have chosen to concentrate mainly on work by authors who have characterized themselves in these terms, but attempts to define the essence and limits of this work would raise further interesting analytic issues which there is insufficient space to go into here. To give just one example, if new literary forms can be seen in part as a necessary move beyond orthodox forms, we would want to know what constituted orthodoxy in particular settings: A dialogue would be less dramatic in a collection of interviews with sociologists than in a scientific journal.

Second, the extent to which new literary forms constitute a technology, a set of techniques for the achievement of reflexive effects should be, and will be, and indeed is being, critically questioned.

6. NEW LITERARY FORMS— A USER'S MANUAL

Here is a selection of new literary techniques you may find useful for achieving reflexive effects. Note that not all of the items in this selection are mutually exclusive nor even distinct from each other.

Asymmetric Lists

"Asymmetric" here means simply that not all of the items in the list are mutually exclusive or even distinct from each other. The form probably originates in Borges' fictional Chinese encyclopedia (cited in Foucault, 1970, p. xv), but the classic instance of it in SSK is Ashmore's (1989) encyclopedia of reflexivity (chap. 2). To get a flavor of the effects of asymmetry, compile a list, include a number of overlapping categories, and make at least some entries refer to each other and some refer to themselves.

Dialogue

This has been the preeminent method of introducing different voices into SSK texts. There are variations in format, but the basic style is not dissimilar to the representation of dialogue in novels. Here is an example of the introduction of dialogue into a text (Woolgar & Ashmore, 1988, p. 2):

> At the same time, other contributors recognise and comment upon some of the difficulties associated with this development . . .
>
> EXCUSE ME, CAN I ASK SOMETHING HERE?
>
> Oh, not you again. What is it?

Notice here that the introduction of different "voices" into the text—a central rationale in many accounts—is taken in a particularly literal sense: Dialogues involve the simulation of spoken conversation and are frequently "chatty" in a way that can be irritating to many.[11]

Plays

(curtain rises)

> **Author:** Apparently an extension of "dialogues," which allows more than two voices to be heard, even though Mulkay's (1984) "The Scientist Talks Back: A One-Act Play" was one of the first actual uses of new literary forms.
>
> **Referee:** Perhaps you should mention some other examples of overtly "dramatic" formats, such as Ashmore (1989, chap. 7).
>
> **Editor:** Good idea.

(exeunt)

Parallel Texts and Happenings

Monologic texts, dialogues and conventional play formats share the catastrophically unreflexive limitation that only one "voice" can be read or heard at the same time.

Parallel texts, by contrast, enable the simultaneous display of different arguments, whether conflicting or harmonious (Ashmore, 1989; Derrida, 1986).

Parallel texts find their dramatic analogue in Case's (1992) conception and use of "happenings" in which at times anarchic cacophony of overlapping voices is created. (To appreciate the effect, attendance at a live performance is necessary.)

Giving Voices to Unlikely Entities

Monologic texts, dialogues, plays, parallel texts, and happenings, however, can all too easily accept the somewhat staid assumption that "voices" be associated with living human agents. Some recent work has rectified this lack of epistemological nerve (cf. Collins & Yearley, 1992) by giving voices to other entities such as dead scientists (Ashmore, 1993), dolphins (Mulkay, 1991a), embryos in the womb (Mulkay, 1991b), and the text itself (in debates with the author and other voices) (Low, 1992).[12]

Reflexive Footnoting[13]

The Book Review

Scientific and Technical Communication: Theory, Practice, and Policy contains a particularly pretentious piece on 'new literary forms' which, despite its claim to be a critical review of this body of work quickly degenerates into pastiche" (pioneered by Ashmore, Mulkay, & Pinch, 1989).

Backstage/Frontstage

A useful technique popularised by Ashmore (1989) and Woolgar (1989; 1992), in which some of the interaction and communication that precedes the writing of the paper is referred to in order to underline the social processes at work in the construction of the text: for example, communications with editors, referees, and so on (see also Cooper, 1997).[14]

Fiction

What characterizes many of these experiments is their use of explicitly fictional forms of writing. This aspect of these new literary forms implies a critique of the distinction between the fictional and the factual, a distinction that constitutes the most basic interpretative prop for the production of scholarly/scientific (nonfiction) discourse.

Quotation

Similarly, the distinction between author and other can be deconstructed by inserting into one's text, and thereby recontextualizing, fragments from other sources. An example of this is the previous entry, extracted from Ashmore's (1989) encyclopedia of reflexivity (p. 66) that parts of this section resemble. The question arises whether this resemblance qualifies the section as a genuine member of the class "new literary forms," or whether it disqualifies it on the grounds of lack of novelty. Hope is at hand, however, for this may well be construed as an example of a . . .

Paradox

To achieve a really authentic "new literary forms" effect, paradoxes are essential. Regardless of the risk of banality, they should be pursued, indicated, and discussed as relentlessly as possible.

Irony

Indispensable part of the new literary formalist's repertoire but easily overdone. Use sparingly.[15]

Wit

If possible.

Self-Reference

Mandatory. Sprinkle liberally throughout.

Narcissism and Navel Gazing

See next section, "Debates."

Ordinary Prose (1)

In certain settings, the decision to avoid experimentation with the form of the text can make a reflexive point; for example, it may represent an assertion (or the testing of an assertion) that such experimentation is unnecessary for the adequate discussion of reflexivity. As such, it attempts both to show and to describe and therefore meets a central criterion for new literary forms (see Cooper, 1997, for an example and discussion of this phenomenon; also cf. the opening sections of Pinch & Pinch, 1988, with their concluding section).

Ordinary Prose (2)

There is, of course, no such thing (see "Fiction" above).

7. DEBATES

It is fair to say that the use of new literary forms has not won universal admiration within SSK. In this section, I consider some of the problems associated with, and criticisms of, this body of work. I suggest that an informed evaluation should avoid conflating reflexivity and new literary forms in the way that some critics have done, especially given, as noted in Section 4, the enormous breadth of approaches and concerns that the former can signify. An awareness of this breadth helps to mitigate against the assumption that the effective criticism of particular techniques would amount to a demolition of the validity of reflexivity as an intellectual issue. Let us begin by looking at some of the issues that relate more to the mode of writing.

First, there is the problem of the alienating effects of some of these stylistic innovations. There is little doubt that many readers find them off-putting (see, e.g., Pinch & Pinch, 1988; Wynne, 1986). The relation that these texts set up with their readers seems to be the heart of the problem here. Latour (1988), in the most sophisticated criticism to date, points to one aspect of this, the existence of "a very naive set of beliefs in the naive beliefs of readers" (p. 168): that is, the assumption that unless attention is drawn to the constructed character of the text, to the contingency of its claims and so forth, then there is a danger of the reader being taken in. The reader must be protected. This can constitute an almost patronizing stance toward the reader, and the effect may be exacerbated by the continual need for the text to refer back to and attend to itself. Whether or not this is perceived as narcissism, the reader can be reduced to the role of bystander while the different voices chat among themselves—the deconstructive work is done for the reader.

The paradox here is that much of this work makes the acts of reading and interpretation themselves topics in a way that most writing does not (see, e.g., Mulkay, 1985, preface). Yet there is a sense in which it has only the vaguest conception of who the audience for this work would be. At its worst, its authors give the impression that they are writing for their own elite community of cognoscenti, from which the reader is excluded.[16]

A further criticism that relates specifically to new literary forms, though it is taken as having a wider significance by some (e.g., Collins & Yearley, 1992), concerns what one might call the political claims that are sometimes made for the genre. The issue is whether bringing in different voices involves a form of epistemological modesty whereby the sociologist, or more generally the writer, refuses to adopt the traditional privileged position of authority within the text. Pinch and Pinch (1988) and Collins and Yearley (1992) have both pointed out that dialogue can be used to simulate plurality while the argument remains in the control of the author.

Gosh. But seriously, who would want to argue with that?

No one. On the other hand, there may be a case for saying that some new literary formalists overstate the case for the antiauthoritarian and liberal potential of the form.[17] But most would be uneasy about the technological determinism of both positions, if we take writing as a technology.[18]

This leads us to some criticisms which also involve questions about reflexivity more generally, and which therefore avoid this restrictive isolated focus on the technology. Of course, there are many who see reflexivity a needless distraction from the real business of empirical research. This is not the place to argue this particular issue in depth, the primary concern being new literary forms, but since they are so often seen as equivalent I will briefly note a problem with one recurrent charge. Collins and Yearley's (1992) central point is that reflexivity (which includes new literary forms) "leads nowhere" (p. 305) and should therefore be abandoned. The assertion points to a potentially complex area of debate: I would want to begin by asserting rather that reflexivity "leads somewhere else." [19] But my main dispute is with the conception of reflexivity that underlies the remark (and the same point could be made in relation to relativism): that is, reflexivity is assumed to be or formulated as a matter of (mere) academic preference. On this account, its "usefulness" can be assessed, and it can be adopted or discarded accordingly. However, this neglects the possibility, suggested in Section 4, that reflexivity may be an unavoidable feature of modernity, of contemporary culture. To construe it as simply a matter of epistemological style is to misunderstand the way in which academic matters are embedded within wider cultural fields.

If this line of argument is followed through, the more interesting questions arise as matters of response and strategy toward reflexivity. I will mention two. First, Latour's point. Latour (1988) accepts the validity of reflexivity as a phenomenon but sees new literary forms as a misguided response to it, a response which he subsumes under the category of meta-reflexivity. Meta-reflexivity entails the attempt for a text to separate from and comment upon itself, to aspire to a metalevel, to escape "the semiotic turn." This, it is said, cannot be done.[20] Rather, one should accept that a story is just a story and adopt an infrareflexive strategy: that is, use rhetorical tricks and devices (such as realism) to persuade readers in the same way that, for example, scientific texts have been shown to do. On this account, to explore reflexivity within the text is essentially pointless, in the sense that it attempts the impossible.[21]

Second, two different articles have made a similar point about the individualism which is implicit in this form of writing. Beer and Martins (1990) commenting on Ashmore (1989) suggest that such work may be a form of "hyperindividualism" and that this lies at the opposite end of the spectrum from the cooperative nature of scientific activity that it studies.[22] They suggest that this may be both empowering and reductive. Collins (1990) brings out the implications of this: for if reflexivity in SSK is seen to arise in respect of the symmetry between scientific and social scientific representation, then the assertion that texts should in some way engage in reflexivity depends on the individual and the individual text being taken as the relevant unit. However, if reflexivity is considered to be an issue for a (scientific) community, then the need to "be reflexive" as we report on empirical matters disappears. Reflexivity can be achieved at the communal level.

If these two criticisms are telling ones, we should be aware of the limits of their scope. Latour's point is aimed primarily at the attempt, which he imputes to meta-reflexivists, to achieve "truer texts," but this imputation is contentious, and it certainly does not represent the totality of what new literary formalists set out to do. The point about individualism, similarly, suggests that experimental reflexive texts are not a necessary response to issues of symmetry, but it does not imply that they are not a valid response, albeit one among many. All that is removed is the idea of compulsion.

8. CONCLUSION

So there we have it. Hopefully, readers now have a clearer idea of what new literary forms are, how to use them, and why they might want to use them. However, bearing in mind the reservations expressed in Section 7 about the alienating effects of this genre, they might be edgy that this slightly more informal tone coupled with an explicit reference to "readers" means that the text is about to fall back into another embarrassing dialogue. This is not the case (yet). My personal conviction is that, for those studying science and technology and indeed for a whole range of intellectual work today, thinking through the implications of reflexivity for one's own practice is invaluable, and that attempts to engage in new forms of writing represent an important attempt to do this. This is not to say that there are not problems to be dealt with. Perhaps the challenge is to give more thought to the reader's position in this enterprise and to develop modes of writing with this in mind.

I suggested at the outset that a key issue for this text was whether this work could be adequately reviewed without recourse to literary experimentation. In other words, what is the relationship between new literary forms and reflexivity? It seems to me that there are two key formulations here. The first takes new literary forms as techniques that can be applied and which of themselves achieve reflexive effects. The second is to insist that reflexivity cannot be discussed without experimenting with the form of the argument. The first is a species of technological determinism, and I have attempted to be critical of it in different ways throughout the chapter. The second is more difficult to assess: Part of the rationale for the form that this chapter has taken was to assess the extent to which experimentation was necessary to do justice to the arguments.

And what's the result? Do you need to use these forms?

Well, of course, it's not that simple. For one thing, if we follow the findings of SSK, the success or otherwise of an experiment is a matter for social negotiation (Collins, 1975).[23] So in this case, the "success" or otherwise of different parts of the chapter is not a matter for the judgement of the author. But of course the issue here goes beyond this, for the idea that this text could serve as some sort of test case should probably be seen more as a rhetorical device for introducing the issues.

How can you say that? You set up the adequacy of different forms of representation as the key issue for the chapter.

And so it has been. Hopefully, the form(s) adopted have brought into focus a number of important issues. For one thing, it attempts to deconstruct the idea that the "voice" behind the text can be unproblematically taken as belonging to the author. This is not the same as simply adding more voices, each expressing different points of view: Rather, it's a matter of trying to show how different genres and conventions of authorship are behind texts (cf. Foucault, 1977). Perhaps this is a way of beginning to deconstruct the simplistic distinction between "new literary forms" and orthodox academic prose; after all, the latter is itself subject to a whole range of conventions. And if this line of argument is followed through, it might mitigate against the reification of techniques and the confusion of technique with forms of knowledge.

So, after all this, aren't you in effect saying that the way things are written is irrelevant?

No, this is not an idealist argument for the irrelevance of techniques and technologies of representation to knowledge: It's an argument against the degeneration of technique into formula. Certain writers begin experimenting with some textual forms that have been comparatively little used within their field; this has the potential to draw attention to a range of questions about reflexivity, textuality, genres, conventions of authorship, and so forth. The problem is that such experimentation can in turn come to be seen as a delimited and definable genre in its own right and thus reincorporated into the stable set of assumptions that it set out to disrupt.[24] The further move can then be made of reducing the diversity of issues that are, or could be, raised about representation to questions about the adequacy of this constructed genre.

So in response to the original question about the adequacy of, and necessity for, new literary forms, you would want to say that a reformulation of the question could stand as an answer?

Who, me?

NOTES

1. Some of its advocates have provided monologic rationales for the use of new literary forms. See, for example, Mulkay (1991a, preface), Woolgar (1988a).

2. It should be noted here that much of the work discussed in this chapter can be read precisely in terms of the aspiration to an overview. On this point, see in particular Latour (1988), discussed in Section 7.

3. In so doing, is an implicit claim being made that knowledge can be discussed independently of and prior to consideration of questions about its representation?

4. See, for example, Woolgar's (1988a) distinction between reflection and reflexion, and Ashmore (1989, chap. 2).

5. Derrida (1991) shows that for all the grandiose claims of continental theory about moving beyond subjectivity/cognition such a move would be extremely hard to accomplish. Indeed, one way of reading his work is in terms of the complex interaction of structure and subjectivity/cognition.

6. Denigration of mere "reflection" notwithstanding; see Note 4.

7. This statement is somewhat contentious in its generality and an adequate treatment of the issue would require lengthy discussion. There are certainly exceptions—for example, Low (1991) and Law (1994). The interesting issue to be explored here is the question of the identity or difference of the researcher in the

field with respect to the author in the text: This chapter should shed some light on why one might wish to support the apparently bizarre assertion that they be thought of as separate entities.

8. As is argued later, the audience has a problematic status in some of this work.

9. See Latour (1988) on the fallacy of truer texts discussed in Section 7.

10. Antecedents for this can be found in the work of both Wittgenstein and Derrida, to name but two. See, respectively, Janik and Toulmin (1973) and Lawson (1985) for discussion.

11. A number of variations are possible here. See, for example, Wynne's (1988) reflection on her own analytic practice, Latour's (1989) highly formal debate, Woolgar's (1993) staging of an imaginary argument between two of his critics, Cooper and Woolgar's (1996) dramatization of tensions between different positions in contemporary research practice, and Derrida's (1995) simulated interview.

12. There are some parallels here with work in actor-network theory. See, for example, Callon (1986). Some dialogues attempt to avoid the assignation of voices to any (stable) identities. See, for example, parts of Ashmore (1989) and Woolgar and Ashmore (1988).

13. This should not be confused with the use of footnotes to supply methodological correctives (Woolgar, 1988a) to claims made in the main text. Rather, the footnotes' capacity for self-reference should be exploited. A good example of this is Woolgar (1989, note 7); see also Cooper (1997, note 19).

14. Not to be confused with an apparently similar device in the acknowledgments of conventional academic papers.

15. More specifically, be sure to use the right kind of irony—reflexive, not instrumental (Woolgar, 1983).

16. In particular, the structure of the most important collection of this writing (Woolgar, 1988c) gives this unfortunate impression.

17. In my view, Mulkay sometimes does this.

18. Perhaps the further point that has been insufficiently discussed is whether the insertion of different voices can be read as an abdication of authorial responsibility: for instance, as a refusal to assert unequivocally without recourse to contradiction, paradox, and qualification.

19. Indeed, Lyotard's (1984) concept of paralogy can be read as suggesting that reflexivity is part of the key dynamic behind the generation of new research paradigms. Woolgar's claims for iterative reconceptualization are in some ways similar (see, e.g., Woolgar, 1992).

20. Nash (1987) makes a similar assertion with regard to literary texts: "Self-reflexivity, for instance, can only make a fool of itself—as writers are often now aware and as the topos of infinite regress shows—since for a text properly to demonstrate, to point to itself, it must stand outside itself and this no text could accomplish however much it wished" (pp. 241-242). It would also appear that the recourse to a metalevel might be in conflict with claims for the liberalism of these texts.

21. Interestingly however, Latour (1992) is full of the textual experimentation of the sort that he here questions.

22. It may be that this tension is manifested in other ways within such work: for whereas the assertion of reflexivity's importance within SSK entails a claim about the symmetry between science and social science, insofar as both are

representational justifications for textual experimentation, it can be formulated in terms of the need to escape the empiricist constraints of scientific representation.

23. The crucial aspect of social negotiation here may turn out to be reader/writer relations.

24. It might reasonably be argued that both advocates and critics share some of the responsibility for this.

BIBLIOGRAPHY

Ashmore, M. (1989). The reflexive thesis: Writing sociology of scientific knowledge. Chicago: University of Chicago Press.

Ashmore, M. (1993). The theatre of the blind: Starring a promethean prankster, a phoney phenomenon, a prism, a pocket, and a piece of wood. Social Studies of Science, 23(1), 67-106.

Ashmore, M., Mulkay, M., & Pinch, T. (1989). Health and efficiency: A sociology of health economics. Milton Keynes: Open University Press.

Bartlett, S. J. (1987). Varieties of self-reference. In S. J. Bartlett & P. Suber (Eds.), Self-reference: Reflections on reflexivity. Dordrecht: Martinus Nijhoff.

Beck, U., Giddens, A., & Lash, S. (1994). Reflexive modernization: Politics. tradition and aesthetics in the modern social order. Cambridge, England: Polity.

Beer, G., & Martins, H. (1990). Editorial introduction to special issue on the rhetoric of science. History of the Human Sciences, 3(2), 163-175.

Bourdieu, P. (1990). The logic of practice. Cambridge, England: Polity.

Callaway, H. (1992). Ethnography and experience: Gender implications in fieldwork and texts. In J. Okely & H. Callaway (Eds.), Anthropology and autobiography. London: Routledge.

Callon, M. (1986). Some elements of a sociology of translation: Domestication of the scallops and the fishermen of St Brieuc's Bay. In J. Law (Ed.), Power, action and belief: A new sociology of knowledge? London: Routledge.

Case, P. (1992, September). Information happenings: Performing reflexive organizational research. Paper presented at Discourse Analysis and Reflexivity Workshop, Sheffield University.

Collins, H. (1975). The seven sexes: A study in the sociology of a phenomenon, or the replication of experiments in physics. Sociology, 9, 205-224.

Collins, H. (1990, March 2). Tu quoque [review of Ashmore, 1989]. Times Higher Education Supplement, p. 20.

Collins, H., & Yearley, S. (1992). Epistemological chicken. In A. Pickering (Ed.), Science as practice and culture. Chicago: University of Chicago Press.

Cooper, G. (1991). Context and its representation. Interacting with Computers, 3(3), 243-252.

Cooper, G. (1997). Textual technologies: New literary forms and reflexivity. In J. H. Collier with D. M. Toomey (Eds.), Scientific and technical communication: Theory, practice, and policy (pp. 270-298). Thousand Oaks, CA: Sage.

Cooper, G., & Woolgar, S. (1996). The research process: Context, autonomy, audience. In E. Lyon & J. Busfield (Eds.), Methodological imaginations. New York: Macmillan.

Derrida, J. (1986). *Glas* (J. P. Leavey, Jr. & R. Rand, Trans.). Lincoln: University of Nebraska Press.

Derrida, J. (1991). "Eating well," or the calculation of the subject: An interview with Jacques Derrida. In E. Cadava, P. Connor, & J.-L. Nancy (Eds.), *Who comes after the subject.* London: Routledge.

Derrida, J. (1995). Language (*Le Monde* on the telephone). In *Points: Interviews, 1974- 1994.* Stanford, CA: Stanford University Press.

Foucault, M. (1970). *The order of things* (A. Sheridan Smith, Trans.). London: Tavistock.

Foucault, M. (1977). What is an author? In D. F. Bouchard (Ed.), *Language, counter-memory, practice.* Oxford, England: Blackwell.

Garfinkel, H. (1968). *Studies in ethnomethodology.* Englewood Cliffs, NJ: Prentice Hall.

Hammersley, M., & Atkinson, P. (1983). *Ethnography: Principles in practice.* London: Tavistock.

Hofstadter, D. (1980). *Godel, Escher, Bach: An eternal golden braid.* Harmondsworth, England: Penguin.

Janik, A., & Toulmin, S. (1973). *Wittgenstein's Vienna.* New York: Simon & Schuster.

Latour, B. (1988). The politics of explanation. In S. Woolgar (Ed.), *Knowledge and reflexivity.* London: Sage.

Latour, B. (1989). Clothing the naked truth. In H. Lawson & L. Appignanesi (Eds.), *Dismantling truth: Reality in the postmodern world.* London: Weidenfeld & Nicholson.

Latour, B. (1992). *Aramis ou l'amour des techniques.* Paris: La Decouverte.

Law, J. (1994). *Organizing modernity.* Oxford, England: Blackwell.

Lawson, H. (1985). *Reflexivity: The postmodern predicament.* Melbourne, Australia: Hutchinson.

Low, J. (1991, April). *Quiet bodies, clean voices.* Paper presented at the Discourse Analysis and Reflexivity Workshop, York University.

Low, J. (1992, April). *Humans and nonhumans in the computer department.* Paper presented at the Discourse Analysis and Reflexivity Workshop, Brunel University.

Lyotard, J. F. (1984). *The postmodern condition: A report on knowledge.* Manchester, England: Manchester University Press.

Mulkay, M. (1984). The scientist talks back: A one-act play, with a moral, about replication in science and reflexivity in sociology. *Social Studies of Science, 14,* 265-282.

Mulkay, M. (1985). *The word and the world: Explorations in the form of sociological analysis.* London: Allen & Unwin.

Mulkay, M. (1991a). *Sociology of science: A sociological pilgrimage.* Milton Keynes, England: Open University Press.

Mulkay, M. (1991b). Intruders in the Fallopian tube—or a dream of perfect human reproduction. *Human Reproduction, 6*(10), 1480-1486.

Nash, C. (1987). *World-games: The tradition of antirealist revolt.* London: Methuen.

Pickering, A. (Ed.). (1992). *Science as practice and culture.* Chicago: University of Chicago Press.

Pinch, T., & Pinch, T. (1988). Reservations about reflexivity and new literary forms, or why let the devil have all the good tunes? In S. Woolgar (Ed.), *Knowledge and reflexivity.* London: Sage.

Ronell, A. (1989). *The telephone book: Technology, schizophrenia, electric speech.* Lincoln: University of Nebraska Press.

Steier, F. (Ed.). (1992). *Research and reflexivity.* London: Sage.

Weber, S. (1982). *The legend of Freud.* Minneapolis: University of Minnesota Press.

Woolgar, S. (1982). Laboratory studies: A comment on the state of the art. *Social Studies of Science, 12,* 481-498.

Woolgar, S. (1983). Irony in the social study of science. In K. Knorr-Cetina & M. Mulkay (Eds.), *Science observed.* London: Sage.

Woolgar, S. (1988a). Reflexivity is the ethnographer of the text. In S. Woolgar (Ed.), *Knowledge and reflexivity.* London: Sage.

Woolgar, S. (1988b). *Science: The very idea.* London: Ellis Horwood/Tavistock.

Woolgar, S. (Ed.). (1988c). *Knowledge and reflexivity.* London: Sage.

Woolgar, S. (1989). A coffeehouse conversation on the possibility of mechanizing discovery and its sociological analysis. *Social Studies of Science, 19*(4), 658-668.

Woolgar, S. (1992). Some remarks about positionism: A reply to Collins and Yearley. In A. Pickering (Ed.), *Science as practice and culture.* Chicago: University of Chicago Press.

Woolgar, S. (1993). What's at stake in the sociology of technology? A reply to Pinch and Winner. *Science, Technology, & Human Values, 18*(4), 523-529.

Woolgar, S., & Ashmore, M. (1988). The next step: An introduction to the reflexive project. In S. Woolgar (Ed.), *Knowledge and reflexivity.* London: Sage.

Wynne, A. (1986, April). *Reading and writing: Sociology.* Paper presented at the Discourse Analysis and Reflexivity Workshop, University of York.

Wynne, A. (1988). Accounting for accounts of the diagnosis of multiple sclerosis. In S. Woolgar (Ed.), *Knowledge and reflexivity.* London: Sage.

Discussion

1. Note the prologue to Cooper's piece. Why is this information given? How does knowing the "pretext" help lend to an interpretation of Cooper's text? More generally, do you think it would be "more objective" to know the complete circumstances under which scientific or technical texts are produced? What factors in the writing process do you think are important to let the reader know? How would a reader of your prose be aided by knowing the elements of your writing process?

2. "Reflexivity," Cooper points out, "can be provisionally characterized as an issue that arises when we address questions of representation: the statements that we make, or the knowledge that we construct about representational practice are themselves representations and thus implicated in what they

describe." Initially, offer an interpretation of this statement. Provide examples of how specific communications practices represent the activity they describe. How do representations of activities (e.g., lab experiments) shape our understanding of the thing in itself? Can one get "outside" linguistic or graphic representations? A critic of the usefulness of reflexivity has argued that it is a little like a bricklayer suddenly ceasing his work so that he may take time to study his trowel. Which view most nearly approaches your own? Why?

3. One of the goals of reflexive textual practices and new literary form is to "disrupt" traditional forms of representation used in scientific and technical communication. What, from Cooper's perspective, is harmful about these representational practices? In what specific ways do new literary forms (NLFs) disrupt representation? How are the tools of NLFs—such as dialogue, parallel texts, irony—in themselves a form of representation? Can you suggest other communicative forms that might be "more useful" in transforming the traditional practices of technical communication?

4. How is the study of scientific knowledge a reflexive problem? What are the central criticisms of reflexive textual practices that Cooper describes? Do you see alternatives to these limitations, or are these practices destined to collapse under their own weight?

5. In what fields or disciplines do you see reflexive issues having the greatest impact? How does the reflexive "problem" manifest itself in these fields? Critics of the social sciences argue that because of inherent reflexive problems in the nature of social and behavioral study, no universal, objective claims and predications can be made about human action. Do you agree or disagree? Why? How might NLFs be a solution to this problem?

6. Cooper ends with an exchange with his omnipresent interlocutor:

   So, after all this, aren't you in effect saying that the way things are written is irrelevant?
   No, this is not an idealist argument for the irrelevance of techniques and technologies of representation to knowledge: It's an argument against the degeneration of technique into

formula. Certain writers begin experimenting with some textual forms that have been comparatively little used within their field; this has the potential to draw attention to a range of questions about reflexivity, textuality, genres, conventions of authorship, and so forth.

In part, this text assumes Cooper's premise that the techniques of scientific and technical communication have, in many cases, simply degenerated into formula. Explain whether you agree or disagree with this assessment. What is the harm in technical communication being dominated by formula? What communicative formulas and standards do you follow in your field or discipline? How do they shape your thinking and expression? What advantages and disadvantages are there to having shared, regulated discourse?

Exercises

1. Cooper provides a "user's manual" for new literary forms. Take a paper that you have previously written, the purpose of which is to objectively render information (e.g., a lab report, set of instructions, functional description, or formal definition), and revise it into a reflexive text using the techniques in the "manual." If you would prefer not to do this with your own work, find a short journal article and assume the authors' identity. In a prologue to the text, instruct the reader how "it came to light."

2. Throughout the chapter, Cooper mentions texts that use new literary forms in their style of presentation (including his own). Referring to the techniques for reading texts in fields in which you are not expert (Chapter 2), write a critical analysis of Cooper's text or another reflexive text. In the conclusion or recommendations section, provide a "reading plan" for someone interested in reading a reflexive text. Consider lending advice about how one should intellectually and emotionally approach these texts, how they are best read (sequentially, at random, closely, apathetically), and how reading a reflexive text compares with reading texts that are common in your

field. Consider what light wrestling with a reflexive text sheds on how scientific and technical texts are traditionally written and read.

3. At the beginning of the semester, form into groups of three or four and provide a short-term (two to three weeks) or term-length "participant observer" study of a laboratory, seminar series, research class, or professional setting. During the course of the study you will need to take notes on the actions of the people you observe. If you own, or have access to, a hand-held tape recorder, you can, with the participants' permission, record what goes on in the research setting. There are two parts to this assignment.

To begin, prepare a brief literature review of a selected number of anthropological and sociological studies of other cultures. In the literature, be careful to note the kinds of artifacts, rituals, customs, social structures, and languages observed in other cultures. Although general texts on anthropological method will do, here are some places in the literature (to which Cooper sometimes refers—his footnotes may also provide inspiration) to start:

▓ James Clifford and George Marcus (Eds.). (1986). *Writing cultures.* Berkeley: University of California Press.

▓ Clifford Geertz. (1973). *Interpreting cultures.* New York: Harper & Row.

▓ Karin Knorr-Cetina and Michael Mulkay (Eds.). (1983). *Science observed: Perspectives on the social study of science.* London: Sage.

▓ Bruno Latour and Steve Woolgar. (1986). *Laboratory life: The social construction of scientific facts* (2nd ed.). Princeton, NJ: Princeton University Press.

▓ Greg Myers. (1990). *Writing biology: Texts in the social construction of scientific knowledge.* Madison: University of Wisconsin Press.

The second part of the assignment is to find the academic culture you wish to study. Consider choosing a discipline with which your group is unfamiliar. Next, target a class (or classes), seminar series, laboratory, or regular disciplinary activity to study. The purpose is to study this setting like studying another culture. Like someone starting a new job, you must concentrate on comparing and contrasting the activities in the research setting to other social activities with which you are familiar. Depending on the length of the study, you can provide your instructor with a series of periodic reports on the status of the project that provide the basis for a more developed oral presentation. When the research is completed, your group then presents its findings in an oral presentation to other class members.

Introduction to Chapter 9

Scientific and technical texts appear "value neutral." A text is "objective" in that it does not appear to represent any system of values or beliefs. During the seventeenth century, scientists promoted research as a neutral activity far outside of, and absent any influence in, the realm of political and religious intrigue. Scientists made discoveries that society could apply— the question of values could be worked out later. Since scientific practice was considered apolitical, the state felt free to allow it to exist and researchers felt free to pursue the subjects they wished. Scientific and technical writing reflected the goal of value-neutral research to appease state and religious officials. Science was portrayed as neutral and in the realm of public reason; values were portrayed as subjective and in the realm of personal impulse.

Our approach to reading and interpreting scientific and technical texts assumes seventeenth century sensibilities. In the seventeenth century, the neutrality of science toward political and religious issues was a progressive solution in defining the relation of science and society. In the twentieth century, however, science and technology are not marginal institutions struggling for survival. Science wields extraordinary social and political influence. Science is ethics. Science is politics. Because science possesses its own power, neutrality can no longer be interpreted as freedom from state and religious authority but as an escape from commitment or as its own instrument of authority. Judgments involving "value neutrality," objectivity, subjectivity, authority, democracy, and power are embedded in scientific and technical writing. But our analyses of scientific and technical texts do not take up the question of ideology or values.

A commonsense notion suggests the more we know about the contexts, relationships, and purposes of the communicative process, the better we know our own choices and practices. To write a better research proposal, for instance, we need to know what areas and concerns are being funded and direct the elements of our proposal to those areas. But if we concentrate on studying scientific texts, how can we determine their underlying basis? In studying the text of a journal article, for instance, you do not go into the laboratory that produced it. Nevertheless the purpose for studying scientific texts is to identify your reactions and reactions of others, to see how they help interpret, and are interpreted by, elements of the text. Examining the construction of sentences, the use of jargon, the placement of visual aids, the organization of the work, and the subject matter—and your responses to these elements—allows you to hold up your presumptions and ideas for examination. In this way you begin to inspect your own writing process.

Bill Keith asks us to study the images and aspects of science, technology, and communication we often use. Keith also introduces us to the elements shared in all forms of communication, such as rhetoric and persuasion. He suggests that "a communicator that takes a rhetorical stance . . . takes responsibility for having a specific purpose in communicating, and designing the communication to fit that purpose." If you accept Keith's notion of "being rhetorical," then scientific and technical communication represents a series of choices not unlike the choices faced—and studied—by writers of all types of literature.

CHAPTER

Science and Communication

Beyond Form and Content

WILLIAM KEITH

The pictures of science we get from the movies are very different from the way it is actually done. We can know that, and yet still find it difficult to get those pictures out of our heads. There is mad Dr. Frankenstein in his laboratory, brave Madame Curie in a white coat bent over a lab table, the countless handsome young men from science fiction movies in the 1950s ready to tackle issues of truth no matter where (or to what monsters) they lead, and endless portrayals of people a bit more than slightly out of touch.[1] The main lesson these representations teach is that science is not like everyday life. It is separate, apart, divorced from the hurly-burly of daily interaction and commerce. Of course, implicitly, we are led to believe that therein lies the strength and power of science: It works so effectively because it is removed from the influences that might distract scientists from truth.[2] In short, we are led to think that science must get a completely different treatment from any other activity; all the assumptions we would make about the role of social, cultural, and psychological factors in any other activity (politics, the arts, business, etc.) are automatically invalidated.

Needless to say, these pictures are false and dangerous ones.[3] They may serve the interests of some scientists at some times, scientists who might like to deflect criticism and divert prying eyes, but for the most part they don't serve anybody's interests. They just make it more difficult to talk and think about science as it really is, rather than in terms of foolish ideals.[4] Nowhere is this more clear than in examining the relationship of communication to science. Communication—written, oral, or otherwise— lies squarely in the realm of the social and the cultural, in the realm of human relationships, motives, and desires. There is very little we can actually do alone; science, like everything else, is a collective enterprise, sometimes requiring a dozen people, often requiring enormous organizations and institutions. For groups to operate, they must at the very least communicate among themselves and with other groups; there may even be more subtle forms of communication at work. So science arises out of a context of communication and is not separate from it. In this chapter, we'll look a bit more closely at the idea of communication, how it figures into science, and ways of thinking about communication that can help those who do scientific communication professionally—including scientists.

THINKING ABOUT COMMUNICATION

There are myriad ways to define and model communication, which present a real obstacle to understanding communication. Although it's something we do every day, it's still a bit of a mystery, in the same way we can walk all our lives without ever thinking about or understanding the physics and mechanics of human locomotion (which is vastly more complex than commonly assumed). If you were responsible for teaching people who walked poorly how to walk, the first thing you would want is to understand walking in a terminology that would help you teach it.

Knowing about the chemistry of terminal efferent synapses might not help much, whereas kinesiology might.

Some ways of talking about and conceptualizing communication are more helpful than others. Let's start with some that most of us are familiar with but that are not really very useful, even if they seem "natural." One common way of picturing communication (especially for electrical engineers!) is in terms of *information:* Communication is the transmission of information from a source to a receiver.[5] It is usually associated with a picture like this:

| Sender | encoder | Channel | decoder | Receiver |

Although this is a very common—and for most people, very intuitive—picture of communication, it is unsatisfactory for many reasons. The main one is that the technical theory of information cannot model meaning, only structure. Because meaning is what, presumably, humans attempt to create when they communicate with each other, this is a fatal flaw. But in a larger and more important sense this picture is not helpful because it is radically incomplete. The terms by which it forces us to talk about communication filter out most of the interesting and important things we need to know about communication in order to be effective communicators. The whole emphasis is on messages and how they can be coded, decoded, and cleaned up. There isn't really any way of talking about the *people* involved in the communication—and people are always involved. Also, notice that there is only one purpose given for communication: the transmission of information. If you think for a few moments about your daily life, you'll realize that you are always doing much, much more than that in a communication interaction, and we'll discuss some of this "more" below.

Another unhelpful way of thinking about communication, which is difficult to avoid, is in terms of the content only. Often, people who have to do professional writing or speaking for the first time assume that it will be pretty easy because the material will suggest its own structure and presentation. They think that the answers to their questions about presentation—"What do I say, to whom, in what order?"—are implicit in the subject matter if they just know it well enough. As one might imagine, this is a recipe for communication disaster. Yet smart people do it all the time, and nowhere is the temptation greater than in scientific communication. In science in particular, we would like to think that the old legal principle applies: *Res ipse loquitur*—the things speak for themselves. But things do not speak for themselves: People have to speak for them. Typically, those operating from the "content" picture think that they have very few choices to make in communicating a subject matter because the subject matter will determine everything. But this is false; we could even generalize that most bad communication results from communicators not taking into account all their choices. No matter how clearly an area of science is understood, there are always many choices to be made in telling someone about it. Of course, if we are accustomed to a particular way of presenting the material, it may not seem like there are any choices because the way we're used to is so "natural." Neglecting to imagine alternatives and choose among them will be highly problematic unless all contextual features are held constant from communication situation to situation, which is virtually impossible.

What are some useful ways of thinking about communication? Let's focus on some of the basic concepts we'll need to use making decisions about how to communicate in a particular situation.[6] These are *audience, relationship, purpose,* and *context.* The first thing one always needs to think about before communicating is the audience. It's pretty obvious that what you say[7] depends on who you are talking to, but most people don't think about how deeply this goes. We can distinguish between expressive and strategic communication: Expressive communication serves to express our ideas and feelings, nothing more. Strategic communication attempts to have some impact or effect on others: You want them to understand, believe, act, accept, reject, and so on. Theses are two general kinds of purposes. If your purpose is expressive, it doesn't matter who the audience is or if there is one; a message in a bottle would be as good as a public speech or an appearance on Oprah Winfrey's show. Truly expressive communication is probably pretty rare.

In most cases, communicators would like to make some kind of difference to an audience, and in that case the specific audience makes all the difference in the world. No matter what your strategic purpose, you won't be able to achieve it unless you tailor your communication to the specific person(s) you're addressing. Dale Carnegie[8] once pointed out that when most people go fishing they want to catch fish (i.e., they are strategic). To get the fish to bite, fishermen must put something on the hook to attract the fish. But what should they put there? (This question is analogous to the issue of communication choices: One wants to affect the audience—but which communication choices will do it?) Carnegie noted that some fishermen put things *they* like on the hook, such as peanut butter. Others put things, such as worms, that fish like (and further, different things to catch different fish) on their hooks. It's pretty obvious who's going to catch more fish, but it is amazing how resistant many people are to this logic; they refuse it and say "It's really just a matter of getting the line attached tightly between you and the fish" or "No, see, the nature of the bait determines what is used, nothing more."[9]

Before going on to expand on the variety of possible purposes in communication, we should briefly consider the concept of relationship in communication. Communication always involves an interaction between two or more people, even if the communication is written and the people are separated by time and space. In fact, as B. Aubrey Fisher has noted, human communication and human relationships are coextensive, for there is never one without the other. The nature of the relationship makes an enormous difference to the kinds of purposes and strategies appropriate to a given communication interaction. Talking to one's fiancée involves very different requirements than talking to a clerk in a store, and most of these differences are attributable to the difference in the relationships. One's specific communication always has embedded in it information about the relationship, from obvious cues such as forms of address ("Darling," "Sir") to more subtle ones, such as a tone of superiority and condescension. A useful way to talk about relationships is in terms of roles. A role is a set of expectations that go along with a person's place in a particular kind of relationship, and so roles frequently come in pairs: teacher/student, lover/beloved, cheater/cheated, persecutor/victim, judge/defendant. There are many, many types of roles, and it is possible to enact more than one at a time. Roles figure into communication in several ways. First, both (or all) communicators have perceptions about the roles of the interactants, and those perceptions determine not only what they will do and say but also what these actions and language will mean. For example, consider the sentence "That's the wrong way to do it." This sentence will take on different meanings according to who is saying it to whom. Imagine it said by a teacher to a student, and then the reverse. Or a son to his father, and the reverse. Or by a homeowner to a contractor, and the reverse. In each case, given the constraints and expectations that go with the role, the sentence takes on a different meaning, has different implications, will tend to get a different response, and so forth.

Second, it's important to remember that roles are not absolute but depend on perception, in terms of both how communicators perceive their own and others' roles. For example, you might find yourself in a group where you have an expertise others lack and suddenly realize that they perceive you as the "teacher" or "expert," whereas you still perceive yourself as just a participant; this difference could certainly cause communication difficulties. Or, as a student, it's pretty clear who's the teacher and who's the student but less clear what these roles amount to. Does taking on the role of "good student" mean that you never ask questions? Always ask questions? Never argue with the teacher? Argue as hard as possible? Obviously, things will work out best when you have a sense of the teacher's perception of the role of "good student" (and "good teacher") and can work from that.

Finally, there are many communication situations where the relationship comes into question in a particular way. In many cases, we must expect the audience to ask "Why are you talking about this subject? What entitles you? What are your motives?" Your perceived appropriateness to be saying something about a particular subject to a particular audience in a particular situation is often referred to as your *ethos*.[10] Ethos can be seen as the appropriateness of trust in the relationship between communicator and audience. Ethos may be an issue of expertise: Do you have the credentials, the knowledge, to be speaking on this subject? Should the audience trust you to know what you're talking about? Few people would believe a carpenter talking about nuclear physics (although he might be credible about carpentry). Ethos may be an issue of motive: Do you have the audience members' best interests in mind? Do you intend to help them or cheat and deceive them? Most people don't trust salespeople because they judge the salesperson's motive as making money, not ensuring that the customer gets the best deal. Ethos may also be an issue of appropriateness: Can *you* fill the role of one who speaks on this issue? Many times, people see it as odd that, for example, a man speaks about the problems of rape or abortion—if he hasn't experienced them (and has no reason to think he will), why would he understand it well enough to talk about it? Similarly, student athletes are going to be unlikely to judge someone credible who has not played college sports—how could they really understand? Of course, it's possible that the man or the nonathlete actually does understand, but the problem is that the audience (quite reasonably) doubts it, and thus the communicator has to do extra work in forming a trusting relationship that a woman or athlete would not have to do.

Thus when communicators address particular audiences, they do so in the context of a relationship, which may preexist the situation but is modified by the communication in it. Now, what are the purposes a communicator might have? Frequently, people new to studying communication are not comfortable with purpose; it's not polite, or it just seems plain manipulative, to have a "purpose" in communicating. That's a natural feeling in our culture, so it's important not to mistake concealed or devious purposes for purpose in general. Actually, it's hard to describe and understand even everyday communication without talking about purpose. Traditionally, there have been three purposes (*officia,* Cicero called them) attributed to communication: persuasion, instruction (information), and entertainment. But these distinctions are probably too crude for most practical purposes, and they invite a serious mistake. Sometimes, instruction, or as we might say today "informative communication," is contrasted with persuasion, and the logic criticized above is engaged: "Well, I'm just trying to convey information, nothing more, so the subject matter (information) will dictate all the important choices." So calling one's communication "informative" can be used as an excuse to ignore the constraints of audience, roles, and ethos. It makes sense, then, that most communicators who see their purpose as "informative" are truly boring, bad communicators. They would be better off seeing themselves as persuasive: They want the audience to care about the information, to understand it, to want to remember it and fit it in with the rest of their knowledge—much more than simply "informing" them; informative communication comes from either laziness (adaptation to an audience and specific purpose takes work) or more commonly from lack of knowledge about the communication possibilities and choices.

Let's call the attitude of taking purposes seriously, of always considering the audience and the context, as being *rhetorical.* A communicator who takes a rhetorical stance thus takes responsibility for having a specific purpose in communicating and designing the communication to fit that purpose. This is not necessarily manipulation, any more than designing a tool that fits the user's hand and task is "manipulating" that tool user. So specifying purpose clearly and precisely is very important. Here's a list (albeit incomplete) of possible purposes:

Open new possibilities of belief or value
Propose change in ideas or action
Build credibility for future persuasion
Establish credibility for current persuasion
Create doubts about opposing ideas/actions
Refute opposing ideas
Create an audience
Build community with audience
Ratify or reinforce community values or ideas
Ask for small changes in belief/action
Ask for moderate changes in belief/action

You can come up with many more, depending on the specifics of the situation. The important point is that when planning communication, whether it is a paper written for a class, a request made to a friend, a proposal of marriage, a memo to colleagues, or a grant made to the National Science Foundation, *if you don't design the communication with a specific purpose in mind, then it won't achieve anything specific* (except maybe by accident). This is where the "informative" speaker goes astray. "Being informative" is not a specific purpose because it doesn't take into account where the audience is starting from (with respect to the writer/speaker and the subject matter) and what the writer/speaker wants the audience to do with the information. A communicator who is being rhetorical takes these things into account.

The final thing that factors into our account of communication is context, or the setting for the communication. There are many ways to talk about context, but it is common to distinguish contexts based on the number of people, their relationship, institutions involved, or the medium of communication. Commonly, the most basic contexts of communication are these:

Interpersonal
Small group
Organizational
Public address
Mass communication

But a great many other topical contexts are also studied:

Political communication
Health communication
Scientific/technical communication
Male/female communication
Intercultural communication

The context will typically interact in important ways with the nature of the audience, the relationships that can be established among communicators, and the appropriate purposes. In the next section, we'll look at scientific communication in particular, try to see how these concepts apply to it, and attempt to determine the nature of scientific audiences, relations among scientists, the purposes of scientific communicators, and the contexts of scientific communication.

SCIENCE AND COMMUNICATION

Since we've established that communication is a natural part of science, we should now consider the various places in science where communication occurs. There are multiple contexts of communication in science, corresponding to different audiences and forms of communication.

Audiences in Science

A traditional distinction is between audiences "inside" science and "outside" science proper. Even though this distinction has been challenged,[11] it is useful for understanding the scope of scientific communication. Beginning with insider audiences, we can divide them roughly into educational and professional audiences, but both audiences tend to be characterized by what they know. Educational audiences on the inside (there are also external ones) are typically sophisticated about science but lack knowledge about a specific topic. For example, physicians frequently attend seminars where researchers teach them about the latest results and techniques in their medical specialty. The physicians are not laypersons or amateurs, but they are still there to learn. Graduate education in science is in the same category; textbooks and articles written for the graduate level presume insider status while still aiming to teach. Most insider education is connected in some way (in the United States) to universities.

Professional audiences may be divided into researchers and practitioners, although this distinction is extremely permeable. Roughly, researchers do basic and (some applied) research, whereas practitioners do applied research and implementation of applications. Basic researchers are most closely associated with the label "scientist," and they are paradigmatically white-coated and laboratory-bound either in the university, private (as Thomas Edison's was), or corporate setting, such as Bell Labs in New Jersey (for electronics) or Bolt, Beranek, and Newman in Boston (for artificial intelligence). Practitioners frequently receive the label "engineer" (whether they are engineers or not) and can be found in many places. They represent an audience inside science to the extent that their professional activity is tied to communicating with other scientists through seminars, professional journals, and the like. Specialization further divides professional scientists of either type into distinct audiences. Mechanical engineers share only a general background with chemical engineers and computer scientists, and although ecologists and geneticists are both biologists, most of what each reads would be inaccessible to the other.[12] The division of scientific audiences according to specialty requires extensive knowledge of the particular science, and such divisions tend to mutate rapidly.

Audiences outside science are typically characterized by a lack of knowledge: They don't know what a specific scientist knows. Communicatively, this difference in knowledge (which, unfairly, is typically characterized as ignorance) creates a gap that communication must bridge. Insider communication typically takes an enormous amount for granted—and gets away with it because the scientists have similar knowledge, education, training, experiences, and so forth. But communication from inside to outside (and vice versa) cannot take all this for granted and so presents itself as more difficult, frequently being characterized as a process of translation. Outside audiences may be divided into three main types: the general public, business audiences, and government/legal audiences. As LaFollette demonstrates in *Making Science Our Own,* the general public has demanded and consumed enormous amounts of information about science since at least the turn of the century. The most obvious outlet for general science communication is the magazine, whose range extends from general, nearly professional magazines like *Science* and *Nature* to specialized magazines on computer applications. There are also many television programs that cater to this audience, typically found on PBS or the Discovery Channel. The members of this audience have a varied set of interests in science: They may simply have a fascination with some topic ("dinosaur crazy"), they may want to be conversant with the scientific issues of the day, they may wish to connect the scientific knowledge (say, about advances in cryptography or archaeology) with a hobby/interest (in political and industrial espionage or Civil War battles), or they may have some application they wish to make of the science (e.g., to personal computing or gardening). There are also foundations that are set up (often by a wealthy, private individual) specifically to fund scientific research that someone thought was important; this should also count as a case of outside communication because scientists applying for funding may be applying to committees of individuals who are not scientists but interested laypeople.

Commercial interest in science constitutes the paradigmatic case of application. Those in business communicate with scientists to find out information and techniques they can apply to their business, to make new products, increase efficiency, or whatever. The business community's interests in science thus tend to be exclusively pragmatic: What can this (knowledge/device/technique) do for me? How can it help me/us, say, make more money, sell more goods, or conduct business more cheaply? Often, the interaction between business and science falls on individuals in the business setting who must assume dual roles: On the one hand, they must be quasi-scientists, conversant with the latest research in their area of expertise and able to talk with others in the area, and on the other, they must represent the interests of the business, weeding out, ignoring, or refusing to support science or research that does not serve the interests of the business. To say the least, their jobs get very complicated.

Scientists interact with the government for two main reasons: The government sponsors scientific research, and the government regulates scientific research. Through the National Science Foundation (NSF), Defense Advanced Research Projects Agency (DARPA), Department of Defense (DOD), National Institute of Mental Health (NIMH), National Institutes of Health (NIH), and many other agencies, the U.S. government has sponsored basic scientific research on a vast scale since the end of World War II. There is not an unlimited amount of money, and not all projects are equally worthy, so the various agencies have to decide who is to be funded. Scientists, in effect, compete with each other by submitting grant applications describing the research they want to do and why it is worthy of being funded. Now, this is clearly a persuasive task but more complicated than one might think. Because having "mere bureaucrats" decide issues of science seems wrong to most people (they don't have the expertise—right?), the government typically employs scientists themselves to review grant applications and make awards. So, if a computer scientist applies for money from DARPA, those who review the grant application are likely to be other computer scientists. Grant writing is thus a mix of inside and outside communication, as the audience consists of insiders who are working for outsiders, and they may not all share the same values, interests, and purposes. The government also regulates science, in part through the funding process (a line of research will die out if no one funds it), and in part through laws about certain types of research. The Atomic Energy Commission regulates any nuclear or atomic research (for safety reasons), and there is a growing movement to regulate genetic engineering research in the same way. For the most part, though, the U.S. government has not tried to "micro-manage" science but only control the general patterns of funding. This may well change in the future.

The legal context for scientific communication has mainly to do with patents, accountability, and expert testimony. Because it is possible to own a discovery, by patenting it, the legal process of obtaining a patent is very important. Additionally, parties may disagree about who deserves the patent on a particular discovery, conflicting patent claims may end up in court. Scientists may also sometimes be accountable for the applications of their work; for example, a chemist who discovers a drug, makes a persuasive case that it has certain effects, and puts it on the market, may be held liable if the effects aren't as promised or if there are negative side effects. Finally, there are many court cases, of all types, in which issues turn on matters of scientific fact and theory. Here scientists may be called in to testify as experts in a particular field. Their audience in this case may be a judge or jury but in any case are nonscientists.

Forms of Communication in Science

The two basic forms of scientific communication are written and oral. Written communication in science takes different shapes depending on context and audience. A basic form for internal scientific communication is publishing, usually in the form of research articles, often called journal articles.[13] Scientific journals are typically distinguished by topic (i.e., there are specific ones for physicists, chemists, biologists, engineers, etc.) and are supposed to represent a forum for the presentation of research and (once the research is accepted) a body of common knowledge for scientists. The form of a journal article responds to the first rather than the second of these purposes. An article should present or describe the evidence for a claim so that readers (i.e., other scientists) can evaluate the truth of the claim and how it fits with other claims about the same topic (i.e., its theoretical implications). In different fields and subfields, however, the nature of evidence is different, and so the presentation of the evidence will be different. Mathematical articles are typically very short, often consisting of a theorem and its proof, for their authors assume that any other information is supplied by the reader. A study of the effect of a certain hormone on humans, however, may be quite long; if it is a double-blind study, many correlations must be presented and explained. There is thus no one way to write a journal article, as the writing must take into account the beliefs and doubts of the audience as well as the standards and types of proof accepted within that scientific community.

Oral communication among scientists, as among everyone else, is typically face to face. (An exception is noted below.) This might be in the setting of a one-on-one interpersonal talk, a small group of interactants, or in a public speaking setting, where one person addresses many. In each of these setting, a smart communicator asks the basic communication questions: Who is the audience? What is my purpose? What is (or should be) my relationship to the audience?

An advantage of interpersonal and small group interactions is that the communicator may have a lot of information about the audience members; in the more public setting, this may not be true (at a professional meeting of chemists, you could expect the audience to be mostly chemists, but you might not be sure how many know or care about the subject of your speech). Purposes in interpersonal communication are typically quite complex. This is due to the layering of purposes: you are managing not only the content of what you want to say but also your relationship to the other person at the same time.

Suppose two people, Ann and Bob, are working in a commercial lab and Ann needs to tell Bob that one of the lab procedures he's using is defective, possibly dangerous. Ann might be tempted to think about this only in terms of the procedure, but that's too simple. To see why, imagine first that Ann is Bob's supervisor. How would their relationship affect the communication? She can just order him to make the change without explanation, which would probably make him resentful or feel at fault for using the procedure even if he wasn't at fault. This may in turn affect his future communication and job behavior, making the workplace less pleasant; Ann would need to find a way to explain the change in a way that respects Bob's integrity and diligence as a lab worker.

Now imagine that Ann works for Bob. She can't order him to make the change, and wants to avoid appearing to subvert his authority, as he might not be willing to listen to an aggressive appeal and has the power to just ignore her. However she puts the issue to him, it will have to be in a way that is respectful of their relative positions. Added to all this is that in a real situation Ann and Bob have a relationship history that figures in each succeeding interaction. Failing to factor in the relationship dimension of communication (which we earlier called ethos) can create a multitude of misunderstandings.

Small group communication has many of the same constraints, along with some others. The advantage of working in groups is that creativity in problem solving is enormously enhanced; it is impossible to predict the precise outcome, but the outcome is almost always more satisfactory than one that an individual could arrive at alone. It is no accident that professions like advertising and litigation, that put a premium on creative thinking about highly constrained problems, rely on group problem solving. The disadvantages of groups are that they take a lot of time and require patience from the participants, as the road to the solution is rarely a straight line. You can think of the communication in groups as having two dimensions: a task dimension and a relationship dimension. The first is the content, or problem, that the group is dealing with; the second is the various relationships among group members. Successful groups try to maximize two qualities in their groups: the maximum amount of input and disagreement with the maximum social cohesion. On the one hand, creative disagreement is necessary for the task dimension: If there is little disagreement or free input from members (as with a leader and a bunch of "yes men"), then there won't be any productive interaction of ideas; it will be equivalent to one person thinking and everyone else agreeing, which is a waste of time. On the other hand, groups must attend to the relationship, or social dimension: If there is little social cohesion—disagreements are taken personally, feelings are hurt, pride wounded—then the group will soon begin to fall apart, with members either refusing to participate or actively working against the interests of the group out of spite. There are numerous techniques for structuring groups to achieve both harmony and creativity in group work.[14]

Public communication, or public speaking, is distinguished by a lack of immediate feedback. In a conversation, by focusing on the other person's nonverbal head-nodding, "um-hums," and so forth you can tell whether or not that person understands, agrees, is offended, and so on. (In truth, though, these clues are often much more ambiguous than we realize.) However, in the public setting, unless people are booing, clapping, or sleeping, you do not really know from moment to moment how things are going and so cannot make adjustments as one would normally do in conversation. What makes public speaking anxiety provoking for most people is this need to plan ahead—and to have the plans be right. For a successful speech, you must accurately gauge the composition of the audience, the relevance of the topic to that audience and their previous knowledge about it, your ethos (relationship to topic and audience), and on the basis of these, the most likely persuasive strategies. Obviously, a key to speaking success is to find out as much as possible about the audience in advance and have thought carefully about it; you achieve little by speaking to your own interests and knowledge.

Written communication in science is the subject of this book; it can take many forms (we have already discussed publications), such as memoranda, grant proposals, and popular articles. For each of these forms, a smart communicator would ask the same basic communication questions: Who is the audience? What is my purpose? What is (or should be) my relationship to the audience? A memorandum can go to one person or many. Most of them end up in the circular file because the recipients, dedicated and busy people, can't see what it has to do with them. In other words, the audience's adaptation necessary to ensure the relevance of the memo is lacking. It is not enough for you to have a specific purpose or plan; that plan needs to be connected.

In grant proposals, the authors (almost always plural) are writing what is essentially a request for money to a public or private funding agency, saying "Here's why you should give us some money." Agencies don't give away money easily or unthinkingly; each government program or private foundation has a specific purpose and will specify the kinds of projects it wants to fund. So the situation is this: Your team has a project it wants to do, and you have researched appropriate grant sources. Now, in writing the grant, you have to find a way of talking about your project that makes it fit with the granting agency's requirements. This doesn't mean making things up or falsifying your plans. Instead, it mean putting the emphasis in particular places and drawing out implications of your project that connect with the granting agency. No matter how worthy your work is, there's no reason the agency should fund it if it is not the kind of thing it funds.

In popular magazine articles, professional scientists must adapt to the knowledge and interests of lay audiences. Obviously, this is completely different from communicating the "same" research information to a sophisticated technical audience. In particular, you must balance comprehensibility and interest. To make the scientific information comprehensible, you have to simplify it to a certain extent, using images, metaphors, and analogies that capture its spirit. Of course, not any old image or metaphors will do; the most successful ones are those that are not only true to the science but connect to the experience and knowledge of the audience. Explaining one technical concept in terms of another is useless. Ball-and-stick models of atoms and molecules represent a certain kind of compromise; they are not particularly true to the physical object, but they show certain relations clearly and are easy for laypeople to visualize. Comprehensibility is thus tied to the audience and so is interest. What makes research interesting to the public? Many different things, having mainly to do with either flights of imagination or technological applications—or both. Enormous space stations capture the imagination because they combine technological applications with a vision of a different kind of society and perhaps a solution to some of our social problems.[15]

THINKING RHETORICALLY:
AN "ALGORITHM"

In the final section of this chapter, we detail a method of thinking about communication strategically, or *rhetorically*. This method has general applicability and can be used for most kinds of communication in most contexts. The first consideration is the kind of critical thinking needed in communication. Many people initially think that what is required is analysis: breaking down the parts of the message, for example, and refining them. A better approach is a *problem-solution* one: thinking about specific acts of communication as the resolutions to specific problems implied by the constraints of audience, context, ethos, and so forth. A good way to see the importance of this is to consider research in expert/novice problem solving. In experiments with a type of problem (say, physics word problems) that novices and experts worked at (freshmen in a physics course and physics professors), researchers looked to see how the problem-solving abilities differed so that the novices could be taught the skills of the experts. One of the most significant findings is that experts spend most of their time on the problem, whereas novices spend most of their time on solutions. Novices typically guess at a solution, find it is wrong, guess at another solution, find it wrong, and so on— basically, trial and error. Experts spend a lot of time thinking about how to set up the problem, and once that is decided the answer usually is found with a few calculations.[16]

In communication, one can see the same pattern. Novices typically concentrate on the artifact, the words to be written or spoken, writing up a draft of a speech or paper, and then tinkering with it. Experts spend a lot of time thinking about the requirements of the communication situation and then know exactly the kind of thing they have to write and can do so with confidence and clarity. The problem for expert physicists or communicators or whomever is that the problem analysis they do is largely tacit, and they have trouble verbalizing what they're doing—they "just do it." The "algorithm" below is an attempt to make the analysis of communication problems explicit. It is not literally an algorithm (more like a set of rules of thumb, actually) but can be used in that spirit. Communicators cannot be strategic until they have thoroughly analyzed their communication situation and understand all the constraints their communication behavior must adapt to. By answering Questions 1-4 below, a communication problem can be defined with enough clarity that Question 5, about the strategies actually employed, can be answered.

1. *What, exactly, is my rhetorical purpose?* (If more than one, specify priority)

    As noted earlier, the more specific the purpose, the more likely it is to be achieved. All possible purposes cannot be listed because they can be as various as communication situations themselves. Still, there are some that arise over and over again and can be used as a starting point for thinking creatively and incisively about purpose in a specific context:

    1. Open new possibilities of belief or value.
    2. Propose change in ideas or action.
    3. Build credibility for future persuasion.
    4. Establish credibility for current persuasion.
    5. Create doubts about opposing ideas/actions.
    6. Refute opposing ideas.
    7. Create/define an audience.
    8. Build community with audience.
    9. Ratify or reinforce community values or ideas.
    10. Ask for small changes in belief/action.
    11. Ask for moderate changes in belief/action.

Two rules of thumb for understanding purpose might be minimization and complexity. First, be sure to have modest goals for any single interaction; the less you ask for, the more likely you are to achieve it. Rational people do not completely change their minds in a single interaction, and communicators would be wrong to expect this; in fact, asking for big changes indicates a real lack of respect for an audience. Instead, to effect really big changes, a communicator needs multiple interactions over time. So the minimal goal of the first time is to get a second hearing. If you can put a hostile or disbelieving audience in a frame of mind to hear more or listen again, this is an enormous success. Second, remember that there are always multiple goals operating on both sides of a communicative interaction; it is never as simple as one would like it to be. For example, in writing a memo proposing a new project, you might be doing (2), proposing a change in action, but because you need to get a group of people together to do it, you might be doing (7), defining an audience of people interested in the particular topic. In addition, because people have accepted you as organizer, (4) is important, as is (3), because they have to think about it and probably listen to a second version of the pitch. Obviously, the analysis of multiple communication goals requires a determination of priority and emphasis.

2. What is the nature of my audience?

Understanding your audience requires two things: relevance and generalization. First, given the topic and purpose of the communication, there are certain relevant things you want to know about the people comprising your audience. Do they agree or disagree with your position? Why? What motivates them? What are their interests? What persuasion have they already heard about this topic? The profile you construct of the same group of people will be different (i.e., they constitute a different audience) when the topic and purpose are different, so these are highly relevant to audience analysis.

It would be nice if you could always survey or question your audience completely in advance to find out exactly the information you need. But this is rarely possible or practical. Instead, speakers and writers are forced to make educated guesses about the views and dispositions of their audiences. They do this by making generalizations for demographic and social information. Of course, these generalizations can be wrong and, to the extent they rely on stereotypes, must be handled very carefully. But with experience, they can be useful tools for estimating the nature of audiences and guiding communication. So, given a topic and purpose, you must ask the following:

- What are the demographics of my audience? (Gender, race, ethnicity, age, politics, religion, education level, socioeconomic status, occupation, geography, culture)
- What do the demographics imply about other beliefs, values, and behaviors relevant to the topic? What other sources of information do I have for this?

▥ What are the various constituencies (i.e., subgroups that share interests, explicitly or implicitly) in the audience, and how are they related to my purpose(s)?

▥ What are audience members' expectations regarding the entire communication experience? What appeals or behaviors will or will not be expected, or are considered offensive? Is this a genre (e.g., a research article or grant proposal), such that there are particular schemes or formats to which the communication must conform? What are the possible roles that the audience expects, and what are the roles that suit my purposes?

> *Speaker Roles*
>   Advisor, counselor
>   Helper
>   Leader
>   Advocate
>   Partisan
>   Salesperson
>   Teacher
>   Expert
>   Antagonist
> *Audience Roles*
>   Judge
>   Jury
>   Client
>   Supplicant
>   Buyer
>   Actor, ones with power
>   Voter, decider
> *Generic Expectations*
>   Occasion and setting
>   Discourse conventions
>   Speaker constraints
>   Audience constraints

What are the sources of resistance to persuasion? (For this audience, in this context)

▥ Inconsistency with their beliefs, actions, values, or behaviors

▥ Lack of communicator credibility

▥ Misunderstanding of message or speaker

▥ Lack of motivation or interest in topic

Remember that while the group of people is a stable thing, its constitution as an audience is very flexible A group of people sitting in a classroom listening to a professor might be defined as a group of students, or potential scientists, or communicators, or professionals-to-be, or men and women, or as patriotic Americans, or as a diverse group with diverse interests, or as excellence-oriented people, and so on—the possibilities are endless. Still, although there may be preexisting expectations as to speaker and audience roles, these are only a starting point, not something set in stone. For example, in pitching a proposal informally to a group of people, you might be expected to be a partisan or salesperson for it; this puts the audience in the role of skeptical consumer, which might make things difficult if you're trying to pitch something new and uncertain. So, as part of your message design, you address the audience as if you were a friend or helper: "We all face this common problem, and here's something to consider doing about it." In this way, the audience is invited to take the role of partner, looking at common interests, rather than as a consumer defending against the interests of the seller.

3. *What information and ideas are part of the rhetorical context?*
For almost any topic and audience, those interested have heard or read something about the topic or genre before. Regardless of the nature or quality of this previous experience, it must be taken into account. Has the reader read many proposals before? On this topic? Are there many rumors about this type of chemical theory, so that I must take into account these rumors as background information for my speech? More generally, as a special part of audience analysis, you must consider the background assumptions of the audience, the things taken to be true. Whether or not these things are true or reasonable, they have to be your starting point. If you are writing a popular piece about superconductivity, you have to begin with the fact that most people understand electricity either as little tiny peas zipping through wires or as fluid flowing through wires. If you want to present a more sophisticated view, you cannot just dive in; you have to start where the audience is and move from there. Consider these questions:

- What beliefs and values are part of the common ground assumed before your discourse begins? That is, what things are taken as "facts" by the audience to which your discourse must respond?
- Do you have credibility? In this context, how important is your credibility as speaker? What is your prior ethos? What are the obstacles to building ethos in your speech?

It is common to speak of prior and concurrent ethos: The first is roughly equivalent to reputation (even if that just means stereotypes that people have about the speaker/writer based on superficial information); the second is built in the process of communicating. Earlier, we spoke of ethos in the context of trust, and building trust is clearly an important part of persuasion. The questions above are very important, since it forces speakers to confront reasons why audiences might not trust them. Remember that these reasons, despite all your good intentions, may seem very rational; if you look at it from the audience members' point of view, you might realize that, knowing what they know, you wouldn't trust yourself either! Almost as a reflex, most communicators attempt to hide the reasons for bad ethos, or objections to the point they're making, as if not bringing them up will cause them not to exist. This is extremely bad strategy. A more effective way to deal with problems of ethos is to neutralize them: Bring them up, give a satisfactory response, and let them go. Combined with credibility building through the communication, this gives you the best possible chance.

For example, suppose that Wayne is pitching a project to his supervisor Laura, a project that does not yet have a clear practical payoff and might be very time consuming. Now, Wayne knows that Laura sees the world in terms of practicality, and so whether or not someone else might not care, she will mind very much that the payoff is not immediately in view. Also, Wayne knows that his history with Laura is one of broken deadlines and work turned in late and that she gets very irritated with this. So Wayne knows that he has two obstacles to overcome: one having to do with the values of the audience and the other with his prior ethos with this audience. By ignoring these obstacles ("Better not mention that!") he ensures disaster because they will be quite present in her mind. His best strategy is to account for them in the way he puts his appeal together, emphasizing the closure he will be able to get, and the reasons why he both wants and will be able to meet the deadline for this project.

4. *What are the rhetorical problems that must be solved?*
Questions 1 through 3 taken together amount to a description of the rhetorical/communicative situation. Answers to them define the set of constraints to which the actual communication must respond. So the analysis of the communication problem leaves you with two questions:

- What burdens are taken on in speaking to this purpose in this situation?
- What are the priorities of these problems?

Jointly these guide the construction of a written or oral message. In the case of Wayne, just discussed, he realizes that he must bear two specific burdens in addition to those demanded by the genre (rigorous argument, correct calculations, reasonable costs, etc.). No one can fully meet the burdens of a communication episode unless these have been thoroughly analyzed, and this can only be done "in your head" by very experienced and skilled communicators. But the rest of us can work on this skill and improve constantly at it.

5. *What rhetorical resources are available, in this situation, for solving those problems?*
Once the problems of the particular communication situation have been analyzed, you then turn to solutions. This book, in a sense, is about the solutions relevant to science, its particular problems and contexts.

SOURCE NOTES

1. Marcell LaFollette has documented these stereotypes in her *Making Science Our Own* (Chicago: University of Chicago Press, 1990).

2. Throughout this chapter I use "scientist" to mean both scientists and engineers, noting differences as necessary.

3. See Steve Fuller, *The Philosophy of Science and Its Discontents* (2nd ed., New York: Guilford Press, 1992), for a discussion of the social dimension of science as the source of error.

4. "I've yet to meet that 'coldly calculating man of science' whom the novelists extol. . . . I doubt that he exists; and if he did exist I greatly fear that he would never make a startling discovery or invention." C. G. Suits, quoted in LaFollette, p. 66.

5. Claude Shannon, *The Mathematical Theory of Information* (Champaign, IL: University of Illinois Press, 1949); L. David Ritchie, *Information* (Newbury Park, CA: Sage, 1991).

6. For any of these, there is, of course, enormous disagreement among theorists about how it is to be properly defined, but these differences won't matter too much for our purposes.

7. Let's allow "say" to stand in for both speaking and writing, since, unless it's otherwise noted, all remarks apply to both. They don't all apply, however, to mass communication.

8. Dale Carnegie, *How to Win Friends and Influence People* (New York: Simon & Schuster, 1936).

9. A problem with this analogy is that it implies that communication is basically one-way (fisherman to fish) and serves only one communicator's ends (the fisherman's), which is certainly how Carnegie saw things. But the points made can easily be generalized to more complex cases, where interaction and purpose are mutual.

10. The terms *ethos* and *ethics* come from different, but related, Greek words. Ethics has to do with (moral) habits of behavior, whereas ethos concerns the character of a speaker.

11. But if they know some *other* science, then they are in the dual role of insiders and outsiders.

12. Phillip Davis and Reuben Hersh, in *The Mathematical Experience* (Boston: Houghton Mifflin, 1981) call this "Ulam's Dilemma" after the famous mathematician Stanislaus Ulam. They quote him as follows:

> At a talk which I gave at a celebration of the twenty-fifth anniversary of the construction of von Neumann's computer in Princeton a few years ago, I suddenly started estimating silently in my mind how many theorems are published yearly in mathematical journals. I made a quick mental calculation and came to a number like one hundred thousand theorems per year. I mentioned this and my audience gasped. . . . It is actually impossible to keep abreast of even the more outstanding and exciting results. How can one reconcile this with the view that mathematics will survive as a single science? (pp. 20-21)

Davis and Hersh conclude that "there will rarely be any single person who is in command of recent work in more than two or three areas" (p. 21).

13. These have been studied in depth by Charles Bazerman in his *Shaping Written Knowledge* (Madison: University of Wisconsin Press, 1987).

14. See Irving Janis, *Groupthink*, 2nd ed., rev. (Boston: Houghton Mifflin, 1983).

15. See Ed Regis, *Great Mambo Chicken and the Transhuman Condition* (Reading, MA: Addison-Wesley, 1990), for a skeptical and humorous account of space stations in the popular imagination.

16. See James Gleick's biography of physicist Richard Feynman, *Genius* (New York: Pantheon, 1992), for a description of someone who was obviously very good at this and left an impression on a whole generation of physicists.

Discussion

1. What does Keith mean by "being rhetorical"? What do you think rhetoric or "rhetorical" means generally? How is rhetoric understood in common usage (refer to Chapter 1 in the text)? Why should a writer purposefully set out to persuade the reader? Should writers clearly indicate what their motives are and how they expect the reader to respond? How is science or technology "rhetorical"?

2. What is ethos? Describe the ethos of your field or discipline to someone unfamiliar with it. What do you think the public perception is of the ethos of science and technology? What function does ethos play in scientific and technical communication? In what specific way can technical writers successfully appeal to ethos to persuade an audience (for a case study of an answer to this question, see Chapter 10, Part II of the text)?

3. In analyzing audiences for science, Keith mentions that traditionally there has been a distinction between audiences "inside" and "outside" science. In your opinion, what would an "inside" audience need to know? Would an "inside" audience need to be experts, other professionals, curious laypersons? Who would compose an "outside" audience?

4. Certain scientific texts—Newton's *Principia,* Lyell's *Geology,* Darwin's *Origin,* Einstein's papers on relativity—are considered some of the most influential works ever written on our thinking about the world. Name some other scientific texts you think are influential. If you cannot name many, why do you think that is? Which of these texts have you read, and for what reason? Are any of these works used in any of the science classes you have taken? If not, why not? If so, how did you analyze them?

5. Keith observes that experts spend most of their time problem-solving in formulating the problem, whereas novices try to get at solutions by trial and error. From an analysis and description of your own writing process, do you spend more time formulating problems or getting at solutions? What aspects of writing do you consider "problems" or "solutions"? From a document that you recently prepared, formulate the steps of

the writing process you followed into a set of problems to be solved. In writing this document why did you formulate or fail to formulate a purpose, determine the nature of the audience, and define the rhetorical context? Why or why not? How could this problem-solving method be applied to other documents?

6. What is the image of science that Keith promotes? How does this image relate to the practice of scientific and technical communication defined in this text? What is gained by you as a student, potential professional, and citizen by revising the image of science?

Exercises

1. Keith offers a list of purposes, contexts, and roles for communication. As a class, make suggestions for additions to these lists, keeping in mind the special problems student writers encounter.

2. In the first discussion question, you were asked to define what Keith means by "being rhetorical." With this definition in mind, find a passage in the readings in Part II or in Chapter 3, Part I, that serves as an example of "being rhetorical." In a brief response paper, citing examples, illustrate what rhetorical attitude you find in the passage. Then, offer suggestions on how to change the text to better achieve its purpose.

3. Keith opens with the claim that "the pictures of science we get from the movies are very different from the way it is actually done." List 5 to 8 pictures or images we get of science from the movies, television, newspapers, or other popular media. Next, list 5 to 8 social or cultural factors that you think influence the practice of science or technology. In a class discussion, compare your lists to those of your classmates. In a brief written response, citing examples, argue for or against the idea that science is like other activities in everyday life. Provide suggestions about better ways to talk, write, or present pictures and images about science or technology.

4. Keith provides an "unsatisfactory" illustration of the communication process. Taking into account the concepts of audi-

ence, relationship, purpose, and context, provide a more useful illustration of the communication process. Given that this illustration provides an ideal model, give a more realistic illustration of your writing process.

5. One could argue that the rapid advance, change, and fragmentation of knowledge lead to the rapid creation of new audiences for scientific and technical communication. Further, upon graduation, practitioners in specialties of larger fields rapidly become laypersons with respect to other specialties in the same field. Consider your own career path over the next 10 to 15 years. In a brief paper, "interview" yourself as a professional 10 to 15 years from now. In the interview, consider whether you think you still possess the "cutting edge" skills you had upon graduation. Consider how you think changes in the past 10 to 15 years have changed how you communicate specialized information. What new audiences and contexts have arisen? In your professional practice, do you think it is important that people in the same field, although not in the same specialty, know basically the same skills and concepts? Do you think increased specialization has helped or hurt your profession? Which communication practices have changed over the years?

Introduction to Chapter 10

Since the 1960s, two opposing but related trends have affected the structure of academic disciplines. The first trend is increasing public interest in how its money is spent. Since the public supports academic institutions with taxes, corporate sponsorship, tuition payments, and contributions, people want to know the relevance of programs receiving money. Academics must explain and legitimate their practices to students, parents, and funding sources. In some instances, esoteric or irrelevant research programs hide behind the label "progress." As disciplinary practitioners are finding, however, the issues of public concern are not adequately addressed by any one discipline's resources. For example, many of the problems that scientists and engineers tackle—treating diseases, finding new sources of energy, developing environmentally friendly ("green") technologies—require input not only from members of different disciplines but from the lay public as well.

The second trend is increasing specialization. To achieve "scientific" status, practitioners in many academic disciplines took up and encouraged a demand for ever narrowly defined areas of research. Increased specialization was taken as a sign of a highly developed research tradition. Academics and professionals speculated that if they could reach a unified theory or get practitioners to apply a uniform set of methods or standards, their fields would gain tangible success, display progress, and acquire influence. The paradox of increased specialization was that many practitioners in the subdisciplines began to call for the elimination of traditional disciplinary boundaries while trying to prove that their own fields had matured into unique, organized research fields.

Recent calls for interdisciplinary (or disciplinary integration) research have been pegged by many scholars, among them Stephen Toulmin and Gerald Holton, as part of the constant swing between "unity and diversity in Western civilization." But the growth in interdisciplinary scholarship over the past three decades—inspired by an economic conceptions of information and knowledge—indicates the emergence of a social movement as opposed to simple intellectual fashion. Recent proclamations of either the end of inquiry—the end of history, the end of knowledge—or the rise of grand unifying theories (physics, genetics, sociobiology) signal the desire to reconfigure traditional methods and forms of knowledge.

Put broadly, the term *interdisciplinary* is defined along a sliding rhetorical scale. On one end, it acknowledges the need for collaborative research on a narrowly defined set of questions, but the research itself does not entail rethinking the disciplinary status quo. On the other end, it refers to eliminating the traditional disciplinary order and asserting a meta- or supradisciplinarity position—a science of science, for example. Out of an examination of the roles and responsibilities of disciplines a new audience for academic discourse has arisen—the interdisciplinary audience.

During the last period of the Mesozoic era, approximately 65 million years ago, the mass extinction of animal and plant life occurred. The question "What killed the dinosaurs?" is still the subject of scientific debate, but recent interest can be traced to 1980. This controversy touches many disciplines—geology, biology, astrophysics, statistics—and has affected many scientific careers. Dale Sullivan's case study analyzes the rhetorical resources that scientists must use to convince interdisciplinary audiences of their views. Scientific and technical communication typically takes place during well-defined occasions. Examining the vagaries of scientific discourse in a time of discord, Sullivan surveys the possibilities of scientific communication in the future—where disciplines collide and audiences transform.

C H A P T E R

Migrating Across Disciplinary Boundaries

The Case of David Raup's and John Sepkoski's Periodicity Papers

DALE L. SULLIVAN

Historically, calls for interdisciplinarity have come either from disciplinarians hoping to invigorate their disciplines or from scholars who encounter a problem that transcends disciplinary lines. The first group are often specialists working within an emerging field in search of legitimacy or specialists within a discipline which has become stagnant and inbred. For instance, when the field of speech communication was in its infancy, Charles Woolbert argued that the emerging field shared territory with such established fields as English, history, law, political science, sociology, education, and philosophy (Woolbert, 1916: 72). Similarly Maxine Hairston, during a crucial time in the emerging discipline of composition studies, called for interdisci-

AUTHOR'S NOTE: This chapter originally appeared as an article in *Social Epistemology* (Vol. 9, No. 2, 1995). Copyright 1995 by Taylor & Francis, Ltd. Reprinted by permission.

plinary ties: "[W]e have to extend our connections to disciplines outside our field—not only to linguistics, philosophy, cognitive psychology, and speech communication, but to less obviously connected fields such as biology, economics, and even the arts" (Hairston, 1985: 279-280). Conversely, specialists within stagnant disciplines also call for interdisciplinarity. Barbara Herrnstein Smith acknowledges that dissatisfaction with traditional definitions of, and methodologies in, literary studies has opened the borders of the domain to traffic from other disciplines (Smith, 1989: 2). Even Stanley Fish, who claims that a scholar can inhabit only one disciplinary mindset at a time, rejoices in the positive effects interdisciplinarity has had on literary studies (Fish, 1989: 20-21).

Whether such calls come from juvenile or geriatric disciplines, they focus on the needs of the discipline. However, the other kind of call for interdisciplinarity focuses, not on the needs of the discipline, but on the need to fully understand a subject which does not fit nicely into disciplinary categories. Cifford Geertz's "Blurred Genres" signals an awareness that the disciplinary boundaries established in the last century are undergoing a reconfiguration. He claims that interdisciplinarity results from the recognition "that the lines grouping scholars together into intellectual communities . . . are these days running at some highly eccentric angles" (Geertz, 1980: 169). Wayne Booth, pointing out that several disciplinary attempts to explain why people change their minds have been limited by their narrowness, advocates a pluralistic approach when he says rhetoricians must "repudiate once and for all the notion of a takeover and embrace rather the notion of a pluralistic set of arts, learning from all relevant disciplines and indeed willing to be absorbed by other disciplines at appropriate moments" (Booth, 1971: 106).

Although Booth sounds as though he has little concern with disciplinary boundaries, at the heart of pluralism is a regard for the domains of disciplinary knowledge. Thus, collaboration is a project that entails reinterpretation without transformation. Stanley Fish's claim that importations from outside disciplines must be translated into the language of one's disciplinary home (Fish, 1989: 19) is consistent with Booth's pluralist approach. Conversely, Arabella Lyon argues that if interdisciplinary projects are to succeed, they "require more than simple importation of texts; the disciplines involved apparently need to share aims and actions (methodologies) if the imported texts are to blend and be productive" (Lyon, 1992: 684).

Steve Fuller also rejects pluralistic notions of interdisciplinarity. Arguing that collaborative projects which "abide by the local standards of all the disciplines drawn upon" are hardly improvements over disciplinary studies, he accuses pluralists of falling into the "fallacy of eclecticism" (Fuller, 1993: 41-42). In place of pluralistic conceptions of interdisciplinarity, Fuller puts forward a theory of interdisciplinarity as interpenetration, "an instance of strategically suppressed disagreement that enables an audience to move temporarily in a common direction" (p. 35).

The two views of interdisciplinarity presented above have been labeled interdisciplinary and integrative approaches respectively (Klein, 1990: 27). Pluralist, or interdisciplinary, approaches follow the metaphor of "bridge building," whereas interpentrative, or integrative, approaches follow the metaphor of "restructuring" (p. 27). These two approaches are really two extremes along a continuous spectrum, for even the most radical interpentrative collaboration will involve people whose experiences and perspectives are informed by their disciplinary training; conversely, it is impossible for specialists from different areas to engage in meaningful ways without some restructuring of knowledge and method. As Julie Klein says, "[Interdisciplinarity] is a process for achieving an integrative synthesis" (p. 188).

Although some theorists favor one approach over another for ideological reasons, both types of collaboration exist and rhetorical studies of both are beginning to appear. For instance, Kaufer and Young, in their discussion of writing in the content areas, describe an instance in which restructuring of a biologist's and a rhetorician's definition of their own expertise took place. They end their article with an observation that captures the "restructuring" mindset: "Both must be willing to travel" (Kaufer and Young, 1993: 102). On the other hand, McCarthy and Fishman, in their "Boundary Conversations," describe a collaborative project that more closely resembles "bridge building": Disciplinary ways of knowing are not broken down but simply juxtaposed (McCarthy and Fishman, 1991: 434). Both of these studies reflect upon the experiences of the writers as participants in collaborative projects.

Rhetorical case studies of interdisciplinary discourse in which the scholar was not a participant are also beginning to appear. One of the earliest to my knowledge is a study of Niles Eldrege's and Stephen Jay Gould's difficulty in accommodating various disciplinary audiences as they presented their theory of punctuated equilibria (Lyne and Howe, 1986). This study brought to light the territorial squabbles that resulted from their making claims which transcended their home discipline. And Debra Journet (Journet, 1993) explores the rhetoric of S. E. Jelliffe who adopted the rhetorical strategy of mixing genres and thereby created an interdisciplinary audience for his theory of psychosomatic medicine. Despite these studies, the literature on interdisciplinary rhetoric is sparse, and few can argue with Klein's assertion that "We would know more about how individuals use these [interdisciplinary] skills if there were more accounts of how interdisciplinarians actually work" (Klein, 1990: 183).

A CASE STUDY OF SUCCESSFUL INTERDISCIPLINARY RHETORIC

In this chapter I analyze a successful example of interdisciplinary rhetoric, an article that was part of an ongoing scientific project attempting to explain the causes of mass extinctions. My purpose in analyzing this paper is to describe the authors' interdisciplinary rhetorical skills. Specifically, I show that the authors were successful in their interdisciplinary rhetoric because of their sense of timing (kairos) and their imaginative projection of an appropriate ethos.[1]

The paper which I analyze was written by David M. Raup and J. John Sepkoski, Jr. It is titled "Periodicity of Extinctions in the Geologic Past," and it appeared in *Proceedings of the National Academy of Sciences, USA, (PNAS)*, 1984. To understand the context, we must turn the clock back. An article which appeared four years before Raup's and Sepkoski's created intense interest in mass extinctions. In June of 1980, *Science* published an article by Luis W. Alvarez, Walter Alvarez, Frank Asaro, and Helen V.

Michel, titled, "Extraterrestrial Cause for Cretaceous-Tertiary Extinction." Reporting their discovery of unusually high concentrations of iridium in rock strata associated with Cretaceous-Tertiary extinctions, Alvarez et al. suggested that the iridium, which is largely of extraterrestrial origin, settled out of the atmosphere after a large meteorite hit the earth spewing tons of pulverized dust into the atmosphere, darkening the earth, cutting off photosynthesis and leading to mass extinctions (Alvarez et al., 1980: 1104). Not unlike the hypothesized meteorite, this article impacted the scientific community with such force that its fallout continues to show up in the journals over a decade after its publication. The Alvarez hypothesis initiated several years of collaborative efforts to ascertain whether or not meteorite impacts have caused mass extinctions.

Raup and Sepkoski contributed to this ongoing project, advancing the Alvarez hypothesis and making a controversial claim of their own. Specifically, they claimed that they had found statistical evidence in the geological record supporting a theory that mass extinctions have happened periodically on a 26-million-year (ma) cycle. The paper is an example of a particular kind of interdisciplinary rhetoric, one which respects expertise and boundaries and yet moves beyond those boundaries. If the success of a paper is judged by the interest and response it generates, then this paper is a very successful interdisciplinary article.

Raup and Sepkoski were not the first to put forward a theory that extinctions were cyclical. Alfred G. Fischer and Michael A. Arthur had published a paper in 1977 suggesting that extinctions occur on a 32-million-year cycle. Their idea had not caught on. Their suggestion, if true, would have been revolutionary, but as Raup says in *The Nemesis Affair*, "Many of us (most in fact) did our best to look the other way. Fischer and Arthur were claiming that the major extinctions of the past 250 million years were evenly spaced, coming every 32 million years. This was anathema!" (Raup, 1987: 107). Given the failure of Fischer and Arthur in 1977 and the success of Raup and Sepkoski in 1984, the question "why?" seems to demand an answer. One part of the answer is that the time was not ripe when Fischer and Arthur made their suggestion.

The Open Door:
Kairos as Rhetorical Timeliness

The first rhetorical dynamic that contributed to Raup's and Sepkoski's successful interdisciplinarity was their sense of timing. In classical rhetoric, the Greek word *kairos* refers to a rhetorical situation that is ripe, an opportunity or window during which otherwise difficult or impossible tasks become possible.[2] When a rhetor grasps the kairos, her rhetoric is kairotic, or timely. Raup's and Sepkoski's paper was rushed into publication in order to take advantage of an open window. In *The Nemesis Affair,* Raup says, "We wanted quick publication, although there was no compelling reason for any hurry" (Raup, 1987: 127). He then explains that he and Sepkoski weren't worried about being scooped, but, he says, "[we] felt like we had something exciting and we were impatient to get it in print" (p. 127). In 1984 (among scholars interested in the geological record and evolutionary change) being able to show statistical evidence to support periodicity of mass extinctions was similar to being able to unravel the structure of DNA in 1953.

The time (*kairos*) was ripe for this paper; many changes had occurred in the seven years since the appearance of the Fischer and Arthur paper; most notably the Alvarez paper about the iridium anomaly at the K-T boundary had appeared in 1980. After the Alvarez paper appeared, several interdisciplinary conferences were held in which the topic of mass extinctions and meteoric impacts had been discussed. Three of these conferences were the Snowbird conference in October 1981, the Dahlem conference in Berlin during May of 1983, and the "Dynamics of Extinction" symposium held in Flagstaff, Arizona, in August 1983 (Raup, 1987: 25). The first is significant because its main topic was the Alvarez hypothesis. At the second, David Raup presented, for the first time and in an informal way, his and Sepkoski's data about periodicity. At the third, Sepkoski presented the data formally. Roger Lewin, a professional science writer, reported on Sepkoski's presentation in the September 2, 1983, issue of *Science,* and so Raup and Sepkoski were in the situation of needing to publish their study rapidly because news of it was already out. In fact, because the Lewin article had mentioned a possible connection with extraterrestrial causes, certain astrophysicists were requesting preprints of the forthcoming article (Raup, 1987: 136).

Other changes had also taken place. Perhaps the most comical was that Alvarez had reported discovering another iridium anomaly in Montana in *Science* 1981, only to find out later that the iridium had not come from outer space, or even from Montana, but from the wedding band worn by the technician who prepared the samples for analysis. In his retraction, Alvarez gave errors of this kind a new name, "wedding-ring anomalies" (Alvarez et al., 1982: 888). However, while retracting his Montana claim, Alvarez reported finding another iridium anomaly, this time associated with the Eocene extinctions. Thus, evidence for meteoric impacts in coincidence with extinctions was mounting.

Furthermore, there were some new tools available. One was Sepkoski's compendium of data on the fossil record of life, which had been put on computer disks enabling quick database searches and statistical analyses. Another important tool was W. B. Harland's *A Geological Time Scale* (1982). According to the review of that book, the Harland time scale is a cutting edge and comprehensive synthesis of available data (Dalrymple, 1983: 944). The combination of a mood of expectation, a more useful compendium of the fossil record, and an updated and more authoritative geologic time scale set the stage for Raup's and Sepkoski's periodicity paper. Furthermore, the audience for extinction papers was larger than in 1977 because the Alvarez paper had been published in *Science* and had transcended disciplinary lines. This conversation was not representative of science as puzzle solving but science in the process of a paradigm shift (from Lyell's gradualism to the view that earth history has been shaped by catastrophes); it was a time of revolutionary science and rapid change.

Raup's and Sepkoski's sense of timeliness seems to permeate the text of the periodicity paper. In several places they refer to the moment or to the rapid process of change. In their purpose statement they say their purpose is to test Fischer's proposition by using "as rigorous methodology as *present* data permit" (Raup and Sepkoski, 1984: 801, italics added). They had the best data available at the time in Sepkoski's compendium, but they knew it was changing. Sepkoski was busy trying to expand the data to accommodate analysis of records for levels more specific than that of the family. Explaining their decision to place extinctions at the ends of stages of geologic time, they say their inference is the best "in the present state of knowledge" (p. 802). At another point, they wish to dismiss a possible 30-ma (million-year) periodicity, and so they say that it "cannot be confirmed with the *present* time scales" (p. 804, italics added). Qualifying their claim in the conclusions section, they explain that the length of the cycle may shift as time scale data improve (p. 805). Furthermore, "at present" Sepkoski's data do not support one geologist's 50-ma hypothesis; in fact, "due to the relatively weak state of the Paleozoic time scale . . . nothing can be said unequivocally at this time" (p. 805). Finally, they call for timely help from astrophysicists when they say, "much more information is need *before* definitive statements about causes can be made" (p. 805, italics added).

The kairotic nature of the article is also reinforced by pronouncements about the importance of the work. They claim that their conclusion is "inescapable" (p. 804), a word that creates the image of prey being cornered, ready to be snared. There is a sense of impending changes in science because, as they put it, "The implications of periodicity for evolutionary biology are profound" (805). Though they do not refer to Lyell or Cuvier, they and their readers know that Lyell's gradualism, which won the day over Cuvier's catastrophism in the early 1800s, was in danger of being overthrown, a possibility that caused even the authors some "philosophical anguish" (Lewin, 1983: 936).

Thus, changes had been taking place and even greater changes were on the horizon; this paper inhabits an opportune moment, a rhetorical kairos. Unlike Fischer's and Arthur's paper that suggested a 32-ma periodicity and languished uncited in 1977, this paper virtually exploded on the scene. Remarkably, just two months after this paper was published, four papers suggesting astrophysical causes for periodicity and one paper showing periodicity in meteorite craters appeared in the April 19, 1984, issue of *Nature*. The first four articles, all by astrophysicists, cite the periodicity paper by Raup and Sepkoski as their first reference, and the fifth paper, by a geologist, cites it as the fifth reference. These papers, printed under the title "Letters to Nature," came in to *Nature* even before the periodicity paper appeared in publication. All of the authors were working from preprints, a situation which caused John Maddox, editor of *Nature*, to reprimand Raup and Sepkoski for their unorthodox behavior. He says, "The most obvious complaint against the system [of circulating preprints] is that it is discriminatory, excluding from the circle of those in the know people who happen not to be on the authors' mailing list" (Maddox, 1984: 685). There would have been no call for John Maddox's reprimand in times of normal science, but in that season of rapid change and kairotic opportunity, Maddox was forced to say something in order to protect a system that is supposed to give voice to science but which in extraordinary times is too slow to keep pace with the changes.

The Inviting Image:
Ethos as Rhetorical Identification

The second factor that contributed to the successful interdisciplinary rhetoric of this article is the authors' projection of an appropriate ethos. In ancient Greek, the words *to prepon* meant "the appropriate"; in relationship to rhetoric, the appropriate changes with circumstances, and so rhetors must be able to adapt to the rhetorical situation.[3] Ethos refers to the persona projected during a speech or contained within a paper. An appropriate ethos, therefore, is a manufactured image or persona that gains attention, elicits trust, and invites participation within a changing environment. In short, it is ethos that causes the audience to identify with the writer or speaker, and it is through identification that consubstantiality is formed, and it is through consubstantiality that people act together in collaborative endeavors (Burke, 1969: 21). Creating identification is difficult enough in disciplinary rhetoric; doing so in interdisciplinary situations is much more difficult.

Raup's and Sepkoski's periodicity article appeared in *Proceedings of the National Academy of Sciences* in February 1984, just four months after it was submitted and just five months after Lewin's report on Sepkoski's presentation of the research had appeared in *Science. PNAS* is published by the National Academy, which is made up of some 1500 people considered to be top scholars in the sciences. The Academy was created by Congress to advise the government on scientific matters. Members of the Academy can publish in PNAS without going through peer review, and because David Raup was a member, the periodicity paper was published without being refereed. Although he claims that only a couple critics have chastised him and Sepkoski for not publishing in a refereed journal, Raup spends three pages in *The Nemesis Affair* (pp. 126-129) explaining their decision to do so. Compensating for its not being refereed, Raup points out that the journal has a quick publication schedule and a large circulation in the United States and abroad. Furthermore, it is a respected journal because it speaks for the Academy, a prestigious "club" that not even Carl Sagan is a member of (Raup, 1987: 164). Another advantage of publishing in PNAS, although Raup does not specifically mention it, is that it is an interdisciplinary journal. Scientists from several disciplines would read it; this is the kind of audience Raup and Sepkoski wanted because the controversy over extinctions was spilling over the boundaries of paleontology and geology into other fields.

The paper, framed by an abstract at the front and acknowledgements and references at the end, is divided into the following sections:

Introduction
Data Base
Measurement of Extinction Rates
Statistical Analysis of the Time Series
  Fourier Analysis
  Nonparametric Testing
  Best-Fit Cycle
Conclusion
Implications

To create identification in an interdisciplinary context, Raup and Sepkoski take on different personae as the paper develops and thereby move the audience from one room in the larger house of science to other rooms. In the introduction, data base, and measurement sections, they assume the personae of orthodox paleontologists. In the statistical analysis section, they assume the roles of expert statisticians. In the conclusions section they combine the two previous personae, and in the implications section they play the role of speculative generalists or amateur astrophysicists. These changing personae make up an appropriate interdisciplinary ethos which invites participation from diverse quarters.

In the introduction, they assume the roles of paleontologists instructing those outside that discipline. First, they make a bold declaration, "virtually all species of animals and plants that have ever lived are now extinct," a claim that may shock outsiders but is presented as a settled issue within the field. They then instruct the reader about the basic assumptions of the field, namely that the extinction process is usually considered a continuous process. Among the articles cited to demonstrate this traditional, orthodox assumption is Raup's own article on cohort analysis, which appeared a couple of years before the Alvarez paper and can be described as containing a conservative view of extinctions. By placing that article among the traditionalists' articles, Raup and Sepkoski signal their own conservatism. They then inform those outside the field, though most are aware, that there is "increasing evidence" that extinctions are short-lived events, and they cite the Fischer and Arthur 1977 paper which Raup had originally considered anathema. What was unspeakable seven years earlier has now found its way into the introductory paragraph of a major paper, but not without qualification. After explaining that Fischer and Arthur used a limited data base and did no statistical testing, Raup and Sepkoski announce their purpose: "The purpose of this paper, therefore, is to test the proposition of periodicity in the record of marine extinctions over the past 250 ma (Late Permian to Recent) by using as rigorous a methodology as present data permit" (p. 801). Having opened the possibility of talking about periodicity by citing the Fischer and Arthur study and having shown the deficiencies of that study, Raup and Sepkoski have opened space for their own news. Surprisingly, the 1980 Alvarez paper has not been cited at this point in the paper, and it isn't cited until the implications section of the paper.

In the next two sections (data base and measurement of extinction rates) Raup and Sepkoski maintain the ethos of conservative paleontologists with progressive methodologies and state-of-the-art material, discussing their improved data base, namely the Sepkoski compendium and the Harland time scale. They still sound like paleontologists, however, because the issues addressed are field specific—the arbitrariness of the definition of "family" (Lewin had called it a mysterious unit in his article) and the discrepancies between the Harland scale and the Odin scale. Furthermore, the discussion of how to measure extinction rates, though sophisticated, is an in-house sort of topic, a subject best left to paleontologists.

However, in the statistical analysis section of the paper, a section that is really the heart of the paper, they assume the role of expert statisticians.[4] This change in persona is signaled when they say, "Qualitative impressions may be misleading. For this reason, we have applied a variety of standard and nonstandard tests of periodicity to the time series" (p. 802). It's as though they come out of the provincial quarter of paleontology with its "nineteenth-century" flavor into the cosmopolitan world of the academy forsaking the vernacular and adopting the lingua franca of statistics.[5]

Raup and Sepkoski act as though they are among peers when they talk statistics. They use technical language usually without defining it: "smooth power spectrum," "first harmonic," "random walk," "composite cycle," and "non-unimodal curve." They carefully explain the statistical procedure they followed to get their results, displaying concern that other statisticians will be able to judge the validity of their procedure. Not only do they discuss their Fourier analysis and their best-fit analysis, they also divide the nonparametric test procedure into three subparts, explaining how they placed several periodic impulse functions on the time series, randomized the real data, and compared the standard deviations of the real data with a distribution formed by 500 simulations (p. 802).

They address issues tied primarily to statistics rather than to paleontology. For example they say, "It can be argued that the necessary minimal spacing of 12×106 years between observed extinction peaks can make random (Poisson) data appear periodic to Fourier analysis" (p. 802), and "It could be argued that the statistical significance of the results could have been generated by periodic elements in the scale itself" (p. 803). They report their results in terms of levels of statistical significance, showing that their tests give results well within $p < .01$ for their claimed 26 ma (million year) periodicity (p. 803). Reporting three major statistical tests and seemingly innumerable variations of those tests, Raup and Sepkoski project an image of expert statisticians: they are knowledgeable about programming computers, about statistical procedures, about possible sources of error, and about levels of significance.

Having established their ethos first as paleontologists (conservative in theory, progressive in methods) and second as statisticians, Raup and Sepkoski have made room for their major claim, which appears in the conclusions section of the paper: "It seems inescapable that the post-Late Permian extinction record contains a 26-ma periodicity, assuming that the Harland time scale . . . is a reasonable approximation of reality" (pp. 804-805). In this short section of the paper, the two previous roles—paleontologist and statistician—are combined. They once again talk like paleontologists, referring to the "Permian-Miocene interval" and the "Early Triassic" (p. 804); but they also continue to use terms like "autocorrelation" and "nonparametric test" (p. 805). They report one last test in this section, one in which they had attempted to find out if the 26-ma periodicity was some kind of statistical shadow of a 52-ma cycle. They claim that their tests do not support the latter. This seeming excursion from the direct path makes little sense unless we have read Lewin's report of the Flagstaff conference. There we find out that Eugene Shoemaker—an expert in meteorite craters—had said that we could "expect to incur a significant [meteor] impact on a 50-million year cycle" (Lewin, 1983: 936). Without specifying the significance of their test, Raup and Sepkoski have set up the final section of the paper, headed "Implications."

As they have migrated through different personae, Raup and Sepkoski have managed to bring paleontologists and statisticians together in one audience. Their last report in the conclusions added geologists to the train, but in this final section of the paper, they anticipate others as well, specifically astrophysicists. They are moving from what Raup calls his "corner of science" (Raup, 1987: 150) to the common parlor, claiming that if periodicity can be demonstrated, "implications are broad and fundamental" (p. 805).

In order to accommodate the astrophysicists, Raup and Sepkoski take on the personae of generalists and of amateur astrophysicists. First, as generalists, they adopt a form of deductive reasoning easily followed by non-specialists. Their reasoning is in the form of a descending logic tree made up of an "if" clause followed by a question which provides a set of alternatives. The second alternative is always the logical choice. For example, after questioning whether the causes (forcing agent) of this apparent periodicity are biological or environmental, they then say, "If the forcing agent is in the physical environment, does this reflect an earthbound process or something in space?" (p. 805). Thus, by gradual removes down the logic tree, they migrate from the ethos of their own expertise to the field of astrophysics, speculating that perhaps the cause is the solar system's passage through the spiral arms of the galaxy, which would, "increase the comet flux" (p. 805). Not until this point, some twenty lines from the end of the article, do they reference the Alvarez paper of 1980 which initiated the conversation they are participating in. They simply mention that their scenario would follow the "Alvarez hypothesis." In this final section of the paper they reference Shoemaker, Alvarez, and Ganapathy, all geologists who can contribute information about meteorite craters and iridium anomalies, but they can not speak authoritatively about larger issues in astronomy. They leave the door open for experts in astrophysics, saying, "However, much more information is needed before definitive statements about causes can be made" (p. 805).

CONCLUSIONS

As I think the above analysis demonstrates, the interdisciplinary rhetoric of Raup and Sepkoski migrates across boundaries. Raup and Sepkoski seem to be cosmopolitan travelers capable of speaking the local dialect of paleontology but also the lingua franca of statistics, able to engage in esoteric methodologies of experts and in the well-worn but reliable methodology of descending logic trees. They are able to become "all things to all people."

Such rhetoric can happen only in special circumstances, when the timing is right. And even then, there is no guarantee of success. Through their skillful manipulation of personae, Raup and Sepkoski create an environment in which identification, consubstantiality, and collaborative work may occur. They build bridges between disciplines and respect disciplinary boundaries while they simultaneously restructure the relationship between the disciplines, getting diverse people to move at least temporarily in the same direction, and adding to a growing body of knowledge within the interdisciplinary project of understanding the history of mass extinctions.

NOTES

1. Most discussions of ethos rely heavily on Aristotle's discussion of it as one of the three pisteis, along with logos and pathos. The literature on ethos is extensive. (See, for example, Halloran, 1982; Miller's and Halloran, 1993; Corts, 1968; Arthur Miller, 1975; Sattler, 1947; Sullivan, 1993.)

2. There are several articles which discuss kairos as it pertains to rhetoric (Poulakos, 1983; Kinneavy, 1986; Carter, 1988; Carolyn Miller, 1992).

3. For more on *to prepon*, see John Poulakos, 1983.

4. Expertise is not exactly the same thing as ethos, though expertise is a kind of ethos. See Geisler, 1992; Carter, 1990. These articles put forth different descriptions of the qualities of expertise. William Rifkin (1989) has developed a theory of expert status as a negotiated concept.

5. Steve Fuller refers to such universal languages as "pidgins," which sometimes evolve from trading zones. He points to Monte Carlo that evolved out of the pooling of expertise and continues to be a body of research to which several disciplines contribute (Fuller, 1993: 45).

REFERENCES

Alvarez, L. W., Alvarez, W., Asaro, F. and Michel, H. V. (1980), "Extraterrestrial Cause for the Cretaceous—Tertiary Extinction," *Science*, 208: 1095-1108.

Alvarez, W., Asaro, F., Michel, H. V. and Alvarez, L. W. (1982), "Iridium Anomaly approximately Synchronous with Terminal Eocene Extinctions," *Science*, 216: 886-888.

Booth, W. C. (1971), "The Scope of Rhetoric Today: A Polemic Excursion," in L. F. Bitzer and E. Black (eds.), *The Prospect of Rhetoric*, Prentice Hall, Englewood Cliffs, 93-114.

Burke, K. (1969), *A Rhetoric of Motives*, University of California Press, Berkeley.

Carter, M. (1990), "The Idea of Expertise: An Exploration of Cognitive and Social Dimensions of Writing," *College Composition and Communication*, 41: 165-286.

Carter, M. (1988), "Stasis and Kairos: Principles of Social Construction in Classical Rhetoric," *Rhetoric Review*, 7: 97-112.

Corts, T. E. (1968), "The Derivation of Ethos," *Speech Monographs*, 35: 201-202.

Dalrymple, G. B. (1983), "Geological Time," *Science*, 221: 944-945.

Fischer, A. G. and Arthur, M. A. (1977), "Secular Variations in the Pelagic Realm," in H. E. Cook and P. Enos (eds.), *Deep-Water Carbonate Environments, Society of Economic Paleontologists and Mineralogists*, Tulsa.

Fish, S. (1989), "Being Interdisciplinary Is So Very Hard to Do," *Profession 89*, Modern Language Association, New York, 15-22.

Fuller, S. (1993), *Philosophy, Rhetoric, & the End of Knowledge*, University of Wisconsin Press, Madison.

Geertz, C. (1980), "Blurred Genres: The Refiguration of Social Thought," *American Scholar*, 49: 165-179.

Geisler, C. (1992), "Exploring Academic Literacy: An Experiment in Composing," *College Composition and Communication*, 43: 39-54.

Hairston, M. (1985), "Breaking Our Bonds and Reaffirming Our Connections," *College Composition and Communication*, 36: 272-282.

Halloran, S. M. (1982), "Aristotle"s Concept of Ethos, or if not His Somebody Else"s," *Rhetoric Review*, 1: 58-63.

Journet, D. (1993), "Interdisciplinary Discourse and "Boundary Rhetoric": The Case of S. E. Jelliffe," *Written Communication*, 10: 510-541.

Kaufer, D. and Young, R. (1993), "Writing in the Content Areas: Some Theoretical Complexities," in L. Odell (ed.), *Theory and Practice in the Teaching of Writing: Rethinking the Discipline*, Southern Illinois University Press, 71-104.

Kinneavy, J. L. (1986), "Kairos: A Neglected Concept in Classical Rhetoric," in J. D. Moss (ed.), *Rhetoric and Praxis*, Catholic University of America Press, Washington, D.C., 79-105.

Klein, J. T. (1990), *Interdisciplinarity: History, Theory, and Practice*. Wayne State University Press, Detroit.

Lewin, R. (1983), "Extinctions and the History of Life," *Science*, 221: 935-937.

Lyne, J. and Howe H. F. (1986), " 'Punctuated Equilibria': Rhetorical Dynamics of a Scientific Controversy," *Quarterly Journal of Speech*, 72: 132-147.

Lyon, A. (1992), "Interdisciplinarity: Giving Up Territory," *College English*, 54: 681-693.

Maddox, J. (1984), "Extinctions by Catastrophe?" *Nature*, 308: 685.

McCarthy, L. P. and Fishman, S. M. (1991), "Boundary Conversations: Conflicting Ways of Knowing in Philosophy and Interdisciplinary Research," *Research in the Teaching of English*, 25: 417-468.

Miller, A. B. (1975), "Aristotle on Habit and Character: Implications for the Rhetoric," *Speech Monographs*, 41: 309-316.

Miller, C. R. (1992), "Kairos in the Rhetoric of Science," in S. P. Witte, N. Nakadate, and R. D. Cherry (eds.), *A Rhetoric of Doing: Essays on Written Discourse in Honor of James L. Kinneavy*, Southern Illinois University Press, Carbondale, 310-327.

Miller, C. R. and Halloran S. M. (1993), "Reading Darwin, Reading Nature; or, On the Ethos of Historical Science," in J. Selzer (ed.), *Understanding Scientific Prose*, University of Wisconsin Press, 106-126.

Poulakos, J. (1983), "Toward a Sophistic Definition of Rhetoric," *Philosophy and Rhetoric,* 16: 35-48.

Raup, D. M. (1987), *The Nemesis Affair: A Story of the Death of Dinosaurs and the Ways of Science,* W. W. Norton, New York.

Raup, D. M. and J. J. Sepkoski, Jr. (1984), "Periodicity of Extinctions in the Geologic Past," *Proceedings of the National Academy of Sciences,* (USA) 81: 801-805.

Rifkin, W. D. (1989), "Beginnings of a Theory of Expert Status," Paper presented at the 1989 Conference of the Society for the Social Studies of Science, Irvine, CA.

Sattler, W. M. (1947), "Conceptions of Ethos in Ancient Rhetoric," *Speech Monographs,* 14: 55-65.

Smith, B. H. (1989), "Introduction: Breaking Up/Out/Down the Boundaries of Literary Study," *Profession* 89, Modern Language Association, 2-3.

Sullivan, D. L. (1993), "The Ethos of Epideictic Encounter," *Philosophy und Rhetoric,* 26: 113-133.

Woolbert, C. H. (1916), "The Organization of Departments of Speech Science in Universities," *Quarterly Journal of Public Speaking,* 2: 64-77.

Discussion

1. Dale Sullivan"s case study points out that during a scientific controversy, traditional disciplines, and audiences change— sometimes radically. Why is the concept of ethos important in understanding how David Raup connects with different audiences? What is the definition of *kairos*? Why is the concept of kairos important in understanding how Raup connects with different audiences? What happens to the relationship between writer and reader during a scientific controversy? How does David Raup convince readers of intra- and interdisciplinary journals that his claims are true? In what ways are the significance of a scientific claim—and responses to it—primarily rhetorical? How does proper timing lend credibility to an idea?

2. At the outset, Sullivan outlines two conceptions of interdisciplinarity. The pluralist model calls for specialists in one discipline to reinvigorate their research by turning to the methods and approaches of other disciplines. On this model, traditional academic disciplines essentially stay intact but widen their scope. The "interpenetrative" model calls for specialists to synthesize their fields of study into a fully integrated approach to a given problem. On this model, traditional

academic disciplines are transformed or completely eliminated. Provide an argument in which you advocate one concept of interdisciplinarity. In your argument, consider how
technical communicators" concepts of audience would be
affected by your position.

3. Given Sullivan"s analysis, draw a portrait of David Raup as a
writer possessing defined rhetorical sensibilities. That is, what
aspects of Raup"s presentation convince audiences that his
claims regarding mass extinction are more likely correct?
Does Raup have a specific purpose in the strategies he adopts?
More generally, in what ways can scientific and technical
communicators capture "timeliness" in their presentations?
Using a current scientific or technological controversy as an
example, which positions regarding it would you consider
"timely" or "untimely?" Explain the criteria for your choices.

4. Which academic audiences do Raup and Sepkoski have to
convince with an explanation of mass extinctions? How does
Raup appeal to those audiences? What part does historical
context play in Raup and Sepkoski"s presentation? How do
they position themselves within the history of geology? How
does the appeal to history insure kairos?

5. Like Keith (Chapter 9, Part II), Sullivan emphasizes the function of ethos in causing the audience to identify with the
speaker. What is the ethos of the audience to which Raup and
Sepkoski must appeal? Sullivan describes an "appropriate
ethos" as a "manufactured image or persona." Considering
that Raup and Sepkoski"s audience is, generally, interdisciplinary, through what process do they create ethos?

6. In the conclusion, Raup and Sepkoski are compared to "cosmopolitan travelers" who are able to speak the languages and
dialects of many disciplines. Still, their ideas may fail to be
accepted unless their timing is right. Sullivan suggests quite
a narrow window of opportunity for successful interdisciplinary rhetoric. What are the implications of Sullivan"s position
for technical communicators who wish to appeal to interdisciplinary audiences? Are claims about phenomena that inter-
sect many disciplines harder to "sell" than knowledge claims
bound within disciplines? Does the acceptance of an explana-

tion in one discipline necessarily satisfy the criteria for the acceptance in another discipline? Provide an example.

Exercises

1. Sullivan"s case study provides a model for examining the function of rhetoric in scientific and technical writing, especially during a time when a new or controversial claim is put forward. Select an explanation of a phenomenon that has recently been the source of intellectual dispute within your discipline. Examples of these disputes include questions regarding whether Pluto is properly classified as a planet, if a gene that determines criminal behavior exists, and if paid political advertising has any affect (as measured empirically) on voters" choices. In a rhetorical analysis and report on selected literature generated by this controversy, provisionally determine the outcome of the debate. In so doing, examine the role that kairos and ethos have in the rhetorical appeals made by the debate participants. Consider how audiences were swayed to take a given position.

2. Referring to Chapter 4 in Part I of the text, perform an audience analysis of Sullivan"s article. Initially, characterize Sullivan"s professional field (rhetoric). Consider what resources he controls, what requirements there are for practice, organizational control, and workstyle. You may wish to refer to Chapter 2 in Part I to help define your response as a reader. To what readers does Sullivan appeal? Does he appeal to readers outside the fields of rhetoric and communication? Do you think an audience of scientists would agree with his analysis of the mass extinctions controversy? Why or why not? Given your characterization of rhetoric as a field and Sullivan as a practitioner, speculate on the requirements for what counts as knowledge within the field, and how these requirements compare to those in your discipline. On the same grounds that Sullivan argues for what constitutes successful interdisciplinary rhetoric, would you assess his analysis as persuasive to an interdisciplinary audience? Why or why not?

3. Sullivan presents an analysis of how scientists appeal to various audiences. Choose two articles on the same subject from a general-audience periodical such as *Time* or *Newsweek* and a somewhat more technical journal like *Scientific American* or *Popular Mechanics*. In a brief response paper, compare and contrast the two articles, considering the audience for each piece and its purpose. Consider the structural aspects of the writing, sentence length, paragraph length, vocabulary, amount of white space, the number of graphics and formulas and the references within and at the end of each article. After making these determinations, draw a profile of the audience for each. What is each audience"s general educational background and expertise?

Introduction to Chapter 11

In a broad sense, most scientific and technical controversies are linguistic. In 1633, the Vatican arrested Galileo Galilei for writing—against the orders of the Church—that the earth revolves around the sun. In other words, Galileo's description of the local universe differed from the Church's. In October 1992, Pope John Paul II made a papal statement vindicating the astronomer. What is interesting here is that the Pope was not so much conceding the obvious—that Galileo was right—as wanting to restore Galileo's standing as a Christian. Specifically, the Pope asserted that because Galileo argued against an absolute reading of the Bible he was a more sophisticated and, essentially, a better theologian than his persecutors. In other words, the Pope considered Galileo's description of the Bible's description of nature superior to that given by the seventeenth-century church.

This most famous of scientific controversies shares much with others—an issue which affects people personally and may threaten (or seem to threaten) health, life, or fundamental beliefs. Science and religion have spurred other controversies: for instance, creationism versus Darwinism; right-to-life issues; and scientific examination of sacred burial sites. More mundane but no less inflammatory controversies surround us: fluoridation, high-voltage electric power lines, secondary tobacco smoke, nuclear power—the list seems to grow longer daily. Both sides of each issue use argument and persuasion to bolster their cases; and at times the language, perhaps most evident in protesters' chants and bumper stickers, obfuscates more than it clarifies. We might expect that scientists and people representing or claiming to represent scientists would do better. Often though, their language, while seemingly more sophisticated than laypersons', is confusing.

The 1991 Persian Gulf War is, perhaps, one of the most interesting cases of control of the media and, subsequently, public opinion in the modern era. Perhaps unalterably, the story of war has been changed. The story is no longer about the repugnance of military action, the devastation of culture, the bombing of ancient cities, and the death of men, women, and children, but of the success of technology. Through a global, cable news outlet, the military presented the images it wanted the world to see, using the language it wanted the world to hear. The power of persuasion and our need as a society to look beyond it were never more clearly evident. In this chapter, Sujatha Raman argues that the military, the press, and the politicians used a kind of description (specifically, terms evocative of cleanliness and precision) that conveyed a picture of the U.S. victory at variance with reality. Chapter 5 in Part I of the text examines the mechanics of persuasion and argument with respect to various functions of language. Taking the Gulf War as a case study, Raman offers additional strategies for analyzing the rhetorical nature of scientific and technical discourse for understanding, and making decisions about, our support of given technologies—and their consequences.

CHAPTER 11

Challenging High-Tech War
Surgical Strike or Collateral Damage?

SUJATHA RAMAN

In this chapter, I discuss how the language of cold war nuclear strategy and the language of the "hot war" in the Persian Gulf have together constructed a particular image of high-tech war. Military precision takes on a new meaning in the electronic battlefield. Now it is the amazing new weapons of war that carry out their tasks like clockwork. Missiles zero in on their targets successfully "delivering" bombs. Things happen by remote control, taking out the messiness inherent in human combat and rendering unassailable victories. I ask here how people who lack direct access to these events can make critical judgments regarding their media representations. For instance, when CNN tells us that what we just saw on our television screens was a U.S Patriot missile successfully destroying an Iraqi Scud, is CNN reporting a "fact"?

The immediate problem appears to be that people lack the expertise to make such judgments. One might think that one would need to know a lot about missile technology—and that would be just the beginning. It is inconceivable that most of us could access, let alone understand, all the relevant technical information that goes into the planning and execution of today's wars. The point I am making here is that it is impossible even for the experts—who do have the information—to make foolproof evaluations. It is precisely because modern technological systems are so complex that no one person can grasp the intricate connections between people's actions and the performance of technical artifacts.

This is not an argument for ignorance. Rather, I argue that the authoritative certainty of military pronouncements can and must be challenged, by looking for alternate interpretations of the same events. In the Gulf War, the morality of U.S. policy depended on the image of a clean war. In the cold war, the morality of conventional war depended on its image of moderation in comparison to the stark horror of nuclear war. Both cases depended also on a particular interpretation of modern technology as infallible. The aim here is to challenge that view by demonstrating the uncertainty of technical knowledge.

THE GULF WAR IN THE MEDIA

Not long after the end of the 1991 Persian Gulf War, cracks began to show in the image of an overwhelming U.S. triumph over Iraq. The prominent stories in the media were confined to whether the political goals were achieved. Should the United States have gotten rid of Saddam Hussein? Was Iraq's military strength, particularly its nuclear capability, essentially untouched? As might be expected, these are contestable issues, and it was not surprising to hear different positions expressed. However, the belief that the Gulf War was an extraordinarily successful exhibition of high-tech weaponry appeared to survive in the eyes of many military experts and peace researchers.[1] Terms such as "smart bombs," "technowar," and "surgical strikes" were routinely used by Pentagon officials, reporters, and various political commentators to accompany the mesmerizing television pictures of electronic "explosions." The language conveyed the idea that this was a clean, bloodless war in which the precision of U.S. technology took center stage, managing to pulverize the Iraqi military without significant harm to Iraqi civilians. The commentary appeared to independently support then President George Bush's claim that "collateral damage" was being minimized.

The actual performance of U.S. weapons in the war is highly controversial. Studies have since identified numerous contradictions in Pentagon information about U.S. bombing attacks, and provided alternate judgments about the performance of the lavishly praised Patriot and Tomahawk missiles. The national newspapers and television networks carried the occasional story on disputes to the high-tech success story, but the controversy remained on the sidelines, never attaining the status of a national issue. Certainly, it couldn't match the hoopla responsible for creating the success story in the first place. When it was recognized that Iraqi civilian casualties were far greater than initially reported and that there had been serious damage to the environment and civic infrastructure, the media seldom made a connection to the performance of U.S. technology. The tale of a high-tech success continues to ensure the earmarking of federal funds for new "strategically superior" weapons programs, even as thousands of defense-related jobs are being cut. Technologies, not people, form the core of the new military. People are dispensable; high technologies—apparently—are not.

Thus far, challenges to the high-tech success story appear to have only caused minimal "collateral damage" to the mainstream viewpoint. Although sophisticated critical evaluations of government, society, or culture are commonplace in the contemporary media, the same cannot be said of technology. The "gee whiz" effect of high-tech displays and the jargon that accompanies their presentation can make it hard for reporters and the public to make their own judgments. The Pentagon's version of the high-tech war "stuck" not only because of the organization's own secrecy and tight control over information (which was truly extensive)[2] but also because of genuine difficulties with critically assessing news reports.

Critical reception is possible—it requires finding controversy where there appears to be none. Behind apparently consensual facts, there often are not only differences of opinion between experts but also agreements on false grounds. One might argue that unearthing them after the fact—as I am doing here—does nothing to change the reality of what happened. However, such criticism can have a cumulative effect on future policy. Interpretations of the past shape policy debates in the present. A particular image of Vietnam as a technical rather than a moral failure came up time and again in Bush's Gulf War rhetoric ("kicking the Vietnam syndrome"). With the Gulf War standing as a technical—and therefore, moral—success,[3] it will undoubtedly offer itself as a paradigm for future wars as well as for national technology policy.[4] In the next section, I describe how the "hot" war in the Gulf was itself influenced by a particular construction of the previous "cold" war.

From Cold War to Hot War: The Attraction of Surgical Strikes

Although the war in the Gulf was "conventional"—that is, it was nonnuclear—it was shaped by cold war thinking about nuclear strategy. Specifically, debates about the distinction between nuclear and conventional weapons influenced public and expert responses to the war. At the outset, there appears to be nothing controversial about a distinction between nuclear and conventional weapons. Hiroshima is ensconced in public memory as heralding the dawn of a revolutionary nuclear age that then came to exemplify the cold war. Although nuclear policy disputes—that is, over what should be done with nuclear weapons—received a good deal of attention during the cold war, the more esoteric arguments over the nature of nuclear weapons and the consequences of nuclear war are still obscure. Central to them is the question of how nuclear weapons differ from conventional weapons, a definition that has been shifting along with innovations in nuclear and nonnuclear military technologies.

The relevance of the nuclear-conventional distinction cannot be summed up by technical facts such as "atomic and thermonuclear bombs work on the basis of nuclear fission and fusion respectively" or in their crudest form, "nuclear bombs yield some $\times$ times energy as conventional explosives like TNT."[5] Even statements that go beyond describing capabilities to describing effects—

"nuclear bombs destroy life through radiation, blast, and fallout, while conventional bombs have more localized effects"—do not give the whole story. These technical descriptions do not provide the context within which the distinction is important.

First, nuclear and conventional bombs are part of weapon systems. Their performance depends on (a) how the other components function and (b) the performance of other weapon systems, including those deployed by the enemy. Second, their effects depend on the strategies through which they are put to use and, in turn, on the way in which the technical plans are themselves implemented. Some nuclear strategists distinguished between nuclear and conventional weapons in terms of what they simply called "usability." Proponents of the Mutual Assured Destruction (MAD) policy in the 1960s considered nuclear weapons too powerful to be usable. The principle of deterrence drew on Bernard Brodie's much-quoted assertion[6] that nuclear weapons could only be "used" to avert wars, not to win them.[7]

Based on estimates of explosive power or yield and the predicted effects of heat, radiation, and blast, these experts concluded that nuclear weapons were unusable. Quite simply, they would cause too much damage for either side to impose its will on the other. If wars are "the continuation of policy by other means,"[8] nuclear war would be the ultimate nonwar. Instead, it would bring complete annihilation, rendering meaningless whatever purpose it was fought for. In the early 1980s, climate scientists put forth the theory of "nuclear winter," which predicted that a large-scale nuclear war would not only kill millions of people but also make the earth uninhabitable. This again reinforced the message that nuclear weapons can serve no rational purpose in combat.

What are the problems with this interpretation of nuclear war? First, the horrific images did not strengthen calls for nuclear disarmament as one might have thought. Instead, they were used to bolster the case for keeping nuclear weapons—and in fact, building bigger and "dirtier" bombs—under the rubric of deterrence. Briefly, this often repeated argument went as follows: Both sides know that even a conventional attack is likely to escalate into nuclear conflict; they also know that all-out nuclear warfare would destroy the world as we know it; since neither side would be irrational enough to take the risk, nuclear weapons paradoxically end up "keeping the peace" between the superpowers. Dissent from this received view was vociferous, but even here there was a nagging problem. The emphasis on the irrationality of nuclear strategy[9] clearly suggests that conventional war can be rational. In contrast to the antiwar movement of the 1960s, mainstream peace protest in the 1980s was preoccupied with nuclear annihilation, setting an extreme yardstick against which destruction in "lesser" wars was implicitly judged.[10] Some critics suggest that this fixation left the peace movement unprepared for the "conventional" war in the Persian Gulf that eventually took place.

A second debate in the 1980s, spurred by further technological developments, is also relevant to the Gulf case. Some strategists, pointing to recent innovations, argued that nuclear weapons were now rationally usable. They argued that the nuclear-conventional distinction was rapidly becoming blurred with the possibility of using nuclear weapons in surgical strikes. In other words, nuclear weapons could be more precisely directed toward military targets. These claims were made on the basis of supposedly revolutionary advancements in missile accuracy. Others, however, argued that it was the newly found precision of missiles that made nuclear weapons special. Nuclear weapons, in this case, were distinguished from conventional weapons not in terms of their explosive power but in terms of their speed and precision in method of delivery.

War has always involved damage to civilian infrastructure and population. Even when wars were officially bounded within a space called the battlefield or "combat zone" as we now call it, violence typically spilled into civilian spaces. However, the brutal experiences of the twentieth century have simultaneously led to widespread awareness and condemnation of war, especially in liberal democracies. Public opinion does not take kindly to large numbers of civilian war casualties. (Some scholars attribute this to television's ability to make vivid the horrors of war, whereas others argue that the style of reportage creates a grand spectacle out of suffering and leaves the public without active strategies of opposition.) In this context, the concept of a surgical strike is attractive because—according to one meaning—it promises to restrict damage to purely military spaces and spare civilian ones. This was the sense in which the term was used in the Gulf War. However, as described below, the term has other meanings that suggest quite different policies.

In the early days of airpower and into the first 15 years of the nuclear age, the dominant attack strategy was all-out war—the very opposite of a surgical strike. Giulo Douhet, Italian theorist of air power, is credited with the argument that a nation could achieve victory simply through the psychological devastation wreaked by aerial bombing attacks on the opponent's territory rather than having to take on and defeat the armed forces of the enemy. This is known as strategic bombing. Until the coming of the atomic bomb in the 1940s, the costs of such a campaign appeared to outweigh the benefits. Promising "more bang for the buck," atomic power appeared to be a relatively cheap way of achieving this capability. The argument for strategic bombing seemed further strengthened with the development of the hydrogen bomb and the intercontinental missile in the 1950s. This meant that war (at least in the gamelike models of nuclear strategists) would involve not only armed forces but entire civilian populations. In these scenarios, the explicit targeting of the enemy's civilians ("city busting," as it was called) common in the two world wars became central to military strategy.

The notion of surgical strikes became popular during the efforts in the mid-1960s to "tame" nuclear weapons. With missiles apparently becoming highly accurate, the United States began to build smaller nuclear weapons with less explosive yield but more precision.[11] The yield of these so-called tactical weapons would be in the range of a few kilotons rather than megatons. Some strategists described the possibility of surgical strikes using these weapons to selectively target and destroy only the Soviet Union's military resources (e.g., weapons in storage or being launched). The economic infrastructure and civilian population would largely be spared. For others, however, surgical strikes simply meant more "limited" strikes—for instance, one that would kill "only" a few million people rather than a whole population. Given the knowledge that nuclear attacks have side effects and would destroy areas around the target through fallout, this was probably more realistic.

The flexibility of the term enabled military officials to justify civilian casualties and still represent the war as a "surgery." During the Gulf War, military spokesmen adopted both positions: that the war was "clean" and that civilian deaths were only to be expected, when confronted with such evidence.[12] Simply demonstrating the falsity of the original claim for a surgical strike was not sufficient to destroy its credibility if its meaning could be shifted.[13] Public critics must therefore realize that technical terms are conceptually slippery.

In fact, I want to argue here that the relevant distinction between nuclear and conventional weapons is fundamentally linguistic. This is not to ignore the physical differences in the structure of the two weapon types. Nor does it take away from the fact that nuclear war will be devastating in the extent and depth of destruction. Rather, the point is to focus on the consequences of drawing a distinction. We have seen the shifts in the grounds by which the nuclear is said to differ from the conventional—from "raw destructive power" or "explosive yield" to "method of delivery" or missile accuracy—until the distinction itself begins to blur. If accuracy is ultimately more important than yield, then conventional weapons become more like nuclear weapons and vice versa. The following two propositions describe the way in which military strategists have invoked this argument to strengthen their case for a new form of high-tech, surgical war.

Proposition 1. If conventional warheads can also be carried on many types of ultraprecise missiles, innovation in accuracy constitutes a revolution in conventional weapons. This amounts to a "nuclearization" of conventional weapons. PGMs (precision-guided munitions), or "smart missiles" as they were called in the Gulf War, represent the premier example of this "other" revolution in weaponry.[14]

Proposition 2. If nuclear weapons are both smaller and more precise due to the highly accurate missiles, they are virtually no different from conventional weapons and can be rationally used in a war. This is the "conventionalization" of nuclear weapons.[15]

Then came the Gulf War and a third way in which the nuclear and conventional worlds collided—this time, though, it was not in terms of mere weapon capability, but in terms of their use. Some uranium was used in U.S. tanks, a fact that was revealed after the war but never gained much attention. In using the fundamental material of nuclear bombs in a conventional guise, this represented a clear case of the blurring of the two worlds. The United States also attacked an Iraqi nuclear facility, an act prohibited by the Geneva protocols. Because it was an attack with a nonnuclear missile, it would not normally be classified as a nuclear strike. However, if one stops to think about it, there is a case to be made for broadening the definition because it does involve blowing up nuclear material (which is why it is banned in the first place).

Challenging Accuracy

Assumptions about missile accuracy were central not only to debates on the nuclear-conventional distinction in the 1980s but also in media reports on the Gulf War. Nuclear hawks arguing that nuclear war could be rational, implicitly accepted the untested claims of accuracy. Likewise, during the Gulf War, reporters and many defense analysts assumed that the "real world," or battlefield, test of accuracy was in fact successful. In both these contexts, the assumption of accuracy was challenged from the margins.

Even before many high-tech weapons of the cold war were "tested" in the Gulf War, some scholars had questioned the belief in their accuracy. Donald MacKenzie's *Inventing Accuracy: A Historical Sociology of Nuclear Missile Guidance*[16] is the premier example of such a scholarly challenge. Among other things, he pointed out the problems of (a) deciding what counts as a successful test of accuracy and (b) extrapolating from test conditions to the conditions of war. Even the most technical aspects of these judgments always involved political choices and constraints. Hence, he argued, they could not be treated as simple technical facts.

With the coming of the Gulf War, it seemed that such skepticism was misplaced. "Smart bombs"—first used in the Vietnam War but much refined since—appeared to be a tremendous success. This view has been challenged in at least two ways. One group of experts argue that there is no natural consensus on what counts as success. A missile's accuracy cannot be readily identified, especially under the chaotic conditions of war.

A second approach maintains that accuracy is itself not important. With respect to nuclear strategy, intelligence analyst Angelo Codevilla argued that simple quantitative analysis—performing headcounts of missile warheads or missile capabilities—is useless if unrelated to a sense of the specific job to be done.[17] According to him, "in the 1980s as missiles moved out of silos, nuclear yield and accuracy became less important than real-time intelligence on the location of mobile missiles, and on-line targeting of offensive warheads" (p. 421). He argued that the worth of any weapon lies in the context of its use, which means that the analyst must take into account the interplay between offense and defense, between shooting at a real target and a synthetic ghost. In other words, information is more important than either yield or accuracy.

In his commentary on Desert Storm, Codevilla claimed that it was "magnificient" and "technically flawless" (obviously assuming that the weapons were as successful as the Pentagon reported) but that it did not constitute a "real" war.[18] Following the 19th-century strategist Carl von Clausewitz, he pointed out that a "real" war requires the careful mapping of political objectives, and the application of means proportionate to the ends. Like some other military theorists who already recognized this before the Gulf War,[19] Codevilla emphasized that an impressive high-tech display does not itself make a war. Thus, it seems that the irrationality of nuclear war (discussed above) applies also to modern "conventional" wars, further blurring the distinction between the conventional and the nuclear.

Amid all this talk about rational war (i.e., the ability of the victorious nation to impose its will on the opponent) we must remember that "non-wars" or irrational wars are capable of producing the kind of destruction and damage associated with "real" wars. The synthetic target that Codevilla dismisses need not be a harmless one. In the Gulf War, the targets were not "ghosts" but often civilians and the infrastructural sources of their livelihood. Hence, I now turn to the studies that strip off the clean, surgical image of the Gulf War.

WAR ON TECHNOWAR

Why should we pay attention to the controversy over the technowar in the Gulf? There are at least two reasons. One, the perceived success of these weapons created and reinforced the idea of the war as "clean." For instance, the February 18, 1991, *Newsweek* cover story was titled "The New Science of War: How Many Lives Can It Save?" The other is that the image of success is used to justify the continuation of expensive, high-tech programs. Patriot and Tomahawk manufacturers requested more federal contracts on the basis of the supposed success of their weapons. Far from stopping with military policy, the shadow of the Gulf War (and of the cold war) also extends to technology and industrial policy more generally. High technology has acquired a special prominence in post-cold-war policy, with numerous business and policy experts claiming that the United States must keep its lead in the area to be economically "competitive." Research programs for "smart" technologies are justified without serious debate on whether they serve human needs.

The public image of Desert Storm was of "smart" bombs, stealth fighter aircraft, and other high-precision weapons. Soon after the end of the war, Air Force Chief Merrill McPeak revealed that the United States used far more "low-tech," or "dumb," bombs in its air attack. In fact, the number of precision bombs was only 7% of the total tonnage dropped! McPeak also said that, on the whole, U.S. bombs missed their targets about 70% of the time. He managed to stem damage to the image of a high-tech success by claiming that the precision bombs alone had a 90% success rate. According to his report, the poor overall success rate was primarily due to the failure of crude "low-tech" (that is, unguided) bombs that hit their targets only about 25% of the time. Thus, while it punctured the image of a clean war somewhat, it did not detract from the idea that "high-tech" is synonymous with precision.

However, the U.S. Department of Defense's final report on the war[20] had much more mixed reviews. One of its findings was that the intelligence agencies could not handle the mammoth amounts of information that were part of the air campaign against Iraq. The report claimed that target restrictions could not be conveyed to the air forces on time, with the result that damage to Iraqi

civilian infrastructure was far more than intended. More interesting, it noted that the agencies involved had been caught in
extended disputes about how the war had been conducted and
how the outcomes were to be interpreted. As I said before, even
experts—those people most closely involved in the planning and
execution of technical plans—rarely ever agree on an understanding of what are highly complex actions. Comprehending the
outcomes of high-tech operations cannot be done on the basis of
straightforward technical rules; they have to be constructed
through language, which means that one ends up with multiple
meanings of the "same" event. The key point to remember here is
that the different meanings do not all have the same status. Some
are clearly more privileged than others, which leaves us with the
challenge of unmasking their power.

So, for instance, even during the war, some people expressed
doubts about the apparent success of the air raids. These tended
to get buried under the blitz of rave reviews. Defense analyst
Pierre Sprey pointed out that the Pentagon was being forced to
retarget several areas where it had hurriedly claimed success.[21]
In a postwar hearing of the Armed Services Committee, Sprey
charged the Pentagon with outright massaging of the data. According to his calculations, the U.S. forces in the first few weeks
of the war spent an average of 24 smart bombs for each successful
targeting of an Iraqi bridge. Television pictures of the air strikes
did not lie—they were merely restricted to those cases of successful hits. What viewers did not see on their television screens
revealed far more about the accuracy of the smart bombs than
what they did see.

Sprey and other former Pentagon officials also presented evidence showing that crude "low-tech" aircraft and missiles were
far more effective than their hyped high-tech counterparts. Journalist Gregg Easterbrook observed that since a thousand-dollar
low-tech weapon was working just as well as a million-dollar
high-tech one, there was no substance to the claim that only
expensive hardware could keep the nation secure.[22] Besides, he
said, by zeroing in on things and skirting people, these smart
bombs were not producing the kind of casualties that could
potentially shock Iraq into surrender. For Easterbrook, there
wasn't enough collateral damage, which was the problem. For

him, the level of sophistication achieved by expensive high-tech weaponry came at the expense of the ability to force defeat on the enemy, one that could only result from extensive civilian damage as suggested by the original theorists of strategic bombing.

Quite apart from the morally reprehensible character of a policy that relies on civilian massacre, it has become increasingly clear that even extensive damage of that sort need not necessarily lead to surrender. Saddam Hussein has managed to hold on to power despite an economy and infrastructure wrecked by the war. Some studies suggest that the so-called war was indeed not a war at all; it was effectively a massacre whose nature was obscured by the televised high-tech spectacle. William Merrin, reflecting on the now infamous—but misinterpreted—claim by a French theorist that "the Gulf War never happened," points out that war involves reciprocity, playing by certain rules. In this case, there was no real engagement between the two sides to merit its label as a "war."[23]

What Is Meant by Success?

A number of figures on success rates were tossed around by spokesmen during and after the war. One obvious problem with these is the verification of the exact numbers. The Pentagon tended to favor inflated success rate figures, some of which the discriminating judge might discount. More interesting than disputes over the exact figures is the uncertainty over what the figures meant. Pentagon sources and analysts were using different definitions of success. Further, some were applying a specific sense of success to numbers derived from another sense. For instance, General Norman Schwarzkopf would cite 80% success rates, giving the impression that the ordnances hit their intended targets this often. It turned out that in Chairman of the Joint Chiefs of Staff Colin Powell's account, 80% success rates simply stood for those bombs that were successfully delivered, irrespective of whether they hit their targets. Note also that even hitting a target need not guarantee success in the sense of completely destroying it.

In the case of U.S. defense missiles (such as the Patriot) it was not clear whether they were successful even when they struck the

Iraqi missile. Reporters hailed the magnificent pictures on our television screens as the successful interception of Iraqi Scud missiles by U.S. Patriots. However, the Patriot's goal is to destroy the Scud before the latter's bomb causes any damage. Military expert and MIT Professor Theodore Postol conducted a detailed analysis arguing that the Patriot was unsuccessful in this respect, that the Patriots typically struck the Scuds only after their warheads had already exploded. A second issue, harder to determine, is whether the Patriot missile that intercepted a Scud was actually responsible for the Scud's failure to deliver its "warhead." In this latter case, a particular Scud's poor design could make the Patriot appear successful.[24] A similar criticism has been made in the case of the supposed success of the Tomahawk missile.[25]

LESSONS FROM
THE STUDY OF TECHNOWAR

Media reports do not pay attention to the nuances of meaning in the effort to bring us "the news." It is important for citizens to note what they do not say as much as what they do.[26] The problem is illustrated in the case of television networks showing the successful working of a smart bomb but failing to show the numerous occasions of failure. Even where a newspaper or a television story seems to present opposing sides of an issue, it is important to remember that there might be other perspectives unrepresented in the debate.

I have suggested in this chapter that the evaluation of technologies is essentially linguistic. Since technical facts shift in meaning, the dogged analyst of technology-based issues must try to uncover the shifts underlying an apparent consensus. This is not an idle exercise. It does not mean that technical claims are simply "cooked up," nor that they have no real consequences. On the contrary, different meanings attached to the "same" fact have different political implications for both policy makers and public group activists. For instance, a sharp distinction between nuclear and conventional war may have kept large sections of the peace movement focusing its energies on the former and neglecting the importance of the latter. On the other hand, some military strategists used the same "fact" to argue for a defense policy that relied on the nuclear deterrent. In blurring the distinction, military hawks argued that nuclear war could be rational. However, peace activists could use the same principle to argue that conventional war is itself irrational.

All of this may suggest that the critical consumer of mainstream policy stories has to spend a great deal of time digging around and excavating alternate interpretations of the technical facts. Only a few people will have the time and resources to embark on this kind of response to the numerous technically complex issues that confront us. However, there are more general lessons to be drawn from this for students and citizens. For one, when confronted with claims such as statistical data on success (or failure) rates, we might ask ourselves—Well, how could the person actually acquire this information? What are the circumstances under which such an observation could be done? If it is a messy situation, as in a war, there are bound to be problems of assessment simply because of difficulties in gathering accurate data and interpreting them.

But more important, we might also challenge the notion that all policy debates have to rely on technical consensus. For instance, in the Gulf case, it makes no difference whether we know exactly how many deaths resulted from the U.S. campaign or the dollar figure of damages to Iraq's infrastructure. The morality of the war should not rest on experts coming to agree on these figures and then deciding if they were too high or low enough. As we have seen, expert consensus is unlikely on these matters and should not presume to colonize all debate on the topic. Personal experiences and observations also make a vivid case and should be allowed to be included as such. After all, the experts are themselves influenced by their personal and collective biases in interpreting the "facts" for our consumption.

NOTES

1. For example, Anatol Rapoport in his *Peace: An Idea Whose Time Has Come* (Ann Arbor: University of Michigan Press, 1992) and Eugene Skolnikoff in

his *The Elusive Transformation: Science, Technology and the Evolution of International Politics* (Princeton, NJ: Princeton University Press, 1993).

2. On this aspect, see Douglas Kellner, *The Persian Gulf TV War* (Boulder, CO: Westview, 1992).

3. With its technical success—a clean war in which only military targets were destroyed—the war gives the United States the moral high ground. While Iraq was the villain that infringed on the sovereignty of another nation-state, the United States played by the rules and set Kuwait (and ostensibly, Iraqi civilians) free.

4. In the debate over Bosnia, politicians like Bob Dole who were calling for air strikes against Serb strongholds invoked the Gulf experience in support of the possibility of surgical strikes. Later on, when cruise missiles were deployed, they did not have the kind of decisive impact that was hoped for.

5. Books on nuclear policy often open with such statements that imply (even if not intentionally) that the difference is that simple.

6. See Gregg Herken's *Counsels of War* (New York: Alfred Knopf, 1985).

7. We must keep in mind that not all strategists agreed on this point. The argument that nuclear war was "unthinkable" prompted a famous rejoinder from Herman Kahn in *Thinking About the Unthinkable* (Tucson: Horizon Press, 1962). He advocated in the 1960s a view that gained prominence in the Nuclear Utilizations Theories (NUTS) of the 1980s—namely, that nuclear weapons were usable in the conventional sense.

8. This is the well-known definition of war proposed by the 19th-century Prussian general and strategist Carl von Clausewitz in his treatise *On War.*

9. For example, Morton Halperin, *The Nuclear Fallacy: Dispelling the Myth of Nuclear Strategy* (New York: Ballinger, 1987).

10. Michael Klare, "The Peace Movement's Next Steps," *The Nation,* 252, no. 11 (1991): 361-363. See also "Movement Gap," editorial in *The Nation,* 253, no. 15 (1991).

11. Martin van Creveld, *Technology and War: From 2000 B.C to the Present* (New York: Free Press, 1989).

12. "This is a war, after all. What do you expect?" being a common response.

13. This might partly explain the failure of former Attorney General Ramsey Clark's campaign against the officials involved in the Gulf War. His monograph (*War Crimes in the Gulf,* edited by Ramsey Clark, 1992, Washington, DC: Maisonneuve Press) documenting U.S. crimes in the war caused barely a stir.

14. The "revolution" in conventional weapons has been discussed by Jorma Miettinen, "Can Conventional New Technologies and New Tactics Replace Tactical Nuclear Weapons in Europe?" in *Arms Control and Technological Innovation,* eds. D. Carlton and C. Schaerf (London: Croom Helm, 1977), and Philip Webber, *New Defence Strategies for the 1990s* (New York: St. Martin's Press, 1990).

15. Reports after the war revealed that the United States considered using such a "mini-nuke" against Iraq.

16. MIT Press, 1990.

17. Angelo Codevilla, *Informing Statecraft* (New York: Free Press, 1992).

18. Angelo Codevilla, "Magnificent, but Was It War?" *Commentary,* April 1992: 15-20.

19. For example, Evan Luard, *The Blunted Sword: The Erosion of Military Power in Modern World Politics,* (London: I. B. Tauris, 1988).

20. U.S. Department of Defense, *Conduct of the Persian Gulf War: Final Report* (Washington, D.C., 1992), cited in David Campbell, *Politics Without Principle: Sovereignty, Ethics, and the Narratives of the Gulf War* (Lynne Riener, 1993).

21. See Kellner, *The Persian Gulf TV War.*

22. " 'High Tech' Isn't Everything," *Newsweek*, February 18, 1991: 49.

23. William Merrin, "Uncritical Criticism: Norris, Baudrillard and the Gulf War," *Economy and Society*, 23, no. 4 (November 1994): 433-458.

24. See William Safire, "The Great Scud-Patriot Mystery," *New York Times*, March 7, 1991: A25; Jeffrey Smith, "Patriot Missiles Less Effective in Israel," *Washington Post*, April 26, 1991: A41; Kellner's *The Persian Gulf TV War* on the Patriot controversy.

25. Eric Arnett, "Awestruck Press Does Tomahawk PR," *Bulletin of the Atomic Scientists*, July 1991.

26. An excellent guide to news coverage by the corporate media is Martin Lee and Norman Solomon, *Unreliable Sources: A Guide to Detecting Bias in News Media* (New York: Carol Publishing Group, 1990).

Discussion

1. Summarize Raman's argument regarding the relationship of the media to our perception of the events of the Gulf War. Give an argument as to why you agree or disagree with Raman's analysis.

2. Much of the controversy about the Gulf War turns, in Raman's view, on a series of definitions. Pick two or three of the examples that Raman uses and analyze them. Do you agree or disagree that the public's understanding of scientific or technological controversy is fundamentally linguistic? What were your impressions of the "success" or "failure" of technology during the Gulf War? Do you think your impressions were shaped by the language of the war? If so, how? If not, why not?

3. Raman claims that blurring distinctions among types of war is a rhetorical tactic used by both military hawks and peace activists. Explain whether you think scientific and technical communicators should take advantage of similar rhetorical tactics in order to convince an audience of a particular position. In arguing your view, provide an example.

4. Wars seem to beget new words for old things—and some would argue that the terms are gradually losing their power, and the real horror of war is somehow sanitized. What in World War II

was called "shell shock" has more recently been termed posttraumatic stress disorder. Are there other terms, in other areas of human endeavor, that seem designed not so much to convey information as to disguise it? Some might argue that such terms are an improvement on the original because they comfort. Do you agree?

5. The war in Bosnia and Herzegovina involved what its participants termed "ethnic cleansing" and what early newspaper accounts of the war stated was the more familiar "genocide"—the systematic destruction of a people. Gradually, newspapers abandoned the latter term and began to use the former. Certainly, they were not aligning themselves with the people enacting the atrocities. Why, then, did they employ their language?

6. The Battle of New Orleans was fought in part because its participants did not realize the peace treaty ending the War of 1812 had been signed. During the Gulf War, Americans saw—on their television screens and in real time—shells raining through Baghdad's night sky. Raman's article suggests that a presentation of the technologies of war may have influenced our understanding (or misunderstanding) of the war. The presentation of the technologies of war was made through a communication technology which was itself almost incredibly sophisticated. Did the communication technology—that is, real-time television pictures—influence your view of the war? How?

Exercises

1. Referring to Chapter 5, Part I of the text, analyze, in a short report, the arguments that Raman gives to support her thesis. First, identify Raman's main thesis and the arguments set forward in defense of her position. Analyze each argument, determining its premises and conclusions, use of evidence, and possible fallacies. From your evaluation of Raman's argument, offer your own argument as to whether the reader should or should not accept her conclusions.

2. In an assignment related to Exercise 1, discuss the linguistic ambiguity and argumentative fallacies Raman points out that military officials and the media engaged in during the Gulf War. Do you agree with Raman's recommendations about our approach to the media? What other recommendations would you suggest?

3. Raman's case study offers a model for examining the function of language in shaping perception and knowledge. Referring to Chapter 5, Part I of the text, perform a linguistic analysis of a scientific or technological explanation as it appears in a textbook, newspaper, or magazine articles and editorials or in literature published by participants. List the terms involved. Consider the style of presentation. Analyze the ways in which language is being used. As the result of your analysis, determine the ways in which facts about a given occurrence or phenomena are established and disputed. Consider in your analysis how the lay public influences, and is influenced by, the use of persuasion in media.

4. Raman claims that blurring distinctions among types of war is a rhetorical tactic used by both military hawks and peace activists. In a report offering recommendations, explain whether you think scientific and technical communicators should take advantage of similar rhetorical tactics to convince an audience of a particular position. Specify what tactics you could use to convince a given audience (which you define), citing a specific case.

Introduction to Chapter 12

In November 1993, President Clinton created the National Science Technology Council, a body composed of secretaries and directors of all the research-oriented departments and agencies in the government. This action was the logical culmination of the claim science and technology are making on fiscal and intellectual resources. By one estimate, half the issues considered by Congress in the past few years involve science and technology, at least indirectly. The House of Representatives has the permanent Committee on Science and Technology, the Senate has two subcommittees whose main purview is science and technology policy, and the executive branch has the Office of Science and Technology Policy. However, in the era of shrinking budgets, privatized research and a bloated scientific workforce, the role of the federal government in encouraging and promoting scientific research has come under fire.

Before World War II, American scientific community was largely separate from the government. American science was based mainly on university campuses; the same universities were the major source of funding. In general, scientists were wary of government intervention, and government saw little need to spend a great deal of money on science. It was scientists who first tried to close the gap. In the late 1930s, a group of nuclear physicists (among them Fermi and von Neumann) who understood the military consequences of recent discoveries in nuclear science warned the U.S. government. In a now famous letter, Albert Einstein prevailed upon President Roosevelt to secure a supply of uranium for possible military uses. Roosevelt responded by creating the first governmental body specifically involved with science: the Advisory Committee on Uranium. Successors followed—the most significant being the National Defcnse Research Committee (NDRC) and the extremely influential Office of Scientific Research and Development (OSRD). None of these agencies threatened the independence that scientists valued and so set a precedent for a national policy dealing with science and technology that allowed scientists considerable freedom.

In 1945, Roosevelt's advisor Vanavar Bush assembled a team of scientists to author a recommendation for government's involvement in postwar science. The recommendation took the form of a report titled *Science, the Endless Frontier,* which called for the creation of what would become the National Science Foundation (NSF). It reads in part,

> [S]ince health, well-being, and security are proper concerns of Government, scientific progress is, and must be, of vital interest to the Government. Without scientific progress the national health would deteriorate; without scientific progress we could not hope for improvement in our standard of living or for an increased number of jobs for our citizens; and without scientific progress we could not have maintained our liberties against tyranny.

The word "tyranny" is particularly significant here, for it reflects the struggle between scientists' desire for intellectual freedom and government's desire to retain limited control. This struggle was in many ways the birth pains of the NSF. The result was (and is) a compromise. The National Science Foundation Act of 1950 determined that the director would be a presidential appointee and that the related National Science Board (NSB), the members of which were also appointed by the president, would be limited to an advisory role. The scientific community, for the most part, was pleased: If scientists were not permitted enormous influence in policy making, they were at least assured of ongoing government support and considerable independence.

The greatest increase in real dollars of government funding of science and technology occurred in the 1960s—in part an effect of the cold war fears aroused by the Soviet Union's launching an artificial satellite in 1957. The 1970s and 1980s saw a leveling of scientific funding in real dollars; the 1990s, so far, have seen diminished resources and economic restraints, and consequently, a greater strain on decision makers. Struck by Vanavar Bush, the compact between scientists and society placed science above politics for the national good. Tobias, Chubin, and Aylesworth revisit that compact and suggest that those seeking jobs in science revisit it as well. The goals of American science, and of American scientists, are debated in light of the redefinition of national welfare.

CHAPTER

Restructuring Demand for Scientific Expertise

SHEILA TOBIAS

DARYL CHUBIN

KEVIN AYLESWORTH

What is America's stake in American science? How do we measure it? And how do we convince employers, the general public, and Congress itself that science is valuable, not just for the products it offers, but for the possibilities it engenders? Along with curiosity-driven research, applied problems, as Robert Sproull used to tell his Ph.D. students, "deserve our respect." Both types of research require a strong scientific infrastructure, sustained funding from a variety of sources, and a steady supply of new talent. If the vagaries of supply and demand

AUTHORS' NOTE: This chapter, from an article originally titled "Restructuring Demand," first appeared as Chapter 7 in *Rethinking Science as a Career: Perceptions and Realities in the Physical Sciences* (Tobias, Chubin, and Aylesworth, 1995) published by Research Corporation, W. Stevenson Bacon series editor. Copyright 1995 Research Corporation. Reprinted by permission.

are to be replaced with strong and certain career pathways for science trained professionals, we will have to explore new ways of restructuring demand. In this chapter we begin that exploration in a way that is more suggestive than comprehensive. We are optimistic because, contrary to much current opinion, we believe not only that scientific skills will be increasingly vital in the years ahead, but that there is a reservoir of goodwill for science that has yet to be tapped. Restructuring demand for scientific expertise will draw on that reservoir and all of our skills.

THE FEDERAL ROLE

The federal government is partly responsible for the supply of scientists. Why shouldn't it be partly responsible for the demand? Since *Sputnik,* production of new scientists has been supported with federal R&D funding (a proxy for private sector demand). From 1959 to 1971, according to the Office of Technology Assessment, this support resulted in a boom in doctoral production.[1] In fact, until the Apollo program was scaled back in 1967, increasing federal support of academic R&D (by 20 percent annually in constant dollars) swelled the number of graduate students on federal fellowships and traineeships. Ph.D. awards declined only after fellowships were cut back in 1969, despite high undergraduate enrollments. The point to stress is this: a federally-induced market for researchers drove Ph.D. production, not private sector demand or changing demographics.

The boom subsided—as they all must—when the demand for more R&D and a supporting infrastructure (faculty expansion and university development) had been met. As OTA reported it,

[By the mid-1970s] social and political priorities shifted away from cold-war-inspired science. . . . By 1974, the proportion of graduate students relying on federal support had dropped from 40% (the 1969 peak) to 25%. Engineering and physical science were the most affected. Fellowships and traineeships dropped 90 percent from 13,600 in 1969 to 1,500 in 1975, and at NASA, DOD, and the Atomic Energy Commission [a forerunner of DOE] research funds dropped 45% in real terms.[2]

The demand spiral reversed itself again in the late 1970s and early 1980s when computer, semiconductor, and energy markets surged. Engineering was the main beneficiary in university enrollments, while overall the number of graduate students with federal support continued to decline.[3]

This historical vignette suggests that the federal role has been to target research problems and protect scientists by insulating them from short-term market forces. Yet, despite these important contributions, the federal government is damned at every turn: if it rescues declining fields through graduate student support, it is accused of mindlessly investing in a supply which will overwhelm demand. If, on the other hand, it responds too vigorously to market signals in new fields, it can amplify the shortsightedness of employers and rob science of a well-distributed (by discipline) base of new graduates. And if it does nothing in fields in which the U.S. appears to be losing its lead, it is accused of undermining economic competitiveness.

We believe there are ways of revising government mechanisms to restructure demand. If federally-supported graduate research assistants and postdocs could be made more independent of their sponsors (as John Armstrong, Truman Schwartz, and others believe they should; see chapter 5), they could pursue productive lines of inquiry on their own and perhaps become immediately employable upon graduation. Fellowships are one way of shifting control of graduate studies to students; traineeships vest such control in institutions. Both types of support could be invigorated, as was recommended by several of the industrial recruiters we queried.

Typically, federal support for graduate students is filtered through an array of research programs, irrespective of how these programs enhance the employment prospects of those being trained. Whole areas of research continue to exist while new areas grow up around them. As a result, young scientists (as we have seen in their responses to the current job market) are unprepared for the fickleness of opportunity and the possibility that their training may be mismatched to future funding. Knowing future funding priorities would be, of course, the best way to predict demand. Harry Wasserman, an organic chemist at Yale University, thinks future demand will be stimulated not by "finding new sources of money to support scientists," but "by finding new science for scientists to do," such as "green chemistry (preventative environmentalism), which applies chemicals at the catalytic instead of at the stoichiometric levels to reduce toxic waste, cascade reactions, and so on.[4]

Another government mechanism for maintaining science and scientists has been the national labs. Historically, the "Big Five" were heavily involved in weapons-related research, but others made significant nonmilitary contributions to basic science by supporting large-scale instrumentation that universities could not afford. With the end of the cold war, the pressure is on to recalculate the value of all the labs in terms of the economy. Some of their supporters are eager to redefine their missions in terms of dual-use technologies, innovations purported to fulfill defense and civilian needs simultaneously.[5] But another approach is to view the labs as a reservoir (albeit an expensive one) of talent and experience.[6] Even if we are justified in asking the federal government to help sustain or restructure demand for scientists, can we link the national labs to the long-term health of science and technology? And do the labs represent the best use of captive talent at current budget levels? Absent pressing military priorities, the national labs could be considered a long-term labor support system. But who will decide whether this is worth doing and how many scientists are "enough?" At a time when the nation's twenty-seven national laboratories and federal research facilities are coming under review, the question is timely.

THE ROLE OF THE PRIVATE SECTOR

What is the role of commerce and industry in matching scientific expertise to jobs? A slew of legislative and executive initiatives encourage corporate collaboration with public and private universities, national laboratories, and state government. But truth be told, incentives such as the Stevenson-Wydler Technology Innovation Act of 1980 (reauthorized more than once) to confer tax credits for private investment in R&D have never had much impact. Either the federal government is considered too unreliable a partner (tax credits may not remain in force from one session of Congress to another), or corporations don't want to risk their R&D portfolios by collaborating with outsiders. A third reason may be that the tax advantage, as permitted by the Congress, is calculated only on increases in research expenditures not on the actual cost of maintaining research.

Many aspects of market demand for scientific personnel were touched on in the proceedings of a symposium held in Washington, D.C. in July 1992.[7] Industry operates within a new set of constraints, participants were told. Set in a global marketplace that is stratified by sector, companies must increasingly rely on multidisciplinary solutions to science based problems. In addition, finite resources require technological organizations to stay within well-planned objectives over longer time frames. Within those constraints, however, the demand for technically-trained personnel who can do multiple tasks and learn others quickly is growing. When companies fail to locate the "complete package" in any one professional ("gold-collar workers," as Curt Mathews of Rohm and Haas calls them), they will rate new applicants on intellectual agility, versatility, and receptivity to new tasks. But how can such multiple skills be introduced into graduate education? Perhaps industry—university collaboration can be justified as much as a training incubator as a way of producing knowledge.

ALTERNATE CAREERS IN
THE PRIVATE SECTOR

There was a flurry of excitement in 1993-94 when a small number of Ph.D. physicists found their way to Wall Street. Their ability to understand "derivatives" in the market (derivatives are highly leveraged instruments whose value is linked to the performance of other assets) made them a "hot item" (and generated a *Time* magazine cover story), at least for a while. More relevant is the quieter story of physicists who went into the venture capital industry over the past two decades. Rather than on Wall Street, they were more likely to be found on the San Francisco peninsula or in Boston with companies like Advanced Technology Ventures. The derivatives story notwithstanding, the possibility that scientists can be valued, indeed prized, for their unique competencies underscores their (and our) interest in increasing the demand for their expertise in other sectors of the economy.

But who will train these scientists for business? Since few companies are eager to retrain,[8] it is all the more important that today's young scientists figure out what industry wants. This means, says John Armstrong, they have to study the industry in general, the would-be employer in depth, and make a convincing case that their skills and background will fit in and enhance the company's efforts.[9] Scientists aren't used to selling themselves in this fashion and business isn't set up to employ science-trained professionals in other arenas.[10] So, there is much to be learned on both sides.

Another arena for more immediate hiring of science-trained professionals in the private sector is manufacturing technology. The stagnation of American industry, wrote Robert Reich in 1983, ten years before he became secretary of labor, was the result of "the management era," when business school graduates, trained in marketing, management, and finance but with no particular technical background, were running American business.[11] If science and engineering converge in the future, as Lewis M. Branscomb predicts,[12] then scientists exposed to the technical problems industries face might provide an attractive new engineering-management cadre.

It is tempting to jump on the "quality management" bandwagon and say, as Reich implies, that American business and industry would be better off with fewer lawyers, financial specialists, and traditional managers, and more science-trained professionals. Bandwagon or not, we agree. An untapped pool can bring new inspiration to business. But, the science community cannot simply wait for future employers to come knocking. To capitalize on demand, it needs to prepare both itself and the next generation of scientists for work in alternate careers. In addition to urging large corporations to support in-house laboratories, academic science should try to demonstrate to private enterprise how useful science graduates can be in business roles away from the bench. This is where restructured supply—a repackaging, if you will—meets restructured demand.

The Self-Employed Scientist

Some science-trained professionals are making it as entrepreneurs. But in response to our questions about alternative futures, few scientists—even those who are unemployed—listed self-employment as an option. In other professions a period of self-employment, as a lawyer in private practice or an educator in consulting, for example, can help a person survive down times or career disruptions. Two things militate against self-employment for scientists: the need for laboratory facilities and the stimulation of a peer group. These might be mitigated by startup loans and by access to computer networks and bulletin boards. But another barrier lies in attitudes and perceptions. Except for the senior scientist who builds an off-site business to develop some spillover technology from research, part-time or self-generated employment tends not to be valued in science.

According to recent surveys, more and more Americans are finding their way into self-employment. While many of these would-be entrepreneurs will not make it financially and will eagerly accept employee status when jobs become available, their periods outside of a salary-paying organization will not necessarily be blots on their records. Until and unless the science community recognizes this kind of self-employment as legitimate and valuable, scientists in transition will have little option but to leave the field.

Academic Science:
Placement and Matching Systems

If, as the American Physical Society reports, 800 U.S. or green-card-holding Ph.D.s in physics were graduated annually in the past few years, and if there were 800 positions for Ph.D. physicists available per year in those years, then the problem of unemployment in physics may not have been one of oversupply, but rather a problem of matching people (and their subspecialties) to jobs. In a nation as vast as ours, with only ad hoc systems (essentially no system) to locate jobs for people or people for jobs, it is not surprising that 200 or more applicants respond to any advertised academic position, and that 199 must be turned down.

In the "bad old days," as women and minorities are quick to remind us, placement of science professionals was too often done informally by students' mentors in conversations with friends and colleagues. With the advent of equal opportunity hiring, however, there is now pressure to advertise job openings and the requirement that search committees at least appear to have diverse applicant pools. What has replaced the bad effects of the old system, if we are to believe anecdotal accounts from our respondents and conversations with search committees, is application overkill thanks to word processing. The vast numbers of applicants per job (more in academe than in industry) are accounted for by the ease with which applicants can tailor and reproduce their resumes. Sometimes applicants do not even go to the trouble of finding out much about the jobs for which they are applying or whether they are even marginally qualified.

What would it take to establish a placement clearinghouse for scientists across disciplines and subfields? Each of the professional associations does this to some extent, and the American Chemical Society, with its dual labor market (academic and industrial), may be the most conscientious. But for the young scientist who cannot afford to travel to meetings (the ACS does waive fees for unemployed members), publications and computer networking may have to suffice. Why not, then, a national matching and placement system similar to that used to assign medical residencies? Medical schools and the hospitals to which they send their graduates as residents have worked out a complicated matching system in which each graduating senior lists five residencies in rank order of preference. Looking over the applicants, the hospital programs select five of the group in their preference order. Then, in a monstrous one-day number-crunching, matching is done. This is most likely too draconian a model for the science community (bear in mind the medical residency "match" is only for one or two years), but something like it might be explored for filling postdoctoral openings.

Certainly some shift in responsibility for placement to graduate faculties is called for. Otherwise, what incentive (apart from kindness) is there for faculty members to try to explore alternate careers for students and work to increase their versatility? Harley A. Thronson, Jr., chairing the Bahcall Committee of the Astronomy and Astrophysics Society, recently concluded that for fifteen years there had been an overproduction of astronomers of 2 to 3 percent annually. Thronson's remedy was that the "fate of a department's past graduates, rather than the training of new ones, become a factor in evaluating grant proposals from any of its faculty members."[13] What's interesting about the idea is that astronomy departments (as well as individual mentors) would be motivated to pay attention to the placement of their graduates, for continued funding would depend on success. Thronson happened upon a truth noted by many of our respondents: graduate professors may be inclined only to place their best students in postdoctoral positions as a way of propagating their own work. There is no collective obligation for the mentor or the department as a whole to place its graduates in jobs.

Giving graduate faculties more responsibility for placement may require training. How much do professors know about the job market? About alternative occupations for the scientists they train? How much do students know about these subjects? What kind and how much training would it take to make a young scientist more skilled at defining problems independently, even across disciplines?

Teaching Postdocs

In addition to conventional postdoctoral appointments, teaching postdocs might profitably occupy (if only temporarily) pedagogically oriented scientists. With an oversupply of Ph.D. scientists and an oversupply of instructors at large state universities (particularly in lower-division physics and chemistry courses), one- to three-year teaching apprenticeships might be a worthy program for NSF or other federal agencies to support. Two models have been tried with some success. Since 1988 the Camille and Henry Dreyfus Foundation has been supporting about ten doctoral scientists per year as teaching postdocs at undergraduate colleges. In each instance the postdoc is teamed with a scholar who directs, inspires, and supervises the new instructor. The fellow benefits from an opportunity to try both teaching and research in a college setting. The mentor benefits from the assistance of a research-oriented Ph.D. who would not normally be available at the college. The cost to the foundation is $50,000 for two years of work, and an additional research start-up grant at the end if the recipient decides to pursue a career in college teaching.[14]

In a similar program, a science education consortia used part of its Pew Charitable Trust funding in the late 1980s to match up postdocs with participating institutions. Faculty of these institutions were relieved of one-half of their course loads in exchange for training and supervising a teaching postdoc. One Ph.D. who took advantage of this opportunity, geologist David Smith, is now running a teaching learning center at LaSalle University in Philadelphia—a fitting and unconventional career step he was emboldened to take because of his teaching postdoc at Colorado College. A teaching postdoc" need not be a formal arrangement. While chairman of physics at the University of Chicago, Hellmut Fritzsche reduced the department's use of first- and second-year graduate students as teaching assistants by using postdocs and older graduate students instead. The benefits were mutual: the grad students and research associates gained valuable teaching experience; students had more mature instructors in class.[15]

There's always the risk, Smith and others say, that teaching postdocs may never find their way back to research. But the desperate need for dynamic science instructors. especially in state universities, is reason to consider expansion of the Dreyfus and Pew models with other sources of funding.

Survival During Voluntary and Involuntary Career Interruptions

We cannot conclude a survey of career prospects in science without making a plea for the scientist whose career is interrupted either by family responsibilities (voluntary) or by years' long inability to get a permanent job (involuntary). Geologist Cathy Manduca is a case in point. Manduca holds a Ph.D. in geology from Caltech. Her current "underemployment," as she likes to call it, is the result of a combination of family responsibilities (two small children) and geographical limitations. Manduca is faced with three challenges: first, how to function as a scientist—that is, to continue to do research—during a period of underemployment; second, how eventually to reenter the job market with a viable curriculum vitae after even a temporary disruption. "Finally," she writes, "it has been important to maintain my self-esteem. And this has been the hardest to do."[16]

To maintain herself as a scientist, Manduca negotiated a position as a continuing research associate at a nearby college that allowed her to write proposals for funding, provided office space, and included access to a research library and some laboratory equipment. She also arranged to do research in laboratories out of state by being in residence for short stints, and at a local business. To stay in contact with the scientific community (and to hear about other research opportunities), she has continued to go to scientific meetings even though she is unable to give papers with her previous frequency.

What is making all this possible, why Manduca is surviving professionally where others in her situation would not, is that her spouse has helped pay for child care, Manduca's trips to meetings and laboratories, and office maintenance costs. To assist others, Manduca suggests establishment of a support program to make it easier for part-time scientists to maintain membership in the professional community for two- to five-year periods. At the very least, productive scientists wishing to return to research after a voluntary or involuntary interruption ought to be eligible for start-up support.

How much would it take to extend placement services to the part-time scientist? To inform local business and industry when someone with a particular kind of training moves into a region? To accommodate scientists in transition on site or during extended working visits at the national labs? At university-industry consortia? It is tempting to dismiss proposals like these as just more entitlement programs at a time when scientists ought to be cutting back on supply, not maintaining it. But the cost of un- or underemployment in science is heavy, both to society which loses trained people and to individuals attempting to keep up in rapidly changing fields.

One attractive feature of programs to help sustain un- and underemployed scientists would be the availability of trained professionals for short assignments. Scientists in transition could be made available to industry, perhaps through a registry, as itinerant "experts" who would bring specialized knowledge into new venues and bridge scientific disciplines. While such consultants are not uncommon at the most senior levels of academe and industry, they are relatively rare at the middle or lower levels where they may be more needed.

Career disruption is difficult professionally, financially, and psychologically, even when it is temporary. The possibility that a temporary disruption might result in a permanent derailment of a career makes the situation even more traumatic. When a scientist loses contact, momentum and confidence may vanish. A support plan would not only assist individuals to stay in science but would also permit the nation to salvage its investment in their training. To do less is to discourage not just the current generation from science, but future generations as well.

CALCULATING THE ADDED
VALUE OF SCIENCE TO SOCIETY

In selling science to the public, the department chair, the company recruiter, the congressional staffer, the agency program officer, and the national associations of scientists may have different priorities. But a more general view must prevail: human resources in science are a national treasure that add value to the world. The issue of "added value" is the critical one. Anyone who understands the process by which the advanced economies of the world have moved from agriculture to manufacturing, and then to the production of knowledge along with goods and services, will agree at least in theory that science as a spur to technology adds value to the economy. But the quantitative measure of that added value is elusive. It is one thing to compute the value of the telecommunications industry in terms of sales and profits, exports, and employment (new wealth); it is quite another to compute the value of its knowledge base as a stimulus to economic growth, the numerous jobs (new sources of wealth) created by the new industries it has spawned, the higher efficiency of business in all sectors that it has made possible—not to mention improved quality of life. Without some measure of "added value" by science and technology to the economy and well-being of this nation, however, the argument for full employment of scientists (and what economists lump under the rubric of "human capital") remains a philosophical one at best.

A first order of business, then, for those who engage in science and technology policy is to attempt to compute, account for, and factor in the added value of science.[17] This involves analyses of the value to the economy of having, for example, the best advanced training in science in the world (affordability and limited access notwithstanding); the benefits to the economy in general that flow from technological innovation; the benefits overall, not just to the industries that profit from them, of advances in computers, lasers, global positioning satellites, automation, transportation, biotechnology, agriculture, and pharmaceuticals, as well as building materials and technologies, and telecommunications; what Jack Gibbons, the president's science adviser, calls in the aggregate science's "social rate of return."[18]

Such a calculation may seem daunting. But comparable valuations have been done in the recent past, and one economist (who won a Nobel Prize for the effort) has attempted to quantify (if only retrospectively) the direct benefits of education, research, and development to technological progress and to the economy.[19] The value of a pristine environment, to take an example from another hard-to-measure sector, is no longer calculated in terms of recreation alone. We measure health benefits and costs, along with new measures, such as the long-term availability (whether visited or not) of our nation's wilderness areas and national parks (called by economists "their option value"). These have become part and parcel of the nation's land-planning metric.

Selling Science, Selling Scientists

An ideal future for science-trained professionals in the U.S. in the authors' opinion would look something like this—a significantly larger percentage of young people, regardless of race, ethnic background, gender, or disability, would be recruited to the study of science. Like today's ROTC and military academy candidates, they would be supported with tuition waivers, monthly stipends, and paid summer work experience. Those who chose to terminate their schooling with a two-year associate's degree would become technicians; those who continued in science through a B.S. or B.A. would not have to repay tuition waivers, no matter what their profession, because it would be understood by the public that science literacy is valuable in all sectors. Those earning degrees at the master's level would have opportunities to do meaningful science-related work. Those earning Ph.D.s would be employed at the bench or in the management of basic or applied research.

Lest this extension of the military-training model to science (mathematics and engineering might also be included) be considered too fanciful or rooted in the cold war, recall Vanavar Bush's original recommendation that 24,000 scholarships be given annually to undergraduates in science. Extending the military-training model still further, graduates in science (at all levels) would be expected to repay their fellowships with some form of science-related service in public institutions (schools, museums, hospitals, national labs), or in the private sector (industry, commerce, banks, environmental clean-up companies, law firms, media organizations).

This scenario assumes a population sympathetic to science, made up of both ordinary people and powerful decision makers willing to pay for a science infrastructure. Just as the public willingly pays for "readiness" in the interest of national security, so it would greet scientific investigation (Unscientific maneuvers," as it were) and a "science corps" of young graduates as investments in national long-term well-being. Some of the vanishing local and regional benefits of military spending (base employment and local contracts) would be resurrected by spending for science. Finally, the media in this ideal future would make science accessible, well-reported, intelligently criticized and, for the most part, celebrated as a national "good."[20]

Why does our scenario seem improbable? One answer common among scientists is that science illiteracy is so widespread in the population at large, and anti-scientism so virulent among a vocal few, as to subvert any appreciation that science might inspire.[21] In Washington it is generally believed that, apart from the space program, "there are no votes in science." This makes it even harder to imagine that the nation would happily sustain science-trained professionals in their careers or invest in new employment pathways for them. But how sure are we that there are no votes in science, or that the public wouldn't support science if it were asked? Does science illiteracy necessarily produce indifference or hostility to the world that scientists do? Daniel Greenberg, editor and publisher of *Science and Government Report,* and formerly of *Science,* thinks not. He recently told a university audience that polling regularly shows that 73 percent of the public consider the benefits of science greater than any of its baneful effects."[22]

Indeed, there is some empirical evidence that scientists may themselves be at fault for not cultivating a support base that already exists. In 1983 sociologist Jon Miller, who reports biennially on public attitudes toward science, studied 287 science policy leaders and found "a woeful lack of interest in mobilizing the 'science-attentive public.' "[23] This was partly because they were unaware of the size of this group (about thirty million, according to Miller's surveys and calculations), and because during the long postwar period from 1945 to 1983 government was willing to respond to the science elite with generous funding. On those occasions when they needed public support, the major disciplinary societies and professional associations tended to focus on their own membership. There was little or no overt effort to identify and mobilize the millions of private citizens interested in science.[24]

Indeed, for 1979 through 1981, only 5 percent of Miller's self-identified "science-attentive public" reported contacting a public official on a science-related matter in the previous year, and most of these contacts were on resource-related, not research-related, issues.[25] The reason for the public's inaction regarding science, Miller insists, was not lack of concern but lack of information as to what the science community would have had them do. The 287 science and technology leaders polled by Miller confirmed this impression. They thought they could go it alone. Given the intense competition for federal resources in the decade ahead (and he saw this beginning in 1983), Miller warned that lack of mobilization of public support would put funding and science itself in grave danger.[26]

Miller's findings are provocative on several grounds, first because he departs from the notion that a "science-attentive public" need be science literate[27] and second because of his identification of a substantial population (19.5 percent of all adults) as science-interested citizens.[28] This indicates that our ideal scenario need not be so farfetched as it first appears if steps are taken to educate and mobilize this population. A second provocative element is Miller's identification of an elitist and preoccupied science leadership rendered inattentive to the broader public by decades of federal support. In his survey, only one of five of the leaders queried had attempted to inform the general public on science and technology issues, with leaders from the university sector being the least likely to have done so.[29]

Mobilizing Support for Science

It is not as if there are no precedents for informing and influencing a science-attentive pubic. Dorothy Nelkin in her book *Selling Science* reminds us that, as early as 1919 with the founding of the American Chemical Society, professional science writers were employed to describe research in language the public could understand.[30] The Scripps Science Service was established in 1930 to do the same, and even in their early years, the American Institute of Physics (founded in 1935) and the American Association for the Advancement of Science had wire services. When it has reason to, industry knows how to sell science and scientists. Aside from merchandising consumer products based on new technologies, industry often calls on scientists to help explain science related issues. The chemical industry has used "advertorials" featuring scientists who are "managing chemical wastes." Westinghouse created the Campus America program in 1976 to train scientists for public debate on nuclear power. The use of scientists in public relations is not the same as building positive public relations for science (and may sometimes have the opposite effect).[31] But the "campaign mentality" does provide a model for influencing public attitudes.

Scientists are sometimes ambivalent about the press, but the press is even more ambivalent about science. There are fewer and fewer newspapers employing science writers, and the weekly science sections are disappearing. It is all but impossible to report on serious science either in the print media or on TV, not because writers are reluctant, but because, aside from health and medicine, business offices, editors, and publishers do not value science enough. Indeed, scientists might well be wary. In an article based on their study of anti-scientism among American intellectuals (see note 21), Norman Levitt and Paul R. Gross note that the "old respect" in which science used to be held "is being supplanted by hostile criticism . . . arising from the just and understandable desire, shared by many intellectuals, that science be democratized."[32]

Of course, the extension of a science-trained work force to groups hitherto excluded from science will bring with it some risk to the habits and traditional values of the work, just as popularization may lead to criticism and loss of prestige. But, properly understood, Levitt and Gross are as eloquent as Gerald Holton in making the case that science, in its constant battle against fanaticism and obscurantism, is a critical support for democratic society.[33]

CONCLUSION

Members of Congress and others are calling for a "new social compact" between science and society, one that contributes to solving the next generation of economic and social problems.[34] The COSEPUP (Committee on Science, Engineering, and Public Policy) report of the National Academy of Sciences, released in April 1995, calls for a balanced blend of research and preparation for diverse career paths in the training of future science professionals, a goal already adumbrated by study commissions of the American Chemical and the American Physical Societies.[35] And thoughtful scientists from all disciplines have nearly conceded—but as yet mainly in theory—that the "old compact" rooted in the cold war and U.S. economic hegemony, in which "science was placed in a special category above politics,"[36] cannot be revived.

No less important than the emerging shift in perceptions and expectations will be shifts in the realities that constrain change: how future federal budgets (and budget-cutting) will affect the amount, manner of dispersal, and criteria for funding of research, including the mix between strategic and untargeted (basic or curiosity driven); how universities will select, train, and direct the next generation of science professionals into certain specialties (and not into others); and whether unrestrained access by foreign nationals to U.S. scientific training and scientific jobs will be allowed to diminish the career prospects of U.S. citizens. In short, the financial support mechanisms and the institutional rearrangements required by the "new social compact" need to be hammered out in relentless debate among all who have, or ought to have, a stake in America's scientific future.

Some readers may be tempted to ignore our perceptions and that of our respondents if they think these don't (yet) correspond to their research areas, their students, or their perceptions. But we believe they do so at their peril. The fortunes of other research areas, other departments, and other students will have an impact on research and teaching in all subdisciplines, and any changes in federal policy and budgeting, even those not immediately targeted at them, will affect the way they do business. They are, in short, part of a larger system, even if they don't think of themselves that way. From this perspective, downsizing and so-called academic birth control, while appealing in the short run, can emasculate what's good about the whole system—the community. In science, as in nature, there is an ecology at work. The science community owes it to itself not to generalize from one node or perch but, rather, to raise the caliber, the productivity, and the utility of the whole enterprise.

Nor ought the science community, in our view, continue to do on an ad hoc basis those things that require a sound empiricism. Issues of careers in science need to be dealt with promptly and responsibly, consistent with the best interests of the young professionals involved and the long-term welfare of the nation as a whole. Failure to do so will make science as a career appear even more risky to those contemplating their futures than it does today. So, we end where we began, with these questions:

How will our nation grow the scientists it needs?
How will our scientists get the work they've trained for?
And dare we leave these matters to chance?

NOTES

1. This and what follows derives from U.S. Congress, Office of Technology Assessment, *Higher Education for Science and Engineering* (Washington, D.C.: USGPO, Mar. 1989): pp. 126-128.

2. Ibid., p. 128.

3. Ibid., p. 129.

4. Harry Wasserman, personal communication to the authors. See also "Chemists Clean Up Synthesis with One-Pot Reactions," *Science* 266 (7 Oct. 1994): pp. 32-33.

5. For a contrasting view, see the widely-reported Galvin Report on alternative futures for the DOE national laboratories presented to Congress, Feb. 24, 1995. The commission, led by Robert Galvin. chairman of the board of Motorola, indicated its reluctance to support the dual-use concept as reported in *Science* 267 (27 Jan. 1995): pp. 446-447.

6. In other countries, such as Germany, national labs are not agency administered or mission dependent, but are engaged in the support of basic research.

7. Preparing for the 21st Century: Human Resources in Science and Technology (Washington, D.C.: Commission on Professionals in Science and Technology, July 1992).

8. Bellcore is an exception. Bellcore's contribution over the past few years has been to put more than 400 Ph.D. researchers (physicists and electrical engineers) through an expensive three-week crash course in software and systems engineering. See "In Sink-or-Swim Environment, Physicists Retrain to Survive," *Science* 261 (24 Sept. 1993): p. 1672.

9. John Armstrong, personal communication to the authors. See also Peter Feibelman's advice to scientists, *A Ph.D. Is Not Enough: A Guide to Survival in Science* (Menlo Park, Calif.: Addison-Wesley, 1993).

10. Vljendra Agarwal of Moothead State's physics department found it hard to identify the personnel officer to talk to at large companies like Honeywell and 3-M about placement of prospective physicists with business minors. One office handles hiring of scientists, another hiring of marketing and management trainees. Agarwal's graduates would fall between the two.

11. Robert Reich, *The Next American Frontier* (New York: Viking/Penguin, 1983).

12. Lewis M. Branscomb, personal communication to the authors.

13. Harley A. Thronson, Jr., "The Production of Astronomers: A Model for Future Surpluses," in *Publication of the Astronomical Society of the Pacific* 103 (Jan. 1991): pp. 90-94.

14. Robert Lichter, executive director, and Harry Wasserman, Dreyfus Foundation board member, personal communications to the authors.

15. Hellmut Fritzsche, personal communication to the authors.

16. The quotations and details come from a memo, written to the authors to answer their queries, and are quoted with Cathy Manduca's permission.

17. For example, see *Research Funding as an Investment: Can We Measure the Returns?* U.S. Congress, Office of Technology Assessment (Washington, D.C.: USGPO, April 1986). The short answer was "no."

18. John H. Gibbons, address to a meeting on "Science in the National Interest," MIT, 7 Feb. 1995.

19. According to economist Robert Solow's analysis, for much of the first half of this century, 80 percent of America's economic growth was due to "capital-independent technical progress"; 34 percent alone to "growth of knowledge" or what Solow calls "technical progress in its narrowest sense." See *Growth Theory: An Explosion*, Robert Solow's Nobel lecture (New York: Oxford University Press, 1987), p. 20. A commentator writes: "Solow's 1957 paper on technological progress changed the focus of growth economies from a crude emphasis on savings to a much-better appreciation of the importance of education, research, and development." Avinash Dixit, in *Growth, Productivity and Unemployment: Essays to Celebrate Bob Solow's Birthday*, ed. Peter Diamond (Cambridge, Mass.: MIT Press, 1990), p. 11.

20. For an opinion on the importance of science writers to science, see William D. Carey, "Scientists and Sandboxes: Regions of the Mind," *American Scientist* 76 (Mar.-Apr. 1988): pp. 143-145.

21. Hostility to science may reside in higher quarters than had previously been assumed. See Paul R. Gross and Norman Levitt, *Higher Superstition: The Academic Left and Its Quarrels with Science* (Baltimore: Johns Hopkins Press, 1994).

22. Taken from a public lecture given at the University of California, San Diego on Oct. 4, 1994. This proportion is fairly stable. See Jon Miller, *The Public Understanding of Science and Technology* 1990 report to the National Science Foundation (Washington, D.C.: USGPO, 1992).

23. Jon Miller, *The American People and Science Policy* (New York: Pergamon Press, 1983), pp. 41-43. Miller defines the science-attentive public as (1) having a self-defined interest in science and technology issues; (2) being knowledgeable about science and technology; and (3) engaging in a regular pattern of relevant information acquisition, i.e., reading a newspaper every day, or most of the time, reading one or more news magazines, one or more science magazines, or watching a television show like *NOVA*.

24. In a compelling "textual analysis" of the testimony of university presidents from the Association of American Universities before congressional committees dealing with research funding over the period 1981-1985, Sheila Slaughter finds the same leaders-to-leaders orientation. Sheila Slaughter, "Beyond Basic Science: Research University Presidents' Narratives of Science Policy, *Science Technology and Human Values* 18, no. 3 (Summer 1993): pp. 278-302.

25. Miller, *The American People*, p. 132. An exception was the zeroing out of the science-education budget at NSF in 1981 by the Reagan administration, which generated a substantial citizen protest, largely because the education community joined in. Pressure of the mobilized public helped, Miller says, to persuade a sufficient number of members of Congress of the value of science education, though the budget was still decimated.

26. According to Miller's figures, federal support for basic research increased from $234 million in 1953 to $2.8 billion in 1968. declined for most of the 1970s, and reached $2.9 billion again only in 1978, and $3.1 billion in 1980.

27. Depending on the definition, the number of Americans who meet a minimum standard of "science literacy" falls between 3 and 6 percent of the adult population. But "science literacy" may not be as important to support for science as "science appreciation" (a phrase allegedly invented by Edward Teller). "Science appreciators" would better correspond to Miller's "science attentive public." For a discussion of these issues, see Morris H. Shamos, "Science Literacy Is Futile;

Try Science Appreciation," *The Scientist* (3 Oct. 1988): p. 8; and "Causes and Effects of Scientific Illiteracy Defined and Explored," an interview with James Trefil, *Chemical and Engineering News* (Mar. 14, 1994): p. 26.

28. Miller's surveys are reported in the National Science Board's Science and Engineering Indicators, 1980, 1982, 1985, 1987, 1989, 1991, and 1993. His data sets are archived at the International Center for the Advancement of Science Literacy, Chicago Academic, 2001 N. Clark St., Chicago, IL 60614.

29. Miller, *The American People*, p. 37.

30. Dorothy Nelkin, *Selling Science: How the Press Covers Science and Technology* (New York: W. H. Freeman, 1987), pp. 133-135.

31. Ibid., p. 146.

32. Norman Levitt and Paul L. Gross, "The Perils of Democratizing Science," *The Chronicle of Higher Education* (5 Oct. 1994): pp. B1, B2. See also Daryl E. Chubin, "Progress, Culture, and the Cleavage of Science from Society" in *Science, Technology and Social Progress*, ed. S. L. Goldman (Bethlehem, Penn.: Lehigh University Press, 1989), pp. 177-195.

33. Levitt and Gross, "The Perils of Democratizing," p. B2. Gerald Holton, *Science and Anti-Science* (Cambridge, Mass.: Harvard University Press, 1994), especially his retort to Vaclav Havel in chap. 6, pp. 145-185.

34. George E. Brown, Jr., put this in writing in his "New Ways of Looking at U.S. Science and Technology," *Physics Today* (Sept. 1994): pp. 31-35; and in "Common Sense, Science, and a Balanced Budget" (presentation to the NAS, Jan. 1995).

35. COSEPUP report, NAS, *Reshaping the Graduate Education of Scientists and Engineers* (Washington, D.C.: National Academy Press, 1995).

36. John Deutsch, speaking as deputy secretary of the Department of Defense, at a meeting of engineering deans, Washington, D.C., 9 and 10, Mar. 1995.

Discussion

1. Briefly sketch the employment outlook for scientists and engineers according to Tobias, Chubin, and Aylesworth. Would, in your opinion, "American business and industry . . . be better off with fewer lawyers, financial specialists, and traditional managers, and more science-trained professionals"? Explain. Do you agree or disagree with the authors' reasoning?

2. Tobias, Chubin, and Aylesworth point out a paradox currently facing scientists. The public mood requires greater taxpayer accountability, both at the federal and state levels. Demands for accountability places scientists and other researchers receiving public funds in the position of explaining the value of their work. Some scientists argue that their work is too

complex for the lay public to understand and cannot be properly explained. Other professionals offer the same argument. Further (according to the authors) "popularization may lead to criticism and loss of prestige." Do you believe science and technology should be "democratized"—that is, explained in a public language, opened to public critique, and changed according to public will? Explain, referring to the arguments forwarded by Fuller in Chapter 7, Part II of the text. What are the benefits and problems you see with your position?

3. Many of you attend state-supported institutions. Even if you attend a private university, many programs in which you participate are directly or indirectly supported by federal and state dollars in the form of grants and loans. Initially, then, what arguments would you give a tax-paying public for why they should, or should not, support education generally and research in your discipline specifically. Why should the state, as opposed to private industry, supply institutions for student and worker training? Should the state formally regulate the number of graduates produced in a certain area (physics, for example) in order to regulate the talent pool?

4. What responsibilities do professional societies (like the American Society of Chemical Engineers) and professors have to practitioners entering their fields? If, for instance, the job outlook for graduates is bleak, should students be actively discouraged from entering the discipline or attending graduate school? Why or why not?

5. What alternative paths to academic research do the authors point out as possible opportunities for science and engineering Ph.D.s? How will having a ready pool of scientists and engineers change the current nature of research? What problems do the authors see with respect to a progressively privatized science? Do you agree? How are science and technology susceptible to, or immune from, change in the market?

6. The authors maintain, "An ideal future for science-trained professionals in the U.S. in the authors' opinion would look something like this—a significantly larger percentage of young people, regardless of race, ethnic background, gender, or disability, would be recruited to the study of science. Like

today's ROTC and military academy candidates, they would be supported with tuition waivers, monthly stipends, and paid summer work experience." Given the authors' further explanation of their reasoning, argue why you think this is or is not a good idea. Could such a program be extended to training in other disciplines?

7. How is the general welfare of the United States tied to welfare of science and technology according to the authors? Explain why you agree or disagree with their position.

Exercises

1. Determine the role the federal government plays in your discipline. In a brief report, document the federal money that goes to support research at your school or in your particular area of expertise. You may look at government documents that account for funding (transcripts from committee hearings can be helpful), examine studies about job and research prospects in your field (in professional and popular journals and magazines, for example), and/or interview practitioners in your field that receive federal grants. From the information you gather, determine what areas of your discipline are getting support and why. Based on your analysis, explain your recommendations regarding whether the federal government should maintain, increase, decrease, or shift its funding to areas of your discipline. From your analysis, and based on predictions of future federal funding (Chapter 6 in Part I and Chapters 7 and 12 in Part II of the text), indicate which areas of your field hold the greatest potential for future employment. Do you agree that your field should head in this direction? Explain your reasoning.

2. In an assignment patterned on Exercise 1, document the role that private industry plays in your field or discipline. You may look at corporate reports, newspaper, magazine and journal articles, and/or interview practitioners in your field about the ways private industry shapes the direction of your field. Based

on your analysis, determine whether private industry should play a greater or lesser role in your field.

3. The authors outline alternative careers paths in science. Based on your interviews, draw a detailed profile of practitioners within your field or discipline, identifying shared characteristics. Compare and contrast the accounts you received with (if applicable) the authors' rendering. Consider, for example, if current practitioners in your field continue to take a standard career path or if alternatives to traditional practice are becoming more common. What factors explain this continuity or change? In drawing these profiles, determine if race, class, and gender act as factors determining career choice. Ultimately, provide a common map of the way these practitioners came into your field.

4. Describe, in a brief essay, the "new social compact" the authors believe should be struck between scientists and society. Referring to Chapter 6 in Part I of the text on the conduct of science policy, how would this new compact influence, or create, current federal policy mechanisms? How is the authors' new compact similar or different in sentiment to the social compact recommended by Fuller in Chapter 7, Part II of the text? Do you think the lay public should have a greater or lesser role in determining science policy? Explain your reasoning.

5. The conduct of science and technology, and their images, have been discussed throughout this text. Traditionally, one of science's hallmark characteristics has been public openness and accountability—scientific knowledge is, theoretically, available to all who seek it and wish to test it. In a response essay, argue, based on a case study or detailed example, how corporate privatization helps or harms the traditional conduct of science. Be sure to clearly define your terms.

Index

About the Authors

James H. Collier is an Instructor of English at Virginia Polytechnic Institute and State University (Virginia Tech) where he acts as head of the Communications and Technical Writing Program for the National Science Foundation Summer Undergraduate Research Program. He has taught technical communication since 1989 and served as a consultant with the university's Writing Across the Curriculum program. A doctoral candidate in science and technology studies, his research interests include the rhetoric and sociology of science, and the epistemological status of interdisciplinary claims about science.

David M. Toomey is a doctoral candidate in English literature at the University of Virginia, where his work involves schizophrenia and modern literature. He has published articles in *Studies in the Novel* and *Southern Quarterly.* He has taught technical communication since 1986 and has been interested in the effects of science and technology upon societies since the sixth grade when he read a little known classic of the space age called *Mike Mars in Orbit.*

*   *   *

Kevin Aylesworth is a general councilor of the American Physical Society and an American Physical Society Congressional Fellow. He has served as a National Research Council postdoctoral associate at the Naval Research Laboratory in Washington, D.C. and founded the Young Scientist' Network in 1990 to counsel policy makers on the job market for scientists.

Daryl Chubin is the division director for research, evaluation, and dissemination in the Education and Human Resources Directorate of the National Science Foundation. He was a senior associate and senior analyst in the Science, Education and Transportation Program, Office of Technology Assessment (OTA), where he was project director for the reports *Federally Funded Research: Decisions for a Decade* (1991) and *Educating Scientists and Engineers: Grade School to Grad School* (1988). He has also authored five books including *Peerless Science: Peer Review and U.S. Science Policy* (coauthored with E. J. Hackett, 1990). He has taught at Georgia Tech, Penn State, Cornell, and Southern Illinois at Edwardsville and is currently affiliated with the Virginia Tech Science and Technology Studies Program at the Northern Virginia Center.

Geoff Cooper is a lecturer in sociology at the University of Surrey. His research interests, which lie within science and technology studies and social theory, focus on aspects of the organization of contemporary knowledge: in particular, the constitution of disciplinary identities, boundaries, and relations; the changing character of research culture; and the practical, methodological, and theoretical implications of such developments for social science.

Steve Fuller is Professor of Sociology and Social Policy at the University of Durham, United Kingdom. He is the founding executive director of the journal *Social Epistemology* and author of three books: *Social Epistemology* (1988), *Philosophy of Science and Its Discontents* (2nd ed., 1993), and *Philosophy, Rhetoric, and the End of Knowledge: The Coming of Science and Technology Studies* (1993). He is completing a book on the origins and impacts of Thomas Kuhn's *The Structure of Scientific Revolutions.* His next major project is to author the *Routledge Encyclopedia of Science, Technology, and Society.*

William Keith is Assistant Professor of Communication at Oregon State University. He is coeditor (with Alan Gross) of *Rhetorical Hermeneutics: Invention and Interpretation in the Age of Science* (SUNY, 1996). He has published articles on rhetorical theory, argument theory, and the rhetoric of artificial intelligence.

Sujatha Raman is currently a research associate at the Centre for the Study of Environmental Change (CSEC) at Lancaster University, Great Britain. She is also pursuing a Ph.D. in public and international affairs at the University of Pittsburgh in Pennsylvania and is interested in how technological innovation is understood in different policy domains.

Dale L. Sullivan is Associate Professor of English at Northern Illinois University, where he coordinates the Writing Across the Curriculum program. He teaches graduate courses in the history of rhetoric, modern rhetorical theory, writing in the disciplines, and the rhetoric of science; he also teaches undergraduate advanced writing classes and technical communication. After receiving his Ph.D. in rhetoric and communication from Rensselaer Polytechnic Institute in 1988, he was a member of the graduate faculties of Michigan Technological University and the University of Nebraska. In his research, he has focused on epideictic rhetoric and its applications in the rhetoric of religion and the rhetoric of science.

Sheila Tobias is author of three books on science education for Research Corporation: *Rethinking Science as a Career: Perceptions and Realities in the Physical Sciences* (1995), *Revitalizing Undergraduate Science: Why Some Things Work and Most Don't* (1992), and *They're Not Dumb, They're Different: Stalking the Second Tier* (1990). She has been a lecturer at City College of New York, Vanderbilt, UC San Diego, Carleton College, Claremont Graduate School, and the University of Southern California and an administrator at Cornell and Wesleyan Universities.